CZECH FEMINISMS

CZECH FEMINISMS

Perspectives on Gender
in East Central Europe

Edited by
Iveta Jusová *and* **Jiřina Šiklová**

Indiana University Press
Bloomington and Indianapolis

This book is a publication of

INDIANA UNIVERSITY PRESS
Office of Scholarly Publishing
Herman B Wells Library 350
1320 East 10th Street
Bloomington, Indiana 47405 USA

iupress.indiana.edu

Manufactured in the United States of America

Library of Congress Cataloging-in-Publication Data

Names: Jusová, Iveta, [date]– editor. | Šiklová, Jiřina, [date]– editor.
Title: Czech feminisms : perspectives on gender in East Central Europe /
    edited by Iveta Jusova and Jiřina Šiklová.
Description: Bloomington : Indiana University Press, [2016] | Includes
    bibliographical references and index.
Identifiers: LCCN 2016011654| ISBN 9780253021892 (cloth : alk. paper) | ISBN
    9780253021915 (pbk. : alk. paper) | ISBN 9780253021939 (ebook)
Subjects: LCSH: Feminism—Czech Republic. | Women—Czech Republic. | Sex
    role—Czech Republic.
Classification: LCC HQ1610.3 .C94 2016 | DDC 305.42094371—dc23
LC record available at https://LCCN.loc.gov/2016011654

1 2 3 4 5   21 20 19 18 17 16

This book is dedicated to all those who have come before us.

CONTENTS

ACKNOWLEDGMENTS

THE AUTHORS WOULD like to thank Indiana University Press, and especially Raina Polivka, the music, film, and humanities editor, and Darja Malcolm-Clarke, the project editor and manager, for believing in this project and helping us bring this work from an enthusiastic proposal to a thoughtfully considered book. We were fortunate to benefit from the close reading and attentive work of the copyeditor Margaret Hogan. And Janice Frisch has been of great help with copyright-related questions.

We would also like to express our appreciation to the two anonymous external readers whose feedback on the earlier version of the manuscript helped sharpen our focus and led to a number of improvements with both structure and individual pieces.

Finally, we are grateful to Iveta's partner, Dr. Dan Reyes, who took time away from teaching philosophy to his students and from his own writing projects to read through and comment on several drafts of the manuscript. His feedback and suggestions significantly improved both the content and language fluency of the present book. As well, we are grateful for Dan's help with translation of several of the chapters originally prepared in Czech.

CZECH
FEMINISMS

INTRODUCTION

Gender, Sexuality, and Ethnicity Issues in the Czech Culture: Past and Present

IVETA JUSOVÁ

IT WAS IN the late 1980s, while studying British and Czech literatures at Palacký University in Olomouc, Czechoslovakia, that I first became aware of feminism and decided to focus my undergraduate thesis on U.S. and British feminist theory. The country was still a socialist state, and feminism was decidedly not considered an appropriate subject of study, nor were there any resources readily available on this topic. But I was in luck. Unbeknownst to me at the time, the Iron Curtain was about to come apart. Through the revolutionary months of 1989, I became acquainted with one of the few scholar-activists in the country who could understand my hunger for anything feminist and could help me with my research: Jiřina Šiklová, the coeditor of this volume. I wrote my thesis in 1990 using the books available at the Gender Studies Library set up in Jiřina's famous apartment-turned–Gender Studies Centre in Prague, likely one of that facility's first beneficiaries. Traveling between Olomouc and Prague to visit the library and center, it did not take me long to develop admiration for the energetic Šiklová.

The early 1990s were times of heated feminist exchanges and public discussions about feminism, and Šiklová's role in making these debates both compelling and possible cannot be overstated. In the context of many prominent male Czech émigrés returning from the West, all nearly uniformly having only derogatory things to say about "feminist ideologues," Šiklová drew on the considerable respect that she wielded with the Czech public (as a dissident and Charta 77 signatory[1]) to speak favorably about women's issues. At the same time, in perceiving mismatches between then widely assumed universals prevalent in Western feminist discourse and the specific situation of the Czech post-socialist context. Šiklová, along with Jana Hradílková, Hana Havelková, and others, developed a consistent critique of "Western-style feminism." In the essays they published throughout the 1990s, Šiklová and Havelková stressed the need to study Czech women's issues in their specific historical, political, and social contexts (Havelková 1993, 64; Šiklová 1993, 80).

Two decades later, in a so-called unified Europe, with the Czech Republic (CR) by and large a proud participant in the European Union's first wave of eastward expansion, Šiklová's call for accentuating the situatedness of our discussions of women's issues continues to be pertinent. This attention to our specificities, differences, and similarities also strongly informs my own ongoing work directing Carleton College's Women's and Gender Studies in Europe semester-long study-abroad program.[2] Guiding U.S. college students in the study of European (including Czech) gender, sexuality, and ethnicity issues, I note every year that students' knowledge brought to the cultural sites, histories, and traditions of Eastern Europe tends to be surprisingly limited. My experience confirms the continued (and perhaps even increasing) relevance of Jennifer Suchland's 2011 assessment of the persistent exclusion of attention paid to the diversity that is the former "second world" within U.S. Women's Studies (but also perhaps U.S. education in general), in spite of overall efforts to "internationalize knowledge production" (838). As Suchland has articulated, while intellectual pathways to certain locations in the world have been instituted within U.S. Women's Studies, there continues to be a lack of focus on the second world in transnational feminism (837).

The peculiar indistinction of the former Eastern European bloc as a supposed "non-region" (as it was proclaimed to be in 1995 by Wanda Nowicka at the World Conference on Women in Beijing) has in some respects been addressed and, one might imagine, remedied. The annual peer-reviewed journal *Aspasia*, dedicated to women's history in Central, Eastern, and Southeastern Europe (CESEE), has been appearing since 2007, offering informative discussions on a plethora of topics relevant to local scholars. The fairly steady stream of monographs and edited volumes devoted to gender (less so ethnicity or class) issues in the region might perhaps even speak to a gradual establishment of a sub-discipline of Eastern European Women's/Gender Studies within the broader field of Women's and Gender Studies (WGS). Relevant articles dealing with the region also occasionally appear in established WGS journals, including the *European Journal of Women's Studies, Women's Studies International Forum,* and *Signs: Journal of Women in Culture and Society.*

These resources are invaluable for those interested in gender-related topics in the former Eastern bloc. Still, scholarly discursive digestion of former Eastern bloc culture and history has not necessarily modified broader public awareness nor tended to have led U.S. WGS students in general to becoming more knowledgeable about the region. Nor has the recent emergence of this wealth of resources translated to a successful reshaping of the prevalent formula (as identified by Suchland) within transnational feminism of "global woman = third-world woman [and] global South = location of transnational feminist analysis" (838). The broader question Suchland posed in 2011 remains relevant: how can feminist scholars best reorient their thinking away from the historical "three-world metageography" (and from the configuration of the three worlds in terms of dichotomies between the first/third and first/second) without treating the former second world as a non-region in the process? (838). Too often, it would appear, the process of transcending this metageography results in the vanishing of Eastern Europe as a specific (while heterogeneous) location, certainly not a result that Allaine Cerwonka seems to have had in mind when questioning in 2008 the usefulness of the "emphasis on difference that runs through the [East-West] discourse" (815). Cerwonka's point is valid that a continued emphasis on the specificity of the former Eastern bloc might contribute to preserving existing East-West cultural hierarchies (817), although, alternatively, being faced with assumptions of sameness, and misread as a result, one's affirmation of this distinction seems like a reasonable response. Clearly the answer to avoiding both a romanticization of cultural difference and a possible re-inscription of global power hierarchies by emphasizing cultural specificity does not lie in ignoring cultural differences and specificities, including relevant national specificities, but rather in affirming these differences in ways that resist dialectical habits of thought.

What do WGS students and scholars—what does transnational feminism—risk missing if the situatedness, or heterogeneity, of the former Eastern bloc is not attended to in transnational feminist discussions? What taken-for-granted assumptions about the subject of Women's and Gender Studies, and more specifically about European women or European gender regimes, will be provincialized or illuminated in new ways in a WGS curriculum that specifically attends to the Czech location in a contextualized and comparative fashion?

In planning and organizing this book project, we started from a conviction that an expanded engagement with the intersections of gender, sexuality, and ethnicity issues in the Czech context,[3] combined with a contextualizing attention to the broader Eastern/East Central European location, might offer a positive contribution to current transnational Gender Studies debates.[4] While we do not presume to pose this volume as an exhaustive study, our engagements here strategically highlight the situatedness of the Czech location in a manner intended to add productively to existing feminist debates, hopefully lending useful expansion to the existing transnational feminist discourse. In these regards several key themes and aims helping us organize this work deserve preliminary discussion here.

Complicating the idea of Eurocentrism. Attending to the specificity of the former Eastern bloc complicates the conceptual lens of Eurocentrism. It is still not uncommon for WGS students from outside Eastern/East Central Europe to conceive of all European nation-states and regions as historically homogeneous: the rising and falling tides of European empire with its colonial ambitions. While there are indeed ways in which the imperial projects of dominant nations affected, shaped, and sometimes benefited even European cultures and regions that were themselves politically, linguistically, and economically dominated, the stories of nations outside the nexus of colonial power and imperial ambition, and their cultural-political horizons, have tended to remain quite different from those of the British, Dutch, or French national subjects.

As addressed by several of this volume's contributors (see especially chapter 1), both in the past and today, the place of the Czech culture within European civilization has not been an established given. Rather, Czechs (similar to other Slavs and Eastern Europeans) have often been historically relegated to Europe's imagined margins. What are some of the implications of this for the history of Czech women's issues? What does it mean for Czech feminism that Czech emancipated women in the nineteenth century, unlike, for instance, their British counterparts, were constructing their emancipation arguments within the broader context of Czech defensive nationalism rather than in the context of imperial ambition? And what are the implications of this nationalism forging its foundational narrative in a story of Czech men and women as presumably "tolerant, industrious and peace-loving" (Herder 1966, 482–83)? What are the characteristics of this "also European feminism" that results from such a historical and cultural situatedness?

Ethnicity. The above-described cultural and political history and accompanying national mythos, as well as World Wars I and II, have played important roles in shaping the ethnic composition of today's Czech population, as compared to the populations of Western European countries, that is, the former colonial empires. Questions of race/ethnicity and their intersections with sexuality and gender in Czech society are rooted in a history distinct from many other European and Western counterparts. Notably, neither plantation slavery nor colonial adventures overseas figure directly into modern Czech history and the demographic shaping of its peoples. Racism in the Czech culture, whether emanating from women or men, manifests itself differently, with its main targets having historically been the Jewish and Romany minorities. Similar to many other Continental European countries, the very term and concept of "race" has different connotations than, for instance, in the post–civil rights movement United States or in the United Kingdom. Nationalism is the main ideology informing these connotations, with the world wars of the twentieth century and, most poignantly, World War II and the Holocaust constituting strongly determining historical events.

Several chapters in this volume directly address questions of the intersections of gender and race/ethnicity in Czech society. Two contributors attend specifically to questions of gender with respect to two of the major ethnic minorities living in the CR today—the Roma and Vietnamese—focusing on the relationships between these communities and the ethnic Czech majority. What are the main challenges faced by these ethnic minorities, and specifically by their women, in the CR? What can these challenges teach us about the ways in which white Czechs conceive of racial and ethnic difference? How do the answers to these questions contribute to our understanding of racism and ethnic discrimination within Europe?

State-socialist gendered subjectivities.[5] The history of state socialism in East Central and Eastern Europe and its implications for women in the region are topics that have received some scholarly attention. This area of knowledge and history, however, appears subject to widespread disregard in public memory and general educational curricula. WGS scholars present a topic in their classes that the U.S. educational system otherwise does not seem willing or capable of covering adequately. Further complicating this field, it is important to remember that each Eastern European country realized socialist doctrines and Marxist-Leninist ideology differently. There were many socialisms and many different perceptions and lived experiences of socialisms—they differed by region and time period as well as by one's situatedness within the regime or one's generation. The contributors to this volume who attend to the specificity of Czech socialism/s suggest broader questions about alternative routes within Europe toward women's rights. What does it mean for our understanding of the history of European and global feminisms that some of the goals of the U.S. and Western European feminist second wave, such as reproductive rights, accessibility to higher education for women, or women's employment, were argued and achieved in socialist Czechoslovakia as part and parcel of the socialist doctrine? And are these achievements automatically diminished by the fact that they might have been reached because they coincided with the needs of a socialist economy? In what ways is our understanding of the historical feminist second wave adjusted when we study the period from the perspective of the Czechoslovak socialist experience?

Post-1989 specificities. Although since 1989 the CR has embraced the opportunity to once again become "part of Europe," many of this volume's contributions addressing Czech gender, sexuality, and ethnicity issues post-1989 make clear that the country's socialist past continues to be a determining element in how women and men regard feminist issues. And just as there were different forms of socialism across Eastern Europe, so too have the post-1989 transitions toward a market economy been organized and implemented differently across the region. The sociocultural and political-economic effects entailed in the transition toward capitalism and the process of the CR's integration into the European Union (EU) are discussed in this volume. And the book also points out some of the lesser-known phenomena influencing and shaping feminist activism and discourse in post-1989 Czech society. These include the return after 1989 of some anti-feminist Czech male émigrés from exile and the uncritical medialization—that is, bringing attention to an issue through the media—of their prejudiced views concerning feminism; the relative popularity of anarchist activism in post-1989 Czech society (especially around the year 2000), and the popularization of feminist positions within this activism; or the fact that unlike in the United States or United Kingdom, women's nongovernmental organizations (NGOs) and Gender Studies programs at Czech universities have been established without a popular grassroots women's movement in the streets.

LGBT expressions and inflections. Much as Western and particularly Anglo-American cultures have long dominated international understandings of feminism's emergences and meanings, something similar appears to apply to the history and discourse of lesbian, gay, bisexual, and transgender (LGBT) rights movements. Attending to the specificities of gay, lesbian, and transsexual issues in Czech society can help answer some of the following questions. How does the story of LGBT rights activism unfold in a social context where homosexuality was/has been discussed in a medical/sexological framework until very recently? What shape does LGBT activism take in a culture where a vocal popular feminist platform is missing? Do feminist, gay, lesbian, and queer movements and discourses necessarily overlap? Answers to these questions, raised by studying LGBT issues in Czech society, can potentially enhance our collective understanding of global gender and sexuality rights movements and discussions.

Czech language. Czech perceptions and conceptions of gender, sexual, and ethnic identity have, of course, historically developed in and within the Czech language. To whatever extent one accepts sexuality as discursively constructed, particular linguistic contexts convey and enforce normative vocabularies of gender in linguistically idiosyncratic ways. Czech is a highly inflected synthetic language with a morphology that is gendered to a much higher degree than English, the dominant linguistic vehicle of feminist thought. What are the implications of international feminist discourse for finding substantial aspects of its conceptual roots formed and articulated in English as an analytic language? And what happens when we think about feminist issues from within a synthetic and morphologically gender-polarized language such as Czech?

While each of these themes are addressed in some substantial detail by one or more of the studies comprising this volume, many permeate across their most direct or immediate context, resonating and reappearing in other chapters of this collection. The above-delineated categories, while helpful as conceptual organizing devices, are porous to each other.

Along with our intentions of organizing this project so as to address these broader strategic themes, the particular cultural-historical and discursive contexts of these studies deserve some further introduction. The history of the Czech women's movement after all is deeply rooted in the history of the modern Czech nation. Toward this end, the remarks that follow discuss the historical context from which these themes unfold and introduce this volume's individual contributions.

CZECH WOMEN'S EMANCIPATION IN THE NINETEENTH CENTURY

In studying Czech women's emancipation, it is useful to begin in the nineteenth century, the time when the modern Czech nation was forming, literally writing itself into existence. Many words and concepts centrally important to any investigation of Czech women's emancipation, including *Čech* (Czech man), *Češka* (Czech woman), and *emancipovaná žena* (emancipated woman), were coined or began to be solidified into their modern usage within the context of the Czech national revival, and their meaning today still bears traces of this earlier imprint. The concept of "Czechness" emerged in the Czech political consciousness during the nineteenth century in relation to and as distinct from Germanness, and this development of a separate Czech national identity was first and foremost marked linguistically. Indeed, the importance of the Czech language-building project in the Czech nation-building movement cannot be overemphasized. While constituting an independent kingdom in the Middle Ages, the Czech lands became part of the Habsburg Empire in 1526, and by the late nineteenth century—as a result of centuries of Austrian economic and political and German linguistic domination—the Czech language was surviving merely in an oral form and almost exclusively among the poorest. Throughout the nineteenth century, the literary Czech language was gradually refashioned through efforts of Czech national revivalists out of the various Slavic vernaculars spoken in the Czech lands, and was mobilized as a rejection of the German language. As Czech words were being adopted to name reality—places and concepts—and as new Czech words were being coined for concepts for which only German words had existed before, more and more territory—of time past, present, and future—was staked out for Czechness (Macura 1995, 40, 54). The Czech language thus played not only a communicative but also a performative role in that it helped posit and construct the Czech nation into existence.

Besides having a linguistic, cultural, and social dimension, the Czech national project quickly developed a strong ethnic dimension as well. Reading nineteenth-century Czech literature leaves no doubt that Jewish and Romany minorities in particular were perceived as ethnically different from Czechs by the Czech population (see Jusová 2010). After all, developing their concept of the nation, early Czech nationalist writers followed the German philosopher Johann Gottfried Herder, whose understanding of national community was centered around the concept of *Volksgeist*—the assumption that every nation distinguishes itself from others by its essence or spirit. While Herder's writing was viewed generally as favorable to the Slavs, and Czech nationalists embraced his ideas enthusiastically, these conceptualizations of European nations also excluded Jews and Roma. While not all nineteenth-century Czech writers condoned these customary suspicious attitudes toward Jews and Roma, the point here is that the terms *Čech* and *Češka* constituted themselves within this historical and discursive context and were marked not only linguistically and by custom but also ethnically as white. Even today these terms and concepts continue to bear marks of this history to such an extent that writing "white Czech" is perceived as verging on redundancy. It is worth noting that the history of the Czech women's movement first unfolded within the context of this linguistically and increasingly ethnically marked national awakening as well.

Similar to other national projects across Europe, nineteenth-century Czech nationalism also had strong gender dimensions, with conventional gender distinctions being viewed and represented as presumably the very foundation of a healthy nation. Czech male nationalists actively coveted the involvement of women as allies, to the point of even writing under women's pseudonyms to create the impression that the movement was supported more broadly by both men and women. But the male patriots' conceptualization of womanhood was far from revolutionary, and the conventional gender distinction between men as active history makers and women as mothers and men's supporters was viewed as "natural," "inherently Slavic," and vital for the survival of the national community.

Such was the context in which the term *Češka* initially took its meaning: as her fellow man's helpmate, possibly even an active agent, as long as the agency was directed toward the common struggle for national well-being. As Jitka Malečková points out in her contribution to this volume on the nineteenth-century Czech women's movement, a significant dilemma Czech emancipated women faced at the time was how to juggle their commitment to the cause of their nation's survival and their growing consciousness that the same commitment sometimes thwarted their desire for self-realization. Rather than rejecting nationalism, many Czech women worked to shape and adjust the emergent national discourse's representation of the ideal Czech womanhood, frequently manipulating the national project in order to achieve specific gains for women. It seems that most Czech emancipated women in the nineteenth century perceived themselves both as women (with specific gendered obstacles to their personal self-determination) and as members of their national community (whose self-determination and well-being was for them a political urgency as well). Overall, they tended to be particularly successful in propagating the agenda of Czech women's emancipation when they could articulate their demands in terms of the good of the whole nation or as part of the larger nationalist struggle against Austrian (and German cultural) domination. To a great extent, this characteristic appears to have stayed with the Czech women's movement well beyond the nineteenth century.

The articulation and negotiation of a Czech national future is not a solitary occurrence in a nineteenth- and early twentieth-century European context. Indeed, in their comparative overview of nineteenth-century women's movements across Europe, Sylvia Paletschek and Bianka Pietrow-Ennker argue that while these movements were marked by local social and political circumstances, they all seem to have had in common that their emergence was "closely connected with other political and social opposition movements" (2004, 331). Paletschek and Pietrow-Ennker point to a strong connection between religious dissent and early women's emancipation in Germany, France, and Britain; links between early anti-slavery and fledgling women's movements in Britain and America; and the co-emergence of national and women's emancipation movements in the contexts of nations struggling for national sovereignty (such as the Czechs or Poles).

Malečková's chapter in this volume also discusses the entry of working-class women into the Czech women's movement in the nineteenth century. As she observes, overall, Czech working- and middle-class women active in women's emancipation efforts tended to cooperate, possibly due to their shared belief in the priority of national over social issues. With that emphasis on unity noted, it also seems that working-class women were less likely to stay blind to the existing social rifts within the nation. This became particularly clear during the First Congress of Czecho-Slovak Women in 1897. While several leading speakers at the congress expressed alarm over what they perceived as a lack of national consciousness among working-class women (who were seen as falling under the supposedly harmful influences of international socialist discourse) and advocated free educational lectures for poor women and philanthropy as solutions, the female factory workers' representative, Aloisie Jirousková, used the congress platform to expose the existing exploitation of working women in both German and Czech factories and scolded the nation that weeps over its burning National Theater but ignores its poorest women (Jusová 2000a, 183).[6]

It could be argued that in the speeches of the 1897 congress, we can already discern two different streams emerging within the Czech women's movement, which seem to overlap with the two streams foregrounded in Marilyn Boxer and Jean H. Quataert's historiography of early twentieth-century European feminisms—one more aligned with the political goals of the middle classes and focused on such issues as women's political rights and the other aligned with the plight of the working classes and a fledgling socialist ideology (1978, 6).

WOMEN'S ISSUES IN THE FIRST REPUBLIC (1918–1938)

In the aftermath of World War I, the defeated Habsburg monarchy was divided into several independent states. This brought Czech nationalists their long-sought goal: the establishment of an independent republic of Czechoslovakia, along with new national sovereignties for Hungary, Romania, and Yugoslavia. Czechoslovakia was formed as a democratic republic uniting the Czech lands of Bohemia and Moravia (formerly under Austrian domination) with Slovakia and Carpatho-Ruthenia (formerly under Hungarian rule). Aligned with the Czechs through mutually intelligible languages and strong cultural ties (although divided by religion), Slovaks, however, soon came to resent the Prague government's reneging on its promise to grant autonomy to Slovakia. Relations deteriorated, eventually leading to the establishment of an independent Slovak state in 1939.

The interwar period (1918–38) in the region was turbulent and marked by a deepening economic depression, workers' mobilization, territorial disputes, as well as political radicalization and an eventual slide toward fascism. Czechoslovakia, however, is usually considered an exception, and historians have praised the republic for maintaining democracy throughout the interwar period. As Alena Heitlinger has expressed it, interwar Czechoslovakia was the only Western-type liberal state in Eastern Europe. It was also quite economically advanced, as the Czech lands inherited two-thirds of the industrial base of the Austro-Hungarian Empire (1979, 3). Although in the end the country was not spared the Great Depression, when compared to the rest of the region, Czechoslovakia (especially Bohemia and Moravia) fared well.

The interwar period in Czechoslovakia, especially the 1920s, was a time of enthusiastic public debates about the meaning of democracy.[7] Soon these discussions became centered on the rights of national and ethnic minorities (Jews, Germans, Hungarians, Ruthenians, Poles) and of women. One of the characteristics that distinguished interwar Czechoslovakia from many of its neighbors was its pro-democratic leadership. President Tomáš Garrigue Masaryk proved a reliable proponent of gender equality. A former philosophy professor and author of books on "humanita" (humanism, humanity) and democracy, which he viewed as a form of government particularly appropriate for the Czechs (Jusová 2000a, 17), Masaryk was also married to a U.S. feminist, Charlotte Garrigue Masaryk, who translated John Stuart Mill's *The Subjection of Women*. The book became highly influential among leaders of the Czecho(slovak) feminist (a term they indeed used) movement at the time.

Melissa Feinberg's study of the interwar Czech women's movement *Elusive Equality*, which focuses particularly on the efforts of the Women's National Council (WNC), demonstrates how Czech interwar feminists made this rhetorical landscape their own. Led by Františka Plamínková and Milada Horáková, Czech feminists presented women's equality as a linchpin of democracy. Arguing along with Masaryk that the Czech nation was "historically conditioned for democracy," they posited that "those who did not support women's rights were in fact betraying their national democratic heritage" (Feinberg 2006, 24). Drawing on the hegemonic discourse that at the time sought to fuse ideas of nationalism, democracy, and internationalism, Czech feminists quickly gained their first demand—women's suffrage (granted in 1920). However, with their next key demand, focused on revising obsolete family law, which dated back to 1811 and still distinguished between husbands as breadwinners and legal heads of households and wives as mothers and caregivers legally responsible for carrying out domestic chores and obliged to follow their husband's decisions, interwar feminists remained unsuccessful (Feinberg 2006, 42). It would be only the post-1948, pro-Stalinist communist government that would adopt a new progressive family law as partly drafted by the WNC's main representative, the lawyer Horáková, who was executed by the same pro-Stalinist regime in 1950.

Besides the feminist movement that developed among sections of Czech professional women and that focused on suffrage and family law, the interwar period witnessed increased efforts on the part of social democrats and communists to organize women workers. The Czechoslovak Communist Party (CCP) enjoyed strong support among women, as did other left-wing political parties (especially National Socialists). As Heitlinger has foregrounded, the founding of the Czechoslovak communist women's conference in March 1921 actually preceded the establishment of the CCP as such, and "of all the parties represented in the Communist International, [the CCP] had the highest percentage of women among its members" (1979, 53). Reviewing the issues discussed at this first conference, the most immediate problems facing working-class women included poverty, unemployment, persecution of strikers, high prices of food, and low wages. According to Heitlinger, "women delegates demanded day-care centers, playgrounds and public dining rooms for children" (53).

Abortion became a hot topic in interwar Czechoslovakia and in the region, although it was not a topic in which the WNC feminists or Masaryk became involved (Feinberg 2006, 154). The law against abortion affected mostly poor women, and it became an issue linked with the working class rather than the middle-class feminist movement. With the economic crisis deepening, the ban on abortion was perceived by many as part of the system that oppressed working people overall, and the public debate on the issue was often framed in terms of saving poor women from back-alley abortions and the children these women already had from hunger (140). In the neighboring Weimar Republic (Germany), which saw a mass campaign to legalize abortion in the 1930s run by communists, social democrats, and independent women activists, the issue was similarly framed as a matter of social justice rather than an individual women's rights issue, and the campaign was presented as a necessary response to the capitalist emergency—the Great Depression (Grossmann 1995, 81).

Just as they remained silent on the topic of abortion rights, most interwar Czech WNC feminists, as well as Masaryk, were fairly conservative when it came to questions of sex and marriage, which were topics widely debated in interwar Czechoslovakia and across Europe. But while Masaryk and most Czech WNC feminists promoted monogamy and/or abstinence, and rejected ideas of sexual liberation, others called for reforms in sex education and even "free love." Karla Huebner's chapter in this volume focuses on this increasing openness about sexuality among early twentieth-century Czechs, and their interest in questions of contraception, sexual technique, and the rights of sexual minorities. As Huebner points out, this openness was typical of interwar urban Europe, especially in the 1920s. Czechs followed the debates among German and Austrian sex reformists, and in 1921, sexology became a field of study at Universita Karlova (Charles University) in Prague, the oldest and most prestigious institution of higher learning in Czechoslovakia. The political left also followed events in the newly established Soviet Union, where the Bolsheviks enacted a revolutionary family law in 1918 making marriage a union of equal partners and easing divorce (Einhorn 1993, 21). In 1920, the Union of Soviet Socialist Republics (USSR) became the first country to legalize abortion on demand. The Russian Bolshevik Alexandra Kollontai discussed marriage as an oppressive bourgeois institution to be abolished under communism and sought to reconceptualize romantic love and childrearing in new communal ways (Einhorn 1993, 30). These developments were eagerly watched in Europe, although under Joseph Stalin, a more conservative family law was passed in 1936, making abortion in the USSR illegal again.

Focusing in her chapter on the Czech surrealist artist Toyen, who experimented with gender and sexual identity both in life and art, Huebner's contribution illuminates "the range of possibilities open to interwar Czech women," especially those who saw themselves as part of an artistic *bohème*, with its cosmopolitan leaning and links to contemporary international artistic and intellectual movements.

CZECHOSLOVAK STATE SOCIALISM AND WOMEN (1945–1989)

World War II interrupted these developments in Czechoslovakia and the region.[8] Following the 1938 Munich conference between Adolf Hitler and the

Western Allies, the Czech borderland region of Sudetenland, with its majority German (and politically pro-Nazi) population, was ceded to Hitler; soon
after, Prague was occupied. According to Lonnie R. Johnson, the Nazi plans
for the Czechs included an assimilation of half of the population, whereas the
other half, especially "the racially mongoloid elements and the majority of the
intellectual strata," would be eliminated or expelled (1996, 214). Only about 10
percent of the Czech Jewish population and an even smaller percentage of the
Czech Roma survived the war, with most of the rest perishing in extermination
camps (Walters 1988, 284). In the aftermath of World War II, millions of Germans were expelled from Czechoslovakia, Poland, and other regions of Europe;
borders were redrawn; and massive "population swaps" took place. As a result,
previously multiethnic and culturally diverse countries, including Czechoslovakia and Poland, became much more homogeneous.

Through the post–World War II negotiations among the victorious powers,
Czechoslovakia fell into the Soviet sphere of influence. The country's population faced the following situation: the 1938 Munich conference was remembered
as a betrayal of the country by the West, the Russian Army had just liberated
most of the territory of Czechoslovakia, and communists were viewed favorably by many as the largest anti-fascist force before and throughout the war.
The Czechoslovak Communist Party enjoyed much popularity after the war,
and the party won an unambiguous victory in the 1946 elections. The party's
rise to absolute power in February 1948 resulted from communists taking advantage of an ill-timed resignation of social democrats and the fall of the coalition government. By 1948, communists had consolidated power in most of
Eastern Europe. While political manipulation and intimidation were part of
this success, in Czechoslovakia, masses of people were also attracted to socialist ideas and to the "Soviet vision of a new social order based on peace, justice,
equality and prosperity" (Johnson 1996, 237).

Through her chapter in this volume focused on women's issues in socialist
Czechoslovakia, Alena Wagnerová discusses the different shapes the Czechoslovak socialist regime took between 1948 and 1989. Of course, socialism/s also
changed in time and took different paths in different Eastern European countries. As Johnson has expressed it, "the fundamental issue at stake was whether
there was 'one road to socialism' designated and dictated by Moscow or many
individual 'national paths' leading to the same goal" (1996, 238). Except for
Marshal Tito's regime in Yugoslavia, which successfully insisted on a policy
of nonalignment with the USSR, most of the new communist regimes were
pulled into the Soviet path toward socialism, which included nationalization

of industry and banks and collectivization of farms—in an effort to prevent future economic depressions—but also centralization of power in the hands of the Communist Party and suppression of dissent. While the German Democratic Republic (GDR, that is, East Germany) and Czechoslovakia followed this course until the 1960s (and then again post-1968), Poland and Hungary resisted the Stalinist path as inappropriate for their national contexts early on, and they maintained some elements of market economy and, in the case of Hungary, liberal government.

Among its many effects, World War II also interrupted activities of the Czech feminist movement. Feminist leaders Plamínková and Horáková were arrested by the Nazis, and Plamínková was executed in 1942. While Horáková survived the concentration camps, she became a victim of the Stalinist showcase trials in Czechoslovakia. Framed as a traitor, she was hanged in 1950. Post-1948, throughout the region, the term "feminism" came to be rejected as designating a bourgeois women's movement that had nothing to offer to women of the proletariat.[9] However, as Wagnerová discusses in her chapter, equality between men and women was, of course, one of the tenets of the Marxist-Leninist ideology followed by Eastern-European communist regimes, although that goal was subordinated to the main goal of communism—the elimination of class antagonism. The communist regimes across the region officially supported equality of the sexes and women's emancipation, although these seldom became a priority in practice. In the Czechoslovak context, both many of the demands articulated by the interwar feminist National Women's Council (such as the new family law) and the demands expressed by communist women (abortion, socialized childcare, end of unemployment) were actually fulfilled after 1948, but in ways that took agency away from women activists and that often instrumentalized women's emancipation for the socialist state's needs. Hana Havelková and Libora Oates-Indruchová speak of the expropriation of the Czechoslovak women's movement's agenda by the socialist state, noting how the state took the management of women's issues on itself and away from feminist activists (2014, 10).

While acknowledging many persisting problems concerning women's issues, most feminist scholars tend to consider the following provisions enacted by communist governments between 1948–89 as having promoted women's emancipation:

1. *De jure equality of the sexes.* In socialist Czechoslovakia, women's equality with men in all spheres of life was enshrined into both the Constitution and

the new family law.[10] However, everyday reality lagged behind the legislation, and traditional gender roles in the family continued to be viewed as natural.

2. *Women's employment.* Communist governments pursued the goal of women's equal opportunity in education and their full employment, following Friedrich Engels's argument that women's subjugation historically resulted from their economic dependence on fathers or husbands. Scholars have pointed out that the goal of women's employment, and of the opening to women of many professions traditionally closed to them, overlapped with the socialist states' demand for the increased workforce urgently needed to reconstruct war-torn economies. Whatever the agenda behind this policy, the end result was, on the one hand, women's overburdening (due to their double burden with household responsibility and the lack of part-time work) and, on the other hand, women's increased sense of confidence and self-esteem (Gal and Kligman 2000, 53). Indeed, reading Pavla Frýdlová's chapter in this volume based on her interviews with Czech women about their experiences with socialism, one gets a sense of both how overburdened women were and also how proud they were of their accomplishments.

3. *Legalized abortion.* As mentioned above, the USSR was the first country to make abortion available on demand in 1920, albeit a short-lived innovation that was reversed between 1936 and 1955 in order to boost birthrates. Communist governments in Eastern Europe liberalized their abortion laws early as compared to the West, although during times when birthrates were dropping, they often passed various pro-natal policies (enacted selectively in respect to different portions of their populations—a matter I return to in remarks on Romany women). The arguments used to promote legalization of abortion in Czechoslovakia, such as to protect socialist women from back-alley abortions, echoed the pro-abortion arguments developed by labor and communist activists in the interwar period. Czechoslovakia legalized abortion on demand in 1956, although until 1986 permission from an abortion committee was required. From across the Eastern bloc, Hungary made abortion on demand available in 1953, Bulgaria in 1956, Poland in 1956, East Germany in 1972, and Yugoslavia in 1977. In Romania abortion became legal in 1957, but the law was subsequently severely restricted in 1966. Comparable changes in the West lagged one or two decades behind.[11]

4. *Efforts to socialize housework and childcare.* Wagnerová's chapter outlines the progress and problems the Czechoslovak socialist state encountered in efforts to deal with women's dual roles as mothers and workers. Failing to make any substantial progress in regard to gender roles in the family, the state promised to ease what continued to be viewed as women's respon-

sibilities by socializing domestic labor and childcare. Nurseries, kinder-gartens, paid maternity leaves, communal canteens, and extracurricular activities for children were established and available either free or for a nominal fee. People welcomed these measures, whose main objective was to reverse falling birthrates, but some of these practices helped perpetu-ate traditional divisions of labor as they were based on the presumption of women as primary caregivers.

Feminist scholars today debate to what extent these kinds of measures could be viewed as "women friendly" or feminist, in spite of the fact that they were enacted with an eye for ameliorating the double burden for women and meeting the demands of the socialist economy rather than with a specific goal of radically restructuring traditional gender roles. A 2007 *Aspasia* forum fo-cused on this issue, and the contributors' views appeared to depend on their conceptualization of feminism. Thus, for Mihaela Miroiu, feminism is an ideology whose goal is women's autonomy as an end in itself. Since women's emancipation was promoted "as a means for communist revolution, but not for women's autonomy and self-assertion," provisions enacted under state social-ism cannot be viewed as feminist (2007, 198, 199). Elena Gapova, on the other hand, points out that individual autonomy (whether men's or women's) was not the goal of socialism/communism, and thus measuring the achievements of communist regimes by this goal might not make sense: "Communism is a collectivist ideology by definition. . . . [It] was not started to incorporate per-sonal autonomy; its social base is mostly in people for whom other values are more important than autonomy, and it worked for gender equality for other reasons than women's (or men's, though this was less problematic) autonomy" (2007, 231). Marilyn Boxer agrees that since socialism has historically been con-structed in opposition to individualism, any definition of feminism that centers around individual autonomy will automatically exclude the history of Euro-pean socialism (2007, 242).

Other feminist scholars of state socialism also call for an understanding of women's emancipation more broadly focused than one centered on achieving women's autonomy.[12] Amy Borovoy and Kristen Ghodsee cite historical exam-ples (including ones from the West) where "women conceptualized feminism and women's welfare in terms of the social good rather than in terms of indi-vidual autonomy" (2012, 155). And Franciska de Haan, Krassimira Daskalova, and Anna Loutfi similarly point out that women across Eastern Europe have often seen "nationalist and socialist projects as necessary for their own eman-cipation as women" (2006, 7). Rather than limiting their focus to those women activists who fought for women's rights by opposing the local, broader collectivist hegemonic political discourses of their time, these scholars also consider ways in which women sought to effect change while working *within* the parameters set by this hegemonic discourse, especially if it emphasized "common good," a premise with which many women identified.

While women's emancipation was often instrumentalized by the socialist state—coopted for political ends other than women's liberation and put to work for the needs of the state—to argue that under state socialism women's issues only made it on the agenda because the state needed women as workers and reproducers risks doing disservice to those countless women (communist or not) who did seek to devise ways to attend to women's concerns.[13] Furthermore, the practice of instrumentalizing women's emancipation agenda is neither the property nor exclusive product of state socialism. Czech women's emancipation efforts were instrumentalized throughout the nineteenth century for nationalist purposes as well. And the agenda of women's emancipation was similarly coopted, for instance, in nineteenth-century Britain for the purposes of colonial expansion, and again more recently in the 1990s–2000s in the United States for the purposes of justifying war. This history leads some scholars to pose questions as to what ends feminism today might be used by the ascendant neoliberal system being promoted in Eastern Europe post-1989 (Ghodsee 2004, 728; Gapova 2007, 234). Still, research also suggests that throughout these different periods and across these disparate geographic areas, there have always been women who objected to the cooptation of women's emancipation where they recognized it—in ways and to the extent that their specific social systems allowed, although the strategies employed by feminists living under Western or Czechoslovak interwar democracy differed from those available to women under state socialism.

POST-1989 WOMEN'S, SEXUALITY, GENDER, AND ETHNICITY ISSUES

In 1989, one by one the communist regimes across the Eastern bloc collapsed, encouraged by Mikhail Gorbachev's reforms of *glasnost* and *perestroika* in the USSR. The Czechoslovak communist government resigned under the mass pressure of the "Velvet Revolution." The dissident and playwright Václav Havel was elected as the first post-1989 Czechoslovak president, and the country set out on a path of political democratization and market liberalization. In 1993, over differences concerning economic reforms, Slovakia seceded from the republic, and the country split into the Czech Republic and Slovakia. The CR joined the North Atlantic Treaty Organization (NATO) in 1999 and the EU in 2004.

Feminist assessments of the post-1989 changes in the region have been mixed. Scholars from many parts of the former Eastern bloc have reported that the new neoliberal regimes installed in the region after 1989 encouraged a re-traditionalization of gender relations, with women being actively pushed into their presumably "natural" caregiving roles (True 2003, 22–23; Blagojević 2010, 184; Marling 2010, 157; Mlinarević and Kosović 2010, 133; Zhuzhenko 2010, 177; Tereskinas 2012, 194). In this period, many post-socialist countries also witnessed attacks on women's reproductive rights, with Poland severely restricting its abortion law in 1992 as a result of the strong alliance between the new political regime in the country and the Catholic Church. While similar assaults on reproductive rights have been unsuccessful in the more secular Czech context, and while Czech women generally have resisted pressures to give up paid work, they have been disproportionately impacted by the neoliberal process of dismantling social welfare provisions, such as public kindergartens. On the other hand, women (and men) can now organize freely, and soon after 1989, women's groups, initiatives, and NGOs started appearing.

Furthermore, after forty years of mostly limited and officially discouraged contacts between East and West women, many feminists from the United States, Canada, and Western Europe started arriving after 1989 in Prague, Budapest, Warsaw, and other recently re-opened Eastern European destinations to study the post-socialist transition, and particularly gender issues. As Simona Fojtová elaborates in chapter 6, misunderstandings abounded between these foreign feminists and women living in the region—as was to be expected after forty years of sociopolitical separation. Through the back-and-forth exchanges that have followed, a new academic sub-discipline has emerged—Eastern/East Central European Gender Studies. English-language anthologies and monographs published as the discipline has solidified since the early 1990s capture the changing topics taken up by this new subgenre of Gender Studies.[14]

The earlier discussions often featuring heated exchanges between Eastern European women and U.S., Canadian, and Western European feminist scholars around disputes concerning power differentials have subsided to some extent. That mode of discourse has generally been supplanted with statistically grounded assessments of state socialism's impact on women's lives, debates on the role of women's NGOs in the region, evaluations of the effects on Eastern European women of neoliberal economic and political transformations in the region, and appraisals of the impact of the EU accession. To some extent, perhaps reflecting the changing state of WGS discourse itself, the early scholarly conversations on Eastern European women operated with a rather essentialist paradigm of womanhood, while the more recent anthologies have sought to be inclusive of masculinity, LGBT, and ethnic issues, and some have also pertinently called for a rehabilitation of, and a renewed focus on, social class as a category of analysis (Ghodsee 2004, 728; Snitow 2006, 290; Linch 2013, 9).

Contributions comprising the second part of this volume focus on post-1989 political, social, and economic developments in the CR, taking up some of these above-mentioned topics in the broader scholarship on Eastern European women while also endeavoring to move beyond them. Included chapters assess the work of Czech women's NGOs; discuss the specific challenges faced by minority, especially Roma and Vietnamese, and also by elderly women in the CR; outline specificities of the Czech gay and lesbian movement; deal with the topic of "post-socialist masculinity"; introduce the reader to gender issues in contemporary Czech and Slovak art; and also study the gendered aspects of the Czech language. This variety of contemporary topics deserves a few additional preliminary remarks.

Hana Hašková and Zuzana Uhde's contribution outlines the main stages in the development of Czech women's NGOs between 1989 and the present. With no sign of local mass women's movements emerging after 1989, mobilizing around women's issues has taken place mostly through small groups. Yet the legacy of NGOs is a contentious topic in scholarship on Eastern European feminisms. As early as 1997, Sabine Lang evaluated the consequences of the "metamorphization" of German women's movements into small-scale NGOs in ambivalent terms, pointing out that one of the results has been the "tendency to translate complex feminist agenda of emancipation into specific single issues," often focused on women's employment (102). In 2004, Kristen Ghodsee criticized U.S. neoliberal donors' domination of women's NGOs in the former Eastern bloc, positing that as women's NGOs in the region have come to depend on this foreign aid, they are encouraged to emphasize certain issues and gloss over others, especially class issues (728). Ghodsee has also pointed out that NGOs are often charged with the task of patching up the holes in social services left by the ongoing dismantling of the socialist state, in this way easing the progress of neoliberalism in the region (738). On the other hand, Jasmina Lukič, Joanna Regulska, and Darja Zaviršek, while acknowledging that women's NGOs in the region face limited resources and lack authority, have stressed their ability to "simultaneously engage in multiple sites in order to facilitate the mobilization of resources, mount new actions and address specific needs" (2006, 4). In their chapter, Hašková and Uhde map the roots and development of Czech women's public organizing in this period, assessing the different pressures varying forms of funding, pre- and post-EU accession, have brought on women's NGOS' work. In the second part of their chapter, the authors focus specifically on the demands of Czech women's organizations concerning care, and especially childcare, applying Nancy Fraser's concept of "non-reformist reforms" (adopted from André Gorz) to their analysis (Fraser and Honneth 2003).

While Hašková and Uhde focus on Czech feminist developments in the form of NGOS, Linda Sokačová's chapter deals with the very different forms that feminist organizing has taken within the context of Czech anarchofeminist activism. With their subversive, non-hierarchical, and anti-institutional stance, Czech anarchofeminists have been skeptical of the reform-oriented approach to women's issues characteristic of established feminist nonprofits, although these activists do not dismiss the work of NGOS altogether.

A number of contributors to this volume—specifically Karolína Ryvolová, Mária Strašáková, and Simona Fojtová (chapters 9–11)—address questions of race and ethnicity in post-1989 Czech society. How do these issues historically compare to issues of race and racism in the United States and Western European countries? As noted earlier, issues of race and ethnicity in Czech society and Eastern Europe are rooted in a history distinct from that of either Western European colonial powers or the United States. Broadly speaking, the term "race" (*rasa* in Czech) has different connotations in Continental Europe than in the post–civil rights movement United States. Confronted with the history of the Nazi extermination of 6 million Jews, hundreds of thousands of Roma, other minorities (handicapped, homosexuals), as well as Slavs, during the years following World War II, "there was a major movement by scientists [across Europe] to discredit the idea of 'race'" (MacMaster 2001, 167). This effort was supposed to be reinforced in socialist countries by the Marxist-Leninist ideology's explicit anti-racist position (163). Practice, however, lagged behind ideology. Avoiding or discrediting the term did not eradicate racist stereotypes, images, or messages. While levels of education and employment among the Roma rose under socialism, they continued to face deep-seated racial prejudice. In socialist Czechoslovakia, and to a lesser extent Romania, Bulgaria, and Hungary, Romany women were also targeted for sterilization, which was incentivized financially or even performed without their knowledge during abortions or Caesarean sections, a practice that continued into the twenty-first century.

After the collapse of communism, as scholars have pointed out, the Roma "were the group most adversely affected by the transition to market economies," as many of them lost jobs (Vermeersch and Ram 2009, 63). Other forms of discrimination faced by the Roma in the CR include placement of Romany children in "special schools" designed for children with learning difficulties, segregated and substandard housing, and increased racially motivated violence from extremists (Koldinská 2009, 258–62). Based on participant observation, interviews, and Romany fiction, Ryvolová's chapter examines challenges faced by Romany women in the CR, focusing on their roles in the traditional community, the connotations of forced sterilization, abuse in the home, as well as LGBT issues in the community.

Turning our attention to the second largest ethnically distinct group in the CR, Strašáková's chapter focuses on the Czech Vietnamese population, especially Vietnamese women. The origins of the Vietnamese community in Czechoslovakia/Czech Republic can be traced back to the 1950s, when the two socialist countries forged strong ties within the Eastern bloc. Today the community counts more than sixty thousand members. Strašáková analyzes the structure of the Vietnamese population in the CR, focusing especially on challenges that Vietnamese women (of different generations) face in their economic, social, cultural, and political integration.

The last of the chapters in this book devoted to the treatment of ethnic minorities in the CR and to migration, Fojtová's contribution discusses trafficking and the work of and challenges facing La Strada CR, an organization striving to assist women and men trafficked today to the CR from the Ukraine, Bulgaria, Romania, Moldova, Belarus, South East Asia, or Vietnam, whether to do sex work, construction, retail, or domestic labor.

Turning to a different topic, Kateřina Nedbálková's contribution focuses on concerns specific to Czech gay, lesbian, and (to a lesser extent) transsexual discourses and activism. Following on the progressive tradition with regards to attitudes toward sexuality dating back to the interwar First Republic, socialist Czechoslovakia was one of the earliest countries to decriminalize homosexuality in the mid-1960s as a result of lobbying by progressive sexologists. The Registered Partnership Act was passed in 2006 (although it excluded the issue of adoption by gay/lesbian couples), and violent acts of homophobia have tended to be rare in Czech society. Overall, the Czech public is considered fairly tolerant toward gays and lesbians, although heterosexuality as the norm is deeply entrenched and social life remains organized around heteronormative principles. Sex reassignment surgery requires recommendation by a sexologist, single status, and sterilization but is covered by national insurance and has been carried out by Czech surgeons since the 1960s. Progressive politics in the

CR—notable as compared to the rest of the region—would suggest an openly vocal and expressive LGBT community, but in reality public presence remains relatively low profile. Discussing the results of two research projects—one with gay men who came of age under socialism, the other with a younger generation of lesbian mothers—Nedbálková's chapter focuses on the forms Czech gay and lesbian organizing takes today and how it compares with the ways in which Czech gays and lesbians socialized before 1989.

In another line of study concerning gendered identities, Iva Šmídová's chapter focuses on questions of Czech masculinity and responds to an increasing interest in what some scholars have called a crisis of masculinity in post-socialist countries. While the unsustainability of the conventional male role is an increasingly visible topic for public discussion, prevailing public and institutional contexts marked by the continued dominance of men, and the mechanisms of the reproduction of male dominance, receive less attention. Šmídová uses the concept of hegemonic masculinity (as developed within the field of Critical Studies on Men and Masculinities) to investigate the mechanisms that continue to bring men to dominance and to understand why structural masculine domination can be perceived by individual men as involuntary and imposed. In this chapter the author explores these issues by analyzing the statements of respondents working in a setting that has long traditionally been professionally prestigious and publicly respected: physicians in the obstetric wards of Czech hospitals.

In the next chapter, turning attention to a group of women often marginalized in feminist and other scholarship, Šiklová's contribution addresses challenges faced by women aged sixty-five and older. Compared to Western Europe, the present cohort of elderly Czech women spent most of their productive lives living under state socialism and fully employed. Thus today they have their own independent pensions. Still, economically, elderly women often find themselves worse off than older men due to structural inequalities long embedded in employment policies and practices. By focusing on the cohort of elderly women, infrequently addressed by Gender Studies scholars, this chapter aims to shed light on neglected issues and advocate for a feminism that would understand itself as a discourse for the variety of walks of life in which all eventually come to play a part.

Bringing the discussion of post-1989 feminism to the arena of contemporary visual art, Zuzana Štefková analyzes the development of gender- and sexuality-related discourses in Czech and Slovak art since 1989, seeking to assess the relevance and impact of these debates on the processes of art production and interpretation. Using examples of contemporary Czech and Slovak visual arts and posing questions about the relevance of the gender identity of an artist, curator, or art teacher, Štefková explores the role of gender in the production of art and artistic meaning.

Finally, Jana Valdrová's chapter is one of the first studies introducing English readers to gender bias in the Czech language. While in the U.S. and British contexts it has become commonplace to discuss the various ways in which traditional English-language practices, such as the use of the generic "he," may be understood as discriminatory, Valdrová has been one of the first linguists to pose similar questions in the Czech context. The path ahead is long in that issues of gender discrimination through the use of the generic masculine, familiar to English readers, are compounded by questions of gender polarization inscribed into the morphology of the Czech language.

Valdrová's contribution sheds useful light on questions concerning the place that English language has tended to play in the operation and development of WGS as a transnational academic field. What are the implications of the fact that the thinking about gender issues that continues to dominate international feminist scholarship is rooted in English as an analytic (mostly morphologically androgynous) language? What happens when we think about feminist issues from within a synthetic and gender-polarized language such as Czech? What are some of the challenges and concerns that emerge in this context and with which Anglo-American feminists (who perceive and think of gender in English-language terms) might not be faced? Or, in the words of Kornelia Slavova and Ann Phoenix, "how is gender reconfigured in the movement from one linguistic and cultural environment to another?" And how do we pay attention to these questions without at the same time overemphasizing or romanticizing cultural difference (2014, 332)? At issue is not only the Anglo-American knowledge gatekeeping in the field of transnational Gender Studies. We must also come to terms with the fact that language, rather than comprising a simple code, is a broader environment which co-structures how speakers experience and embody gender and other lived concepts (Descarriers 2014, 566).

It is our hope that together the variety of studies and inquires comprising this volume contribute toward a better-formed picture of the many factors and dimensions of Czech and East Central European feminism/s both today and in some of the defining moments leading to the present. Readers should gain a substantive picture of the Czech context, from a gendered and intersectional perspective, while being challenged to rethink feminist knowledge assumptions from within an East Central European and Slavic perspective. The relevance and topicality of the book is underscored by the ongoing emphasis within Gender Studies on broadening and diversifying feminist scholarship and on exploring alternatives to the Anglo-American–centric trajectory previously so common to WGS discourse. After all, feminism that is adequate to the challenges before us needs to be in touch with itself as well as attuned to the world around it.

NOTES

1. Charta 77 (Charter 77) was a document written and signed by 242 Czech political dissidents and their sympathizers in 1977. The document criticized the Czechoslovak communist government for human rights violations, and its dissemination was forbidden.

2. The Women's and Gender Studies in Europe program was affiliated with Antioch University until 2016 when it was transferred to Carleton College.

3. While the Czech nation shared much of its twentieth-century history with the Slovak people (the two nations were part of Czechoslovakia between 1918–1938 and 1945–1993), this volume focuses primarily on the Czech Republic (CR). Slovakia exhibits many national, cultural, geopolitical, and religious specificities beyond the scope of this volume, which deserve to be treated on their own terms. Slovakia was part of Czechoslovakia until the end of 1992 and became independent in January 1993.

4. See chapter 1 for a discussion of the terms "Eastern Europe" and "East Central Europe."

5. Although some scholars use the terms "communism" and "post-communism" descriptively when referring to Eastern European countries' socialist past, I find the terms "socialism," "state socialism," and "post-socialism" more adequate. Communism was presented as the distant goal of an ideal, classless society of equals, which Eastern bloc societies were to reach one day in the future, while socialism was the transitional stage those societies had to presumably go through while trying to achieve the communist ideal. I do use the term "communist" when referring to "communist regimes" to highlight the leading role of Communist Parties in those regimes.

6. Abstracts of the speeches presented at the congress were published as a supplement to *Ženské listy* [Women's Journal] 1.11 (1897).

7. See Melissa Feinberg (2006, especially 6–10) on the debates in interwar Czech society about the meaning of democracy. As she points out, for Czechs, democracy was both "a set of political ideas that would help create a just system of governance for all and . . . also the form of governance that would best enable the Czech nation to flourish" (7). Soon it became apparent, Feinberg notes, that there was no one single vision of democracy in the Czech nation, but this ambiguity was actually part of the reason the term could operate as a unifying concept (7).

8. During World War II, Slovakia became an independent state aligned with the Third Reich, and Ruthenia was partially annexed by Hungary. After the war, Slovakia and the Czech lands were reconnected again in a single country (until the end of 1992), while Ruthenia became part of the Soviet Union.

9. Marilyn Boxer dates the origins of the socialist/communist rejection of feminism as bourgeois to the turn of the twentieth century, and she points to the German socialist Klara Zetkin's role in this history (2007, 242). Boxer also notes the irony, in the context of this history, of the post-1989 rejection of feminism in Eastern Europe as presumably too closely associated with socialism and communism (245).

10. For a detailed discussion of the various iterations of the Czechoslovak socialist family law, see Barbara Havelková 2014, 33–42.

11. The United Kingdom liberalized its abortion law in 1967, the United States in 1973, Sweden in 1974, France in 1975, Italy and Norway in 1978, the Netherlands in 1984, while in West Germany abortion remained unconstitutional but became available in restricted cases in 1976.

12. This debate mirrors similar discussions among Arab and other postcolonial feminists. Most notably, Saba Mahmood has questioned some of the assumptions underpinning Western liberal feminist conceptualizations of agency as oppositional, as well as the liberal understanding of self-realization as always necessarily linked to individual autonomy (2005, 5–11).

13. On this issue, see Kristen Ghodsee's research in the Bulgarian context (2012) or Wang Zheng's research in the context of communist China (2005).

14. The anthologies include *Gender Politics and Post-Communism* (1993), *Ana's Land* (1997), *The Politics of Gender after Socialism* (2000), *Women and Citizenship in Central and Eastern Europe* (2006), *Gender Politics in the Expanding European Union* (2008), *Women and Gender in Postwar Europe* (2012), and *Postcommunism from Within* (2013).

PART 1

GENDER ISSUES IN CZECH SOCIETY PRIOR TO 1989

1 SITUATING CZECH IDENTITY

Postcolonial Theory and
"the European Dividend"

IVETA JUSOVÁ

In 1993, THE publication of *Gender Politics and Post-Communism: Reflections from Eastern Europe and the Former Soviet Union* marked one of the first post-1989 English-language scholarly anthologies on Eastern European women. The express aim of Nanette Funk and Magda Mueller in editing their collection was to provide discursive space for women from post-1989 Eastern Europe to directly voice their perspectives and to "explain" to Western readers the situatedness of Eastern European women's issues. From newly enabled (post-1989) encounters across borders, the situation appeared to call for explanations on both sides.

Along the lines of Simona Fojtová's observations (addressed in greater detail later in this volume), throughout the 1990s, misunderstandings abounded between feminists from "the West" arriving in newly reopened Eastern European destinations and the women who had resided there all along. The initial impulse on the part of North American and Western European feminists traveling to the region seems to have been to look for the familiar in the unfamiliar, and the ensuing misrecognitions were often resented by Eastern European women writers and activists. The North American feminist academic discourse at the time—featuring both well-articulated postcolonial critiques and significant discussion concerning long-neglected intersections of race and gender—would seem to include a number of relevant cautions against presuming a universality of women's experience. Yet Western feminism's post–Cold War sojourns to the East curiously appeared to leave these lessons behind, to find them somehow inapplicable. Eastern European women were perceived as white and (more or less) European—and these surface appearances perhaps invited expectations for similarities rather than differences with mainstream Western feminisms. "They just needed to catch up with the West" was the initial as-sumption, although it was gradually replaced with a more tentative approach, following the first, often disorienting clashes and disappointments. The domi-nant strands of feminist discussions of difference in the United States at the time flowed along the lines of race or sexual orientation. In the Czech Republic (CR), and other countries of Eastern Europe, however, there were women who looked like the feminists arriving from the United States and Canada (predom-inantly of white European ancestry) but who still insisted on their specificity and difference. These women, while acknowledging that, yes, women and men were indeed treated differently in Eastern Europe, were not even necessarily convinced that feminism was needed.

It is fascinating to compare the 1993 anthology by Funk and Mueller, pub-lished soon after the dissolution of the Cold War barriers, with Joanna Regul-ska's and Bonnie G. Smith's 2012 *Women and Gender in Postwar Europe*, writ-ten two decades later. Clearly, Regulska and Smith found themselves facing a very different Europe than had Funk and Mueller in the early 1990s, one much less visibly divided along East-West lines perhaps, even if one also more in-ternally differentiated. Indeed, already in 2000, Susan Gal and Gail Kligman noted an increasing convergence between East and West concerning women's issues after 1989, and in 2008, Allaine Cerwonka even suggested that the con-tinued emphasis on differences between East and West in scholarship dealing with Eastern European women risks further entrenching the existing power differentials and gulf between Eastern and Western feminists (814). Regulaska's and Smith's 2012 anthology seems to be responding to these calls as it repre-sents post–World War II Europe comprehensively, interweaving voices from across East and West, North and South in a single volume. Differences within the same countries or regions are underscored, almost to the same degree as differences and similarities among the regions. While recognized as inherently demographically plural, Europe is also nudged here discursively in the direc-tion of being recognizable as one. This narrative cross-weaving and integration seems inspired by the editors' recognition of the continued undesirable asso-ciations connected with the idea of a separate East (and the continued nega-tive ramifications for countries of being relegated into the East), as much as by the actual economic and political integration of the region through contin-ued European Union (EU) eastward expansion. The question remains to what extent this project of (nuanced and differentiated) discursive reunification is reflected in "reality." Addressing specifically the question of post-socialist con-texts, Regulska and Grabowska could write in the 2012 anthology that "many post-state-socialist states are now considered part of the 'developed' world." But they also immediately add that "the old divisions—based on the east and west of Europe—persist, and make activists and scholars raise questions about the specificity of east European feminism" (212).

ARE THESE EUROPEANS?

The persistence of the East-West demarcation—especially conceptually and in terms of cultural imagination—intrigues me as a Czechoslovak-born WGS and humanities scholar who has been bringing U.S. WGS students to the region for the past eleven years. Study abroad involves crossing borders and experiencing cross-cultural encounters in foreign settings. Throughout these physical and intellectual processes of transition, cultural associations, stereotypes, and pre-conceived notions (some that we might not have even been aware of possessing) become triggered more intensely than when learning about a subject at home. Available scholarly works, including political and sociological analyses of the region, such as the ones mentioned above, help ground students' learning about Eastern Europe in facts and history, although these studies do not necessarily account for or counter the cultural associations through which these facts will be filtered and interpreted in students' and other travelers' minds. Neither do they always sufficiently address the global power relations within which U.S. students' cross-cultural learning in the CR, and other Eastern/East Central European countries, takes place.

By the time we arrive in Prague, after already having spent several months in two or more Western European cities, some of my students curiously report expecting Czech people to be "slightly darker" with "prominent facial hair" (in the case of men) and "sexually virile" (again specifically regarding Czech men). Students recognize that these are "racialized images absent in my mind when thinking of Western Europe," and are curious about where these preconceptions might be coming from. Leaving Prague, some students have commented, self-reflexively and sincerely yet with clear value judgment, on their perception of Czech fashion as backward ("stuck in the 90s time warp"), the population as too white and homogeneous, Czech gays and lesbians as insufficiently politically active, feminists as too straight, and people in the streets as staring at our gender-variant and racially mixed group too much. The fact that these value judgments of perceived "cultural delay" are harbored by otherwise generally well-prepared liberal arts college students who are encouraged in their curricula to question these kinds of presumptions and who overall make a conscientious effort to be

culturally sensitive, makes these observations even more provocative and telling. As far as cultural imagination and mental mapping is concerned, the CR
and Prague (geographically, of course, located to the northwest of Vienna) continue to be perceived as rather precariously and incompletely situated within
Europe, despite political and economic analyses that appraise the CR as being
one of the most solidly "arrived in Europe" from among the post-socialist countries. My students' perceptions of the CR, somewhat irrespective of the facts
they learn about the country, appear filtered through expectations and preconceptions disposing the Western viewer to evaluate the cultural differences encountered as inherently inferior or wanting.

Reflecting on these continuing East-West divisions in our mental geography, and, more importantly, on the stubborn hierarchy projected onto these
divisions, I find Larry Wolff's 1994 *Inventing Eastern Europe* invaluable, even
though the picture of Eastern Europe painted there is rather monolithic.
Guided by Edward Said's postcolonial framework but paying close heed to the
specificity of Eastern Europe, Wolff reminds us that the idea of Eastern Europe, accompanied by traditions and habits of conceptualizing the region as
backward, is much older than the Cold War. He traces the invention of Eastern
Europe to the Enlightenment, when the previous conventional mental orientation for thinking about the European Continent along a North-South axis
(characteristic of the Renaissance) was gradually replaced with a new West-
East orientation. Wolff makes a convincing argument that "Churchill's demarcation of a boundary line 'from Stettin in the Baltic to Trieste in the Adriatic'
followed a line that was drawn and invested with meaning over two centuries"
(4). If the invention of Eastern Europe as the "complementary other half of
Western Europe" (4) predates the Cold War by two centuries, it is then perhaps
less of a puzzle why the hierarchically organized West-East demarcation would
prove so persistent, even with many Eastern European countries now officially
integrated into the EU.

Combing through eighteenth- and nineteenth-century German, British,
French, and Austrian accounts of real and fictitious voyages into the Eastern
"shadow" lands, Wolff delineates how the region gradually emerged and solidified as a mediating cultural zone "between European liberty and Asiatic
despotism" (7). What the eighteenth- and nineteenth-century travelers seem
to have found particularly off-putting and worth remarking upon—besides the
perceived "filth and misery," serfdom, and sexual promiscuity—was the mix-
ture (today we would say diversity) of races, nations, cultures, and customs.
Phrases such as "an inconceivable melange," "a motley aggregation of primi-

tive people," and "a racial mish-mash with strong Asiatic elements" proliferate in the excerpts quoted by Wolff, with frequent references to "swarms of Jews" (369, 28). This racial, cultural, and national heterogeneity, clearly assessed as inferior, combined with the incomprehensible (to Westerners) Slavic, Hungarian, and Romanian languages, helped produce the impression of the East as a land of nonsense, paradox, and unresolved contrasts.

Focusing mostly on British, German, and French accounts, Wolff captures the West as gazing at the East, but, of course, the East has long been looking back. The following quotation from a short story written by the late nineteenth-century Czech nationalist writer Gabriela Preissová demonstrates that Czechs, Moravians, Slovaks, and no doubt others from among the "motley of incomprehensible races and nations" were well aware of the gaze and perceived it in terms of lopsided power relations.[1] A fictional Viennese baroness, who comes to witness a harvest celebration and be entertained by seasonal workers' national dances, is depicted as objectifying Moravian workers through her folklorist's curious gaze:

> "Ranger, ask them to sing something for us," the baroness said. "I am
> much interested in studying such originalities. What nation is it?"
> "They are Slovaks," the ranger answered with his neck bowed, "mostly from
> higher Hungary."
> "Do they speak Hungarian?" the baroness inquired, looking around through
> her monocle.
> "No, madam. They speak a Slavic language similar to Czech.". . .
> "The ladyship wishes to hear one of your songs."
> "Something national," the baroness added. (1896 [1889], 95, my translation)

Preissová represents the baroness unsympathetically, as a critical caricature of nineteenth-century Austrian urbanites whose interest in understanding the people of the empire did not go beyond their folklorist curiosity about the songs they did not understand and the costumes they collected.

It is interesting to compare how Western travelers of what perhaps now seems like a distant past once perceived Eastern Europe with what their counterparts say today. While in the eighteenth and nineteenth century visitors complained about the region as presumably excessively racially diverse, today it is often the opposite. My American students regularly comment on the racial uniformity of the Czech population. Whereas in the past Westerners seem to have been preconditioned to value homogeneity, and they assessed Eastern Europe as inferior because of the perceived excess of diversity that they encountered there, U.S. students today have increasingly been acclimated to valuing diversity and multiculturalism, and they find the Czech lands inadequate once again, although this time it is for the perceived lack of diversity of the population. There is certainly some truth to this perception, although the relative ethnic homogeneity must be first and foremost understood in its historical context of post–World War II reconstruction in Eastern Europe reliant almost exclusively on the labor of local populations, in contradistinction to late-colonial and then postcolonial political-economic migrations in the West. Against such a backdrop, shaped through four decades of local continuity with relatively little broader geographic migratory influences, the East inevitably has come to feature some noticeable demographic homogeneity.

But beyond any complaints of "lagging behind" in terms of overt multicultural mix, Eastern/East Central Europeans, including the Czechs, continue to be othered in other ways as well—and often this othering is articulated in gendered and sexualized language. Wolff discusses how in the past, Eastern Europe was perceived as sexually promiscuous and a place to explore and enact forbidden sexual fantasies (1994, 57). The sense of the region's primitiveness and backwardness, in fact, rested to a large extent on presumptions about its population's sexual profligacy. While the region had become effectively closed off to Western visitors after 1948, following 1989 (speaking specifically of the CR again), the perception of sexual promiscuity was quickly picked up again and reconstructed by (and for) Western travelers. As Timothy M. Hall has articulated it, "Soon after the Velvet Revolution in 1989, tourists from neighboring Austria and Germany began visiting cities in what was then Czechoslovakia. They were drawn not only by curiosity about their neighbors . . . but also in increasing numbers by a growing sexual mystique around 'Eastern', Slavic women and men, seen as wild, passionate, uninhibited—in some ways more primitive and natural than the restrained and civilized Germans" (2007, 458). Of course, this exoticizing rhetoric also served as an alibi for sexual exploitation purchased from the standpoint of significant economic advantage. Since 1989, the CR, and especially Prague, has become a major producer of pornography, particularly gay porn, and Anglophone and Germanophone male sex tourists have poured into what many of them perceive as "sexual paradise" (459) in search of cheap sex with not only local (and other Eastern European) women and gay men but, apparently, also local heterosexual men. Hall further notes, "Part of the Western gay fantasy of Slavic sexuality since the early 1990s derives from the relative availability in post-socialist countries of heterosexual-appearing men who are willing to engage in sex with other men" (458). The position of Czechs, women and men, as mostly providers of sexual services rather than paying clients would seem to reinforce their place among "the rest" rather than on an equal footing with the West.

While during socialism Czech and other Eastern European women were often represented in the West as asexual or masculine, as gray and shapeless workers, today, in contrast, not only are Czech women represented as highly sexualized but Czech men seem to figure in the Western cultural imaginary mostly as feminized. In this context, Jacqui True's consideration of the post-1989 Czech economic and political situation through the prism of gender and sex representation is quite perceptive. She explores the ways in which Czech men are placed disadvantageously "in subject positions relative to Western men in global capitalism" (2003, 114). Examining local advertisements for Western European products and companies, True notes how Czech men are commonly constructed in them as "secondary, incomplete subjects, not yet rational or masculine enough to 'return to Europe'" (114). True's observation is congruous with Boris Buden's 2010 insights, in "The Children of Postcommunism," about the infantalization of post-socialist societies in Western spectators' comments.[2] Buden ponders the preponderance of metaphors of immaturity and childhood in the Western "jargon of postcommunist transition," noting the irony faced by Eastern European subjects: one day they are being celebrated for toppling totalitarian regimes, only to be declared "still in diapers" politically the next. Buden suggests there is no ambiguity regarding whose interests are served here: "There is no relation of domination that seems so natural and self-evident as the one between a child and a guardian, no mastery so innocent and justifiable as that over children," and he speaks of the childhood metaphor as "a symptom of the new power relationship" between the self-proclaimed mature West and the immature post-communist East. The combination of rendering Eastern Europeans as politically immature and childlike while simultaneously representing them in sexualized ways—alternately as a pre-subjective, uninitiated novice and as a fetishistic object of pseudo-pedophilic attraction—makes for a strangely disabling relational expectation with Western influence. In the meantime, Czech men, especially Czech male politicians, try to compensate and "catch up" with what the West represents to them as dominant (and mature) masculinity, often doing so on the backs of their divorced wives and accompanied by new, young trophy wives.

The Czech land has been feminized for Westerners as well, particularly in the immediate post-1989 period, when it was often represented as a virgin territory, in a language that harks back to that used by Western colonizers of overseas territories of the distant past. Anne McClintock and other postcolonial scholars have explored the long tradition of ways in which male colonial agents' travel to new continents and unexplored territories was often narrated and expressed as "an erotics of ravishment" (1995, 22). McClintock continues: "For centuries, the uncertain continents—Africa, the Americas, Asia—were figured in European lore as libidinously eroticized" (22). Similarly, as True has pointed out, the Eastern European markets have been represented as "the adventure playgrounds for male managers, investors and professional risk-takers." In 1993, *Playboy* described Prague as a "great multinational orgy of buying and selling" (Bruce Jay Friedman, quoted in True 2003, 23). True summarizes perceptively: "The capitalist push eastward allows these men to claim 'virgin territory' and to reassert their western hegemonic masculine identity *vis-à-vis* the 'wild, wild East'" (23). In the meantime, the land and country's wealth are being misappropriated and much of it placed in the hands of foreign investors. By 2000, 30 percent of Czech industry and 25 percent of Czech banking were foreign owned, and "the trend was towards even more local banking and industry coming under foreign control" (Ramet 2007, 24). And according to the 2011 Investment Climate Statement on the CR, issued by the U.S. State Department, "more than eighty percent of the Czech economy is now in private hands . . . [and] most major state-owned companies have been privatized with foreign participation."[3]

EASTERN/EAST CENTRAL EUROPEAN LOCATION AND THE POSTCOLONIAL DISCOURSE

If Czechs, other Slavs and Eastern Europeans in general have been historically appraised by "Europeans proper" as only precariously connected with the cultural life and heritage of the continent, how have the Eastern Europeans themselves perceived their location in relation to Europe? As Vladimír Macura has summarized in his essay "Dream of Europe," "Throughout their history, Czechs have seen themselves as, variously, standing at the center of Europe, at the edge of Europe, or as forming a bridge between the 'civilized' West and the 'barbaric' East" (2010, 13). At some historical periods, especially post-1948, Europe came to figure as a hostile, degenerate world, and the (official) Czech sight was cast in the direction of Russia. At other periods—indeed, most of the time—Czechs sought to write themselves into Europe's very center. Being relegated in the Western mind to the margins, Czech intellectuals have persistently claimed the center instead, embracing the term and concept of Central (or East Central) Europe. Macura, for instance, quotes the former dissident and post-1989 politician Petr Pithart: "Eastern Europe is shifting sands . . . the fragile edge of the European continent, a crumbling edge falling away and disappearing from Europe. I understand Eastern Europe as a fully realized 'spiritual Balkanization,' Central Europe as a sober, skeptical but nevertheless tenacious will for synthesis" (21). And analyzing Václav Havel's dissident writing, Timothy Garton Ash points out that Havel used the term "Eastern Europe" when the context is negative or neutral and "Central" or "East Central Europe" when the context is positive (1989 [1986], 184). Furthermore, most Czech writers have historically represented this claimed geographic centrality as coming hand in hand with a presumed historic role for the Czech culture as the depository of the most authentic European values, in a position to renew, when needed, "moribund Western civilization with an influx of Slavic values" (Macura 2010, 13).

After 1989, as the CR came to view itself as competing with other post-socialist nations for NATO and especially EU memberships, the Slavic attribute (a connection with Russia) became de-emphasized, while the concept of Central Europeanness was fully embraced and manipulated. The objectives have been strategic: to distance their nation, in the eyes of Western donors and institutions, from Eastern Europe, with its continued associations of cultural, economic, and civic backwardness. Similar efforts to shake off associations with the East appear to have been shared by all former Eastern European bloc countries (Burgess 1997, 63; Kovačević 2008, 9; Veliković 2012, 166). Inclusion into the "European club," and the requisite transition to a market economy and its supposed promises of riches, thus seems to require adopting and mastering the rhetoric of Eastern backwardness, combined with a simultaneous vehement disassociation from the East.

The location of the Czech lands in the presumably backward Eastern Europe, although mitigated to some extent by Czechs' desire and ability to discursively relocate themselves to Europe's center, calls for a reflection on the applicability and possible usefulness of a postcolonial theoretical framework for discussions of the Eastern/East Central European, and specifically Czech, situation. Thinking of my U.S. students, typically with no prior experiences with the so-called Second World, arriving in East Central Europe can be disorienting without some effort at a careful mapping of the situatedness of this geopolitical and cultural-historical demarcation in relation to the First and Third Worlds. The concept of Eurocentrism, through which U.S. students tend to view European cultures overall, is only partially useful here as it obfuscates power differentials between the West (the United States and Western Europe) and the Eastern/East Central European location.

Adjectives like "backward" and "barbarian" in the above-mentioned travelers' accounts of Eastern Europeans inevitably echo the all-too-familiar discourse of inferiority produced by Western writers and colonial administrators about African, Arab, or Asian native populations. The fact that throughout the eighteenth and nineteenth centuries most Eastern European nations (with the exception of Russia, itself an empire) were subjugated under powerful Western European empires suggests further parallels with former colonies. As Jitka Malečková reminds us in this volume, from the sixteenth century into the early twentieth, the Czech lands and people were dominated by imperial neighbors. It took a century-long grassroots language, culture-, and myth-making project before the nationalist discourse grew into the dominant cultural and political discourse in Czech society, which, opportunely situated by the shattering of Habsburg Austria at the end of World War I, culminated in the foundation of independent Czechoslovakia in 1918. The emergent and triumphant Czech national formation in a way foreshadowed the unraveling of colonial influence later in the century, with Western European imperial powers proving unable to indefinitely sustain overt political, economic, and religious domination beyond their constituent national borders.

Writing about Poland, another East Central European country that, similar to the Czechs, experienced centuries of domination by European empires, Clare Cavanagh insistently advocates for the application of postcolonial theories and language to the context of Eastern Europe.[4] Cavanagh reminds her readers that "there have been European empires with *European colonies*. . . . And yet, only one European country, Ireland, has generated a sizable literature in critical theory on its troubled colonial past and semi-postcolonial present" (2004, 84, 85; emphasis added). Other scholars reflecting on these questions have pointed out that the intra-European geographical location of (what today are) Eastern European countries is inconsistent with the overseas aspect so crucial to colonial dynamics (Regulska and Grabowska 2013, 173), although discussing the case of the eighteenth- and nineteenth-century Russian Empire, Marc Ferro has challenged the criterion of overseas expansion as a necessary characteristic of modern colonization (1997, 2). Wolff's implicit comparison between the historical Western European treatment of Eastern Europe and of overseas colonies is also instructive and worth noting here. Wolff specifies that while clearly perceived as backward, "Eastern Europe was located *not at the antipode of civilization, not down in the depths of barbarism, but rather on the developmental scale* that measured the distance between civilization and barbarism" (1994, 13; emphasis added).

Studying East Central "also European" cultures certainly works to provincialize and decenter some of the givens in contemporary debates about the history/ies of European colonialism. What are the implications for our understanding of the history of European imperialism and Eurocentrism that Czechs, similar to other Eastern Europeans, have been often historically relegated to Europe's imagined margins, and that their place in Western cultural imagination has to some extent mirrored that of the oriental, the colonial, the native? Europe is not the product of one nation, one people, a single party, an economic bottom line, one master race, one dominant gender. Even within Europe, there is the West, East, North, and South.

Turning attention toward more recent and present-day circumstances, Madina Tlostanova (2012), Nataša Kovačević (2008), Vedrana Veliković (2012), Hana Červinková (2012) and others have also pondered the potential fruitfulness of bringing a critical postcolonial lens to bear on post-socialist Eastern European experiences and discourses. Are there overlaps, they ask, between some of the dilemmas faced and experienced by postcolonial subjects on the one hand and the so-called post-socialist subjects on the other? And would the discourses and disciplines that have developed around each of these historically, geopolitically, and culturally specific paradigms benefit from mutual cross-pollination?

In her contribution to these scholarly inquiries and efforts, Tlostanova shifts the emphasis away from situations of direct colonial expropriations of land and resources (colonialism) and toward "mind colonization" or "colonization of knowledge and being" (what she calls "coloniality"). Tlostanova here draws on the conceptual framework developed by Walter Mignolo and other members of the decolonial collective (2012, 132). Distinguishing between two types of modernity, the liberal/capitalist (as represented by Western Europe) and the socialist/statist (as represented by the former Soviet bloc), Tlostanova argues that each has had its own kind of coloniality (137). The term "decolonial option" then refers to intellectual, cultural, and epistemic efforts on the part of those historically subjected to "mind colonization" to delink from modernity and coloniality (whether liberal/capitalist or socialist/statist) and to develop their own paths, creating something different (138).

Other scholars of post-socialism use the postcolonial theoretical framework that goes back to Edward Said in their efforts to disrupt Western mainstream representations of the region and to critique the continued Western monopoly on knowledge production as such. Kovačević, for instance, has made use of Said's concept of Orientalism to critique the ways in which some scholars have deployed orientalizing metaphors and discourses of Eastern Europe's presumed racial inferiority and backwardness, in their efforts to rhetorically naturalize their dismissal of Soviet and Eastern European socialist pasts and justify the teleology of presumably inevitable neoliberal capitalist globalization (2008, 16). "I suggest," Kovačević writes, "that the 'othering' of Eastern European communism was aided, among other things, precisely by the existing discourses on Eastern European racial inferiority, barbarism and overall backwardness." (16). In this context, I also find pertinent Červinková's observation and argument that the category and field of post-socialism/post-communism were first established after 1989 by Western anthropologists as a "project of [Western] epistemological dominance and subjugation" (2012, 159). Červinková posits this main epistemological distinction between the postcolonial and post-socialist categories: "Postsocialism is an orientalizing concept through which western anthropologists constructed postcommunist Europe," whereas "postcolonial theory is a result of an indigenous project of critique" (159). The promise of the use of a postcolonial lens by Eastern European scholars, then, is that it might help articulate a critical local Eastern European standpoint/s on post-1989 social and political developments, ideally delinked from both the Western and former Soviet hegemonic narratives.

THE CONCEPT OF THE "EUROPEAN DIVIDEND"

Any effort to study Eastern/East Central European societies through the grid of postcolonial (or decolonial) theory needs to include a serious consideration of questions of race and ethnicity, and not only in the analyses of East-West relations but also in investigations of racial arrangements within Eastern European societies themselves. The continued Orientalization/infantalization of Eastern, including East Central, European cultures, populations, and lands adds another dimension to the already registered and studied (yet persisting) types of European racisms, including the "old" (but persistent) anti-black, anti-Semitic, and anti-Romany racisms, and the newer anti-immigrant "racism without race" of Étienne Balibar.[5] Encountering expressions of the Orientalizing attitude from Western commentators or facing violence when traveling for work to the countries of the "European core"[6] does not stop Eastern/East Central Europeans, including Czechs, from subjecting those vulnerable to consideration as lower on the geographical and economic rung to similar Orientalizing and racializing attitudes. The Czech Romany population serves today as the main geographically internal group against whom ethnic Czechs affirm their whiteness and

Europeanness. The concept of Central Europe or East Central Europe also suggests Czechs' willingness to assert their Europeanness by delinking themselves from the idea of the East while continuing to Orientalize those located further east (rather than flatly rejecting the pattern of Orientalizing the East—or the South for that matter—as such). Milica Bakić-Hayden has called the phenomenon of projecting the pattern of being Orientalized onto others as "nesting orientalisms: a pattern of reproduction of the original dichotomy upon which Orientalism is premised. In this pattern, Asia is more 'East' or 'other' than eastern Europe; within eastern Europe itself this gradation is reproduced" (1995, 918). Taking this into consideration, we could thus argue, using Allaine Cerwonka's terminology, that (non-Romany) Czechs are "flexibly raced," less white and privileged in some contexts but more white and privileged in others. Their geographic location contiguous with European powerhouses and their (however precarious and not always historically recognized) "flexible" whiteness does afford the (non-Romany) Czechs certain important privileges as compared with immigrants into Europe from former French, British, or Dutch overseas colonies or even with inhabitants of countries further East in the region.

Reflecting on these privileges, I want to introduce the term "European dividend." I here borrow from critical masculinity studies, which distinguish between hegemonic and non-hegemonic masculinities. While "non-hegemonic" men might fail to embody the model of dominant masculinity and might in fact occupy a subordinate structural position in relation to it, they still enjoy a share in patriarchal power through what Raewyn W. Connell calls "the patriarchal dividend," as long as they stay complicit with hegemonic masculinity (1995, 79; also see Iva Šmídová in this volume). Similarly, my notion of the European dividend refers to a share in geopolitical privilege afforded East Central Europeans like the (non-Romany) Czechs through their geographic location and their (relative) whiteness. Overall, Czechs have access (or a promise of access) to a share in the global political, economic, and cultural privilege and power wielded by Europe as such. This access seems preconditioned by their willingness to help maintain Eurocentric and capitalist attributes and to recognize the European powerhouse, even if they themselves have been at various historical periods, and continue to be today, disadvantaged by the very same Eurocentric attributes and marginalized or exploited by the very same European powerhouse. They thus structurally inhabit a non-hegemonic, peripheral (but still) European position.

Economically, Czech citizens as a group are relatively better off than citizens of most postcolonial, non-European nations (the traditional subjects of postcolonial studies), and they benefit from a still fairly strong welfare state, which provides national healthcare, free education through graduate school, paid maternity leave and parental leave benefits, as well as fairly robust unemployment and national pension benefits. Furthermore, the CR has been accepted to both NATO and the EU, and Czechs can move freely inside "Fortress Europe," a privilege most former colonial subjects can only dream of. Politically and institutionally, the Czechs' integration into the EU seems to mark a tentative acknowledgment of their Europeanness—"their" land (although increasingly expropriated from underneath them by transnational companies and foreign "investors") is currently nested within the second of the three concentric rings cast around the "European core."[7]

David Theo Goldberg reminds us in his discussion of "Euro-racisms" that "Europe continues to be considered by the bulk of Europeans as the place of and for Europeans historically conceived" (2006, 352). Unlike the Jews, Roma, or Tatars, and today immigrants from postcolonial countries, ethnic Czechs have historically been recognized as the rightful inhabitants of the Czech lands. Becoming accepted as "fully European" is not for ethnic Czechs a matter of having to challenge the historical, entrenched nationalist "blood and land" conceptualization of Europeanness that continues to make it difficult for former colonial subjects (and the Roma) to be acknowledged as Europeans. Rather, the main challenge faced by ethnic Czechs is having their homeland and culture recognized as falling within the political-geographic-cultural space of Europe. As long as that land/culture falls within the borders of Europe, ethnic Czechs will be considered "autochthonously" European (that is, native Europeans). The anxiety over being part of Europe for Czechs has to do to a great extent with the question of how the physical, political, economic, and cultural borders of Europe might shift in the future—after all, they have shifted before many times—and whether the Czech territory/culture will fall outside or inside of these future borders.

That the situation is different for Roma has been exposed through such cases as France's and Italy's expulsions of thousands of Romanian and Bulgarian Roma in 2010 despite the official legal presumption of ethnically blind travel for all citizens of EU countries. The so-called Canada-Czech Republic visa and Roma affair of 2009, wherein Canada imposed visa obligations on Czech citizens in an effort to limit the exodus of Czech Roma into Canada, exposed (besides continued Czech discrimination against the Roma) similar limitations to the presumed ethnically blind travel principle for EU citizens (Guild and Carrera 2013, 13). Where East Central Europeans such as the Czechs might have been officially accepted as European citizens with their countries' EU accession, that gesture does not seem to necessarily equally extend in practice to the Romany populations of these countries. Even with the accession of their countries of citizenship to the EU, the Roma continue to face discrimination—whether they stay in Eastern/East Central Europe, including the CR, or try to act on their (presumably ethnicity-blind) European citizenship rights and travel searching for work. The Eastern/East Central European Roma, with noticeably less access to the privileges of ordinary citizenship, thus demonstrate how the European dividend is not shared equally even among its supposed recipients.

The concept of the European dividend can also help explain the specificity of Czech women's (and feminists') location. As Kornelia Slavova has pointed out in reference to the academic field of transnational/global feminism, despite numerous differences in their experiences, Eastern European women have shared with Third World and black women their criticism of the Western mainstream feminist "assumptions about the universality of feminist goals across cultures" (2006, 245). Similar to Third World/postcolonial women's efforts (as articulated by Chandra Talpade Mohanty 1984), East Central and Eastern European women have been involved in the double project of simultaneously "subvert[ing] established Western feminist models while construct[ing] their own feminist identity and politics" (Slavova 2006, 247). Also analogous to the situation of feminist (and other) scholars in postcolonial regions, Eastern/East Central European women continue to be placed in an "asymmetrical position to Western feminists" as "they become transmitters of Western knowledge but not creators" (Marina Blagojević, quoted in Slavova 2006, 248).

While in relation to the U.S. and Western European feminist establishment, Eastern/East Central European, including Czech, women and feminists might be in a non-dominant, non-hegemonic position, they still also find themselves in a position to exclude others from full Europeanness by refusing to recognize them as Czech on the grounds of their race, ethnicity, or migrant status. Being recognized as autochthonously European provides white Czech women with access to some privileges they share with their Western European white sisters—and that could be propitiously discussed in terms of the European dividend concept. At least within their own national context certainly, the European dividend gives Czech feminists the power to define Czech womanhood in ethnocentric terms, excluding some from the definition of Czech, and thus also European, womanhood. After all, Czech women's emancipation discourse and movement shares its nineteenth-century history with the Czech nationalist movement, which conceptualized the Czech nation along the lines of a specific ethnic and linguistic community, excluding other ethnicities considered foreign or non-European, such as the Jewish or Romany people (Jusová 2005, 64). It is likely this history of the Czech women's movement—its close interconnection with Czech nationalism—that explains its continued conceptualization of Czech womanhood as ethnically distinct. As several other chapters in this volume point out (Malečková, Hašková and Uhde, Ryvolová, Strašáková), with some exceptions, Czech feminism has tended to demonstrate a persistent lack of recognition of (and too often also a lack of welcome toward) ethnic differences among Czech women. As they exclude for instance Romany women from Czechness, Czech women effectively exclude them from Europeanness as well.

Taking the above into consideration, where Czech and other East Central European feminists can and have contributed to transnational feminist debates by highlighting the ways in which women's sources of oppression differ in postsocialist and Eastern European circumstances, they (and we) would at the same time benefit from taking to heart lessons from (Western, Third World, Eastern/ East Central European) women of color concerning intersections of gender and race/ethnicity. To put it bluntly, there is a need for Czech women (and allied scholars and activists) to start paying closer attention to differences, including ethnic and cultural differences, among women who live in the CR, and help redefine the Czech nation and Czech womanhood (and, by extension, Europeanness) along non-ethnic lines. Such a move would amount to "delinking from modernity and its myths" (including the myth or race/ethnicity), following the challenge posited by Tlostanova (2012, 131). Further questioning is needed regarding the ways in which the existing racial/sexual/cultural hierarchies continue to be used to make groups of people feel inferior and thus perhaps less ready to resist their proletariatization and the expropriation of their land and resources by what Tlostanova has called "the winners of modernity" (134).

In her discussion of the feminist concept of location, the European Continental philosopher Rosi Braidotti has pointed out that our location "is not a self-appointed subject position but rather a collectively shared and constructed, jointly occupied spatiotemporal territory." As Braidotti emphasizes, since much of our location escapes self-scrutiny, the politics of location requires "an intervention of others" (2011, 16). Feminists from different regions of the world can learn about their own blind spots as they dialogue with others and as they themselves highlight new significant categories of difference for transnational/ global feminist scholarship and practice to take into consideration.

NOTES

1. Moravia is a historical region within the Czech Republic (CR) bordering Slovakia.

2. See the introduction, note 3, on socialist/post-socialist versus communist/post-communist terminology.

3. http://www.state.gov/e/eb/rls/othr/ics/2011/157266.htm.

4. Between 1795 and 1919, Poland was divided among Prussia, Russia, and Austro-Hungary.

5. Balibar's term "racism without race" (1992), and similarly David Theo Goldberg's "raceless race" (2006, 356), refer to the continued reality of anti-black racism in Europe even as the post-Holocaust continent hesitates to apply the term "race" in relation to people.

6. Vedrana Velicković, among others, has collected examples of such violent reactions to Eastern Europeans arriving, post-2004, in the United Kingdom, the Netherlands, and France (2012, 171).

7. See Balibar's 2005 discussion of French and German politicians' comments about current Europe as consisting of "three concentric circles": "The core countries with a single currency (some columnists call this first circle 'Euro-land'), the broader circle of other European countries which cannot or refuse to adopt the euro, and the 'periphery' which is not 'part of Europe' but should be as closely associated as possible with it, for economic and security reasons" (12).

2 THE IMPORTANCE OF BEING NATIONALIST

JITKA MALEČKOVÁ

From its emergence and well into the twentieth century, the Czech women's movement was arguably defined by its close connection with nationalism. Women's emancipation found its articulation as a part of the national movement. Consequently, the "woman question" was incorporated into the national project, while issues of the nation were central within women's emancipatory activities. The close relationship between the Czech women's and national movements—emphasized by both male and female contemporaries (Jonáš 1872, Krásnohorská 1881, Viková Kunětická 1919) and noted by Czech as well as foreign scholars (Havelková 1995, Hendrychová 1992, David 1991)—has been mostly evaluated as beneficial for women.

In other national contexts, scholars have pointed to the often contradictory character of the relationship between gender and nationalism: "While it is men who claim the prerogatives of nation and nation-building," Tamar Mayer (among others) has noted, "it is for the most part women who actually tend to accept the obligation of nation and nation-building" (2000, 2). In anti-colonial nationalisms of the nineteenth and twentieth centuries, women represented the sacred spiritual domain of the nation, embodying national traditions that had to be protected from the polluting effects of the outside world. Although women may have used national rhetoric in their pursuit of emancipation, male nationalists still believed that women's emancipatory aspirations had to be curtailed (Chatterjee 1993, 116–57). Within imperial powers, women often fought for their own rights while at the same time supporting the colonial enterprise and presumed European superiority over other races. Some British feminist writers, for example, adapted and used an imperial discourse to legitimize their feminist projects, even if this strategy ultimately often limited the subversiveness of their feminism (Jusová 2000b, 299).

The Czechs (including their historians) like to view themselves as a civilized nation whose democratic inclinations have been reflected in the equality of its women with men. I have argued elsewhere that, rather than being a reflection of the actual historical situation of Czech women, this myth of gender harmony was created in the context of the nineteenth-century national movement (Malečková 2000). Nevertheless, by the early twentieth century, it had become such an integral part of the Czechs' self-perception that it forced male patriots to include women in the newly formed civic nation and its legislation, most notably the Constitution of the new Czechoslovak Republic in 1920. The Czechs, including Czech feminists, have thus tended to emphasize collaboration between men and women, rather than women's separate struggle for emancipation or other axes of struggle prospectively dividing the nation. Ethnic fights, for instance, have not been absent in modern Czech history. Yet mainstream Czech historiography has presented them as something extrinsic to the Czechs, forced on them by external forces—whether Habsburg rule, Nazism, or the actions of Czechoslovak Germans (see Třeštík 1999).

Furthermore, instances of Czech racism have been largely portrayed as being limited to small groups of extremists and have generally remained unexamined as part of the nation-forming processes.[1] Studies dealing with anti-Semitism commonly assess Czech anti-Semitism of the nineteenth and early twentieth centuries as prevailingly "non-racist" (Soukupová 2007, 35; Goldstücker 1999, 147). Given this tendency to idealize both Czech nationalism and Czech women, it perhaps should not be surprising that so far the place of women in late nineteenth- and early twentieth-century Czech racism has also been neglected in the framework of Czech historical scholarship.[2]

Examining the relationship between the Czech women's and national movements in the late Habsburg Empire, this chapter considers whether the effects of nationalism on women's efforts for emancipation were indeed as positive as presented in existing literature. The first part of this study outlines the Czech women's emancipation movement from its emergence to the establishment of independent Czechoslovakia in 1918. The second part analyzes nineteenth-century Czech women's attitudes toward the most relevant ethnic and racial Others at the time—Germans and Jews.

Since 1526, the Bohemian Crownlands—Bohemia, Moravia, and Silesia—formed a part of the Habsburg Empire, and after 1867, of its Austrian half, Cisleithania. The Habsburg rule did not suppress the memory of the independent medieval Czech Kingdom, which had flourished especially in the thirteenth and fourteenth centuries, and of the early fifteenth-century Hussite movement for religious reform (an early forerunner of Protestantism). The defeat of the uprising of the Czech estates in 1620 was followed by a forced conversion to Catholicism of the Czech population, among whom Protestantism had grown strong roots.[3] As a result, by the end of the nineteenth century, the majority of Czechs were Catholics, although the Czech Protestant past, combined with the association of the Austrian Habsburgs with Catholicism, contributed to often lukewarm and ambivalent attitudes toward religion in general among Czechs. The reforms of the Habsburg Enlightenment absolutism (a form of absolute monarchy inspired by the Enlightenment) in the eighteenth century brought centralization and Germanization. During that time, the Czech estates lost the last remnants of political power, as their functions were taken away and given to imperial civil servants appointed by the Habsburg rulers. German became the official language.

Perceived as a threat to the very survival of the Czech nation, these Habsburg reforms actually contributed to the emergence of a Czech national movement. In the late eighteenth century, the first generation of Czech patriots started to study the Czech language, culture, and history, and they attempted to win over the nobility, including noble women, for the Czech national cause. Since these efforts mostly proved to be futile, the next generation of patriotic intellectuals, who in the 1810s and 1820s saw their mission in "awakening" the whole nation, instead strove to gain the support of their middle-class female compatriots. The obvious goal, common in other national movements as well, was to produce nationally aware mothers who would educate their children in Czech and in a patriotic spirit.[4] Given that the group of Czech patriots was rather small and could not find other allies, women also became potential partners in the national struggle.[5] Patriotic activists in the 1830s and 1840s, such as the Frič family or the dramatist Josef Kajetán Tyl, encouraged women to participate in theater performances, literary salons, and patriotic balls, all conducted in Czech. These men welcomed, supported, and occasionally even invented stories of women's own educational and literary activities. For instance, the famous poet František Ladislav Čelakovský not only published poems under the female pseudonym of Žofie Jandová in order to prove that Czech women could write excellent poetry in Czech, but also revised and edited the works of one of the first women who did write in Czech.[6]

Czech women thus entered public life in the first half of the nineteenth century in the context of increasing patriotic activities and of attempts, on the part of male intellectuals, to secure women's support for the national project.

Women became engaged in literary and educational activities and expressed similar concerns as men for the fate of the national community. During the 1848 revolution—a wave of political upheavals that spread across Europe and included the Habsburg Empire—some Czech women even directly took up arms while others organized public meetings. In the wake of these revolutionary events, Czech women founded their first short-lived organizations influenced by the spirit of pan-Slavism.

The beginnings of an organized Czech women's emancipation movement are conspicuously associated with the efforts of a man, Vojta Náprstek. Influenced by his stay in the United States after the 1848 revolution, Náprstek, upon his return, began lecturing in Prague on the progress of women's rights in Britain and America and, together with the writer Karolína Světlá, founded Americký klub dam (the American Ladies' Club) in 1865. This and other early women's associations focused on charity and education, and their leaders included the wife of the prominent politician František Ladislav Rieger, as well as well-known women writers such as Světlá and later Eliška Krásnohorská.

By this time, the Czech society had started to debate the "woman question," which from the beginning carried a strong "patriotic" aspect. As one of the male journalists put it in 1872: "I do not want to claim that the cause of a full equality of the sexes should be put in the front of our national program in the Czech Lands; we have on agenda questions *equally* important for the education, welfare and future of the population in our countries" (Jonáš 1872, 109, 111; emphasis added). Krásnohorská, who fought for the establishment of a girls' secondary school (gymnasium) as a step to their access to universities and professions, emphasized that "the woman and the Czech questions resemble each other like sisters" (Krásnohorská 1881, 6). She claimed that Czech men should understand and support women's efforts because they had been through a similar experience: just as German professors considered the Czechs unworthy of higher knowledge because of their presumed intellectual inferiority, narrow-minded men similarly considered women to be destined by nature to eternal intellectual subjugation (27).[7]

In the 1890s, the women's movement began to establish its standing as a mass movement. The geographical and social expansion was accompanied by a differentiation in women's goals as well as by attempts at unification. While the majority of women's organizations around the country were rather moderate in their goals and typically limited to charity and cultural patriotic activities, the period also witnessed the emergence of more radical feminist views and working-class women's organizations.

Up to this point, the Czech women's movement was primarily a middle-class affair. Czech noble women participated in it only exceptionally in the earlier period. Throughout the 1860s, women from working-class families had been merely objects of middle- and upper-class women's organized activities. More conservative women favored charity, while the mainstream movement advocated self-help and preparation for paid work. In the late 1880s and 1890s, however, working-class women, aligned with social democrats, started to organize and even published an independent journal in the Moravian capital, Brno. Still, up to the early twentieth century, middle- and working-class women active in women's emancipation efforts tended to cooperate. This collaboration, which distinguished the Czech women's movement from its West European counterparts, can be explained by the Czech women's shared belief in the priority of national over social or class issues. Cooperation across political allegiances was also characteristic of the Czech Women's Club in the early twentieth century, whose leaders included an active member of the National Social Party and a social democrat, alongside the first Czech female doctors of philosophy, medical doctors, and teachers.

The first decade of the twentieth century was a period of increased politicization that brought the pursuit of political rights to the forefront of women's demands. Some women preferred to work within existing political parties. Others, perhaps for the first time, put their gender interests above those of the nation and succeeded in gaining the support of some men for their efforts to get a woman elected to the provincial assembly, the Bohemian Diet. Although new legislation drafted in Vienna denied women either passive or active voting rights,[8] some categories of women could still vote, and women were not explicitly excluded from passive voting for the Bohemian Diet, as such a situation had not been anticipated by lawmakers. The Committee for Women's Voting Rights, led by Františka Plamínková, used this opportunity to call on parties and the public to support a female candidate and to fight the exclusionary election reform advanced by the Austrian government.[9] The election of a woman to the Bohemian Diet, the committee argued, would become a patriotic manifestation, showing Vienna the unanimity of the whole Czech nation in defense of its rights (Honzáková 1935, 61–67).

The Czech political scene was, relatively speaking, favorably disposed toward women's emancipation. The Social Democratic Party had moved away from its initial position of rejecting women in working-class associations in the 1870s to advocating, at the turn of the century, for female suffrage and even nominating a female candidate for the Diet. The rising National Social Party and the Progressive Party, popular among the intelligentsia, supported women's political rights as well. The Progressive Party was led by the future Czechoslovak president Tomáš Garrigue Masaryk, who had since the 1880s openly criticized the double gender standard and defended the equality of women.[10] Masaryk fought for equal educational opportunities for women and maintained close ties with the Czech women's movement up to the outbreak of World War I (Neudorfl 1990). The only explicit opponents to women's emancipation were thus the Catholic parties and the already marginal Old Czechs. The Young Czech Party was not exactly known for its interest in women's emancipation. Yet, ironically, it was its candidate, Božena Viková Kunětická, supported also by the National Social Party and the State Rights Progressivists, who became in the 1912 by-election the first woman elected to the Czech Diet (though ultimately not permitted to take office). Czech politicians clearly understood the importance of the "woman question" and of the opportunity to gain additional votes for their parties by supporting or nominating female candidates. It is likely that the agitation and activities of the Committee for Women's Voting Rights, with their strategic presentation of the election of a woman as a patriotic act, also contributed to the parties' near unanimity on this issue.

Perhaps even more surprising than this early success in electing a woman to a political office was the choice of candidate. A respected writer, Viková Kunětická was a feminist and seen as such by her contemporaries. It could be even said that her feminism occasionally bordered on open misandry. In her 1897 novel *Medřická*, for example, she described a poor woman teacher who opted to become a single mother despite condemnation by society and the danger of being fired from her teaching post. The role of the man in the novel is practically that of a drone: after his biological part in conception is completed he disappears from the narrative. Yet Viková Kunětická's feminism was paradoxical. She repeatedly distanced herself from the organized women's movement and criticized it for presumably depriving the nation of children and women of their highest mission—motherhood. She was particularly critical of the English women's movement and described its fight for suffrage as "a brutal degradation of womanhood" (1919, 71). When elected to the Diet she somewhat moderated her criticism, but it seems clear that she used references to the women's movement rather pragmatically. Overall, Viková Kunětická was foremost a nationalist, and she unfailingly stressed that the national interest always came first for her. Thus she boycotted an international women's conference in Budapest to protest the treatment of Slovaks and other Slavs in Hungary (25–26). Perhaps this very combination of strong nationalism with her distance from the organized women's movement is what best explains the support she received from more conservative Czech political parties.

To be sure, it was quite common for Czech women at the time to put national above gender concerns. On the international scene, for example, representatives of the Czech women's movement consistently emphasized Czech (or Slavic) interests, and Plamínková fought for independence from the Austro-Hungarian section of international women's organizations. Similarly, Czech women's attitudes toward national and ethnic Others were also shaped—and occasionally almost predetermined—by mainstream Czech nationalism.

The Germans were the most relevant Other for both the Czech national and women's movements. Since the beginning of the national movement, patriotic intellectuals had been constructing a Czech identity and history, creating literature, and demonstrating the maturity of the Czech nation and its right to exist specifically in opposition to the Germans. However, the relations and balance of power between the Czechs and Germans were far from uniform or static. Throughout the second half of the nineteenth century, Czechs had been expanding economically and demographically to such an extent that by the end of the century, they could hardly be considered a "non-dominant" nation in the Bohemian crownlands. Economically motivated animosity increased in the later part of the nineteenth century, and ethnic conflicts escalated in the late 1890s, when the short-lived Badeni's Ordinance of 1897 required civil servants in Bohemia and Moravia to know both German and Czech, disadvantaging Germans who frequently had no knowledge of the Czech language.

While relations on the official, institutional and ideological levels of national(ist) organizations were unfriendly at best, actual daily contacts and experiences of Czechs and Germans ranged from conflict to passive cooperation, dealing in commerce and even intermarriage. Gary B. Cohen has documented not only the "voluntary segregation" of organized Czech and German social life and politics in Prague but also many cases of residential, economic, and personal contacts that cut across ethnic conflicts (1981, 123–39). Ethnic divisions played a major role in education, and both Czechs and Germans insisted on maintaining separate systems of schools. While German parents (of both Christian and Jewish heritage) tended to overwhelmingly prefer German schools for their children (132–34), education conducted in Czech was a primary concern for Czech patriots throughout the nineteenth century. As late as 1913, a booklet titled *A Czech Child Belongs in the Czech School!* expressed strong hostility against the Germans, calling them reckless enemies who tear out the maternal tongue from Czech children's mouths (Titĕra 1913, 15–16). Yet Tara Zahra has also suggested that in spite of the centrality of children to the Czech and German nationalists' agendas, the practical actions of Czech and German parents were often marked by a certain indifference toward nationalist campaigns. This was reflected, for instance, in frequent exchange stays of Czech children in German families and vice versa, especially in linguistically mixed areas, as well as in the practice of sending Czech children to German and German children to Czech schools to enable them to learn the other language (2008, 2, 19–32).

Czech women's organizations, as a rule, did not cooperate with organized German women in the Bohemian Lands, even when they shared similar interests and views on women's emancipation.[11] Instead, they saw each other as rivals. Czech women's organized efforts throughout the nineteenth century did not necessarily aim only (and perhaps not even primarily) at improving women's knowledge but rather at creating a Czech alternative to German education and, sometimes, to specific German schools.

As for German and German-Jewish women's associations in Bohemia, their network was quite widespread, and they tended to be divided by class and religious allegiances. The liberal Prague German women's groups were led mostly by wives or daughters of prominent Prague German leaders (Cohen 1981, 175). The most important among these was the Prague Women's Trade Association (Prager Frauen-Erwerb-Verein), founded in 1869. The most radical German women's organization was the Women's Progress (Frauenfortschritt), founded in 1894 (Horská 1983, 728, 734). Jewish women's organizations, such as Smichower israelitischer Frauenverein (the Israelite Women's Association of Smichov), were also perceived as rivals to Czech women's organizing efforts, primarily due to their Germanness. This attitude toward the Jews in Bohemia was consistent with that of the mainstream Czech national movement.

Whether they admitted it or not, however, Czech women were influenced and often inspired by the German women's movement. Thus, for example, the Czech Women's Trade Association was founded in 1871, two years after its Prague German counterpart. In the early twentieth century, when promoting the establishment of the Czech Women's Club, the preparatory committee explicitly emphasized that the endeavor was stimulated by the news about the founding of the German Ladies Club in Prague. "In our progress," the committee stressed, "we cannot stay behind other nations and particularly our closest neighbors"; further, they spoke of the Czech women's duty to outshine other women in education (see Czech Women's Club 1901, 5–6).

Božena Viková Kunětická's views largely reflected the suspicions and prejudices marking Czech women's attitudes toward German women. Immediately following her election to the Diet in 1912, she expressed her surprise at being complimented by German women in Bohemia (Viková Kunětická 1919, 48, 51). A year later, however, she complained about "the deep-rooted German antagonism toward the Czechs and particularly Czech minorities on the occupied territory" (65). In contrast, in February 1918, she downplayed German women's concern about the oppression of the German minority in Bohemia, and sarcastically wished the Germans at least thirty years of the kind of "freedom" that Czechs had experienced for centuries (131). Continuing in the same vein, Viková Kunětická emphasized that the Czech nation would never violently deprive Germans in the Bohemian Crownlands of their "variously acquired" possessions. "We are not afraid of the circle of Germanness begirding us from all sides like a thorn crown, in Bohemia, Moravia and Silesia. We will only prevent its thorns to get deeper into our blood and thus will pronounce against it the natural verdict of withering [odumírání]" (132).

Viková Kunětická was certainly not a "typical" Czech woman. Yet, as a public figure, writer, and speaker (and future senator of the Czechoslovak Republic), she had the power to reach and influence a broad audience, and thus her views, including those on ethnic and racial issues, deserve attention. Iveta Jusová has noted a racialized aspect in the work of Viková Kunětická, linking the author's contempt for the rural lower classes, portrayed in her work as inferior and threatening to the quality of the Czech nation, to the growing influence of anthropo-sociological theories in the late nineteenth century (Jusová 2010, 76–77). And Robert B. Pynsent (2004) has explicitly described Viková Kunětická's nationalism as racist, citing various examples of derogatory depictions of Jewish characters in her novels, ranging from dishonest, greedy, and dirty to degenerate.

Characteristically Viková Kunětická often used negative Jewish stereotypes in stories or novels whose main focus was not anti-Semitism. For instance, in her novel *Vzpoura* (*Revolt*), the heroine goes to buy a coat and passes a row of shops with Jewish names on their fronts only to be brought to tears by a greedy Jewish shopkeeper. The image, presented in a by-the-way manner, clearly demonstrates deeply ingrained prejudices against Jews. In 1919, Viková Kunětická wrote a more explicit article on "The Question of Race" [*Otázka rasy*], in which she emphasized the importance of race in general and for women in particular. Here she praised the "Slavic race," contrasting it with "the race without a state"—the Jews, whom she depicted as archenemies of the Czechs and of Czechoslovakia and also as the leaders of world socialism (Heczková and Svatoňová 2012, 278–81).

Czech anti-Semitism of the turn of the century was not a new phenomenon.[12] Yet, the 1890s brought a qualitatively new phase of anti-Semitism, characterized by the changed situation of the Czech nation on the one hand and the concurrent development of several types of anti-Semitic activities on the other. An economic campaign in provincial towns of Central Bohemia to discourage the population from buying from Jewish merchants culminated in the 1890s in the "Svůj k svému" (Support Your Own) campaign (Kieval 2000, 189; Kieval 1988, 66). Furthermore, the Jews, traditionally identified with German speakers, were often perceived as agents of Germanization, which became particularly relevant in the period of increased struggles over the language around the Badeni's Ordinance. Following the elections of 1897, Jews were accused of being agents of socialism, when, in response to the nomination of an anti-Semite by the Young Czech Party (a traditional ally of the Czech Jews), the Jews in Prague chose to support the Social Democratic Party instead (Kieval 1988, 68). Finally, in 1899, a Jew, Leopold Hilsner, was accused of a ritual murder of a young woman in Polná, leading to the (in)famous "Hilsner affair," considered the peak of Czech anti-Semitism at the turn of the century (see Goldstücker 1999).

Czech political parties and public figures were divided in their attitudes regarding the Jewish question. The Realist Party, led by Masaryk, became an ally of Czech-identifying Jews after 1897. Masaryk, who criticized the "blood libel" and Hilsner's murder conviction, has come to be seen as a symbol of the Czech struggle against anti-Semitism (Kieval 2000, 198). The National Social Party, similar to other radical nationalist parties in late nineteenth-century Europe, employed anti-Semitic rhetoric. However, as T. Mills Kelly observes, their anti-Semitism was pragmatic and flexible; for example, they distinguished between "Czech-Jews," whom they accepted as members of the Czech nation, and "Jew-Germans" or German Jews, whom they viewed as its enemies (Kelly 2006, 62).[13] The journalist and Catholic priest Rudolf Vrba, author of numerous anti-Semitic pamphlets, represented the extreme end of the Czech nationalist spectrum. In his extensive 1898 book *Národní sebeobrana: Úvahy o hmotném a mravním úpadku národa českého* (National Self-Defense: Reflections on the Material and Moral Decay of the Czech Nation), Vrba, influenced by the anti-Semitic views of Eduard Drumond and August Rohling, attacked what he presumed to be the Jewish domination of the world and of the Czech Lands. In a chapter on "The Slavery of the Christian Woman" (363–86), Vrba described

Czech women both as failing to fulfil their roles as mothers of the Czech nation and as victims of the Jewish "slave trade" (trafficking in women).

Another anti-Semitic work, *Český lid a český žid: časové úvahy* (The Czech People and the Czech Jew: Timely Reflections), was published by Jaroslava Procházková in response to the 1897 elections. Procházková here argued for a "conscious" or "educated anti-Semitism," which would defend Czech interests against the alleged Jewish rule over Czech enterprise and "Jewish moral influence" on the Czech population. Yet the author also referred to the unchanging Jewish physiognomy and "Jewish particularities," presumably visible even to those who have no knowledge of phrenology (1897a, 12–13, 16). The booklet was in line with similar contemporaneous publications that tried to influence specifically Czech women to support Czech businesses and discourage them from buying from Jewish merchants (Frankl 2007, 223). While this booklet, along with other anti-Semitic works of the turn of the century, has received some scholarly attention (Frankl 2007, 222, 235; Soukupová 2007, 40; Kielal 1988, 69–71), curiously, no details are given in the existing scholarship about its author.[14] In fact, although published under a female pseudonym, the booklet was actually written by a man. To be sure, it was not uncommon to use pen names while writing on the "Jewish question" (Mikulášek 2000, 137); however, these were usually male pen names. When the early nineteenth-century Czech patriot František Ladislav Čelakovský used a female pseudonym to write poetry, his motivation was to demonstrate the advanced character of the Czech nation and its women. In the case of the booklet published under the name of Procházková in the late nineteenth century, on the other hand, a female pseudonym was used for a different purpose: to reach and affect women. The author of the pamphlet, writer and journalist Jan Misárek (*Masarykův slovník naučný* 1929, 975), used this *nom de plume* in another work in which he dealt with the role of women in Czech nationalism. Suggesting his agenda to manipulate Czech women readers, here he explicitly mentioned the leading role of men and their power to make women into what men want them to be (Procházková 1897b, 4, 18–20).

Little is known about real women's opinions on the Jewish question, apart from views some of them, like Viková Kunětická or Benešová, expressed in literary works (Pynsent 2004, 2010; Jusová 2010). No attention has been paid to women's participation in the Svůj k svému campaign. In 1906, the Czech Women's Club, a representative body of publicly engaged Czech women, published their own booklet titled *Svůj k svému*. Although the booklet appeared under the club's name, it was apparently written by the leading representative of the women's movement of the early twentieth century, Františka Plamínková, together with Marie Tůmová (Honzáková 1935, 67). The booklet, one of several pamphlets with the same title, encourages the public, particularly women, to support Czech commerce and industry. Women should buy Czech goods from Czech stores, instead of "foreign" goods from non-Czech stores, where "non-Czech" mostly refers to Germans and includes Jews. The booklet focuses on economic arguments and does not dwell on presumed characteristics of Jews, their appearance, or way of life. However, in the rare cases when Jews are explicitly mentioned, the examples are telling: the Jews are represented as the almost exclusive beneficiaries of the home production sector of the economy, which exploited the poorest workers in horrifying ways. It is this exploitation, the booklet claims, that enables Jews to offer lower prices, to the disadvantage of the presumably more moral Czech entrepreneurs (Czech Women's Club 1906, 10–11). Although Honzáková later argued that the goal of the booklet was to inspire Czech businessmen to acquire the good qualities of the Jews, not to incite hatred toward them (1935, 67), and Plamínková herself was of Jewish origins, the booklet and the club's activities in support of Czech enterprise can be considered a part of the anti-Semitic nationalist campaign of the time.[15]

The few examples noted here certainly do not represent all Czech feminists or women. There were other voices heard, and Czech women also participated in defense of Jews.[16] It does not seem that women were exceedingly engaged in the anti-Semitic movement—at least judging from the fact that the authors of anti-Semitic political pamphlets, literary works, and articles in the anti-Semitic press were mostly men.[17] However, women were far from exempt from the excesses of nationalism, and their role in anti-German and anti-Jewish campaigns deserves more research.

To summarize, the Czech women's movement in the nineteenth and early twentieth centuries was part of a broader national movement directed against Habsburg political rule and the cultural impacts of German-language imposition. There is no doubt that publicly active Czech women displayed the same kinds of nationalist attitudes as their male counterparts. At times, they were able to pragmatically use their patriotism to promote and forward their interests as women, when, for example, they got a female candidate elected to the Diet. The close connection with nationalism clearly brought Czech women benefits, namely the support of (some) Czech men and their acknowledgment of the relevance of women for the national project. Unlike male nationalists in many British, French, and other overseas colonies, Czech men as a rule did not harbor a need to protect Czech women against foreign impacts by keeping them away from public life. The Czechs' internalized belief in their nation's inherent democracy and its reflection in the largely inclusive treatment of Czech women led to the incorporation of the principle of women's equality in the 1920 Constitution of the Czechoslovak Republic, although, as Melissa Feinberg (2006) has recently shown, this equality had its limits and contradictions.

As a part of the Habsburg Empire, which was, in the last period of its existence, assertively engaging in a colonial/imperialist enterprise, the Czechs also belonged to an imperial power. Some Czech businessmen and members of professions, such as architects, teachers, and medical doctors, benefited from the opportunities created by the Austrian occupation of Bosnia and Herzegovina. Still, given that these new provinces were inhabited by Slavs, the Czechs' interactions with the local populations tended not to lead to racist attitudes.[18] Czech nationalism and racism were instead directed against internal Others. With the development from a nation "under threat" to a self-confident Czech nation in the late nineteenth century, instances of Czech nationalism would become more consequential and potentially more dangerous. Women participated in manifestations of anti-German nationalism and anti-Semitism. In this respect, they followed the lead of mainstream Czech nationalism, divided as it was in its attitudes toward Others. Neither all Czech male nationalists nor all feminists were violently anti-German or anti-Semitic. However, extremist views did exist within Czech feminism, and they circumscribed its overall potential, showing a little-known effect of nationalism on the women's movement.

NOTES

1. For a useful overview of literature dealing with racism in Czech national history, see Frankl 2007, 5–10.

2. Some attention has been devoted to Czech women's attitudes toward the Jewish question in literary studies, most notably by Robert B. Pynsent (2004, 2008, 2010), who has pointed out the anti-Semitism of some Czech feminist writers. See also Jusová 2010.

3. The term "estates" refers to social groups into which Czech and other European societies were divided and which were represented in medieval and early modern assemblies.

4. The founder of a patriotic school called "Budeč," Karel Slavoj Amerling believed that women should get better education not only as mothers but also for their own sake, "to develop as human beings" (quoted in Volet-Jeanneret 1988, 67–71).

5. Despite the enkindling of national consciousness in the second half of the nineteenth century, less than 63% of the population of Bohemia and around 70% in Moravia identified themselves as Czechs in 1890 (*Ottův slovník naučný* 1893, 6:122; 1901, 17:638).

6. On Čelakovský and the writer Josefa Pedálová, see Macura 1995, 128–35.

7. This does not mean that Czech women always found support among men. Some male intellectuals—and not only the most conservative ones—considered women's in-

volvement in public life an "aberration" or "a profaning of woman's nature" (Pech 1969, 321–23). When in 1867 Světlá presented her article on women's education to her friend, famous poet and editor Vítězslav Hálek, he refused the argument, claiming that women should stay at home and learn only how to be wives and mothers (Volet-Jeanneret 1988, 254). And Krásnohorská established the Minerva gymnasium (secondary school) for women in 1890 without any official assistance: a number of prominent Czech men, such as Julius Grégr, the founder of an influential women's journal (*Ženské listy*), and the Old Czech party leader Rieger, who had endorsed his wife's more moderate educational efforts, refused to support her (Brabencová 1996, 210).

8. The term "passive voting right" refers to the right to be elected while "active voting right" is the right to vote.

9. By the 1908 elections the committee both came forward with its own candidate, Marie Tůmová, and tried to persuade political parties to nominate women. This effort resulted in two more female candidates, though none of the women was elected in the end.

10. Masaryk's American wife, Charlotte, who participated in Czech women's emancipatory activities and translated John Stuart Mill's *The Subjection of Women* into Czech, had a strong influence on Masaryk's thoughts on women's emancipation.

11. An exception was the Association of St. Ludmila in the 1850s, which had no national goals and joined together Czech and German upper-middle-class and a few noble women.

12. Modern Czech anti-Semitism has to be understood in the broader European context as well as the development of the Czech national movement (Frankl 2007).

13. The term "Czech Jews" refers here to those Jews who supported Czech, rather than German, political parties in Bohemia.

14. Alexej Mikulášek (2000, 132–33) is exceptional in that he names Jan Misárek as the author of the pamphlet but without mentioning the female pseudonym he used.

15. T. Mills Kelly emphasizes that not all those who supported Czech businesses at the expense of German and Jewish businesses purveyed anti-Semitic rhetoric (2006, 17).

16. This was the case, for example, of the writer Růžena Svobodová.

17. In newspapers, the names of the contributors often did not appear, but those that appeared were male. See also the pamphlets and other anti-Semitic works cited by Frankl 2007 and Mikulášek 2000.

18. To be sure, Czechs occasionally revealed a feeling of superiority over the local population. Women's attitudes to the Balkan population would also deserve further research.

3 THE CZECH 1930s THROUGH TOYEN

KARLA HUEBNER

LATE ONE FREEZING night in the 1920s, a group of young Czech avant-gardists stood on a Prague street bidding one another adieu after lingering over a glass of wine. One, an artist known familiarly as Manka, lived with her sister at the Smíchov train station, so a cab was called for her. Her friends seated her in the vehicle, but before it could drive away, she opened the window, threw her arms around theoretician Karel Teige's neck, and in a mournful voice informed him, "Farewell! I am a sad [male] painter" (*Já jsem malíř smutnej*).

The poet Jaroslav Seifert recalled later that Teige replied that the artist "should just sit nicely in the corner, we all wished from the heart that 'he' would sleep well. And good night!" S/he didn't hear this, because "the car had already driven away and carried the sad paintress [*malířka smutná*] off to Smíchov" (Seifert 1999, 156).

This anecdote, about the artist who would become famous under the genderless pseudonym Toyen, is but one of many references in avant-gardist memoirs to Marie ("Manka") Čermínová's intentionally unstable gendering. Born in 1902 in Smíchov (an industrial suburb of Greater Prague), Toyen joined the interdisciplinary Devětsil group in 1923 and was later a founding member of the Prague surrealist group. This highly visible figure provides us with numerous avenues through which to explore interwar Czech women's relationships to gender and sexuality. She came of age during a period of intense Czech feminist activity, spoke in the masculine gender, dressed in ways not limited to the traditionally feminine, expressed her attraction to women, and has become known for her sexually transgressive art. She could even be said to embody an ungendered, revolutionary sexuality (Huebner 2008, 2010a, 2013; Sternstein 2006). While Toyen was thoroughly unconventional in her ideas, art, and self-presentation, a focus on her nonetheless enriches our understanding of the broader Czech context during the 1930s by illuminating the range of possibilities open to interwar Czech women. This chapter considers what it meant to be Toyen, and conversely what it might have meant to be a Czech woman who was not Toyen.

COMING OF AGE IN THE HEYDAY OF CZECH FEMINISM, WORKING IN A PERIOD OF STAGNANT FEMINISM

Czech feminism, which was extremely active and successful during Toyen's childhood and youth, provides an important context for the artist and her contemporaries. While during most of the nineteenth century Czech women had few rights and little opportunity for education or for well-paid work outside the home, they, like women in other industrialized nations, formed a home-grown feminist movement (see Jitka Malečková's chapter in this volume). Beginning largely from bourgeois circles and with modest goals, in time the Czech women's movement came to involve a wider range of social classes and became more daring in its demands. Its close relationship with nationalism, however, proved a mixed blessing. *Fin-de-siècle* Czech feminist rhetoric asserted that Czech men must sympathize with the cause because they too were oppressed. While this strategy appears to have garnered widespread support from men, including nationalist politicians, it separated Czech feminists from their Bohemian and Moravian German and Jewish sisters.

Prior to World War I, few Czechs could have imagined that they would emerge from the conflict in a democratic state independent of Austria-Hungary; rather, most sought greater autonomy and power within the framework of the Habsburg monarchy. That Czechoslovakia came to be founded was due in part to a small group of wartime Czech and Slovak activists abroad but chiefly to the destructive effect of four years of war, which ultimately discredited the Dual Monarchy in the eyes of its peoples. The military collapse and political disintegration of Austria-Hungary in October 1918 thus led to the creation of several successor states, of which Czechoslovakia was one. With independence, Czech feminists achieved many of their goals, a success due not only to the hard work of first-wave feminist groups but also to the longtime support of Czechoslovakia's first president, philosopher Tomáš Garrigue Masaryk, and his American wife and notable translator of John Stuart Mill's *The Subjection of Women*, Charlotte Garrigue Masaryk. Tomáš Masaryk's Progressive Party had supported women's suffrage, and during most of the period 1905–1915, his journal *Naše doba* (Our Era) carried a monthly column on women's issues. The 1918 Washington Declaration, which proclaimed the founding of Czechoslovakia, announced: "Women shall be placed on equal footing with men, politically, socially, and culturally" (7). The new Constitution followed up on this promise, stating, "Privileges due to sex, birth or occupation shall not be recognized" (41).[1] Czechoslovak women officially gained the vote in 1920, whereas (by way of contrast) French women would not vote until 1944. Other gains included easier access to divorce, abolition of the requirement that female civil servants be unmarried, and recognition of female civil servants' right to the same salary as men. Masaryk's support of feminism continued throughout his presidency, which lasted nearly the whole of the First Republic (1918–38). During this period, Czech women expanded their occupational options, even becoming well-known pilots and racecar drivers. Not surprisingly, the First Republic prided itself on its attention to gender equality (David 1991; Feinberg 2006; Garver 1985; Huebner 2011; Neudorfl 1990).

While growing up in these transformational times, Toyen and her urban Czech contemporaries experienced the apex of a national feminist movement. They studied subjects previously closed to girls, played sports previously restricted to males, and heard adults discussing women's suffrage. They began to wear corsetless undergarments and filled in for male workers during World War I. In other words, their experience, while specifically Czech, was comparable to that of women in other countries with strong feminist movements, such as Britain, France, Germany, the United States, and the Scandinavian countries. As Melissa Feinberg notes, however, Czech feminists distinctively "emphasized equality over difference" and avoided the maternalist rhetoric present in many other early twentieth-century European women's movements (2006, 25).

The little we know about Toyen's youth reflects the emerging gender politics of her time. Probably of working-class or petit-bourgeois origin, in her youth the artist worked for a time in a soap factory but was nonetheless able to attend UMPRŮM, Prague's celebrated school of the decorative arts. Rather than marrying, she embarked on significant artistic partnerships—first with Jindřich Štyrský and later with Jindřich Heisler—that may or may not have included partnered sex or conventional romance. While Toyen would become in many ways an exceptional woman, her choices about both employment and personal relationships were shaped by larger societal circumstances. Becoming a working artist was compatible with interwar gender expectations. While remaining single was less common, it did serve to safeguarded her career.

Although First Republic Czechoslovakia was a relatively successful democracy during its twenty-year existence, the Masaryk and Edvard Beneš governments did not fully succeed in realizing the gender-equal state guaranteed in the Constitution. While feminists and legal scholars struggled to revise inherited Austrian legal codes relating to family law, that project never came to satisfactory resolution (Feinberg 2006). Simultaneously, feminist momentum worldwide slowed, perhaps in part due to earlier successes, and Czechoslovakia was no exception. Once women gained the vote, feminist organizations tended to collapse or contract. In 1922, more than fifty existing Czech women's associations united to form the Ženská národní rada (Women's National Council). Furthermore, Czech feminists continued to link feminism to nationalism, and to emphasize messages about temperance and sexual "purity," rendering feminism less appealing to the internationally minded jazz-age generation (David 1991; Garver 1985). Women of this generation largely continued to value marriage but were also interested in sexual pleasure, contraception, and recipes for cocktails (Huebner 2011).

Even as internationalism grew in popularity among Czechs during the 1920s, national identity remained important, and Feinberg argues that interwar Czechs saw both female suffrage and a gendered family structure as vital supports for the nation. Thus, while interwar Czechs generally believed in women's right to intellectual and political equality, they saw women's rights as subordinate to the rights of family and nation. As elsewhere in Europe and America, most Czechs believed that gender roles were defined by nature. Furthermore, many Czechs expressed concerns that double-income families took jobs from the unemployed, a view that gained increased importance in the economically troubled 1930s. Even so, most women worked outside the home at some point, and throughout the interwar period nearly a quarter of Czech women had jobs. Professional women such as Toyen were unusual not in that they worked outside the home but in that they had true careers.

How, then, did Toyen and other Czech women artists fit into this increasingly dynamic but still unequal world? Toyen herself was something of a New Woman—she worked, wore pants, and smoked—and like many women she attended UMPRŮM (Academy of Arts, Architecture and Design) rather than the Akademie výtvarných umění (Fine Arts Academy) in Prague. But while many Czech girls had enjoyed access to college-preparatory education since the 1890s, had begun receiving university degrees at the turn of the century, and by this time were well represented in art and design schools, few women were particularly visible on the Prague art scene. Mentions of female artists in First

Republic journalism are relatively scarce. Departing from the conventional trends of the time, Toyen was a member of the avant-garde. The only other women known to have joined Devětsil were the dancer Mira Holzbachová and the columnist Jaroslava Václavková, while the only other woman in the original Prague surrealist group, Katy King, was more a supporter than an active poet. Toyen was the only female visual artist in either group during the interwar period (Huebner 2013).

Many Czech women—such as Emilie Paličková, credited with the revival of Czech lace and embroidery—worked in design. Several women's groups in the fine arts existed, including Kruh výtvarných umělkyň (Circle of Women Visual Artists). Its members exhibited actively—some also internationally—but their exhibitions were mostly publicized in periodicals directed specifically toward women, such as *Eva* and *Ženský svět* (Women's World). They were best known in feminist circles, and due to their interest in themes relating to women's lives and tendency to exhibit in all-women shows, their work was often categorized as "feminine" art. In contrast, Toyen's membership in the predominantly male Czech avant-garde provided her not only with a supportive peer group but also one that was well covered in the press (Pachmanová 2006; Huebner 2013).

SPEAKING IN THE MASCULINE GENDER, DRESSING IN A MASCULINE STYLE

Fellow members of the Czech avant-garde often commented on Toyen's use of the masculine gender, which struck them as odd. As we have seen, the poet Seifert recalled how one night she exclaimed, "Já jsem malíř smutnej"—I am an unhappy male painter—rather than the gender-appropriate "Já jsem malířka smutná." Architect Karel Honzík, too, noted Toyen's use of the spoken masculine, giving the example "Byl jsem na výstavě, řekl jsem, že přijdu do kavárny" (I [male] was at the exhibition, I [male] said I'd go to the café), which contrasts with the feminine *Byla jsem . . . řekla jsem* forms (Honzík 1963, 50).

For English speakers who may be unfamiliar with grammatically gendered languages, this all may be puzzling (for more on this question, see Jana Valdrová's chapter in this volume). Yet English is actually unusual among Indo-European languages in its lack of grammatical gender. While in English forms like "paintress" and "sculptress" have largely vanished, and verb forms never distinguish gender, the Czech language includes three grammatical genders: masculine, feminine, and neuter. Since nouns, adjectives, and past participles all reflect gender, the sentence "I am a sad painter" spoken by a woman would normally be "Já jsem malířka smutná" whereas a man would say "Já jsem malíř smutnej." Czech children learn from infancy to refer to themselves in either masculine or feminine constructions, and thus for Toyen to use male linguistic forms was a much more difficult feat (and much more startling to her listeners) than for an English-speaking woman to call herself an actor rather than an actress. If we accept what Benjamin Lee Whorf termed linguistic relativity, or in other words the idea that linguistic structure and the structure of thought are deeply intertwined, each influencing the other, then the Czech language's emphasis on gender is in notable and significant contrast to English's relative gender neutrality. The English language (and perhaps Toyen too, if we take her use of the masculine to be intended as de-gendering rather than masculinization) significantly strips away the linguistic announcement of gender difference. It can be argued that absence of grammatical gender helps level the field. However, in a world with both male and female (not to mention intermediate) possibilities, it can also be argued that gendered languages offer speakers and listeners a potentially beneficial ongoing awareness of gender difference and identity. Some Czech women, in fact, assert that feminine forms, such as the surname ending "-ová," which recognizes a woman's presence by having the surname change, convey recognition of Czech women's equal status.

Toyen's undeclinable pseudonym also functioned as a de-gendering strategy. It was decidedly non-Czech and may have come from the French *citoyen,* itself a masculine noun (Le Brun 2001, 132). Fellow Devětsil member Adolf Hoffmeister made witty use of both the artist's pseudonym and Czech grammatical gender in his 1930 caricature *Ten-Ta-To-yen,* drawn for the cover of the weekly Prague arts paper *Rozpravy Aventina.* The caricature's very title provides a grammar lesson, defining "that male, that female, that neuter" being. Visually, Hoffmeister presented Toyen wearing trousers but casting a skirted shadow.

Clothing was, indeed, a mutable signifier for the artist. As a young factory worker, Toyen wore coarse cotton pants, a man's corduroy smock, a turned-down hat of the type worn by ditch-diggers, and "ugly shoes." Seifert, who first encountered her at that time, noted that in those days women didn't ordinarily wear trousers. Indeed, when Toyen came to join the Devětsil group, she wore "dainty pumps" and stylish openwork stockings (Seifert 1999, 52–55). Nonetheless, Honzík recalled her as often wearing a man's suit and shirt, a beret, and walking with a "careless, swaying gait" that suggested, "I don't care what you all think of me." Her hands were usually in her pockets, and there was often a cigarette in the corner of her mouth (1963, 50). Generally, Toyen's male associates

Figure 3.1. Adolf Hoffmeister, *Ten-Ta-To-yen*, cover of *Rozpravy Aventina* 5:23, March 5, 1930. Used with permission.

recalled her appearance as unusual and as departing from the gender norms of the period.

While contemporaries perceived Toyen's personal style as out of the ordinary, neither trousers nor "mannish" styling in themselves were that uncommon for young urban Czech women of the First Republic. For instance, the 1929 bilingual text *Civilisovaná Žena—Zivilisierte Frau*, which accompanied an exhibition on the modern woman, presented designer Božena Horneková's "new conception of women's garments," which were based on wide over-the-knee pants (Uchalová et al. 1996, 33–34). Throughout the 1930s, women's magazines regularly featured images of women wearing pants for leisure and sport.

Cross-dressing, as opposed to merely wearing pants designed for women, was more problematic. Ordinances against cross-dressing appear to be linked to the mid-nineteenth-century rise of the modern European industrial city, in which single adults often lived far from their families of origin and were able to create new and sometimes non-normative sexual and gender bonds, practices, and communities (Stryker 2008, 31–34; Bullough and Bullough 1993, 122). In a number of national contexts these nontraditional lifestyles became the target of new ordinances, which were perhaps more vigorously enforced early on (for instance, the French painter Rosa Bonheur had to obtain police permission to cross-dress) than during the interwar period. Central European women in general seem to have had relatively little trouble cross-dressing between the wars. In Vienna, it was not illegal for women to wear men's clothes, and the only excuse for police involvement was if the women were disrupting the peace. Similarly, a cross-dresser in Budapest was not arrested despite her ex-lover's starting a fight, because the police decided she had not broken any laws. In Germany, laws against cross-dressing were apparently enforced laxly, although arrest was always possible (Young 2004, 71–72). It is likely, however, that cross-dressing was less problematic for women than for men. In the summer of 1933, the homophile journal *Nový hlas* (New Voice) observed that recent incidents in Prague involving men wearing women's clothes had generally resulted in a week in jail ("Poznámky" 1933, 80).

ATTRACTED TO WOMEN, ATTRACTIVE TO MEN? GENDER AND SEXUALITY IN THE FIRST REPUBLIC

Toyen unquestionably presented herself differently than most of her contemporaries. She asserted that she was attracted to women and claimed that her partnership with Jindřich Štyrský was platonic, although the two were known to have amassed a large collection of erotica. Seifert recalled that she asked him to translate a cycle of Paul Verlaine's lesbian sonnets, three of which Štyrský later published in his sex-focused *Erotická revue*. Yet the perhaps lesbian artist was repeatedly described by her male associates as very attractive and had numerous male admirers. The artist Alén Diviš allegedly harbored an unrequited love for Toyen for many years. The architect Bedřich Feuerstein, who proposed she be named the Muse of Devětsil, was also rebuffed. Poets Seifert and Vítězslav Nezval were both enamored of her for a time as well (Seifert 1999, 158–59). Did gender ambiguity add to Toyen's appeal within avant-garde circles? And to what extent were gender ambiguity or homosexuality acceptable in interwar Czech society at large?

These questions cannot presently be fully answered. During the first half of the twentieth century, the concept of gender "inversion" meant that same-sex desire and gender variance were often thought to be closely associated (McLaren 1999, 87–109). However, there is evidence that interwar Czech society was relatively open to variations of sexuality and gender identity. This was a highly literate population that discussed a wide range of topics in print. Interest in matters relating to gender, sexuality, and the body grew from earlier activity on behalf of feminism, health, eugenics, and sex reform. Broadly speaking, "sex reform" dealt with contraception, abortion, venereal diseases, marriage counseling, divorce laws, homosexuality, and rights for unwed mothers and their children, as well as improvements in sex education and sexual technique. Czech discourses on sex and sexuality were usually tied to questions of hygiene and social reform, as well as to discourses about gender, women's rights, and class. This was typical of early twentieth-century sex-related discourses in Europe as well as in the United States (Huebner 2010b, 28).

Interwar Czech discourses on gender and sexuality are relatively understudied, especially in English-language scholarship, and while they drew on international ideas, those ideas were filtered through a complex set of conflicting desires for modernity, internationalism, and Czechness. The German and Austrian situations provide useful background for the study of Czech sexuality, as German was widely understood by Czechs, although ethnic tensions and Czech nationalism limited the degree to which Czechs chose to use the German language. While Czech sex reformism was not identical to German sex reformism, there were close ties to the German movement, and Czech writers and activists paid close and often critical attention to German ideas (Huebner 2010b, 29). Scholarship on sexuality in nearby countries also suggests ways in which the Czechs' attitudes and experiences may have differed from those of their neighbors. For instance, Stephen Brockmann (1994) argues that Weimar sexual cynicism was connected to the disintegration of the German family, but interwar Czechs may not have experienced an equal level of anxiety about the family nor felt a great degree of sexual cynicism.

After World War I, sexologists and reformers internationally moved away from focusing on taxonomies of "perversion" toward studying "normal" (primarily but not solely heterosexual) behavior. Likewise, popular sex education emphasized discussions of happy marriage and its positive eugenic potential (McEwen 2003, 137). To some extent this related to eugenic efforts and efforts to promote childbearing and parenthood, strong in many European countries during this period. Public acceptance of sex education also came from the belief that nineteenth-century anti-pornography and obscenity laws had repressed healthy sexuality, causing rather than preventing so-called degeneration, theorized as physical and mental devolution (Dean 2001, 230). Czech-language texts on sexuality, whether translations or Czech originals, were numerous during the First Republic. Czech periodicals were not shy about advertising texts relating to sexuality and often provided detailed lists of the contents. This suggests a strong popular desire to learn about, as well as to be titillated by, sex (Huebner 2010b).

One reason Czechs expressed an interest in learning more about sex was that birth control was not cheap and consequently abortions were frequent (Balkenende 2004, 142; Feinberg 2006, 129–58). Up to about 1925, the Communist Party provided the strongest support for a liberalized abortion law that did not leave the matter entirely up to physicians—who might support abortion for medical reasons but generally did not condone it publicly (Balkenende 2004, 230). Later, socialists and others gave vocal support to abortion reform as well. Leftists typically saw the prohibition of abortion as a class issue, since working-class women had limited access, while wealthier women could receive them from venal doctors who would break the law for the right price. Popular opinion remained mixed on abortion, but sex reformism helped increase awareness and acceptance of birth control (Balkenende 2004; Feinberg 2006, 129–58). By the mid-1930s, advertising for birth control could be found not just in sex-reform publications but also in mainstream women's magazines (Huebner 2010b, 36).

Male homosexuality, and to a lesser extent bisexuality and lesbianism, had begun to be discussed publicly in the Czech lands during the 1890s. In 1924, František Jelínek's *Homosexualita ve světle vědy* (Homosexuality in the Light of Science)—the most voluminous book on the subject published during the First Republic—provided readers with an overview of famous homosexuals in history and claimed many famous Czechs to be homosexual. During the early 1930s, two magazines, *Hlas sexuální menšiny* (The Voice of the Sexual Minority), founded in 1931, and its successor, *Nový hlas: List pro sexuální reformu* (New Voice: Journal for Sexual Reform), which lasted until 1934, provided readers with timely information about the lives and concerns of sexual minorities (Seidl 2007, §9.2; Huebner 2010b). Covering homoerotic literature, legal and social events, and developments relating to the largely male homosexual and bisexual community, the magazines often reported on meetings of the Československá Liga pro sexuální reformu (Czechoslovak League for Sexual Reform or ČLSR), a branch of the World League for Sexual Reform, and the Osvětové a společenského sdružení Přátelství (Enlightened and Social Association "Friendship" or OSSP), a Prague-based social club inspired by German homosexual organizations (Seidl 2007, §5.2, §5.2). In the early 1930s, several Prague "gentleman's clubs" advertised in the homophile press. While extensive study of public reception about the emergence of these venues has not been undertaken to date, it appears that for the most part they were tolerated and, although subject to sporadic annoyance from the police, not actively persecuted (Huebner 2010b).

While *Hlas* and *Nový hlas* included lesbian and bisexual topics, these were sparsely covered, mainly by writer Lída Merlínová, and it appears that Czech women were less actively involved in sexual minority reform efforts and social groups than men. Even so, in July 1932, the OSSP reported that it would be establishing a women's group, and by September that group was meeting in Prague. Furthermore, access to German-language lesbian publications such as *Ledige Frauen* (Unmarried Women), *Frauenliebe* (Women-Love), *Blätter für Ideale Frauenfreundschaft* (Pages for Ideal Women's Friendship), *Garçonne*, and above all *Die Freundin* (The Girlfriend) would have been relatively easy for savvy Czechs.

Czech sexual minorities, like those in Germany, came more into the open with the establishment of new interwar governments. Early in the First Republic, the Czechoslovak state had moved toward decriminalization of homosexuality as part of its post-independence revisions of the criminal code. Sections of the proposed revisions relating to homosexuality were approved in 1925 and discussed the next year at the First International Congress for Sexual Research in Berlin. The recommendations did not, however, become part of Czechoslovak law. The reasons for this are unclear but may relate to the similar failure of attempts to revamp family law (Cornwall 2002, 325–26).

While some liberalization of popular attitudes toward homosexuality may have occurred during the First Republic, with the approach of World War II, the Czech press focused considerable negative attention on homosexual scandals in Czechoslovakia, especially when these could be connected to Sudeten German nationalism.[2] As the political situation heated up, Czechs apparently increasingly chose to view homoeroticism and homosexuality as an ethnic German characteristic rather than as common to both Czech and German populations (Cornwall 2002, 2012). This suggests that while sexual and gender minorities could be tolerated when times were good, under stress scapegoating was still likely to occur.

GENDER AND SEXUALITY IN THE ARTS

Toyen's partnership with fellow artist Štyrský predated the pair's membership in Devĕtsil and continued until Štyrský's death in 1942. The two were considered a duo. However, while Toyen was almost the only woman in either Devĕtsil or the Prague surrealist group, she was not seen as Štyrský's follower or property. Seifert later recalled, "It first appeared that the young painter painted somewhat in the shadow of her older friend. It soon became evident, however, that this was not at all the case" (Seifert 1999, 155). Contemporary accounts discussed the two artists' work in mostly equal terms, and publications usually reproduced their work with equal emphasis. Nor did gender usually surface in reviews, with the exception of a 1931 text that called Štyrský "more intellectual" and Toyen "more lyrical, more decorative" (Pečírka 1931). But such stereotyping was unusual in discussion of this pair, and most art writers did not regard Toyen as partaking of feminine traits.

Indeed, to some extent Toyen and Štyrský were perceived as exchanging gender attributes. Vítĕzslav Nezval, for example, wrote, "Štyrský was her soul and her female element, because Toyen, who after a certain time dressed like a boy, refused, when she spoke of herself, to use the feminine endings, in order to demonstrate her human and artistic equality" (1965, 130). In addition to describing Toyen's masculine-coded traits, Nezval noted Štyrský's "seemingly meek" and somewhat "feminine" side (133). The critic Václav Nebeský also considered Štyrský to represent a more feminine element while Toyen was the more virile (1937, 18). This notion of balancing "masculine" and "feminine" polarities was common in Central Europe and is reminiscent of the Asian concept of yin and yang.

Toyen and Štyrský shared a strong interest in the erotic, which they regarded as an important realm of human life that required thorough study and exploration. Malynne Sternstein has theorized that adoption of a genderless pseudonym not only de-gendered Toyen but created "a fully sexualized being where only a gendered one stood before" (2006, 113). Secretive about any actual sexual relationships she may have had with either men or women, Toyen was never secretive about desire itself, and she explored transgressive and what we might call today queer sexualities from the start of her career as when, for instance, she painted an orgy scene. Although the activities depicted in that early painting were heterosexual, the theme of group sex clearly rebelled against societal norms (Huebner 2010a).

In what ways, then, might we consider Toyen's art transgressive or queer? Polish scholar Magda Szcześniak's recent reflection on the question "What is a queer image?" offers a useful starting point. Stating that the first answer "seems obvious—queer images portray lives of non-normative sexualities and document the existence of ever-changing LGBTQ communities from the present and past," Szcześniak adds images created by queer creative figures and suggests also images dear to specific queer constituencies, such as Douglas Sirk melodramas or portraits of David Wojnarowicz. Yet she finds her list unsatisfactory and asks us to imagine what else might constitute queer imagery: "What would happen if instead of limiting ourselves to identifying queerness in the creator of the image and/or its content, we start looking for queerness in the image itself—its construction, form, modes of circulation, social functioning?"[3]

If we consider these parameters, Toyen's works fit easily into Szcześniak's first two categories, as Toyen can be considered a queer artist whose oeuvre includes queer themes. For example, after her early orgy painting, Toyen went on to depict scenes of lesbian encounters, phallic toys, bondage, and women who are part animal.

Regarding norms for such work, erotic art and literature were published with relative freedom during the First Republic, provided certain rules were followed. Czechoslovak censorship was usually more political than sexual, although the censorship scandal following the 1929 publication of the Czech translation of the Comte de Lautréamont's *Les Chants de Maldoror* made clear that erotica should be published carefully. It could be publicly advertised but had to be sold by subscription with notices that the material was not to be made available in libraries or to children. This requirement did not hinder Toyen and Štyrský from publishing sexually explicit work. In 1930, Toyen added erotica to her types of book illustrations—projects that included Aubrey Beardsley's *Venus and Tannhäuser*, Felix Salten's *Josephine Mutzenbacher: Memoirs of a Viennese Tart*, D. H. Lawrence's *Lady Chatterley's Lover* (all 1930), and Pierre Louÿs's *Pybrac* (1932). Likewise, from 1930 to 1933, Štyrský published the journal *Erotická*

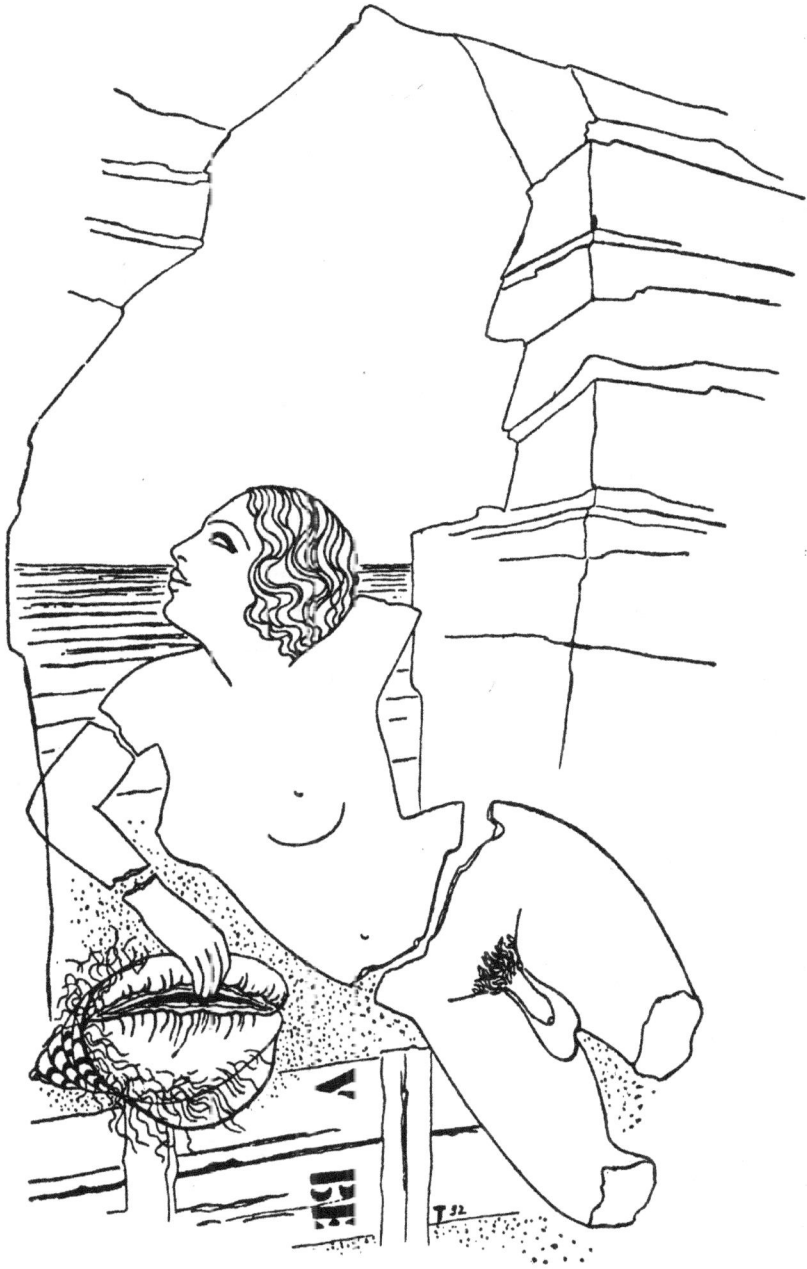

Figure 3.2. Toyen, untitled drawing, 1932. © 2015 Artists Rights Society (ARS), New York / ADAGP, Paris.

revue, which included not only sketches by Toyen but exuberant erotic drawings by various other well-known Czech artists of the time (some anonymous, some not). The cartoons and private drawings of interwar Czech artists indicate that many of them were able to address gender and sexuality in humor and fantasy. Thus, Toyen's erotic illustrations were not perhaps queer in terms of circulation and social function but were part of what defined Czech avant-garde erotic art. Queerness of construction, form, circulation, and social function developed perhaps more gradually in her work. Toyen's later surrealist art, while less explicit than the early erotica, would manifest an intensely sensuous vocabulary of queer desire, filled with imagery of labia, tongues, and vaginal openings. These images were largely produced in France after 1947 but were foreshadowed in 1931 by a remarkable sketch of a woman's face with labia in place of eyes and mouth.

The abundance of material on sex and sex education during the First Republic suggests that Toyen's exploration of the erotic, while not typical of female artists of her generation, was generally congruent with Czech cultural attentiveness to sexuality at this time. Toyen's interest in eroticism, although unusual in its extent and expression, was intimately related to her historical and geographic location as an urban Czech forming her artistic personality during first a period of economic boom, avant-garde optimism, increased opportunities for women, and sex reformism, and then a period of economic crisis, restriction of women's employment, and relative social conservatism.

How, we might ask, does Toyen resemble or differ from sexually and/or gender-transgressive figures now embraced as part of transgender history? Today, the category of transgender embraces identities, practices, and embodiments that were sometimes firmly separated and sometimes conjoined in interwar sexology (Stryker 2008; Bullough, Bullough, and Elias 1997, 15–19). If Toyen thought of herself as a lesbian, then she does not quite fit today's understanding of transgender. If, on the other hand, she considered herself to be genderless or a man in a woman's body, then she does fit within today's concept of transgender/transsexual. As Toyen resisted making statements that would allow us to categorize her more specifically than as a queer artist interested in transgressive sexuality, it is best not to try to pigeonhole her. Instead, Toyen enhances our understanding of transgender history as an example of an early twentieth-century Central European Slavic artist considered biologically female but who chose, with fairly strong social acceptance, to present herself as gender-ambiguous. It is true that artists tend to be allowed a wider range of behaviors than the average person. The fact that Toyen was an artist thus somewhat complicates the issue, as her ambiguously gendered self-presentation should be considered in light of her enthusiastic reception within avant-garde groups. Still, Toyen provides an interesting window into what was possible for a talented, non-normative Czech woman of her generation.

CONCLUSION

In sum, during the First Republic, advances in equality were achieved, although both men and women noted the need for further progress. Educated people were generally sympathetic to feminism and sex reform, but the increasingly influential communists considered these issues and the rights of sexual minorities subordinate to class struggle. Early twentieth-century Czech attitudes toward gender and sexuality were also always in complex dialogue with "German" attitudes, whether "German" meant Austrian, German, or Sudeten. This resulted from the Czech lands' historical position within the Austro-Hungarian Empire, the existence of a large ethnic German minority in Czechoslovakia, and German and Austrian prominence in sexology and psychoanalysis. With Czechs having had historically a highly ambivalent relationship with their German neighbors, it is not surprising that while they kept up with scientific and reformist developments in the German lands, in the later 1930s, many Czechs came to view homosexuality as a "German vice."

Studying Czech culture of the 1930s with a focus on Toyen enriches our understanding of options that existed for talented, gender-nonconforming women in the First Republic. These options clearly widened in the post–World War I context of a young, newly independent democracy, priding itself on its tolerance of open sexual discussions and experimenting with women's equal rights, although for most Czech women, especially those following the more conventional trajectory of marriage and motherhood, the possibilities would still remain circumscribed by the Czech nation's eagerness to emphasize the needs of the national community over those of individuals. As Melissa Feinberg has noted, as the 1930s progressed, Czechoslovakia gradually shifted from its early focus on individual rights (including women's rights) to a more "authoritarian democratic" regime in which individual citizenship became subservient to the nation's perceived needs (Feinberg 2006, 223–28). The earlier relative tolerance of sexual and gender experimentation did not alter dominant ideas about the importance of family and nation completely, suggesting Czech society's middle position between individualist and collectivist cultures. While in Czech society the individual is valued, as in strongly individualistic societies, twentieth-century Czech culture repeatedly placed a higher value on collective good than was typical for highly individualistic societies like the United States and Britain. As Feinberg points out, democracy is a process rather than something ever fully achieved, and anxiety about the potential of sexual and gender equality to change our ideas of marriage and family is a worldwide problem for democratic societies (228–29). Given that cultures around the world vary widely in their focus on individual versus collective good, Czech efforts to find a middle path—even though historically not always successful in defending individual rights—provide both useful models and important cautionary tales.

NOTES

1. An English-language publication of the Washington Declaration, officially the Declaration of Independence of the Czechoslovak Nation by Its Provisional Government, is available in several downloadable formats at https://archive.org/details/declaration ofindooczec. The 1920 Constitution of the Czechoslovak Republic is available at https://archive.org/details/cu31924014118222.

2. The term "Sudeten Germans" refers to the ethnic German population of interwar Czechoslovakia's northwestern, western, and southwestern border regions. Many of these Germans developed Nazi sympathies in the 1930s, and this population as a whole was expelled after World War II.

3. For Magda Szcześniak's 2013 call for paper submissions for *View: Theories and Practices of Visual Culture*, see http://www.critical-theory.com/submit-papers-queer-images/.

4 WOMEN AS THE OBJECT AND SUBJECT OF THE SOCIALIST FORM OF WOMEN'S EMANCIPATION

ALENA WAGNEROVÁ

WOMEN'S EMANCIPATION, OR more precisely the realization of women's full equality with men, was an integral and, from the point of view of Marxism-Leninism, key part of the political program of socialism.[1] Following Czechoslovakia's political takeover by the Communist Party in 1948, women's emancipation came to be viewed, in a manner similar to that emphasized within other countries of the socialist bloc, as an essential aspect of the social changes needed to achieve the equality of all. As such, social policy with a focus on gender was implemented from above as part of the official state agenda. Women did not figure here as the subjects of their liberation but rather as mere objects of an already set ideology of liberation. And state governing powers expected that women would accept this role and organize their lives accordingly. However, people under any regime tend to resist becoming passive objects of political decisions. Perhaps not surprisingly, women living under the authoritarian regime of Czechoslovak state socialism sought to stretch the system, sometimes working with and other times in opposition to it. They sought to create livable lives for themselves while minimizing the negatives and maximizing what they saw as the positives of the socialist regime. It could be said that they emancipated themselves alongside, rather than according to, the state's dictates. The German poet Friedrich Hölderlin once compared the state to a wall encircling a garden (1979, 41). While flowers and fruits in the garden might be captured within its walls, they continue to flourish nevertheless. Along the same lines, actual life in the shadow of Czechoslovak state socialism's wall was more colorful and varied than this power structure would seem to allow at first sight.[2] And the structure of the system itself slowly changed in response to interactions with and tensions exerted from below.

A similar back and forth between actual people's lives/actions and ideology characterized the quiet drama, across four decades, in which the Czech socialist model of women's emancipation evolved. It was a never-ending struggle to turn from an object to at least a partial subject of change. The main engine of this drama was not theory but rather the lived practice of "real gender equality," by which I mean the form of gender equality as it was lived and experienced (rather than theorized about) in everyday life. This practice of "real equality"— often ignored today because its understanding requires an intimate acquaintance with the situation in the country at the time—needs to be considered when assessing the socialist model of women's emancipation or comparing the position of women in the two main forms of European industrial society, capitalism and socialism. A sufficiently varied understanding of the fundamental differences in the interactions between political power and lived life under these two systems is needed, and more nuanced understandings along these lines should serve as relevant sources of knowledge for today's feminist theory.

In the West, the second wave of feminism, as it emerged in the 1960s, was formed from below, with feminist activists developing their positions, expressing their critiques of the status quo, and stating their demands for change.[3] A clearly articulated and popularly embedded program was necessary for the grassroots feminist movement to be taken seriously and have a chance at success. Whereas the socialist regime called on women to accept and fulfill the assigned program of their liberation, in Western countries (and also in Czechoslovakia of the interwar period) women were in the driver's seat, so to speak, petitioning the power structure to meet their demands. This grassroots pressure served also as an engine in forming feminist theory. Fundamentally, that theory was not as much about formal gender equality before the law, which was more apropos and pressing in the West, where legislation concerning women's legal standing lagged behind the socialist countries.[4] Rather, the main contribution of (Western) feminist theory was in its focus on women's right to interpret the world freely and outside masculine norms, and to make decisions about one's life accordingly. The rights to define and name are decisive instruments of power, and this aspect was missing in the socialist emancipatory model. It could not form here because circumstances were different and the contraposition of the masculine and feminine perceptions of the world was not recognized as the dominant dichotomy here—perhaps partly because men's position was to some extent "weakened" under socialism by the nationalization of the means of production, which, importantly, stripped men as a social group of their economic power.

It could be said that since political power in the West has accepted (some) feminist demands and started fulfilling (some of) them "from above" through such means as European Union (EU) policies and benchmarks, women to some extent are now turning from subjects into objects of emancipation within the EU as well. In the meantime, the political system is adopting the demands in ways that do not jeopardize its existence, with the end result being that the radical idea of transformation of the entire social system, as it was originally envisioned by Western feminists, has been amended to simple reforms of aspects of the system. While it cannot be denied that some feminist demands have been met, this kind of mainstreaming does amount to a great extent to working with the same technocratic masculine rules, even if stretching them. This is particularly true about the post-1989 situation. In a political space framed as a victory of capitalism over socialism, an opportunity was wasted to learn equally from women's emancipatory models as they developed not only under capitalist but also under socialist regimes. Too often the entire body of social and political thought and practice that happened under socialism is viewed in terms of a failed experiment that presumably has nothing to teach us besides mistakes to avoid.

THE MARXIST-LENINIST THEORY
OF WOMEN'S EMANCIPATION

While Czechoslovak state socialism is often correlated to the Czechoslovak Communist Party's seizing power in February 1948, during the interwar period of democratic Czechoslovakia, a strong and quite heterogeneous women's movement developed across various social groups, ideologies, and political programs. The recent book on Czechoslovak women's emancipation under socialism (1945–89) edited by Hana Havelková and Libora Oates-Indruchová focuses on the ways in which some of the strategies and programmatic issues originally developed in the context of the Czechoslovak interwar liberal women's movement managed on occasion to resurface during the state socialist periods. In this section, however, I focus specifically on the Marxist-Leninist theoretical underpinnings of Czechoslovak state socialist programs of women's emancipation, as they first developed within the framework of Czechoslovak (and Soviet) socialist/communist movements. While riddled with problems due to its prioritization of social class over other issues, the Marxist-Leninist discourse did provide some officially endorsed arguments and positions that women could invoke and utilize during the 1948–89 period.

According to Marxism-Leninism (in its reading as a more nuanced and less monolithic discourse than was often presented to the Czechoslovak public), women's liberation is a necessary part of human liberation and thus one of the central tenets of the socialist revolution. While for Vladimir Lenin women's issues never were primary, and he opposed the idea of autonomous women's organizations, he insisted that the proletariat cannot become free unless women are free (1961, 364). Thus the progress of women's emancipation comes to be viewed as a criterion of the success of the socialist revolution. What Marxism-Leninism also assumes is that women's emancipation requires a fundamental transformation of the entire social system and cannot be achieved without that transformation, understood in terms of eliminating the antagonism between labor and capital. Eliminating private property of the means of production was considered a necessary precondition for transforming the social system, including gender relations. According to Friedrich Engels, the capitalist accumulation of the means of production means a historical loss for women as a social group. When women become incorporated into the socialist labor force, becoming economically independent of men, their positions would be transformed once again. In practice, although not in theory, the sphere of employment came to be viewed as the central sphere of women's emancipation, and the progress of women's liberation was measured in terms of the incorporation of their labor capacity from the "unproductive" private domestic sphere into the sphere of economic production.

Note that housework was regarded even by the classics of Marxism-Leninism as nonproductive labor, as it did not produce measurable values.[5] Here Marxist-Leninist theory remained entirely under the sway of the classic economists of early capitalism, such as Adam Smith and David Ricardo. Western capitalism itself oddly persists in this view as well, as not even today is work carried out outside of the labor market included in the gross domestic product (GDP) of any industrialized country in the world, despite long-term discussions on this topic. With domestic work being traditionally done by women, its removal from the sphere of economy amounts to rendering women's work invisible. In its underappreciation of reproduction and care as economic categories, and its failure to account for their economic and social significance, the Marxist model of women's emancipation (in a manner similar to that occurring under capitalism) shows its greatest limitations. At the same time, as the Czechoslovak socialist model was being put into practice and as most women worked full time, housework and women's reproductive roles did gain some attention and recognition. As the sociologist Libuše Háková pointed out in 1970, it was impossible to overlook the fact that women's reproductive roles had specific effects on their employment and that women thus could not be reduced as easily as men to a labor force only (≤43). The time put into housework, reproduction, and care is tremendous and is generally believed to far outnumber the hours invested in "productive" labor. The world of paid labor thus de facto lives on the work done for free, and socialism, as put into practice, did not change this reality. What was different was that under socialism this unpaid work was not appropriated for capitalist accumulation but rather was put in the service of the entire "socialist house" and therefore did not have an immediately exploitative character.

Some Marxist theorists, especially August Bebel, were well aware of the problem of unpaid domestic labor, and they thought that transferring labor from home to social institutions, combined with a collective rearing of children, would solve the problem. This requirement became one of the main postulates of the Marxist model of women's emancipation, and it was being realized in the form of workplace and school canteens, nurseries, kindergartens, organized free afterschool activities for children, laundromats, and "Liberated Household" services, all set up with the goal of freeing women from domestic work.[6] The classics of Marxism did not consider the idea of a redistribution of housework between men and women; this was beyond their historical framework. But not even during the actual realization of the socialist model or after the 1960s, when Czechoslovak sociology began to develop again and a slew of empirical studies appeared on the topic, did housework labor redistribution come to figure as a major topic in public discourse, even though the issue of "men's help at home" was researched to some extent. For instance, Háková sought inspiration in the Swedish sociologist Edmund Dahlström's (1967) conceptualization of men's and women's roles as equivalent rather than complementary, but no serious social debate developed around this topic. And in popular literature of the 1960s and 1970s, one could still find passages, articulated by psychologists, praising the presumed "ingenious polarity of male and female sexes" (*Encyklopedie* 1972, 110). Marxist theory here remained behind the developments taking place in the more progressive societies of the West (especially Scandinavia) in the 1970s, although Czech/Slovak men at the time were likely more involved with family life than their peers in many Western contexts.

The question of what the change in women's position meant as far as men were concerned also remained beyond Engels's or Bebel's (and their later followers') horizon. There were various empirical surveys conducted addressing men, but the questions focused on their perceptions of women's positions, especially women's full employment. The men were never asked how women's changed status, and particularly their economic independence, with the related loss of men's traditional role as the family breadwinner, affected the perception of men's function in society.[7] One wonders to what extent the overall strengthening of men's status and the marginalization of women after 1989, accompanied by the sexism with which many Czech men responded to questions of feminism, might be connected to this neglect of the "men's question" prior to 1989. It is as if these men were unconsciously reacting to their experience of "real women's emancipation" under socialism, and as if they somehow felt that the socialist system had benefited women more than men.

Looking back, socialist society shows much ambiguity concerning men's social position. On the one hand, the power structures of the Czechoslovak Communist Party were authoritative, paternalistic, and patriarchal. On the other hand, the normativity of masculine patterns of behavior was fundamentally weakened by the nationalization of the means of production. Traditionally throughout history, men's patriarchal domination has been tied to and sustained by men's economic power. Even today, women own merely 2 percent of wealth globally.[8] In this sense, the nationalization of wealth under socialism meant a historical loss for the male sex, just as the emergence of capitalist private property had meant, with Engels, a historical loss for the female sex. With capitalist ownership of the means of production eliminated, Czechoslovak socialist society developed into an egalitarian society, without large class disparities, and people were generally not categorized into groups on the basis of accumulated capital at their disposal.

While the Marxist-Leninist thesis that women's emancipation and the liberation of all humans are closely tied together and achievable through a transformation of the social system might seem convincing, its further elaboration as a theoretical concept came to be hindered by ideological dogmatism, and the practical results of this principle's application in the end exceeded its theoretical development.[9]

THE REALIZATION OF THE SOCIALIST MODEL OF WOMEN'S EMANCIPATION

The socialist model of women's emancipation, as formulated by the classics of Marxism-Leninism and their followers, started to be put into practice in Czechoslovakia in 1948, after the Communist Party took power and Czechoslovakia became part of the socialist bloc.[10] While it is true that the program of women's liberation was being applied "from above," the social climate was highly favorable to these changes and the topic was broadly discussed. The call for full equality between men and women could be found already in the 1944 May Manifesto of the anti-fascist resistance group Předvoj (The Vanguard) and, more importantly, in the first official document of the restored Czechoslovak Republic, the so-called Košice Government Program, issued in the spring of 1945. Similarly, the new family law of 1949 was already being prepared in the interwar period, well before the 1948 communist takeover. The family law as it was finally implemented in 1949 in fact highly benefited from the earlier preparatory work done by the lawyer Milada Horáková, a key representative of the Czechoslovak pre–World War II women's movement, who was later during the Stalinist showcase trials sentenced to death and hanged (for more on Horáková, see Feinberg 2006, 211–19). This new family law was immensely progressive for its time, equalizing men and women in all spheres of family and labor law.[11] It came to mark the legislative direction of the new political system in terms of women's emancipation. Also, for the first time in the history of Europe, in 1947 a woman—the engineer Ludmila Jankovcová—became a cabinet-level member of the Czechoslovak government as the minister of industry.[12]

The pre-1948 discourse on the "woman question," as it was unfolding still under free democratic conditions, developed along the lines of mostly leftist solutions, as they had been discussed by the avant-garde before World War II. The atmosphere of these discussions was no doubt marked by the long tradition of the Czechoslovak women's movement, in which women's liberation was understood as an integral part of the emancipation of the whole nation. In this tradition, women were expected to view themselves first and foremost as members of a larger national community in pursuit of its self-determination, and their options, goals, and strategies tended to be circumscribed by that larger community's struggle against its oppression. While before 1918 these oppressive forces were represented by the Austro-Hungarian Empire and during World War II by Nazi Germany, under socialism this role came to be played by the Communist Party bureaucracy.

The 1948 February takeover by the Communist Party did not constitute a smooth transition in the tradition of the Czech women's movement. It marked the end of a free democratic debate and the inauguration of the rule of ideology, which, however, came to take on different forms over the course of the next forty years. Overall, we can distinguish three main periods in the history of the realization of the socialist model of women's emancipation in Czechoslovakia, which, however, are not strictly separated from each other but rather sometimes overlap in various ways:

1. *The period of the model's dogmatic implementation, 1948–56.* The reigning assumption was that the "women's question" had been solved automatically through the socialist revolution. The end of this period coincided with the so-called political thaw, following Josef Stalin's death in 1953 and the historical 20th Congress of the Soviet Communist Party in 1956, marked by Nikita Khrushchev's critique of the cult of personality. Under the sign of this overall political relaxation, the first public debate on abortion took place in Czechoslovakia, leading to its legalization in 1957.

2. *The period between 1957/58 and 1969, during which Marxist ideology was increasingly confronted by the lived reality.* The discipline of sociology was restored and the first empirical studies on women's position in society were conducted. This discussion developed along the lines of "searching for the original meaning of the revolution" by reformist communists. The forceful termination of the Prague Spring in August 1968 (when the tanks of the Warsaw Pact entered Prague) put an end to public debates concerning women's position as well, with some of these discussions still continuing until 1970–72 under the increasingly tense atmosphere of the so-called Normalization.

3. *The period of Normalization, starting around 1970, with the status quo maintained.* With the arrival of the so-called real socialism, even theoretical reflections on women's issues stagnated. Changes that were implemented during this period, such as the extension of the maternity leave to twenty-eight weeks and the establishment of parental leave and maternity allowance, were of an entirely pragmatic character. These measures tended to reinforce the traditional model of family and the role of women as mothers.

1948–1956/57: THE PERIOD OF A DOGMATIC IMPLEMENTATION OF THE MODEL

The initial, relatively short period of Czechoslovak state socialist gender politics was marked by the rule of ideology and (until Stalin's death) by Stalinist terror. Life was being forced to fit the framework of a set ideology. The main goal in play with respect to women's liberation was women's full employment. Women's role as workers was perceived as primary, while their role as mothers was secondary, taken care of, so to speak, "on the go." This understanding was reflected also in the relatively short paid maternity leave of twenty-two weeks.

The introduction of women to the workforce was paradoxically eased by the history of the Nazi occupation, during which Czech women (Slovakia was a separate state during World War II) of a certain age who were either childless or had older children had been forced to work. This was the first time in Czech history that women entered traditionally male professions, such as serving as tram conductors or drivers. To young women who underwent this forced labor deployment, the experience, however strenuous, also opened a new view of the traditional women's role.[13] About one third of them stayed employed after the war. They were joined by other women who entered the labor force as part of women's work recruitment campaigns after 1948, while even more women went to work after the 1949 monetary reform, when a second paycheck became indispensable for most Czech and Slovak families.

In 1948, women in Czechoslovakia made up 37.8 percent of all employed, a high ratio for Europe at the time. In the next ten years, the percentage rose to 42.4 percent (*Statistická ročenka ČSSR 1958–1972*, quoted in Köhler-Wagnerová 1974, 34) and was accompanied by a quick growth in levels of women's education. In Marxist theory, women's employment was never discussed as the goal but rather as a means toward their emancipation. In the pragmatic Czechoslovakian reality, however, women, along with the countryside population, represented the largest reservoir of labor needed for postwar reconstruction. As the concept of women's emancipation was rigidly implemented, soon the means became the end itself and women's employment came to be conceived of as emancipation achieved. As Antonín Zápotocký stated, "Working along with men, women best demonstrate their emancipation" (quoted in Köhler-Wagnerová 1974, 17).[14]

Tapping into the reservoir of women's labor meant that Czechoslovakia was able to avoid inviting foreign guest workers, which was the main way of dealing with postwar labor shortages in most Western European industrialized countries, many of which were trying to send "their women" back to the home after the war. Statistically, between 1948 and 1964, women's employment in Czechoslovakia rose by 750,000 women as compared to only 79,000 men entering new jobs. Even as late as 1964, women made up 94.2 percent of all new employees (Fukalová 1967, 67). However, along with these dramatic changes, problems began to emerge. The Czechoslovak labor market was highly inflexible at the time, offering only full-time employment (48 hours/week), and at most workplaces work began at 6 or 7 AM. Part-time positions were practically nonexistent, with the limited exception of some jobs with more flexible hours like school teaching. The long working week meant that women with children were overburdened. Of course, theoretically, as in the ideas of Engels or Bebel, domestic work and childcare were supposed to be socialized and institutionalized, and traditional housework was to practically disappear. At the beginning of the 1950s, these ideas were still remembered in the form in which they had been discussed in the 1920s by Czech leftist avant-garde architects (influenced by French modernist architects like Le Corbusier). The so-called *koldům*, or collective house, represented what was considered an ideal solution. It concentrated under one roof all social necessities, including a canteen, nursery, kindergarten, laundromat, and facilities for leisure-time activities, such as a swimming pool and gymnasium. However, while several of these collective houses were designed and some even built, the expense turned out to be unsustainable, and practice once again left theory behind.

In a similar vein, the idea of collective childrearing, according to which the family was supposed to only supplement the upbringing of children in socialist institutions, was realized only partially. Throughout the 1950s, nurseries and kindergartens where children would spend most of the week, going home only for weekends, were promoted as the most advanced form of childcare, especially for women working on shifts. Society, however, rejected this model, and only 15 percent of all children attending nurseries went to the week institutions, with the percentage dropping to 5.1 percent by 1965 (Dunovský 1971, 155). Even day nurseries remained fairly unpopular. According to 1965 statistics, only 9.3 percent of children under the age of three were placed in day nurseries (Svoreňová-Királyová 1968, 13).[15] With paid maternity leave limited to only twenty-two weeks, the usual age of children first admitted to nurseries was six months, which was widely considered by the public as too early. Gradually, an improvised solution to the problem of small children started emerging in the form of three-generational families, a solution favored and necessitated by the housing shortage. Retired grandparents took care of children to the age of three, when children would be admitted to (free, state-provided) kindergartens.[16] Young families would often wait for the birth of their first child until a grandmother had retired and become available to care for the infant. Some, especially college-educated women, would hire an older woman to care for their children. Women were thus devising various strategies to overcome the rigid ideological premises, demonstrating much more flexibility and resourcefulness than the entire bureaucratic system.

The debate about abortion that emerged on the pages of newspapers and magazines in 1955–56 could be considered the first real breakthrough of lived reality into the ideological schema. While ideology assumed that under socialism every conceived child could be born, contraception was practically nonexistent and the reality of illegal abortions, with all of their consequences, was impossible to hide or ignore. Of course, the main argument for legalization was not "my body, my choice" but rather that it was beneath the dignity of the socialist woman to have to resort to traditional midwives and bear the consequences of back-alley illegal interventions. After all, advocates argued, legal abortion was an old demand of the traditional leftist women's movement.

With the church marginalized, there were almost no anti-abortion voices in the debate, and deliberations concluded with a legalization of abortion by Act 68/1957, implemented in 1958. However, the law required each case to be approved by a local abortion committee, and appearing before the committee was often uncomfortable, even humiliating, because here too the system stood above the individual. Still, the abortion committees did approve over 90 percent of requests. Finally, in 1986, the committees were abandoned, and abortions were permitted until the twelfth week of pregnancy.

As for the number of abortions performed in socialist Czechoslovakia, it varied between 61,000 abortions for 235,000 births in 1958 and 99,000 abortions for 228,000 births in 1968. The number peaked in 1969, with 102,000 abortions for 222,000 births (*Statistická ročenka ČSSR 1958–72*). In the five years of the biggest baby boom, the abortion-to-birth ratio was between 55,000/191,000 in 1975 and 68,000/153,000 in 1980, when the birthrate started declining. In the 1980s, the national abortion rate started increasing, reaching the maximum in 1990 with 111,000 abortions for 130,000 births.[17] It is noteworthy that in periods of social unrest and change, such as in 1968–69 and 1988–89, the abortion rate increased, quite possibly indicating that women were in this way responding to the climate of insecurity.

In the 1990s, the number of abortions in the Czech Republic started to decline—partly due to the increased availability and use of hormonal contraception. Simultaneously, the birthrate started declining sharply as well, to a mere 93,000 in 2003 (with 42,000 abortions performed that year).[18] And as in many other post-socialist countries, the Czech Republic witnessed an (unsuccessful in the Czech context) attempt to restrict the abortion law in 2003.

1956/57–1969: TRANSFORMING THE DOGMATIC CHARACTER OF THE MODEL

The second stage in the development of the socialist model of women's emancipation was characterized by attempts to adapt the model to the reality on the ground. The lived reality of socialism began to overtake ideology, and, after years of dogmatism, the entire society underwent reconstruction. The question of women's position in a socialist society became the focus of lively public debates, lasting throughout the 1960s, with the needs and interests of women themselves finding their way to the center of these debates. Women were asserting themselves into the position of subjects of emancipation, and its goal was no longer restricted to achieving full employment but was broadened to ensure that "women are not excluded from participation in economic, social and political life just because they are women" (Fukalová 1967, 88). The first empirical studies into the questions that were emerging at the time played an important role. While Engels remained the main theoretical source, after crediting him, authors now frequently followed with a "but," highlighting the differences between advanced socialist society and Engels's context.[19] The first of these empirical studies were not authored by sociologists but by physicians and demographers, because sociology as a discipline in Czechoslovakia was only beginning to be reconstituted.[20]

A pediatric congress in Bratislava in 1961 can be considered one of the key events during this period. It tackled for the first time the problem of psychological deprivation and its impacts on children placed in institutional care, especially the weeklong institutions.[21] It was during this year that week-nursery use peaked, although they still constituted only 15 percent of the overall use of nurseries (Dunovský 1971, 155). The public reception of the problem of psychological deprivation led to the consideration of women's double burden and to the gradual recognition of the importance of maternal care. This then resulted in the extension of paid maternity leave to twenty-six weeks in 1968, and in 1969 to the introduction of a state maternity allowance for the second child until its first birthday.[22] The center of childcare moved back to the family again, with the collectivist institutional care only supplementing it.[23]

But even in this propitious context, while women's double burden was discussed, the idea of changing the traditional division of labor in the family remained unexamined. According to surveys conducted during this period, housework took women 4.9 hours per day on average (*Statistická ročenka ČSSR* 1958–72; see also Lippold 1967), and women's employment continued to grow, with women making up almost 46 percent of the labor force in 1968. Also, the gradual increase in women's educational levels, which began to rise in the 1950s, continued throughout the 1960s until the gender gap was closed. In the 1970s, more women than men graduated from high school. And while in 1963 women earned 44.7 percent of technical degrees, in 1970 it was 50.2 percent.[24] Finally, the number of women with college-level education grew from 23 to 31.3 percent during this period. Even with these changes, however, the average woman's salary continued to reach only 66 percent of a man's, and women's high levels of education were not reflected in their representation in leadership positions. The highest percentage of women in leadership, 30.1 percent, was in municipal services, while only 9 percent of leadership positions within academia were filled by women, who also represented merely 1.6 percent of company directors (Köhler-Wagnerová 1974, 53).

In politics the situation was similar. In 1971, of the 115 members of the powerful Central Committee of the Czechoslovak Communist Party, only 8 were women (7%), while in the politically inconsequential Parliament, women represented 25 percent (Köhler-Wagnerová 1974, 54). Throughout the entire socialist era, women, with the exception of Ludmila Jankovcová, did not fill any political positions of real significance. While this reality to some extent reflected how difficult it was for women to navigate and advance within the Czechoslovak Party structures, not many women were attracted to the notion of entering these structures with their detached modes of operation. Women, on the other hand, could be found anywhere it was possible to do meaningful public work, such as in trade unions, organizing child recreation, and so on. And they were highly engaged in political work any time it was expressed in the form of civic movements, such as during the Prague Spring and later in the Czech dissent, especially Charta 77.[25]

As the possibility of economic reforms along the lines of market principles were being debated during the second half of the 1960s, questions surfaced about the economic efficacy of employed married mothers' labor, with some arguing that state childcare costs were exceeding the economic value of children's mothers' labor (discussed in Fukalová 1967, 96). This argument met with a negative response on the part of women, who saw it as an attack on the principle of equality and an attempt to return to an outdated social model. At the same time, women continued to highlight the overload put on their shoulders, noting the insufficiently developed public services and infrastructure, and only 21 percent of them agreed that women had achieved equality with men (*Mínění žen* 1972). Women's responses to the question of whether or not they wished for their daughters to work outside the house is characteristic of attitudes from this period. While almost 84 percent of women answered yes, 39 percent added, "but not where I work" (Němcová 1971, 12).

1969–1989: THE PERIOD OF "NORMALIZATION" AND "REAL SOCIALISM"

The twenty-year period starting with the forceful suppression of the Prague Spring in August 1968 and the onset of the so-called Normalization was characterized by stagnation in both general discussions about and proposed solutions to women's issues. Theory more or less returned to dogmatic Marxism, and the public for the most part (with the exception of dissidents) became politically resigned to the status quo. It is in this period that the term "real socialism" was introduced and, not without irony, "real equality."[26] Only the recognition of the value of the maternal role continued to grow, with regular increases in maternal allowances and, in 1988, the extension of paid maternity leave from twenty-six to twenty-eight weeks. In 1989, an additional three-year parental leave and allowance were introduced. Some politically dissenting women used the maternity leave as a sort of shield against a possible job loss or as a way to retreat from the public sphere. The political situation thus could possibly have contributed to the rise in birthrate between 1970 and 1979.

In contrast to official politics (failing to significantly represent Czech women even today), during this period women were actively engaged in civic opposition, especially the Charta 77 movement. Between 1977 and 1990, almost 30 percent of Charta spokespeople were women,[27] and quite a number of women were also involved in (illegally) typing Charta materials and secretly (and illegally) transporting them, often in strollers or shopping bags. Also, still before November 1989, through the grassroots activities of the group Prague Mothers, the first nonprofit, nongovernmental organization in Czechoslovakia came into existence, working in the field of ecology.

While Czechoslovakia (and most of the socialist bloc) was undergoing this period of political stagnation, many Western countries were witnessing the emergence and height of the second wave of feminism in its many different forms. With the second wave, public consciousness concerning women's issues was gradually beginning to change in the West, though lived reality continued to lag behind theory. In Czechoslovakia, the situation under Normalization was the exact opposite. Theoretical discourse on women's issues stagnated, but in the practice of everyday life, under the radar of ideological supervision, unsystematic and unstructured "real equality" continued to develop.

There are also many indications of different effects of the repressive regime under Normalization on women and men. While women continued to experience the double burden (although infrastructure and supply of products improved during this period, thus making things easier for women responsible for shopping), they appeared to be as a group better psychologically prepared to deal with political repression in the public sphere by relying on their inner strength (True 2003, 72; Gal and Kligman 2000, 69). Traditional cultural respect wielded by women's roles, and especially motherhood (for those who became mothers), provided to some extent a source of protection unavailable to men, such as when women opted to go on (paid) maternity leave when their jobs were threatened. Men, on the other hand, socialized as they continued to be to look for self-realization mostly at work, saw fewer alternatives for self-realization if they lost their professional position or were banned from publishing, and they seemed overall less flexibly positioned to deal with the repressive political situation (True 2003, 72).

But even women living the taken-for-granted equality were not prepared for the post-1989 surge of Western feminist thought into Czechoslovakia. In the subsequent political climate, which interpreted the fall of socialism unambiguously as a victory of capitalism, there was no space to critically reflect on socialism's deficiencies or its achievements in relation to women's emancipation. What happened instead was a certain colonization of the lived reality of women's lives under crumbling socialism by Western feminist theory, which certainly was, especially in terms of its theoretical scope, advanced as compared to the socialist model of emancipation, which was stuck, to some extent, in Marxist-Leninist dogma. However, in the process, the lived reality of the socialist system became, at least temporarily, completely devalued and de facto expropriated from those who had lived it. This happened especially as many scholars (including Czechs) were uncritically applying the criteria of Western feminist theories (created under and for different social circumstances) in their assessments of the socialist past.

Women's marginalization and the strengthening of masculine models of behavior post-1989, especially in the first decade of the renewal of capitalism, again lent relevance to the Marxist-Leninist question of the relationship between women's emancipation and the ownership of the means of production. Unfortunately, no serious public debate around these issues developed. Jiřina Šiklová's efforts in bringing about the *Pamět' žen* (Women's Memory Project), initiated in the early 1990s and realized in the following decade, focused on women's experiences under socialism and was meant as a sort of rescue act, to capture and preserve the reality of women's lives during the forty years of the Czechoslovak socialist era.

CONCLUSION

It is certainly paradoxical to consider that a nondemocratic, authoritarian socialist regime opened many opportunities to women as compared to Western democratic regimes during the same period. While women's emancipation under Czechoslovak state socialism did not reach into important and fundamental areas such as prejudices around sex roles, especially in the family, there were also noteworthy achievements, which included:

1. Legislatively guaranteed equality of men and women before the law, in all aspects of life and work, starting in 1949; legalization of abortion starting in 1958; and decriminalization of homosexual acts in 1961.

2. High levels of educational attainment among women, their integration into the workforce, and their economic independence from men. Even post-1989, despite some politicians' predictions, no mass return of women to the home has taken place, and Czech women continue to value their employment highly.

3. Women's statutory independence from men, a process that is still unfinished in many Western countries.

4. Women under socialism were not treated as sex objects, certainly not to the extent they are under consumer capitalism. The importance of this reality for women's "real emancipation" often remains overlooked despite the fact that the degradation of women as sexual objects is considered by many feminists the most obvious vehicle for maintaining the subjection of women. The decreased status of women after 1989 and the "reconstitution" of the woman's body as public property, including in the forms of prostitution and sex tourism, are clearly connected.

The post-1989 disintegration of the socialist regime in Czechoslovakia marked the end of the development of the Marxist-Leninist model of Czech and Slovak women's emancipation. This, of course, should not mean an end to critical reflection and public debate about that system's achievements and shortcomings. The reality of people's experiences under socialism should not be excluded from feminist discussions as if this stage of women's emancipation never existed or was in some way negligible, although such denials and dismissals are unfortunately still encountered with some frequency.

NOTES

1. I use the term "emancipation" with some caution as it seems to imply a process for which society can create circumstances (such as equal rights for men and women) but the realization of which is an individual achievement. Yet the possible alternative term "equality" does not capture the complexity of the topic, and "emancipation" seems more appropriate. In her recent book-length study on the Czechoslovak women's movement between 1945 and 1955, Denisa Nečasová similarly hesitates to use the term "women's movement" when discussing post-1948 Czechoslovakia (2011, 17, 248) and finds the term "feminism" entirely inappropriate for the socialist period, during which the term gained intellectual and bourgeois connotations (21, 380).

2. A convincing testimony to this reality can be found in the oral history project *Pamět' žen* (Women's Memory Project), the Czech part of which was realized between 1996 and 2003. Women of three generations were interviewed as part of this project. See Pavla Frýdlová's chapter in this volume.

3. Western societies at the time were dominated by a type of normative, hegemonic masculinity and (in some cases) machismo that in Czechoslovakia did not, post–World War II, develop to the same extent, as its full development there was interrupted by the change of the social system. It is not without irony that forms of this demonstrative masculine type of power and its other face—the degradation of women to sexual objects—started appearing in the Czech Republic after the return of democracy and capitalism post-1989.

4. For instance, while family law that equalized both partners was passed in socialist Czechoslovakia in 1949, in West Germany such a law was not passed until 1977.

5. See also Alena Heitlinger's critique of Engels's failure to consider reproductive and domestic labor as productive (1979, 19).

6. In the Czechoslovak context, this problem was first studied by Jiří Musil (1961).

7. For more on this topic, see Alena Köhler-Wagnerová 1974, 71.

8. See Valeria Sodano (2011): "98% of wealth on earth is in the hands of men, and only 2% belongs to women; the 225 richest persons in the world, who are men, own the same capital as the 2,500 million poorest people; of these 2,500 million poorest people, 80% are women" (291).

9. In the GDR (East Germany), an effort to interrogate this theory was attempted by a private group of scholars (becoming semiofficial in 1982) from Humboldt University and the Academy of Sciences, headed by Irene Dölling, which was, after 1989, gradually transformed into today's Center for Interdisciplinary Gender Studies at Humboldt. In Czechoslovakia, on the other hand, during the period of Normalization, sociology mostly stagnated, partly because many competent sociologists were either banned from research and publishing (Libuše Háková, Jiřina Šiklová) or emigrated (Irena Dubská), and the situation in the humanities was characterized by a turn to dogmatism.

10. The model's realization was based on the same premise in both Slovakia and the Czech lands, although in Slovakia the process was slower and reflective of its specific context.

11. The family law of 1949 abolished the former function of the head of the family, ended the previous duty to state a child's legitimate or illegitimate origin on the birth certificate (thus equalizing legitimate and illegitimate children), and allowed freedom of choice in deciding on the last name in marriage.

12. See "Ženy ve vládách: 1. díl—Československo" (Women in Governments: Part 1—Czechoslovakia), http://www.cpssu.org/view.php?cisloclanku=2004060501.

13. Many women interviewed for the oral history project *Pamět' žen* reflected on this experience.

14. "Ve společné práci s muži dokazují ženy nejlépe svou rovnoprávnost." Antonín Zápotocký (1884–1957) was a leading functionary of the Czechoslovak Communist Party and the Czechoslovak president between 1953 and 1957.

15. According to Svoreňová-Királyová, nurseries became most widespread in GDR.

16. In 1965, roughly half of all children attended kindergartens in Czechoslovakia (Svoreňová-Királyová, 13).

17. See Český statistický úřad [Czech Statistical Office], 2001, www.czso.cz.

18. See Kocourková 2007. The statistics provided for the period until 1992 cover the entire Czechoslovakia; after 1992 only the Czech Republic.

19. We could cite two articles by Libuše Háková, both published in the communist monthly *Nová mysl* (New Thought), as classic examples of this sort of change in thinking. While Háková's earlier, article, from 1961, is written entirely along the official party line; her later, 1966 article is written under the sign of the above-mentioned "but" followed by the author's list of complaints against the status quo.

20. The results of many of these empirical studies, focused on a range of aspects of women's lives, were published in the academic journal *Demografie*, especially by Vladimír Wynnyczuk and Jiří Prokopec. These studies were straightforward but methodologically correct, and their relevance is given by the large sample with which the authors worked.

21. A path-breaking work in this context was conducted by pediatricians and psychologists Marie Damborská, Jiří Dunovský, Josef Langmeier, and Zdeněk Matějček on the theory of deprivation.

22. The length of paid maternity leave in Czechoslovakia was twenty-two weeks between 1964 and 1968, twenty-six weeks between 1968 and 1987, twenty-eight weeks between 1987 and 1988, and twenty-eight weeks for the first child and thirty-seven weeks for the second child between 1988 and the present. Besides paid maternity leave, in 1989 the state also introduced a parental leave (a provision still in place) during which either the mother or the father can stay at home with their child for up to three years without losing their job and while collecting parental benefits from the state.

23. F. Bánhegyi focused on this issue in his *Sociólogia súčasné rodiny* (1967).

24. In West Germany, on the other hand, an overall low level of girls' and women's education and qualification was still cited as a problem of emancipation as late as 1971.

25. Charta 77 (Charter 77) refers to a group of Czech political dissidents who signed and supported the 1977 document Charta 77, which was critical of the Czechoslovak communist government.

26. Practically the only exception in this theoretical lacuna was the first Czech study of two-career families under socialism by Ivo Možný in 1983.

27. During this period, there were eleven female and twenty-six male spokespeople for Charta 77.

5 WOMEN'S MEMORY

Searching for Identity under Socialism

PAVLA FRÝDLOVÁ

THE 1989 LIFTING of the Iron Curtain in Czechoslovakia was accompanied by heightened expectations with regard to the production and distribution of knowledge. Perhaps nowhere were these new opportunities more highly anticipated than in the area of Women's Studies. At that time, many feminists from Western Europe and North America rushed to the supposed "backward" region of Eastern Europe under the flag of global sisterhood, frequently judging the position of women in the East on the basis of their own social and cultural experiences and norms. Some of these Western visitors saw women in the region as not emancipated enough, while others brought with them exaggerated ideas about something called the "socialist woman."

In 1995, during two-week-long discussions among women from both Eastern Europe and the West, all aboard the transcontinental train taking us through Siberia to the Fourth Women's Conference in Beijing, we, the Czech delegation, became particularly aware of the importance and urgency of reflecting on and articulating the uniqueness of our experiences under socialism. The sociologist Jiřina Šiklová, founder of the Gender Studies Centre in Prague, formulated the idea into a project proposal: women from the former Eastern European bloc should trace the lives of women who lived under socialism and study the question of women's identity under socialism.

Numerous women's organizations from post-socialist countries immediately expressed an interest in participating in the Women's Memory Project, although funding was a limiting issue from the start and would prove an unsurpassable obstacle for many. In the fall of 1996, our Prague group started interviewing Czech women, and gradually we were joined by colleagues from other countries, who, like us, were willing to spend much time fundraising and grant writing. Only the East German team managed to receive state funding for the project.

In 1998, with the support of the Heinrich Böll Foundation, the Czech, East German, and Polish teams cooperated to pilot the project and to work out its methodology. In the following year, with funds from Open Society, a weeklong workshop was organized on the Croatian island of Brac, attended by teams from six countries (the Czech Republic, Slovakia, Poland, Germany, Croatia, and Serbia). An agreed-upon mandatory methodology, a long-term plan, and principles of cooperation were developed and adopted by consensus. It was decided that the project would be directed from Prague, where all of the interviews and their transcripts, along with the accompanying materials, would be archived, while at the same time each team would proceed independently according to its abilities. In subsequent years, teams from the Ukraine and Montenegro also joined.

The aim of Women's Memory was to capture the history of women under socialism in its complexity, from international and interdisciplinary perspectives. We wanted to challenge the established myths and clichés about the "socialist woman," often represented one-dimensionally as some kind of heroic, female tractor driver. Our goal was to document the life experiences of women of three generations born between 1920 and 1960, and we were interested above all in their life strategies and their personal methods of survival.

QUESTIONS OF METHODOLOGY

Already our first interviews made clear that it would be impossible to limit our questions to the socialist period, as many of our interviewees' childhood and youth unfolded in the pre-socialist period, and the changes that happened in their lives post-1989 were important to discuss as well.

More crucial was the question of our overall methodological approach. Our methodology, as it developed through our conversations, was inspired by feminist developments in the social sciences that challenged the traditional, male-dominated interpretation of the world and emphasized women's personal experiences. As a result, many feminist researchers use narrative and biographical methodological approaches in order to capture and give expression to those personal experiences. History is here no longer understood simply as a series of events but more as an outcome of interactions among individuals. It is the meaning and significance attributed to events by individuals that retroactively shapes and forms historical "reality." Thinking along these lines, we decided on a technique of oral history interviews. Rooted in oral transmission of knowledge and in family narratives, this approach seemed particularly suitable considering our interest in lived experience rather than "objective truth."

While we initially drew on the lessons and experiences of other related projects, our own specific methodology was shaped by and changed through the actual process of interviewing. Methodological issues were also discussed during five international workshops. While respecting cultural, religious, and historical differences among teams from various countries, we felt it necessary to establish an agreed-upon common ground that would later enable us to compare the project results internationally. From the beginning, we emphasized an interdisciplinary focus, understanding that the complexity of relations between socialism and gender issues could never be fully grasped from the exclusive perspective of any one single discipline. Each national research team therefore included women from various disciplines, including sociology, history, linguistics, psychology, philosophy, ethnography, anthropology, and journalism. Additionally, one of the project's unique aspects and strengths, in our view, was that it sought to address the broader public (rather than just the academic community) in the related countries.

Much attention was paid to the process of interviewing, understood in terms of an interaction between the interviewer and the respondent requiring mutual trust. We saw it as essential to seek to equalize the position between those involved in the interview, especially since the purpose was not just to collect "data" but also to work with women in the direction of reflecting on their/our identities. While the basic structure for the interview would be prepared in advance, this was used only as a helpful outline that we kept at the back of our minds. We felt that the ideal situation was one where the interviewed woman would feel that she was setting the direction of the story she was sharing. Most of the interviews would take several hours, and often several meetings were required to complete the process. This was a time-consuming and demanding task, and it would have been impossible to complete without a deep commitment on the part of the team members.

From the beginning, we also recognized the importance of selecting the right women to interview. While each life story was important to us, not every woman was able or willing to tell it. Searching for women to interview, we often relied on the snowball method and on personal recommendations, as trust was important; without it, it would be difficult to ask about such intimate issues as sexual relations, childbirth, abortion, family planning, and so on. Needless to say, full anonymity of the respondents was guaranteed.

The women who were interviewed included a farmworker, typesetter, nurse, librarian, physician, lawyer, photographer, pilot, and many others. Although we were clear from the beginning that this was not meant to be a completely representative sample of the female population of each country concerned, we did attempt to strike a relative balance among the social circles and age groups of the women chosen. The most urgent task was to interview the oldest generation. It was obvious that this generation—then in their late seventies and early eighties—was not going to be with us for much longer. We did not want to allow the circumstances that had shaped their lives as women to be forgotten, or, equally bad, to be unnecessarily distorted by later second-hand interpretation. That this age group represented the first economically independent generation of women added importance to the task of engaging and including them. Never before had there been a generation that, thanks to the socialist regime under which most of their lives unfolded, came to experience a complete economic independence from men.

PROJECT RESULTS

During the ten years of our work on the project—marked by a perpetual struggle for funding—over five hundred biographical interviews were conducted and transcribed, and most of the transcripts are now archived in the Gender Studies Centre in Prague.[1] Each of the national teams handled the research results differently. Some teams, such as the Serbian, Croatian, Montenegrin, and Czech groups, produced documentary films, radio programs, and popular books addressing broader public (see the appendix to this chapter for more information), while others, such as the Slovak team, published the project results in the form of scholarly monographs (see Kiczková et al. 2006).

Beyond the published results, there is another dimension to the concept of "research output" with projects like this: the process of consciousness-raising among the women who participated in the project. Many of the women interviewed were genuinely surprised that anybody would be interested in hearing their stories, and for many this was their first opportunity to recapitulate their lives. The interviews enabled them to see themselves from a new perspective, and the very fact that others were interested in their lives boosted their self-confidence.

As we transcribed the interviews, sifted through the material, read other researchers' interviews, and discussed them in workshops, we were learning what multiculturalism really means, while the clichés about the gray uniformity of life in East Central Europe were being rapidly eroded. The interviews made it abundantly clear that women under socialism did experience a form of emancipation, although one that must be understood in terms of its essentially non-Western uniqueness. While women in the West had to struggle long and hard for many of their rights, the paternalistic socialist states ruled by communist governments provided many of these rights through policies and directives from above. After all, women's equality was guaranteed by the communist constitutions and (theoretically) was integral to that political platform's package of social and economic change. Still, one of the leading questions for our project was to assess how these legal directives and statements of principle were actually applied in practice in everyday life.

THREE ASPECTS OF WOMEN'S EMANCIPATION UNDER SOCIALISM

So, how was the socialist form of women's emancipation unique as compared to what feminists from the West have come to know? There are at least three aspects to this uniqueness: economic independence, access to and attitudes about education and/or professional competence, and women's independent social identity. We arrived at this list through the process of interviewing ninety Czech women born before 1930, of different ethnic backgrounds (including Czech-German, Romany, and Jewish), as well as various professional and social backgrounds, who came both from urban areas and the countryside.[2] These women lived through and participated in some of the major social and political events of the twentieth century, including World War II, the communist takeover, the Cold War, the 1968 Soviet occupation, and the Velvet Revolution of 1989.

Across Europe, World War II was a turning point in the history of women's employment. It was during this period that significant numbers of women from various social backgrounds joined the paid labor force. But unlike in the West, where women were subsequently encouraged to return to the household, many women in the socialist region continued to work even after the war. And a subsequent reorganization of the Czechoslovak national industry and agriculture, when part-time employment became practically nonexistent, led to almost full employment among women. Throughout the 1950s, the model of a double-income household gradually became the social norm as well as an economic necessity. As a result, the concept of "housewife" almost entirely disappeared. Indeed, working on the Women's Memory Project, we did not meet a single Czech woman who spent her entire adult life caring for her children and husband.

Most women described themselves in the interviews largely in respect to their activities and achievements in their professional and public, as well as private lives. Notably, they tended to speak of their heavy workload positively, highlighting a diligent and conscientious attitude toward work as an important attribute and expressing pride in their ability to manage their full load. For the generation of Czech women born in the 1920s, postwar enthusiasm was characteristic, with its accelerated study, work brigades, Sunday shifts, and so on. Most of the respondents, accustomed as they had become to hardship and self-sacrifice from World War II, considered the heavy workload and discomforts connected with postwar shortages as an inevitable part of the building of the new republic, and they accepted the double shift (home and work) as a matter of course.

We also tried to track down women featured on the covers of magazines from the 1950s and 1960s: crane operators, tractor drivers, pilots, and exemplary workers in socialist industry and agriculture, or, as they were called at the time, "work heroines." We managed to find and interview some of them. Whatever direction their life stories took since the time of the feature articles, they were all proud of their professional achievements. For instance, one story was of a private seamstress who changed course and became a crane operator, proudly managing the whole construction from the height of her crane cabin.

Their salaries were not negligible either, although the gender gap in salaries did persist under socialism. Slávka N., a full-time dance instructor born in 1935, commented on this issue:

> It bothered me that the principle of equal financial remuneration and of equal status of women at work was not followed in practice. Often, a woman perfectly capable of filling a leadership position could not do so simply because men were still considered the family breadwinners who presumably needed to earn higher salaries. Women, whether married or not, were expected to be able to manage on a smaller salary, even if they were doing more work. I felt it as an injustice toward women. If a woman has the required qualification and skills, why shouldn't she be hired for a job over a man who might perhaps have the qualifications but whose skills might not be 100 percent? This always bothered me and it still bothers me today. (*Všechny naše včerejšky II* 1998, 163)

Many of our respondents found much inspiration in their strong grandmothers and mothers, whom they saw as role models. In their effort to live up to these models, however, they often overlooked that older traditions of gender roles were entirely different, and that the pace of their own lives and their workloads could not be compared with those of their mothers' and grandmothers' generations. It is also impossible not to see that this one-dimensional emphasis on and celebration of hard work helped facilitate the socialist regime's hiding and legitimating the overload of, and discrimination against, women. The socialist model of emancipation provided women with the opportunity to find self-realization at work, but it did not decrease their load at home. Men, raised by the previous generation of mothers, who were mostly housewives, were accustomed to full service at home, and they often did not understand that they should be involved equally with their wives in domestic chores and childcare. As Anna K., an office clerk and translator born in 1920, expressed it:

> My husband was used to not having to do anything at home. He was part of the generation where mothers were at home and children did not have to help. My mother-in-law, for instance, was really surprised that I would not clean my husband's shoes. At my house, everybody had to clean their own shoes. Later, when we had a child and I needed help, my husband would say: "Manage as you can, you are the mother—do as if I weren't here." And his behavior was like this as well. He would take our son for a short walk on Sundays, but that was the extent of his help. Otherwise, when he watched TV and our son would ask him something, he would yell that he is disturbing him. . . . During [our] divorce, he wanted the custody of the child, but the report sent to the court from our son's school said that at school they did not even know him. (*Všechny naše včerejšky* 1998, 18)

Our respondents did not question the value of hard work. Doing so would diminish the positive self-evaluation of their own identities and past achievements. Yes, they did feel overburdened at certain periods of life—especially when their children were growing up—but they never perceived themselves as victims of a regime. Instead, they emphasized their abilities and resourcefulness. They were proud at how they had managed everything, although they did not hide that it was difficult. Jitka R., a teacher born in 1934, said:

> In 1958, I went back to work. I started working as a schoolteacher, and I must admit that this was the most stressful period of my life. I had to take my sons to school and to catch a bus every morning. This meant that I had to wake them up, feed and dress them, and go running to school with them. We would run every morning; the last part was through a small park—the teacher was at the door and I would say: "Boys, quick, you can run the rest on your own!" And I would already see my bus coming from around the corner. I would run to the bus stop, jump on and ride to my school. In stress all the time, not to miss the bus, not to be late; well, it was a nightmare. (*Všechny naše včerejšky* 1998, 96)

No matter what their social backgrounds, the interviewed women without exception shared a desire for education, and some expressed a sense of lack of fulfilment if they did not, for whatever reason, achieve the education they had desired. The respondents did not necessarily see education as the most important part of emancipation, but they perceived it as a way to get further in life. For this generation, education was a fundamental life value. The librarian Pravomila M., born in 1925, perhaps expressed it best:

> My grandmothers did not have the opportunity to study. Village women went to school only irregularly when they were not needed on the farm. They had two books to read in—the dream book and the prayer book. My mother achieved primary education. She was an avid reader, reading at night with a candle under the blanket—mostly popular calendars and novels that told stories about simple Prague folk. . . . I have achieved secondary education, and my daughter, the great granddaughter of my grandmother, is a college student. Our reading standards are much higher too.[3]

After all, virtually all Czech feminists of the past, whether Eliška Krásnohorská or Františka Plamínková, considered education a key instrument and precondition for women's emancipation.[4] While the Women's Memory interviews conducted in other participating countries do not show the same emphasis on education, almost all of the Czech respondents sought to reach at least a high-school diploma. For many of them, their education was interrupted by the war, which further increased their determination to finish. And it was also the availability of education that they considered the greatest achievement of the country's postwar development. Most of the women who did not finish high school never stopped seeing this as the major failure of their lives. These women tended to be particularly insistent in ensuring the education of their daughters and granddaughters.

Not all of them, however, found their partner to be supportive. For instance, Antonie S., a factory worker born in 1923, noted, "There was one thing that bothered me about my husband. I wanted to get a high-school diploma. It would take a year of prep school, and then I would have to go to school in the afternoon for three years. But he went on about how he would not care for the children for me. I couldn't leave them at home all alone, and I didn't know anybody in Prague, so I had to give this up" (*Všechny naše včerejšky II* 1998, 49).

More surprisingly, one generation later, Hanka, an accountant born in 1949, reported a similar experience:

> When my first son was born in 1972 and I was on maternity leave, I felt that I was not using my time well and wanted to study at college, but my husband

categorically rejected the idea. Why should his wife have higher education than himself? And why should he, a married man, share house chores with me? You got married, you wanted kinds, he would say, so now take care of them instead of running around and commuting to school. I was really unhappy about this at the time, and I continue to think till today that I should have been more persistent and should have fought harder for my education. . . . This was the first time in our marriage that I felt that my husband put limits on what I wanted to do. Although later he came to see that he made a mistake, by then it was already too late—there were new responsibilities. (Frýdlová 2007, 141)

THE DOUBLE BURDEN

The major negative consequence of women's economic independence during the socialist period was an overburdening of women. Women acquired their professional roles without any decrease in their domestic workloads. As Alena Wagnerová discusses in the previous chapter in this volume, in the early 1950s, the socialist regime assumed that public services and a collective lifestyle would solve the issue of women's double roles. Some of the social service projects as they were designed and practiced at that time sound almost incredible today. A shopping service was available: ordered food was delivered to the house every day for a nominal fee. Lunches were provided in factory canteens and school cafeterias for a nominal price. Families were offered housing in communal, state-owned houses for a small rent. All services related to laundry, washing, cleaning, and so on were provided through a centralized, nationwide, state-run company called the Liberated Household. Leisure time was also taken care of. Each workplace ran recreational facilities (such as ski lodges in the mountains) where families of the employees could spend their holidays. All school children spent several weeks of the school year in the mountains and summer camps. Needless to say, all these activities and facilities included proper ideological and political training. The idea behind them was to minimalize the traditional role of the family in society and consequently free a woman for her participation in collective production.

The awakening from the socialist dream came sooner than expected. The predominant orientation of the Czech economy toward heavy industry led to the stagnation of the so-called nonproductive sector of services. The growing problems of the national economy in the early 1960s—especially in the services area—had the most dramatic impact on the female population. Again it fell on women to cope. Furthermore, issues arising from the new male and female roles in socialist society remained unaddressed. It was not until the late 1960s, a period of relative political freedom, that these issues emerged in the public arena. Some surveys conducted at that time demonstrated that an average "socialist woman" had an extremely limited amount of leisure time compared to her male partner. This resulted in a decreased quality of life and consequently led toward gender inequality. The turning point in most women's lives, the point when her inequality would become particularly pronounced, was the birth of her first child. Thus it is not surprising that in the 1960s, the national birthrate started to dramatically decrease. One of the measures introduced by the state to counter this trend was a gradually extended maternity leave. By the end of the 1980s, the state provided six months of fully paid maternity leave plus up to three years of guaranteed job security along with state benefits, an arrangement that is still in place today.

One of the ways in which many women responded to their overburdening was by lowering their professional ambitions. That a woman worked was accepted without question, but whether she could or should occupy a leadership position at work was a different matter altogether. As a result, women often took the longest maternity leave possible and had their children in close sequence in order to spend three (with one child) to nine (with three children) years at home, some of it on full pay and without losing their jobs or benefits.

When listening to women who spent most of their lives fulfilling both roles—full-time employment and housework/childcare—it becomes clear that efficient management of time was essential, as was incorporation of grandparents into childcare. The help of grandparents with kids, such as in picking them up after school and taking them to various extracurricular activities, or caring for sick grandchildren, was made possible by an early retirement age, which, perhaps also reflecting a gender bias about care-giving, was several years lower for women than for men.[5]

Interviewing women born in the 1920s and 1930s, we expected that the issue of overburdening would emerge as a leading theme in our interviews. To our surprise, this did not happen. Only when explicitly asked did the women delve into the difficulties of managing their dual roles. The range of strategies for dealing with these often-conflicting positions turned out also to be wider than expected. Furthermore, while women did emphasize the hardships and difficulties they had faced, especially when their children were young, they seldom presented themselves as victims of the regime, let alone of their partners or family. Instead, they highlighted their courage, resourcefulness, and pride in themselves. They clearly took their full employment for granted, and the achievement of economic independence was for them a fundamental and desired part of their lives.

There is one more unique aspect of our respondents' experiences: the women we interviewed did not derive their own social status and identities from the identities of their partners, husbands, fathers, or brothers. In their life stories, their partners' social or professional identities seemed to have played a marginal role. We conducted interviews with physicians, teachers, librarians, journalists, nurses, and lab assistants, but also with many factory workers, cooperative farm workers, and "simple" women with little education. They all talked about themselves as teachers, farmers, or workers, but not as wives, although most of them were married and had children. They took for granted that they were fully employed and simultaneously were mothers, wives, and daughters taking care of aging parents. Managing all of these duties was an important source of self-confidence for them, and sometimes also a source of their sense of superiority over men, who did not manage as much in spite of men's burdens having been lighter and their opportunities greater. In the minds of our respondents, women's emancipation had been achieved; they took it for granted as something that did not need to be mentioned.

This does not mean that the respondents failed to experience manifestations of inequality between women and men. With men's attitudes and expectations often lagging behind the changes in gender roles, many of these emancipated, economically independent, professionally fulfilled women reported disappointing experiences in their intimate relationships. The statement of one of them, that "men often see women as their servants," along with the reports from women of being told by their husbands, "you are the mother, so take care of things," were not unique, and many marriages ended (usually after the children grew up) in divorce.

CONCLUSION

Socialism left behind a relatively high standard of emancipation ("real emancipation") in Czech society. Its main characteristics included a high level of women's education, their taken-for-granted participation in the sphere of work, and economic independence. However, no major change took place in the social understanding of women's traditional roles as mothers and wives, and childcare and housework remained women's responsibility. The state provision of long maternity and parental leaves (mostly taken by mothers, only minimally by fathers), along with a very low number of mothers of small children who work and the nonexistence of part-time work, have further reinforced this state of affairs. In recent years, the Czech Republic has experienced a serious shortage of kindergartens. Considered a relic of socialism, in the post-1989 period the number of state kindergartens was cut down almost by half. As a result, many mothers today cannot return to work after their parental leave ends, and their career therefore often ends too.

The Women's Memory Project was meant, among other things, as a challenge for women to think of themselves outside of traditional schema.[6] The experience of women, written down and archived, might not only serve as an inspiration for generations to come but can also help us to reflect critically on the continuing masculine model of Czech society. Ideally, the project will help us understand the specificity of women's experiences and approaches to life. It will contribute to discussions of men's and women's roles in society, and hopefully help bring about necessary changes in obsolete gender stereotypes.

APPENDIX: SELECTED PUBLICATIONS AND PRODUCTIONS BASED ON THE WOMEN'S MEMORY PROJECT INTERVIEWS

In Czech

Frýdlová, Pavla. 2006. *Ženská vydrží víc než člověk, XX. století v životních příbězích deseti žen* [A Woman Endures More Than a Human: The 20th Century in the Life Stories of Ten Women], based on interviews conducted for the project *Paměti žen* [Women's Memory Project]. Prague: Nakladatelství Lidové noviny and Gender Studies Centre.
———. 2007. *Ženám patří půlka nebe* [Women's Half of the Sky]. Prague: Nakladatelství Lidové noviny and Gender Studies Centre.
Paměti romských žen: Kořeny I—Memories of Romany Women: The Roots. 2002. Brno: Muzeum romské kultury. Five interviews with Romany women of different generations; in Czech and English.
Válka očima žen [War through Women's Eyes]. 2005. Gender Studies Centre and Czech Radio, 10 30-min episodes.
Válka v paměti žen [War in Women's Memory]. 2005. Film documentary. Gender Studies Centre and Česká televize, 57 min.
Všechny naše včerejšky [All of Our Yesterdays]. 1998. Prague: Gender Studies Centre. Twelve interviews with women of three generations from the first phase of the project.
Všechny naše včerejšky II [All of Our Yesterdays II]. 1998. Prague: Gender Studies Centre. Twelve interviews with women of three generations from the second phase of the project, accompanied by short reflections by the project participants.
Žily tady s námi [They Lived Here with Us]. 2006. Prague: Gender Studies Centre and Czech Radio, 7 30-min episodes. Stories of German anti-fascist women in Czechoslovakia.

In Slovak

Kiczková, Zuzana, et al. 2006. *Pamat' žien: O skúsenosti sebautvárania v biografických rozhovoroch* [Women's Memory: The Experience of Self-Formation in Biographical Interviews]. Bratislava: IRIS. An analysis of interviews conducted by the Slovak Women's Memory Project team.

In Serbian and Croatian

Borovi i jele: Sječanje žena na život u socijalismu [Pines and Firs: Women's Memories of Life under Socialism]. 2002. Film documentary. Zagreb. 58 min.

Dijanić, D., et al. 2005. *Ženski biografski leksikon: Sjećanje žena na život u socijalizmu* [Women's Biographical Encyclopedia: Women's Memories of Life under Socialism]. Zagreb: Centar za ženske studije.

Sjećam se [I Remember]. 2004. Kotor: ŽINEC. Twelve interviews with women from Monte Negro.

Ženski identiteti [Women's Identity]. Between 1999 and 2005, several volumes of biographical interviews and autobiographies by women philosophers, politicians, and sociologists were published in Belgrade.

NOTES

1. Most of the interviews were transcribed, producing about twenty thousand pages. The transcripts are archived along with additional materials (brief biography, protocol, summary), and an index is available for the Czech transcripts.

2. Czech Romany women were interviewed by colleagues for a related project. These interviews with Romany women of different generations have been published (in Czech and English) as *Paměti romských žen: Kořeny I—Memories of Romany Women: the Roots* (Brno: Muzeum romské kultury, 2002).

3. From an unpublished interview conducted by Pavla Frýdlová, February 23, 1998.

4. Eliška Krásnohorská (1847–1926) was a Czech writer and founder of Minerva, the first women's grammar school in Central Europe. Františka Plamínková (1875–1942) was a Czech politician, journalist, and women's suffrage activist killed during World War II.

5. Until 1996, the retirement/pension age for women was fifty-seven. If a woman raised one child, her retirement age decreased to fifty-six; with two children, it decreased to fifty-five. The age of retirement for all men was sixty. Starting in 1996, the retirement age for both men and women has been increasing, and the number of children no longer factors into it.

6. For more on the Women's Memory Project, visit www.womensmemory.net.

For selected publications and productions based on the Women's Memory Project interviews, see the appendix to this chapter.

PART 2

GENDER ISSUES IN CZECH SOCIETY POST-1989

6 CONTESTED FEMINISM

The East/West Feminist
Encounters in the 1990s

SIMONA FOJTOVÁ

Throughout the years Western European and American feminists
have had the opportunity to seek and define their program, to choose
and discuss it. We could only accept or, in exceptional cases, reject
the political program given to us. That being so, please give us time
for our self-discovery. I would not like to see the women of Central
and Eastern Europe merely taking over Western feminists' views and
again imitating someone else.

> JIŘINA ŠIKLOVÁ, former Czech dissident, sociologist,
> prominent gender scholar, and the initiator and
> cofounder of the Gender Studies Centre in Prague

Do Czech women need feminism? *Yes*, I think we do need feminism.
The point is which kind of feminism. Feminism as a label standing
for a collection of claims about women's oppression in the male-
dominated patriarchal order, deepening in the Czech Republic
already quite powerful channels of hostility, is not particularly
welcome. Each of us should work on her or his own feminism—try
to choose, construct, and reconstruct arguments and perspectives
according to our needs, ways of understanding, maybe even tastes.

> JIŘINA ŠMEJKALOVÁ-STRICKLAND

Contemporary Western feminism is already trying to cope with the
challenges posed by Western women, primarily women of color and
poor women, who feel it doesn't sufficiently address their realities. It
took white, middle-class feminists a long time to stop talking about
power only in terms of patriarchy—to accept that "men oppressing
women" is perhaps too simple a formula, to give up celebrating
sisterhood and begin celebrating differences, and to attempt to move
beyond a binary us-and-them mentality. If we begin to listen to
Eastern European voices, we are taken even further in this direction,
and find ourselves in entirely new territory.

> LAURA BUSHEIKIN, describing her experience
> in the Czech Republic in the early 1990s

The differences of opinion alluded to in the above passages take us back to the post-1989 period, which witnessed the dissolution of borders, the celebratory tearing down of walls at the collapse of communist regimes across Eastern Europe, and the unmaking of a cultural-political landscape that had for a lifetime largely blocked dialogue between women of the East and West. As addressed in several of the preceding chapters, Czechoslovakia of the communist era (1948–89) was marked by tight government control of social research activities. Even though the position of women in Czechoslovakia of that time was publicly discussed and addressed through research, women's emancipation was seen mostly in terms of legal equality and equal labor force participation and was also viewed as having been accomplished to a great extent. The different perspectives on women's/gender issues that had started to develop in Western Europe, the United States, and Canada as part of the feminist second wave, including those focused on questions of sexuality, sexual orientation, or gender identity, were long rejected as "bourgeois" and considered dangerous to the communist regime.

After the fall of communism in 1989, expanded discussions about women's issues and feminism began to emerge. Even though a vocal and popular feminist platform was missing in Czech post-socialist society, women's issues became a subject of interest among women writers and intellectuals, who gradually started advocating for the necessity of studying gender. The interest in feminism unfolded in a context of international exchanges and contacts through which Czech women engaged with feminists from Western Europe, the United States, and Canada, who were arriving in the region in large numbers to study local women's situations. In the often-heated cross-cultural exchanges that unfolded throughout the 1990s, and in which misunderstandings abounded on both sides, "feminism" became a highly contested term and was often represented as a Western import.

These cross-cultural exchanges were complicated by the way feminism was being represented in the popular Czecho(Slovak) media at the time.[1] In the early 1990s, the Czech media delighted in ridiculing feminism, often giving platforms to returning chauvinistic male Czech émigrés, who warned Czechs to stay away from "feminist ideologues." Consider, for instance, the following comment from an interview published in 1992 in the noted Czech weekly *Respect* with one of the most prestigious Czech-Canadian émigrés, writer Josef Škvorecký:

> One of the worst things that can happen to a good idea is when a madman à la Lenin turns it into a basis for an ideology. . . . The most recent example of this process, which we have experienced firsthand here [in Canada], are

the latest adventures of American feminism. The idea of women's equality in all aspects of life has been turned into the ideology of women's superiority, whose spokeswomen and spokesmen . . . represent a typical "vanguard" of feminism, in the most extreme case openly lesbian or radically anti-male. (quoted in Šmejkalová 1998, 15; my translation)

Or see another example from an interview with émigré Otto Ulč, published in 1992 in the esteemed daily *Lidové noviny* (The People's Newspaper) under the title "Zabíjejte novorozené chlapečky! Neklid na lesbické frontě" (Kill Newborn Baby-Boys! Unrest on the Lesbian Front). Ulč here describes the delegates of a lesbian congress he had presumably attended as "frowning, irritated, insulting and aggressive, suggesting injuries. Witnesses saw that the ladies not only raised clenched fists in a revolutionary greeting, but with two fingers they were making a scissors motion, cut, cut. Passerby men, even owners of the most peaceful penises all ran away, in fear for their manhood" (quoted in Sokolová 2005, 34).

Local women activists and intellectuals who were interested in women's issues found themselves responding to two very different discourses and constituents—on the one hand, they faced derogatory and dismissive representations of feminism in the Czech media; on the other hand, they fielded inquiries and questions from an influx of feminist scholars arriving in the region (and especially Prague) to study post-socialist women. On the positive side, the fact that productive relationships had already started developing between Czech and foreign feminists in the early 1990s (tensions notwithstanding) is exemplified by the story of the founding of the Gender Studies Centre in Prague. While the Czech sociologist and former dissident Jiřina Šiklová played a key role in conceptualizing and founding the center, the startup money was provided by Ann Snitow, the founder of the Network of East-West Women (NEWW), and the center's feminist library initially relied heavily on book donations acquired through the NEWW.[2] Later the center received long-term support from the German foundation FrauenAnstiftung, funding that was acquired in 1992 with the assistance of Czech-German feminist Saša M. Lienau (Hašková 2011, 148). Yet aside from the largely successful collaborative cross-cultural relationships such as those surrounding the Gender Studies Centre, the debates between Western and Czech (and other Eastern European) women throughout the 1990s were often marked by frustrations and misunderstandings, as well as by disputes around power and difference.[3]

Often described as contentious and confrontational, these cross-cultural exchanges focused on the relevance of Western feminist analysis in post-socialist societies (Drakulić 1991; Šiklová 1993, 1997a, 1997b, 1998; Havelková 1993, 1997; Einhorn 1991, 1993; Wolchik 1991, 1995; Šmejkalová-Strickland 1993; Busheikin 1993; Funk 1993, 2004; Occhipinti 1996; Heitlinger 1996; Snitow 1997a; Renne 1997; Ferber and Raabe 2003; Ghodsee 2004; Nash 2002; Argent 2003, 2008; Slavova 2006). In the views of many scholars, appeals to global sisterhood remained unanswered in most post-socialist societies in Central and Eastern Europe after the fall of communism. Scholars noted the absence of vibrant feminist mobilizing and advocacy for women's rights, and analyzed why women's movements in Eastern Europe did not become a strong social force in the process of transformation. The negative public attitudes displayed toward feminism in Eastern Europe became one of the most discussed issues among Western feminist scholars, and the communist legacy served as an explanation for Eastern Europeans' alleged apolitical attitudes and antipathy toward feminism. Throughout the 1990s and early 2000s, many scholars were posing questions such as, Why were Western feminists being perceived as culturally insensitive and feminism understood as a form of theoretical imperialism rather than an emancipatory force? Why were Eastern European women exhibiting so much resistance toward feminism?

Among the former socialist countries, Czechoslovakia became associated with the most pronounced resistance to Western-style feminism. For example, Barbara Einhorn suggested in 1991 that Czechoslovakia may have "the strongest resistance to an explicitly feminist grouping" as compared to the other former socialist countries (29). Reflecting on her research stay in the 1990s, Rebecca Nash similarly noted that Czech women were seen as lacking gender consciousness and feminist activism: "Feminists, East and West, often remark on gender inequalities in the Czech Republic, and on what they see as a lackluster response to the situation on the part of leading Czech women academics. . . . While in Prague, I regularly encountered other American women (from tourists to long-term residents to diplomats to fellow researchers) puzzled by what they interpreted as acceptance of or indifference to large-scale subordination at work, in politics, the media and the household" (2002, 303). In 1996, the Czech historian Jitka Malečková also commented on anti-feminist sentiments among the Czech public and argued that "the reaction of both men and women, the public as well as the academics, towards the very terms feminism, women's movement and Women's Studies is generally negative" (101).

Now, more than twenty years later, the commonly debated question from the 1990s about the possibility of feminism coming to life in Eastern Europe, and specifically the Czech Republic, seems to have been answered. When we look at the changing academic, social, and cultural landscapes that reflect growing gender consciousness and a feminist ethos, it is apparent that feminism has taken root. In contrast to the 1990s, the new millennium has offered a steady growth in Czech feminist scholarship, a burgeoning institutionalization of Gender Studies programs at Czech universities, and an increased presence and influence of women's nongovernmental organizations (NGOs). Moreover, a significant change has also become visible in the portrayal of feminism in public discourse. The post-1989 attacks on feminism in the Czech media have lost much of their original vitriol as well as mass support, and in the past several years the Czech mainstream press has even started featuring pro-feminist articles. This change is also evident in other post-socialist countries. As the feminist historian Maria Bucur observed in 2008, "whereas feminism was deemed an exotic foreign import in the 1990s, the emergence of a definite feminist sensibility can be seen in the realm of popular culture in post-communist Eastern Europe [today]" (1388).

Given the transformation of feminism from a Western ideology of questionable relevance to an established academic field and important perspective of analysis, why return to the earlier debates about the applicability of feminism in Eastern Europe? My aim in revisiting the East/West dialogue about feminism is to complicate the commonly accepted academic assessment of the 1990s in the English-language scholarship, according to which Czech women rejected feminism. Also, in many accounts of these conversations about feminism, the communist past is used as an explanation for the lack of feminist mobilizing and gender consciousness. Yet I believe there is another way to understand the dialogues and a different story to tell.

The challenge with respect to Western feminism in the 1990s was particularly evident in the English-language writings by Jiřina Šiklová, Hana Havelková, and Jiřina Šmejkalová, all of whom expressed concerns about the relevance of Western feminist concepts for the post-socialist context. Šiklová emerged as the most critical voice on Western feminism at the time, and she has since become "the most frequently translated and esteemed 'Czech Feminist' in the popular Western imagination" (Argent 2003, 38). Although English-language texts by Šiklová, along with texts written by sociologist and philosopher Havelková, became the most anthologized, Šmejkalová's work remains less known despite its importance for understanding the East/West debates on feminism. While Šiklová, Havelková, and Šmejkalová questioned the relevance of Western feminist theory for Czech women in different ways, they shared important commonalities in terms of how feminism could take into account Czech specificity.

Drawing on the work of Šiklová, Havelková, and Šmejkalová, I argue that even though top-down women's emancipation by socialist states did create specific conditions through which Eastern European women approached (and reproached) feminism after 1989, feminism did not become contested solely because of the communist legacy. Czech women's experiences with socialism did not necessarily lead to their perceived rejection of feminism; rather, these experiences exposed the limitations of the applicability of liberal Western feminism to the Czech context. Contrary to the dominant academic assessments, I argue that their critiques should not be seen as a rejection of feminism but as a call for a cultural and political situatedness of feminist analysis relevant to Czech women. Pointing out differences in social, political, and intellectual experiences, Czech gender scholars have argued that feminism conceptualized only as seeking equality between men and women simply did not resonate with Czech women.

The East/West differences and disagreements over the meanings of feminism thus exposed a need for new forms of analysis, and I want to argue that intersectional theory offers a form of analysis relevant for the post-socialist situation of Czech women. Frequently deployed in acknowledgment of differences among women, intersectionality not only questions the exclusive theoretical focus on gender but also offers a commitment to situatedness. Still, even as intersectionality has broadened the focus of Western feminist theorizing beyond patriarchy to examine how gender intersects with race, class, sexuality, ability, and other identity markers, issues of nationality and the role of the state, and especially of the communist regime, have received less theoretical attention. Given the primacy of national identity and the top-down emancipation of women by the Czechoslovak communist regime, Czech scholars' critiques suggest that intersectional analysis that specifically investigates how gender intersects with nationality and the role of the communist state would provide a particularly appropriate lens through which to examine the situation of Czech women.

To be sure, calls for attention to be directed toward the situatedness of feminist analysis are not new. Similar suggestions have previously been made as women of color and lesbians in the United States, as well as Third World women, challenged Western feminist notions of universal oppression, the uniformity of women's experiences, and a global theory of patriarchy. Czech resistance to Western feminism can be seen as a way to continue the critiques by women of color that have challenged the subject implicit in Western feminist thinking, a subject that normalizes the experience of white, middle-class, First World women (hooks 1984; Trinh 1989; Mohanty 1984).

Drawing on Chandra Talpade Mohanty's insights into the construction of Third World feminism, Kornelia Slavova has argued that Eastern European feminisms have followed a similar trajectory of deconstructing and constructing: "On the one hand, they are critically appropriating and subverting established Western feminist models, while on the other hand, they are striving to construct their own feminist identity and politics" (2006, 247). In this respect, when Czech women questioned the relevance of Western liberal feminism, it was their way of challenging the Western-produced category of woman, as well as the first step in their efforts to develop their own feminism. Czech women's critiques of Western liberal feminism in the 1990s can thus be seen as contributing to ongoing attempts to assess the relevance of Western feminist theory beyond national borders, and the East/West feminist exchange can serve as a case study for building future feminist coalitions across those borders.

NEGOTIATION RATHER THAN NEGATION OF WESTERN FEMINISM IN EASTERN AND CENTRAL EUROPE

As noted above, when Western scholars searched for recognizable signs of a feminist movement in post-socialist Europe in the 1990s, they did not find much indication of feminism coming to life. Instead, they saw multiple manifestations of anti-feminist attitudes among both the general public and intellectuals, and a lack of vibrant feminist organizing, mobilizing, and advocacy. Many scholars focused on the communist legacy as an explanation for this alleged antipathy to feminism. In the introduction to *Ana's Land: Sisterhood in Eastern Europe*, Tanya Renne, for instance, summarizes the main reasons for anti-feminist sentiments in post-socialist Eastern Europe: "[Feminism] is seen either as an imported Western ideology to be rejected out of hand or as an old communist principle to be proudly refused. People of the region are painfully familiar with the use of the women of the Communist Party to spread the propaganda of their governments" (1997, 2).

More specifically in the Czech context, scholars were pointing out that the Czech communist government not only endeavored to discredit feminism as a Western ideology but also appropriated the independent Czech women's movement from interwar democratic Czechoslovakia (1918–38) for the government's own purposes. Viewing the communist legacy as the main source of feminist antipathy, Melissa Feinberg, for instance, contends that "in the Czech case at least, current attitudes toward feminism can only be explained as a legacy of Communism, which gutted the democratic Czech feminist movement and took its language, its organizational structure, and even its magazine for itself" (2006, 10). Feinberg's book, which details the history of the Czech feminist movement in the first half of the twentieth century, in fact diverges from the view which was prevalent in the 1990s that Czech women exhibited a historical antipathy to feminism and that "independent feminism is relatively new to Eastern Europe" (Renne 1997, 2). Mapping out the women's movement in democratic Czechoslovakia, Feinberg discusses the political influence and intellectual authority of Czech feminists in the interwar period and argues that "their story also serves to remind us that the lack of popular sympathy for feminism in Eastern Europe today is not something intrinsic to the region" (2006, 10).

The Czechoslovak communist government not only effaced the memory of the feminist history of the first Czechoslovak Republic by appropriating aspects of the Czech feminist movement, but it also implemented state policies that resulted in forced emancipation of women. Such policies overburdened women by mandating that they work outside of the home in addition to being mothers, wives, and full-time housekeepers.[4] Czech critics and Western feminists have rightly exposed the alleged equality of Czech women as almost singularly a matter of economic emancipation that served the political interests of the regime. Thus, in response to those who pointed out the strong presence of women in the socialist labor force and interpreted it as a sign of achieved economic equality of women under socialism, others challenged such egalitarianism and claimed it was actually forced emancipation that necessitated mandatory engagement in paid labor. Hana Havelková summed up these critiques: "There is a sense that women's emancipation, defined as full employment, was achieved under socialism but that no one really benefited from it" (1993, 65). Rather than becoming liberated and fulfilled through paid employment—as many Western feminists envisioned for Western women—Czech women became overburdened. As Šiklová explained, "It was necessary for women to enter the workforce, and thus the majority of women did not regard the involuntary 'choice'—the possibility or necessity of gainful employment—as an opportunity for self-realization or self-assertion" (1997b, 76).

While economic independence and social participation became core concepts of women's liberation in Western feminism, they were not seen as relevant goals for many Czech women after 1989 given women's triple role under communism. If the second wave of Anglo-American feminism focused on bringing women into the public sphere through paid employment, education, and political participation, Czech women had already achieved these goals under state socialism to a certain degree because they were obliged to participate in the public sphere not just through paid labor but also via their roles as citizens. As Alena Heitlinger has pointed out, "Throughout the communist period, women's role was defined as a unity of economic, maternal, and political functions; a counterpart to this threefold role has never been spelled out for men" (1993, 95).

Czech scholars have not only questioned the relevance of the goals and priorities of Western liberal feminism, such as women's economic emancipation and political participation, but have also questioned the strategies and language many Western feminists used to achieve such goals. Along with associating Western-style feminism with the discredited politics of the former communist regime, scholars explained the perceived negative associations between state-sponsored women's emancipation under communism and Western feminism in terms of the language used and the forms of advocacy prioritized. The Western feminist rhetoric and the forms of organizing it called for seemed to be reminiscent, in the eyes of many post-1989 Czech women, of discredited socialist emancipatory slogans. As Šiklová explained,

> When Western feminists ask us how many times we have demonstrated against our government, against the discrimination of women in employment, or against lower pay, we are at a loss as to what to say. We have not demonstrated; we do not revolt as women. In this country, the political struggle for women's rights has not been included in our program. Czech women were obligatorily organized for too long; hence, they tend to connect liberty with the liberty not to be organized in any way. (1997b, 79)

Because Czech women were expected to be politically engaged under communism, Šiklová views the communist legacy as an explanation for their current disinterest in public and political involvement. Yet her explanation for the lack of public involvement does not necessarily imply a disinterest in women's issues. Šiklová simply sees small, grassroots women's organizations, rather than the large-scale political activism characteristic of second-wave Western feminism, as an appropriate venue for addressing women's issues in post-socialist Czech society.

Rather than rejecting feminism in its entirety, many Czech writers have questioned particular Western feminist goals, strategies, and theoretical frameworks, expressing instead a demand for a feminist discourse that is culturally relevant to the situation of Czech women. In 1993, Šiklová spoke of concerns about the significance of Western feminist concepts in the post-socialist context and warned: "No identity, let alone a feminine one, can be imported. The absence of feminism in theory and practice cannot be corrected by merely accepting the experiences and ideologies of the Western feminist movement" (80).

As illustrated through the epigraph quoted at the top of this chapter, Šiklová envisioned the possibility of a feminism that would be informed by specifically Czech conditions. While Šiklová cautioned against the uncritical adoption of Western feminist frameworks, Havelková also stressed the limited relevance of Western feminist theory due to the differences between Eastern and Western contexts: "There are many strong arguments that women's experiences in post-totalitarian societies constitute the basis for a different practical-philosophical approach to the women's issues, one that differs considerably from the model of feminism derived from the political context of western societies" (1993, 63). And Jiřina Šmejkalová-Strickland underscored the divergent intellectual histories in Eastern Europe and the West that gave birth to different theoretical approaches to women's issues. She argued that while psychoanalysis, Marxism, and post-structuralism became important theories in the West, these theoretical traditions did not resonate in the Czech intellectual milieu (1993, 16).

Some scholars questioned the applicability of Western notions of women's liberation from their prison-homes in the post-socialist context: "'The treatment of the family by white [Western] feminists . . . has taken the family to be a significant, if not the primary, source of women's oppression.' . . . This approach has been criticized by Black and Third World feminists . . . as culturally and historically embedded; it is no surprise then, that it is highly problematic when applied to Eastern Europe" (Occhipinti 1996, 18). And still other scholars have probed the limitations of Western feminist concepts of liberation and oppression. While examining the emergence of women's NGOs funded by Western aid, Kristen Ghodsee urges us to interrogate the forms of feminism imported into Eastern Europe (2004, 749). Overall, the post-1989 East/West debate over the meanings of feminism helped articulate questions concerning the dominant assumptions about the universality of feminist goals across cultures and exposed a need for new forms of analysis and activism.

As mentioned earlier, intersectional theory offers a new form of analysis relevant to the situation of Czech women. Given the history of exclusions in feminism, intersectionality has been deployed as a way of redressing these exclusions and acknowledging differences among women.[5] However, the prevalent Western focus on race, class, and gender as intersecting lines of oppression does not necessarily provide a relevant framework for Czech women since their difference stems from the political systems of communism and nationalism. As Laura Busheikin put it in 1993, "now it has become fashionable in the West to talk of 'race, class and gender' as intersecting lines of oppression, but this doesn't offer a framework which can fully account for East European women's experience" (74). Many of the critiques by Czech scholars reflect a similar notion. Havelková, for instance, wondered skeptically, "what are we, Czech women with respect to the categories of race, class, and gender? We experience neither race nor class oppression and we still do not consider gender oppression a priority" (1997, 59).[6] And reflecting on class as a key analytical category in Western feminism, the historian Jitka Malečková explains why class has not become a relevant theoretical perspective for either contemporary Czech feminism or the early Czech women's movement: "In post-communist societies, the concept of class often has a negative connotation, reminiscent of the simplified orthodox Marxist (ab)uses of the term" (2009, 264).

Given the interconnectedness of women's issues with Czech national interests and the political system of communism, scholars and activists need to move beyond single-axis feminist analyses in order to understand the situation of Czech women. While the prevailing intersectional approach connecting gender, race, and class might not necessarily offer relevant categories of analysis for all Czech women, theorizing the relationship between gender and nation would certainly provide a useful intersectional framework.

BEYOND GENDER AS A SINGLE CATEGORY OF ANALYSIS: THE INTERCONNECTEDNESS OF WOMEN'S AND CZECH NATIONAL ISSUES

As acknowledged above, Czech and other Eastern European women have not been alone in questioning the dominant concepts underpinning Western feminist theory. In her article, "Looking at Western Feminisms through the Double Lens of Eastern Europe and the Third World," Kornelia Slavova examines the similarities in critiques of Western feminist theories expressed by Third World feminists and women in post-socialist Eastern Europe. As she argues, "Their visions and revisions of Western feminist theory . . . pose similar questions about the validity of certain assumptions and theories that attempt to embrace 'global' feminist developments, such as: the universality of feminist goals and methods, 'the equality of rights' agenda, the role of patriarchy, and the easy alliance between feminism and Marxism" (2006, 246–47). While Slavova's comparative analysis is a welcome contribution, little attention is paid in her essay to the differences that exist among Eastern European women. Yet there is a specificity to the Czech women's movement that differentiates its approach to women's issues in the Czech historical context from other Eastern/East Central European countries. Aligning women's issues with Czech national interests has historically been a characteristic feature of the Czech women's movement. This dimension is tied not only to the socialist experience but also to the history of the early Czech women's movement in the nineteenth century and to the Czech feminist movement during the First Republic.

Given the Czech struggle for national independence from the Habsburg monarchy in the nineteenth century, there is a long history of Czech women's service to the national cause. Historians of Czech women's issues, such as Malečková, have examined this relationship. Malečková has characterized the early Czech women's movement, which was closely aligned with the struggle for national independence, as a movement of middle-class women focused on achieving full equality in education and access to professions. Moderate in its character, the women's movement for the most part did not encounter violent opposition and was mostly supported by Czech male politicians and intellectuals. In her earlier work, Malečková highlighted two characteristics of the Czech women's movement: "The prevailing subordination (or better connection) of women's aims to the interests of the whole nation, and the role of men in the women's movement, namely their active support of women, and women's deliberate collaboration with them. From its early beginnings, the Czech women's movement, emerging as a part of the national movement, shared a common 'enemy' with the latter—Austrian rule and authorities, and Germanization" (2004,187).

The emancipation of the Czech nation and the emancipation of Czech women became inextricably linked in the nineteenth century, and similarly the democratic process during the First Republic, with its emphasis on egalitarianism, was intertwined with the feminist movement for equality in the first half of the twentieth century. Indeed, due to the convergence of feminism and nationalism, Czech women gained some rights—such as legal parity—with less struggle than women in other countries. For example, as Melissa Feinberg notes, "In the Czech lands, women got the vote only after a few years of work. Their rapid success was certainly not typical in Europe" (2006, 11). Although not all rights were achieved so quickly by Czech feminists in the First Republic—abortion rights and progressive changes in family law were accomplished only later under communism—Czech feminists secured a high degree of political influence and intellectual authority in the first half of the twentieth century.

Czech nationalism not only helped shape Czech women's approaches to women's issues but has also had an impact on the relationship between Czech women and men. Much of the scholarship on the early Czech women's movement points out how the interconnectedness of women's and Czech national issues resulted in Czech men's historical support of women's equality. Likewise, the democratic principles and egalitarian ideology of the First Republic extended to include equality for women as well. As Malečková has argued, "This view of the early women's movement and its favorable acceptance by the mainstream Czech national society had implications for the present as well: it suggested that in the post-communist Czech Republic men were women's allies rather than obstacles to women's equality" (2009, 263). Moreover, in Malečková's view, showing the strength of the earlier women's movement served as an important legitimizing mechanism for contemporary women's movements in many post-socialist countries because "it showed that the movement for women's rights and equality was neither a Western import, nor could it be identified with the official women's organizations under communism" (264).

Demonstrating that Czech feminism was indeed a historically homegrown product rather than a foreign import (which, of course, does not mean that Czech women and feminists worked in isolation from the rest of the world) became especially important in the context of the post-1989 East/West feminist encounters. The history of the early women's movement could offer Czech women a local building block for creating their own contemporary feminist movement, an important opportunity considering the concerns expressed by Czech scholars throughout the 1990s about uncritically importing Western feminist theory and strategies. We should not understand these scholars' critiques as a rejection of feminism but as a call for a different theoretical framework. And considering that national identity has been historically constructed for Czechs as their primary identity, I have suggested that intersectional analysis, one that specifically investigates how gender has historically intersected with nationality and the role of the communist regime, might be a particularly appropriate lens through which to examine the situation of Czech women.

Placed in a unique position between the West and the rest, the Czech context invites a new analytical perspective given the specific Czech dimension aligning women's and national issues. It can serve as a useful case study for examining how gender intersects with nationalism. Moreover, analyzing gender issues from a Czech perspective and in the Czech context can enrich Gender Studies debates still dominated by Anglo-American and Western European influences. As the editors of this volume have suggested in their introduction, attending to the situatedness and specificity of the Czech context can suggest new angles and approaches to existing feminist debates, and can lead toward acknowledging new concerns from which feminists globally could benefit.

NOTES

1. In 1993, Slovakia separated from Czechoslovakia, and the country split into the Czech Republic and Slovakia.

2. Ann Snitow remembers the NEWW contributions to Prague's Gender Studies project in her short piece "Appendix: A Postscript to Laura Busheikin" (1997a).

3. I use the term "Western feminism" as a shorthand referring to the variety of feminist discourses as they were perceived as "arriving" in Eastern Europe from the United States, Canada, Britain, and Western Europe in the 1990s. This is also how the term was used by many Czech and other Eastern European women writers at the time. I do not mean to suggest that feminist theory and philosophy are exclusively Western phenomena in their origin or usage. For a critique of the notion of feminism as a Western concept, see, among others, Aili Mari Tripp 2006. Numerous examples of women's activism in Central, Eastern, and Southeastern Europe (collected in Franciska de Haan, Krassimira Daskalova, and Anna Loutfi, eds., *A Biographical Dictionary of Women's Movements*) clearly demonstrate that, whether calling themselves feminist or not, women's movements have a long history in the region.

4. With the exception of those with a medical condition or those on maternity leave, women under socialism did not have the choice of not working long-term. Czech women had the highest employment rates among the socialist countries. The result was the much-discussed double burden of mandatory paid employment and unpaid household duties.

5. While many black women writers in the late nineteenth and early twentieth centuries addressed both issues of gender and race, intersectionality is most often associated with U.S. black feminist theory of the late 1970s and 1980s. The 1977 manifesto of the Combahee River Collective, a U.S. black feminist lesbian group, stressed the importance of integrating gender, race, class, and sexuality into feminist analysis. Many other U.S. feminist scholars examined multiple forms of discrimination and theorized the intersection of race, gender, class, and sexuality, especially hooks (1984); Davis (1981); Hull, Scott, and Smith (1982); Smith (1983); Moraga and Anzaldúa (1983); Zinn and Dill (1994); and Crenshaw (1989, 1991). While the concept itself had been used earlier, the term "intersectionality" was coined by Kimberlé Crenshaw and has been associated with her work, specifically her 1989 article "Demarginalizing the Intersection of Race and Sex: A Black Feminist Critique of Antidiscrimination Doctrine, Feminist Theory, and Antiracist Politics." Building on earlier U.S. black women's challenges to feminist exclusions, Crenshaw's criticism extends to legal discourse, which has also failed to address the multidimensionality of black women's experiences. Therefore, Crenshaw advocates for an intersectional approach, which treats race and gender as intersecting rather than mutually exclusive categories of analysis and experience. Intersectionality has also been used as an analytical perspective in areas other than feminist theory, and it has been adopted to address a variety of exclusions other than race, such as class, sexuality, ability, and nationality. Even though Crenshaw developed intersectionality as a theory that highlights race, some European scholars have taken the concept in other directions. For a transnational deployment of intersectionality and the importance of local contexts, see Helma Lutz, Maria Teresa Herrera Vivar, and Linda Supik 2011.

6. Havelková's "we" in this quotation constructs Czech women as a racially homogenous category and as white. Even though the presumed "Czech woman" for many Czech feminists seems to be white (and thus race-less), some feminist scholarship has begun to question the whiteness of this "we." For example, two articles in this collection focus on women of color in Czech society. Examining specific issues that Romany and Vietnamese women face in their communities and in Czech society, Karolína Ryvolová (chapter 9) and Mária Strašáková (chapter 10) highlight the need for an analysis of both gender and race.

7 CZECH WOMEN'S NGOs

Women's Voices and Claims in the Public Sphere

HANA HAŠKOVÁ AND ZUZANA UHDE

In this chapter we build on our long-term study of women's public organizing in the Czech Republic (CR).[1] Our focus is on nongovernmental organizations (NGOs) that operate with an explicit agenda of advocating for gender equality or improving the position of women in Czech society. We begin by mapping the roots and development of women's public organizing in the CR during the post-1989 transformation, with particular attention to how the Czech situation has differed from the Anglo-American situation, where feminist NGOs and academic feminism/s first evolved in the context of the feminist movement "out in the streets." Our chapter goes on to examine the CR's 2004 European Union (EU) accession and the effects of this development on women's public organizing. Finally, in the last part of our discussion, we focus specifically on the claims and demands of Czech women's organizations concerning one of the core feminist issues—care. In particular, we consider how Nancy Fraser's concept of "non-reformist reforms" might apply to our analysis of Czech women's groups' approaches to the topic of care (and more specifically childcare) while endeavoring also to illuminate a deeper understanding of some of the strengths and weaknesses of current women's organizing in the CR.

Our investigations and findings draw on an analysis of thirty-eight semistructured interviews carried out between 2003 and 2005 and three group discussions conducted in 2004, 2005, and 2009. We also include the results of twelve semi-structured interviews on the topic of childcare we conducted in 2008–9 with representatives of Czech majority-population women's organizations and Romany women's groups, as well as migrant organizations.[2]

WOMEN'S ORGANIZING IN THE "POST-SOCIALIST" CONDITION

As in many other Central and Eastern European countries, a number of women's organizations and informal groups were active in Czechoslovakia between the two world wars, and the Czech women's movement dates back to the nineteenth century. It was in the interwar period that Czech and Slovak women gained the right to vote and women's education began to be systematically promoted. However, the women's movement in the region was significantly curtailed by German occupation during World War II, and in the aftermath of the war, the ascendance of state socialism played a dominant hand in shaping and limiting the organizing opportunities for women's activism.

As Alena Wagnerová discusses in more detail in this volume, soon after World War II, civic organizing became controlled by the state, and the agenda of women's emancipation was subsumed under the broader socialist program. Some of the key feminist issues (e.g., abortion rights, access to publicly funded childcare, women's participation in the labor market) were addressed at the Czechoslovak state and semi-official state levels; however, other issues of considerable concern to West European second-wave feminism (e.g., domestic violence and sexual harassment) remained unaddressed in public debates.

The pre-1989 public discourse and practices had a profound impact on women's organizing after 1989, including providing a pretext for hampering feminist and other kinds of women's organizing through the "anti-communist" ideologies that dominated the post-1989 transformation period. As a result, as Alena Heitlinger put it in 1996, 'most Czechs mistrust utopian and emancipatory ideologies, associate concepts such as 'women's emancipation' and 'women's movement' with the policies of the discredited communist regime, are disinclined to engage in collective action, regard themselves as strong women rather than as victims, assign a highly positive meaning to motherhood and family, and perceive feminism to be anti-male" (77). Marie Čermáková and Hana Havelková have noted that, not only among the general public but even in academia in the 1990s, feminism was usually defined narrowly as women trying to imitate men, as the eradication of differences between the sexes, or as the emancipation of women through work that threatened femininity (1995, 3–4).

Nevertheless, in the early 1990s, when numerous public and political initiatives, groups, and organizations were formed, about seventy women's public groups were established (Čermáková et al. 2000, 34). Compared to men, women were more active in public and civic associations than in formal politics. As in other countries in the region, in the CR women's groups were first founded as "interest" or "self-help" groups, including groups oriented around specific social problems, professional organizations, branches of international organizations, and women's groups connected to political parties, churches, social movements, and the academic scene. In some cases these organizations were established by women who had emigrated from the country before 1989 and who had personal, firsthand experience from their time in Western European countries, the United States, or Canada. Many of the groups were supported through personal friendships with feminists from abroad, while others were formed as branches within larger international women's organizations (Hašková 2005, 1083).

In the beginning, women's groups and organizations tended to lack experience, wider societal recognition, and contacts with other political actors. Moreover, they were typically very small and relied on volunteers, often ceasing to exist after the departure of the leader. The only exceptions to the rule of small membership were a few women's groups connected to churches and political parties, and the Czech Women's Union, which had a large membership base from its socialist past, including in regions outside the country's two largest cities.[3] On the whole, the activities of women's groups remained fragmented during the 1990s, although some interconnecting coalitions and umbrella organizations were formed. The Czech Women's Union tried but failed to establish a national congress of women, as most of the other women's groups took a skeptical view of the union because of its pre-1989 history (Wolchik 1995, 10). That initial skepticism notwithstanding, a decade later the Czech Women's Union would become one of the three founding members of the Czech Women's Lobby, a national branch of the European Women's Lobby.

During the first half of the 1990s, women's organizations were generally funded by international organizations, by bilateral development aid from the West, or by private foundations whose support was rooted in personal ties. Available financial resources included both project funding and the more coveted developmental funding, that is, long-term funding covering the entire scope of activities of an organization, its development, personnel, and equipment (Hašková 2005, 1085).

Generally throughout the 1990s Czech women's groups were not in direct contact with the formal political and decision-making sphere, and the media were not particularly interested in their activities either. A breakthrough came when they began cooperating with left-wing women members of Parliament in

1997 to interpellate the prime minister. This questioning addressed criticism coming from women's organizations that the CR was failing to meet its commitments from the Fourth World Conference on Women in 1995. The United Nations (UN) deadline for the CR to submit a report on gender equality in the CR was fast approaching and the EU accession process was in full swing. The interpellation was successful and resulted in the establishment of the first Czech governmental body to promote equality for women and men (Pavlík 2006, 133).

Earlier on, Nadace Gender Studies (the Gender Studies Foundation; currently called the Gender Studies Centre), with the largest local Gender Studies library and a curriculum center that developed the first teaching programs in the field of Gender Studies in the CR, was established in the apartment of sociologist Jiřina Šiklová in 1991. At the beginning the library was mostly supported by gifts from allies in the United States (e.g., financial support from the Network of East-West Women, a Books for Prague campaign organized by the University of California at Santa Cruz). Subsequently, thanks to Saša M. Lienau, the Gender Studies Foundation won long-term support from the German foundation FrauenAnstiftung and hired its first staff. For many years, FrauenAnstiftung (and after its transformation Heinrich Boell Stiftung) remained the most important donor of the Gender Studies Foundation. It was not until 1998 that the first university Gender Studies program was established in Prague, with the financial support of the U.S.-based Ford Foundation. While in the early 1990s the activist and academic sectors were interconnected, after the first university Gender Studies program was founded, the organization Gender Studies abandoned its initial academic focus in favor of becoming a networking point for feminists. As Simona Fojtová's chapter in this volume discusses in some detail, throughout the 1990s, representatives of Czech women's organizations outside and inside the academic sphere had a highly ambivalent relationship with feminism. Still, research carried out by Lenka Václavíková-Helšusová (2006, 178) and Blanka Nyklová (2013, 57) has shown that this negative attitude toward feminism within Czech women's activist and academic scenes has gradually changed.

Toward the end of the 1990s, the first phase in the development of women's public organizing in the post-1989 CR came to a close. Financial resources and ideational support from the United States, Canada, and Western Europe played a crucial role. During this time, organizations dedicated to women's rights firmly established themselves, and some activists gradually adopted a feminist and politically engaged identity. By the end of this phase, Gender Studies had become established as a recognized university program of study and discipline, and—already under the sway of the accession negotiations with the EU—the first steps were taken toward establishing state gender equality bodies.

MOVING TOWARD SHORT-TERM PROJECT FUNDING

The EU negotiations, initiated in 1996–97 and completed with the CR's accession to the EU in 2004, had a profound influence on the environment in which women's organizations operate in the country today. Changes to how women's organizations were funded intensified the process of formalizing women's groups in the region, bringing both the positive and negative effects of NGO-ization (Kapusta-Pofahl, Hašková, and Kolářová 2005, 40–45; Einhorn 2005, 1031–32; Lang 1997). Many organizations became professionalized, project-oriented, and reform-oriented. The EU, Czech state authorities, and the foundations selected by these authorities to organize EU-funded project competitions in the CR became the most important donors supporting project grants, while foreign and other international agencies, which had provided funding in the region during the 1990s, moved further east. Professionalization has resulted in women's groups becoming formally registered organizations, with offices and employees providing the expertise and skills required by donors. Project-orientation means that the activities of women's organizations are now conducted with clearly defined objectives, budgets, and timelines that tend to follow the priorities identified by the donors. Reform-orientation means that women's organizations work to improve existing institutional structures step by step and to provide services that are likely to be supported by donors. These processes have served to increase the influence of formalized women's organizations on institutional changes in the country, but they have also led to the marginalization of women's groups focused on non-mainstream issues and of organizations explicitly opposed to the processes described above (Hašková 2005, 1098–99; Kapusta-Pofahl, Hašková, and Kolářová 2005, 44–50). The availability of European funds has resulted in an increase in the number of organizations implementing projects that deal with gender equality. In the NGO sector, these projects started to be implemented not only by NGOs focused specifically on women's issues but also by NGOs focusing more generally on the development of human resources, civil society, equal opportunities in the labor market, human rights, minority rights, and environmental issues. Private firms and agencies providing requalification training have also been successful in applying for this funding.

While women's organizations tended to view the new funding opportunities from the EU Structural Funds between 2004 and 2006 as "the golden era of projects," highlighting the ability to employ larger staff, they evaluated the next wave of funding through the Operational Programme of the European Social Fund (ESF) between 2007 and 2013 more negatively. The organizations criticized the ESF Operational Programmes for their narrow focus on the labor market (supporting mostly requalification training). Furthermore, with the field of equal opportunities for men and women ultimately not included among the priority areas of the Czech state's subsidy policy, the ESF Programmes (with their almost exclusive focus on the labor market) became de facto the only source of funding for Czech women's NGOs.

Both waves of European funding have presented Czech women's NGOs with the need to engage in new and untested strategic networking and cooperation with entities such as private firms, agencies providing requalification, and NGOs focusing primarily on issues other than gender equality. In practice, these partnerships have usually not lasted beyond the duration of the project. Moreover and importantly, the changes in funding connected with the EU accession have resulted in a shift in the topics and activities taken up by Czech women's organizations (Hašková 2005, 1098–99). In the era of ESF projects the emphasis on topics related to women's participation in the labor market has increased while other crucial topics have been pushed to the margins.

Ondřej Císař and Kateřina Vráblíková stress that the EU accession process increased the domestic opportunities for political activity of women's NGOs and that this shift took place at the institutional and cultural levels (2010, 213–15). At the institutional level, not only was the Czech state required to harmonize its legislation with that of the EU (including the implementation of gender equality directives), but it was also obliged to establish governmental bodies focusing on gender equality. These bodies were then required to cooperate with women's NGOs. For example, since 1998 government ministries have had to actively engage, seek advice from, and cooperate with women's NGOs. In 1999, the Government Council for Equal Opportunities between Men and Women was established, and one year later the Committee for the Elimination of All Forms of Discrimination against Women was formed. Both bodies consist of representatives of women's NGOs and of the ministries, along with experts (the former body also has representatives of major Czech employers). Furthermore, since 2001, there is at least one official at each ministry who is responsible for attending to the issue of equal opportunities. However, Petr Pavlík has criticized these bodies for their inactivity, lack of decision-making power, motivation, expertise, and even for their abusive behavior toward women's NGOs (2006, 135–38). At the cultural level, the EU has acted as a "certification agency," helping to determine which political demands would be recognized as relevant. Certain issues (such as gender discrimination in the workplace, work-life balance, and domestic violence) have finally begun to be acknowledged as relevant political problems. As documented and observed by Charles Tilly and Sidney Tarrow, if a movement attempts to push through its agenda in a particular national political system, the likelihood of its success increases greatly if this agenda is in line with internationally recognized norms or if it overlaps with the agenda of important international organizations such as the EU (2007, 215; see also Císař and Vráblíková 2010, 210). Nevertheless, some Czech women's NGOs associate this kind of increased social recognition of a certain issue with the flattening of that issue. In the case of domestic violence, for instance, this has resulted in the gender dimension of the issue being ignored.

Císař and Vráblíková also stress that EU accession has increased the opportunities for formalized women's organizations to mobilize at the supranational level since they are now able to interact directly with EU institutions (2010, 215–17). The establishment of the Czech Women's Lobby (CWL) was an important milestone in this respect. The CWL, which is the representative body of Czech women's organizations and a group that explicitly endorses feminism, currently consists of twenty-eight women's organizations, most of which were already operating in the late 1990s. The CWL engages in collective lobbying and releases joint statements, serves as a coordinator between Czech women's NGOs and the Czech decision-making sphere, and functions as a pool of experts on issues related to gender equality and women's rights. The beginnings of this organization date back to the pre-accession period, when the European Women's Lobby (EWL) called on the candidate countries to establish their own national representative bodies.[4] Because the EWL originally contacted the conservative Union of Catholic Women (UCW), Czech feminist organizations were reluctant to join the EWL. Moreover, some of them had been part of the Karat Coalition (since 1997) and argued that Karat would better represent their interests at the supranational level.[5] Pragmatic reasons (and especially the better prospects of the EWL to succeed in lobbying than Karat) resulted in the UCW, the Czech Women's Union, and the Gender Studies Centre establishing a Czech network in 2004, which a year later became a member of the EWL and called on other organizations to join. Because the position of the UCW on abortion and same-sex partnerships differed from that of the EWL, the UCW withdrew from the CWL. Another contested issue was prostitution, which opened a debate among the

CWL's member organizations over the abolitionist approach of the EWL. Further heated debates in the CWL ensued over the preparation of a recommendation and petition regarding the direction of family policy in the CR, which the CWL decided to prepare in response to the rejection of the Barcelona targets by the cabinet of the CR.[6] Because of the disagreement over the priority of childcare facilities, some members of the CWL refused to add their signatures to the recommendation by the CWL. With the gradual consolidation of the CWL and its growing membership base, Czech women's organizations started communicating and lobbying directly at the European level, either through the EWL or through individual members of European Parliament. Another important milestone came with the entry of Czech women's organizations into strategic court cases, both in the CR and at the European Court of Human Rights.

The first Women's Congress organized in 2013 in Prague underscored the diversity of existing women's organizations. The organization of the congress was initiated by Fórum 50% (a Czech NGO supporting equal participation of women and men in politics and decision making), Národní kontaktní centrum—gender a věda (National Contact Centre—Gender and Science, a Czech NGO contributing to building gender equality in science and research), and others. With more than seven hundred participants, the congress provided important networking opportunities. While the 2013 congress drew particular attention to the barriers to women's participation in the labor market, the 2015 congress focused on gender and the media. The main challenge for future congress meetings is to focus more on the multiple disadvantages faced by Czech women from different social and ethnic backgrounds and to move beyond the CR's borders to address solidarity with those who suffer from poverty globally.

To sum up, the period around and after the accession of the CR to the EU brought a radical transformation of the sociopolitical environment for Czech women's organizations. The processes of NGOs' professionalization and projects and reform orientation have marginalized those activities and topics that are not the central interests of the EU (the most important donor in the sector) or of Czech ministries and agencies, such as the National Training Fund and the Civil Society Development Foundation, through which European funds are distributed. Despite these developments, which have resulted in a thematic reorientation of some women's organizations and have overshadowed certain issues in the Czech public debate, European funds did significantly increase the amount of money available to women's organizations and led to the subsequent entry of many new entities, including private for-profit organizations, into projects focusing on the equality of men and women. The period since

2007 has been perceived as a period when European funds for gender equality have become limited primarily to organizations working in the field of the labor market. At the same time, this period has also seen the entrenchment of the network of women's organizations, and especially of the CWL, a body that explicitly endorses feminism and whose influence can today already be clearly seen in lobbying and public deliberation. A major challenge for Czech women's organizations continues to be a greater emphasis on the intersection of multiple disadvantages and on building solidarity with marginalized groups inside and outside the CR.

CARE MOVES TO THE FOREGROUND

Problems related to the gendered division of labor and the distribution of care have been part of feminist struggles since the end of World War II. However, in the CR, after 1989 gender inequalities related to care were sidelined when the prevailing anti-communist ideology negatively labeled and dismissed these issues as relics of state socialism. Furthermore, at that time, women tended to take for granted that public childcare services would continue to be available or even expand. It was only once the availability of childcare facilities significantly decreased that women's organizations started to prioritize this issue.

During the first decades after World War II, care was regarded as a public issue in Czechoslovakia. Public daycare facilities and other services supported by the state were introduced, with the goal of liberating households from housework and care (Bezouška and Vytlačil 1963, 328). However, by the 1960s groups of experts, along with the Czechoslovak Women's Union, had begun to assess critically the unsuccessful socialization of housework and the consequent double burden faced by women (Háková 1966, 559–60; see also Wagnerová in this volume), and they called for longer maternity leave while maintaining existing state support for childcare facilities (Hašková and Uhde 2009, 95; Hašková and Klenner 2010, 275–76). After the Prague Spring in 1968, in the period of Normalization, which was characterized by the strengthening of the authoritarian regime and general societal apathy, support for (rather conventionally conceived) women's gender roles in the family increased. Maternity allowances for full-time mothers were introduced and their length was gradually extended up to a child's age of three. Their amount, however, has never been allocated or intended to allow for maintaining an independent household and rather counted on the male income in the family. Since long interruptions to employment posed only low risk to the job security of mothers, and since having a two-career family was rare in Czechoslovakia (a two-career family differs significantly from a two-income family, the latter of which became a norm and dominant practice in Czechoslovakia), the practice of mothers staying at home with the first child until the birth/s of the second (and possibly subsequent) child/ren significantly increased during Normalization. The sequencing of periods of study, care, and employment in a woman's life course became the dominant practice instead of allowing a woman to combine productive and reproductive work during her lifetime (Saxonberg, Hašková, and Mudrák 2012).

The post-1989 public discourse labeled state support for childcare outside the family a "communist invention." This eventually resulted in a significant drop in the availability and affordability of daycare facilities and further strengthened re-familialist policies, that is, policies which turn away from previously established incentives for women to combine paid work with caregiving toward incentives undermining women's employment and shifting the care work back to families. The previous and still operational re-familialist developments from the period of Normalization help explain why there were no public protests after 1989 when the state ceased to fund nurseries and the majority of nurseries quickly disappeared. Post-1989 explicitly re-familialist policies included extending maternity allowances for full-time mothers to up to four years. These policies, coupled with post-1989 developments in the labor market under a market economy, are the main reasons why today the CR is one of the countries in Europe where motherhood has the greatest negative impact on women's participation in the labor market.[7] Moreover, today's women with young children are more vulnerable to precarious working conditions and contracts and long-term unemployment, a situation which radically differs from the pre-1989 model of permanent work contracts and one lifelong job (albeit interrupted by relatively long childcare periods since the 1970s) or, in most cases, no more than a few jobs over a woman's life (Saxonberg, Hašková, and Mudrák 2012, 40).

Although a fairly large number of women's organizations were established in the 1990s, they mostly focused on topics other than care. Those women's organizations that did focus on care policies in the 1990s issued statements advocating for the right of women to care for their children in the home (Wolchik 1991, 205; Saxonberg 2003, 233). The conservative National Center for the Family was the most successful NGO in influencing the direction of post-1989 Czech family policies during this period, thanks to its close ties with the Christian Democrats, the only party that consistently focused on family policy in the 1990s.

At the end of the decade, it became clear that long-term unemployment among mothers was rising steadily, and the CR was criticized by the EU for neglecting to adopt an active employment policy. The fact that the birthrate slowly started rising again (after a precipitous drop in the early 1990s) also served to encourage women's organizations to take an increasing interest in issues of care and specifically childcare. Moreover, many women activists who have recently been lobbying for childcare policy changes belong to the generation that was in their teens in 1989, and they themselves became mothers only in the new millennium (women's average age at first birth increased from a "socialist" twenty-two to a post-socialist twenty-eight). Consequently, in the new millennium childcare began to figure more centrally in political and media discussions. However, the issue of childcare today tends to be framed through work-life balance arguments that put to the fore the need for women to participate in the labor market. As a result, attention commonly gets deflected away from other relevant issues, including the different types of challenges faced by various groups of women. Moreover, organizations focusing on minorities typically do not define the issue of (child-)care as a priority, arguing rather that there are other, more urgent problems.[8]

Neither migrant-focused nor Romany organizations would become visible in the Czech public sphere until the late 1990s (Leontiyeva et al. 2006; Černá et al. 2002). The interests of Romany women are mostly represented in conjunction with Romany family interests, aimed especially at children rather than at women themselves. There are four organizations that declare themselves representatives of Romany women's interests (Manushe, The Working Group of Romany Women under the Council of the Government of the Czech Republic for Romany Community Affairs, Athinganoi, and Romea). In terms of care, children's education and socialization are their most visible agendas. Of course, both of these are strongly gendered issues because women are primarily responsible for the education and socialization of children in Romany families (Uhde et al. 2009, 39–42; see also Ryvolová in this volume).

As the CR is increasingly becoming a destination rather than transition country for migrants, the number of migrant-focused organizations has grown (Leontiyeva et al. 2006; IOM 2012). In general, gender inequalities are not perceived as a primary issue among these groups although a small number of organizations, such as the European Contact Group or, more recently, the Association for Integration and Migration, do focus specifically on women migrants. As with most women's organizations, activist groups representing migrant women are dependent on project funding. With regard to care, issues such as access to social security and other social benefits, access to public health insurance and healthcare, the status of illegal migrants, and the recognition of migrants' right to private and family life receive significantly more attention than childcare. When it comes to children, the focus is on primary education as a means of integration (Uhde et al. 2009, 36–39).

A broader coalition between majority and minority women's organizations has yet to be formed, although both Romany and migrant women have representatives in the CWL. The recent campaigns for the right of migrants to public healthcare insurance and to protect the rights of domestic migrant workers are signs of positive developments in this area. The question is to what extent majority women's organizations reflect the problems and needs of minority groups of women. Majority women's organizations predominantly focus on white, middle-class women, and the work-life balance dilemma is interpreted mainly from that point of view. Organizations focusing on women migrants do not define childcare as one of their most important issues, and organizations concerned with Romany women do not view the issue of childcare in terms of gender equality, instead linking care to issues of poverty and exclusion (Hašková, Uhde, and Pulkrábková 2011, 70–72).

WHAT IS TRANSFORMATIVE IN THE CURRENT CARE CLAIMS?

Attending to the affirmative and transformative strategies of claim-making, as described by Nancy Fraser, offers us a potentially useful lens for examining the efforts of Czech women's organizations. In analyzing justice claims in terms of political orientation, Fraser distinguishes between affirmation and transformation (1997, 11–40). Arguing that affirmative strategies deal with individual aspects of injustice insufficiently, Fraser first advocated for transformative strategies that would go directly to the roots of injustice.[9] In her later work, however, she recognized that this distinction is contextual rather than absolute, and she also became aware of the difficulties connected with the implementation of transformative strategies. Following the work of André Gorz, Fraser then argued for "non-reformist reforms," combining the radical content of transformative strategies with the practicable assertion of affirmative strategies (Fraser and Honneth 2003, 78–82). Non-reformist reforms are progressive steps that question the roots of existing structural injustices and set a path toward radical transformation of these structures in the long term. In the remainder of this chapter, we use Fraser's notion of non-reformist reforms to assess and foreground those elements of current care claims that we believe can lead, in the long run, to a deeper transformation of social structures and an improved functioning of Czech society.

The articulated needs and claims of different groups of women in contemporary Czech society should be the starting point for any transformative politics. Following public debates on care we focus on the criticism and claims of women's majority, migrant-focused, and Romany women's groups in the CR. We cannot analyze all publicly articulated care claims; rather, we focus on the most visible ones that have a shared basis among the different kinds of women's groups and organizations. We analyze how these groups tend to frame their care claims through the lens of affirmative and transformative strategies, and explore how the ways in which strategies are conceptualized either contribute to or obstruct a more radical transformation of the contemporary organization of care in Czech society.

Childcare Institutions without Multicultural Diversity

Claims made by Czech feminist organizations for financial and spatial access to institutional childcare are usually formulated in a work-centered and gender equality framework. In line with the Barcelona and Lisbon Treaties adopted by the EU member states, these requests are regarded as a means to improving women's labor market participation and consequently promoting gender equality. Our research shows that claims for childcare institutions are also articulated in a work-centered framework by migrant-focused organizations. These organizations tend to regard the availability of childcare institutions in terms of an opportunity for mothers to work outside the home, as well as an integration opportunity for children. On the contrary, gender-conservative organizations tend to stress claims for wages for care, as a strategy of overcoming the devaluation of care while prioritizing home-based maternal care.[10] And Romany women's groups with whom we have conducted research are mainly interested in overcoming the marginalization and even exclusion of older preschool and young school-age Romany children from childcare and education. Their goal is to get a better education for their children as a way out of the circle of poverty and exclusion. Nevertheless, they also emphasize the importance of family care for young children and the child's right to parental care, which is voiced as part of the struggle against the forced placement of Romany children in institutions of foster care.[11]

Articulating their claims, Czech feminist organizations tend to argue that society is responsible for childcare, and they criticize the re-familialization, individualization, privatization, and commercialization of childcare, as well as the absence of men in childcare. However, they usually do not pay sufficient attention to specific problems faced by Roma, migrant women, or families with disabled children. This is the case of gender-conservative organizations as well.

Migrant-oriented organizations and Romany women's groups do not articulate their claims in terms of combating gender discrimination, even though they do point out the burdens on migrant and Romany women resulting from childbearing responsibilities. Discrimination based on these groups' marginalized status is seen as the main problem, while other power relations (e.g., gender relations) are not articulated as pressing issues. Nevertheless, the lived gendered experience of migrant and Romany women is an incentive behind some important activities organized by migrant-oriented organizations and Romany women's groups.

Our research shows that although calls for childcare facilities are formulated across all of these organizations, there remains the problem of different framing by majority and minority women's groups. Childcare institutions could have a transformative social potential, and we see the path to fulfilling that potential as lying in joint debates about the claims for childcare institutions as formulated by different groups. These requests and arguments can be reframed in such a way that they would reduce both gender and other inequalities in society. The calls for quality state-funded childcare facilities can become transformative social agents—if they emphasize the inclusion of all children, including immigrants and ethnic minorities. Otherwise, the existing inequalities between majority and minority or between citizens and noncitizens are reproduced, and no deep social restructuring is initiated. Furthermore, the calls for quality childcare institutions (for all children) need to be combined with calls for an improvement in the working conditions and pay for childcare workers. In order to think about childcare institutions in terms of non-reformist reforms, it is important to address the issue of who works in these institutions and under what conditions.

The Issue of Men's Participation in Caring

Although the different kinds of organizations discussed above generally all agree that men should be involved in care (with the exception of migrant-focused groups, which tend to leave this issue aside), how they frame their arguments around this topic varies. While gender-conservative organizations and Romany women's groups often center this issue in terms of the moral value of parenthood, feminist organizations articulate it within the frames of work-centered arguments and gender equality. Gender-conservative organizations as well as Romany women's groups stress the child's right to have both parents' care, and they highlight the positive value of fathers' active participation in childcare so that the children might advantageously have access to each gender model. On the other hand, feminist organizations emphasize men's participation in childcare in terms of rights and responsibilities—as a way to support women's participation in paid employment as well as a way of challenging and disrupting the feminization of care as a presumably less valuable activity.

The moral value framing of parenthood emphasizes the fathers' right to care for their children and the child's right to paternal care. Good intentions notwithstanding, the emphasis on the right of children to both male and female parents' care is potentially discriminatory against lone-parent families and families that do not fulfill the heterosexual norm. Fathers' care rights are demanded mainly at the legislative level through equal legislative provisions for both parents, although not through a quota system. On the other hand, the gender equality framing used by feminist organizations stresses both the right and responsibility of men to care for their children. This involves calls to introduce a father quota in the parental leave scheme. Although the interpretative frame of the moral value of parenthood emphasizes the right of children to paternal care, which a father quota would also support, gender-conservative organizations tend to reject this and present it as incompatible with the rhetoric of free choice. The different framings of the claims for paternal care by individual organizations thus reveal differences in the principles behind their arguments.

It could be argued that there is transformative potential to framing the call for men's participation in caring by using arguments of gender equality. However, the strategic use of work-centered arguments by feminist organizations to legitimize their claims for a father quota may have the unintended consequence of reinforcing misrecognition and devaluation of caring activities. As it stresses the value of women's participation in paid employment, it unwittingly affirms the secondary value of unpaid activities such as caring. Nevertheless, if the demand for men's participation in caring is conceptualized as a moral entitlement without simultaneously putting the same emphasis on men's responsibility for caring and gender equality, the unintended consequences will be the reproduction of an unequal gender division of responsibility for care and the reinforcement of inequalities between the heterosexual two-parent family and lone-parent and gay and lesbian families.

Flexibility within a Work-Centered Society

Our research suggests that Czech majority women's organizations devote considerable attention to the issue of flexible forms of employment as a strategy for resolving the work-life balance dilemma. However, if the "family-friendly employment" argument is exercised exclusively in connection with women, such a framing could disadvantageously impact women's bargaining power with employers or reduce the eventual benefits currently realized through women's pensions. Feminist organizations use the frame of gender equality in order to eliminate the association between the employment model of mothers and flexible forms of employment, which are still construed as secondary forms of jobs as compared to the uninterrupted employment trajectory of full-time work. They highlight the need to make these forms of employment available to both men and women, and to support both men and women in using family-friendly forms of employment. Nevertheless, since the calls for flexible forms of employment are articulated within a work-centered framework that does not question the dominant work paradigm (equating work only with paid employment), another prospective hierarchy is produced in the process between parents and nonparents.

Conversely, gender-conservative organizations tend to link the demand for flexible forms of work to their call for valuing care by means of providing women with the opportunity to combine home care and paid employment. Some of these groups argue for wages to remunerate caring for children paid by the state (as opposed to benefits or paid care leaves associated with dependency). Their arguments thus symbolically question the market logic of work valuation, although these organizations tend to articulate their claims within traditional gendered frameworks. While their argument opens up the possibility of a redefinition of the dominant work paradigm, it also reinforces the traditional gender division of labor, ultimately boosting the male bias in the labor market, with men representing the ideal of an independent, market-oriented employee and women the ideal of the dependent caregiver. Romany women's groups tend to stress other priorities than the employment of women. Instead, they emphasize the value of family in Romany communities. Thus they question the presupposition of the work-centered society, although mostly in traditional, gender-specific ways. Finally, for migrant women, employment is often the only means of staying in the CR legally. The migrant-oriented organizations' focus therefore tends to be on criticizing the fact that obtaining a residence permit is conditional upon having an employment contract and that its validity is tied to a specific employer. The issue of flexibility for migrants centers around the disentangling of the residence and work permits.

The idea of reducing working hours, raised by many organizations arguing for flexible forms of employment, contains a transformative potential, but this potential can be fulfilled only if it is universally framed. The current demands for flexible forms of employment within the work-centered framework tend to reinforce the status quo, discriminating against women (and to some extent parents in general) in the labor market. Contrary to most Czech feminist organizations we have researched, gender-conservative organizations and Romany women's groups actually do question the overall organization of work-centered society, although they typically do so only in the gender-specific situation of caring for children, implicitly reinforcing the link between care and femininity.

CONCLUSION

In this chapter, we first outline the historical development of Czech feminist and women's public organizing in the "post-socialist" condition, and then focus on analyzing care claims, as care has been a central feminist issue and yet was left aside during the capitalist transformation of the CR in the 1990s. Nevertheless, at the end of the 1990s, the issue of care resurfaced among Czech feminist and women's NGOs and other informal groups. We analyzed care claims articulated by Czech majority women's and feminist organizations, migrant-focused organizations, and Romany women's groups. We focused in particular on those elements of their claims that obstruct or support a deeper transformation of social structures, especially in relation to the gender patterns of care practices and responsibilities. Nancy Fraser calls these gradual steps, which combine the feasibility of affirmative demands with the radical implications of transformative demands, non-reformist reforms. Although we point to the possible unintended consequences of some current care claims, we argue that there is potential for the development of non-reformist reforms of the social organization of care, especially childcare. Calls for institutional childcare can be transformative when they combine gender equality agendas with demands for the inclusion of children from marginalized groups. The demands for men's participation in caring can be transformative too, provided they connect rights and responsibilities for care. Finally, calls for a flexible employment model can be socially transformative if decoupled from work-centered understandings of sociability. Pinpointing, analyzing, and comparing the different discursive frameworks used by different kinds of women's groups and organizations in articulating their care claims makes it possible, we believe, to identify barriers to developing their transformative potential.

NOTES

1. This research was supported by the Program of Support of Perspective Human Resources of the Czech Academy of Sciences; by the grant project "Intersectionality in Sociological Research into Social Inequalities and into the Impact of the Economic

Crisis on Employment" (Czech Science Foundation, grant no. 15-13766S); and by institutional support RVO: 68378025.

2. Based on our agreement with the researched groups and partners, the collected data were anonymized.

3. The only women's organization that existed in the era of Normalization, the Czech Women's Union, was established to represent Czech women well before 1989.

4. The EWL associates women's organizations across Europe and cooperates with European institutions to lobby for gender equity and various women's interests.

5. The Karat Coalition represents organizations focused on women's human rights and gender justice in Central and Eastern Europe and Central Asia. It works at the national and international levels, advocating for policy change and awareness raising.

6. EU member states committed to fulfill the Barcelona targets in 2002, which stipulated that by 2010 they would ensure the availability of childcare facilities for at least one third of children under the age of three and 90% of preschool children aged three or older.

7. The Organization for Economic Cooperation and Development, OECD Family Database, 2012, chart LMF1.2, www.oecd.org/social/soc/oecdfamilydatabase.htm.

8. We focus mostly on childcare in this chapter because it is the issue to which the attention of Czech women's organizations shifted at the turn of the millennium. Other related topics, such as elderly care and household work, are of interest only to a relatively small (although growing) portion of these organizations.

9. According to Fraser (1997), affirmative strategies of redistribution tend to focus only on the redistribution of outcomes and do not address the structures and institutional contexts that generate these patterns of redistribution. Affirmative strategies of recognition tend to focus on group identities without questioning the creation of the meaning of difference.

10. Based on our research of Czech women's organizations we differentiate between feminist and gender-conservative organizations. While both focus on women and address gender inequalities, gender-conservative organizations build on gender essentialist assumptions and advocate for maintaining traditional gendered divisions.

11. This part of the chapter is also based on interviews and research we conducted as part of the projects mentioned in note 1. As stated above, based on our agreement with the researched groups and partners, the collected data were anonymized.

8 CZECH ANARCHOFEMINISM

Against Hierarchy and Privileges

LINDA SOKAČOVÁ

CZECH ANARCHOFEMINISM BEGAN to emerge very soon after the political realignments of 1989. At that time, with four decades of an interventionist state socialist system having undermined the trust in state powers for many Czechs, Marxism as an emancipatory project had lost legitimacy, while the new post-1989, pro-Western capitalist regime did not put an end to, and rather seemed to deepen, political corruption. With Marxism having exhausted its persuasive force and new official political outlets not trusted either, anarchism became an attractive alternative, especially among segments of young Czech men and women. Anarchism's suspicion of the state, combined with its anti-capitalist but non-Marxist agenda, strongly appealed to many Czech activists who were throughout the 1990s and early 2000s intent on finding or inventing a distinctly new third way.

Already in the 1990s, some of the groups that were part of the Czech anarchist and autonomous movements began availing themselves of the topics of gender inequality as well as spiritualism and ecofeminism. Czech anarchofeminism peaked during the years 2001–5 with the activities of Anarchofeministická skupina (Anarchofeminist Group, AFS), previously known as Feministická skupina 8. března (Feminist Group of the 8th of March, FS8B), and the *Bloody Mary* magazine. After 2005, Czech anarchofeminism—along with the entire anarchist movement—began to decline. While this chapter mostly uses the past tense when discussing Czech anarchofeminism, reflective of the fact that the above groups have disbanded, it should be noted that a number of ideas arising from anarchofeminism continue to flourish in the Czech public discourse, both left-wing and mainstream.[1]

This chapter is significantly informed through the study of texts produced by these groups, already existing academic publications dealing with anarchofeminism, and individual interviews I conducted with (former) members of these groups and advocates of the Czech anarchofeminist movement overall.[2] The objective here is to introduce the reader to Czech anarchofeminist organizations and other groups whose principles were similar to anarchofeminism. The chapter focuses on the broader social context that gave birth to these organizations and on their goals, as well as on their influences on the anarchist and broader autonomous movements and on mainstream feminist organizations. The observations in this chapter are informed both by my expertise as a sociologist who has researched Czech and global political movements and by my experience as a cofounder and former member of AFS.

THE GENESIS OF CZECH ANARCHOFEMINISM

Czech anarchofeminism seeks to combine anarchist and feminist ideas. The concept of anarchofeminism has attracted those activists from Czech autonomous, anarchist, and anti-fascist movements who accept the feminist critical thesis of an unequal social position between men and women while disagreeing with the anarchist argument that these inequalities can be successfully remedied through an anti-capitalist revolution. At the same time, anarchofeminists also challenge the thesis that the unequal women's position can be solved by focusing on gender issues alone. Rather, they consider questions of class and ethnic inequality and discrimination as crucial. Indeed, some supporters of anarchofeminism have argued that liberal, institutionalized feminism, focused on individual rights without foregrounding the individual's place in society, helps to produce new power disparities and sometimes furthers inequalities emerging through economic globalization. They point out the disparities emerging between globally traveling "professional feminists" and everyday women with limited opportunities.

As noted above, the roots of Czech modern-day anarchofeminism can be traced to activist efforts in the 1990s, although these were only first, initial steps. After 2000, the interest in the movement increased, partly due to the readiness of anarchofeminism to address new topics of everyday life, such as family, raising of children, violence against women, and the role of language in society. Anarchofeminism started working with the concept of human rights while insistently critically foregrounding the role of economic institutions and capitalism. The structure of anarchism changed as well when it was combined with feminist principles, becoming more attractive to those who might have felt uncomfortable in older anarchist organizations, which previously had revolved around dominant, and mostly male, personalities.

Anarchofeminism attracted feminist activists who took issue with the by then fairly well established Czech liberal-feminist organizations. Anarchofeminists criticized mainstream feminist organizations for over-relying on academic debates, for their uncritical positions toward class inequalities, and for their efforts to join the existing status quo rather than structurally change the system. Anarchofeminists were also devising new, engaging means of advocating anarchofeminist ideas, including direct action, street activism, and direct appeals to the public.

FS8B and AFS also found inspiration abroad, such as in the U.S.-based anarchofeminist collectives of the 1970s, including the Black Rose and Siren, who had embraced the bonding of feminism and anarchism. Likewise, the Czech groups drew inspiration from German, French, and Spanish contexts, especially the Spanish Mujeres Libres, founded in 1936 and organized specifically around working-class women's issues. As for texts, *Quiet Rumours: An Anarcha-Feminist Reader* served as an important source of knowledge.[3]

The history of anarchofeminism in the post-1989 Czech Republic (CR) can be divided into the following periods:

1. The 1990s: activities of the feminist collective organized around *Vicca* magazine and the Luna group.
2. 2000–2005: the foundation and early work of the FS8B and *Bloody Mary* magazine. The "golden age of Czech anarchofeminism."
3. 2006–present: gradual dissolution of organized anarchofeminism.

A number of authors who have written on Czech anarchofeminism, such as Jitka Kolářová and Marta Kolářová (who are sisters), were members of the anarchofeminist collectives that emerged around *Vicca* magazine and the group called Luna in the 1990s. Vicca was a feminist collective consisting of women and men, who published (between 1993 and 1996) a magazine of the same title focused on issues of spiritualism, witchcraft, and ecofeminism. Members also discussed the position of women within the anarchist movement and looked for ways to strengthen that position. The women's group Luna (with its zine *Esbat*), founded around 1995, further emphasized gender issues, pointing out the dominant position of men and the patriarchal patterns in anarchist collectives. One of the major topics for anarchism and anarchofeminism at the time was ecology, partly because environmental issues—generally ignored and suppressed before 1989—were finally becoming prominent in the Czech public discourse. Czech anarchists participated, for instance, in the blockade of the Temelín nuclear plant. These early groups laid an intellectual and ideological foundation for the later, more prominent FS8B, as well as the *Bloody Mary* collective:

> *Vicca* was a revelation for me. I started feeling feminism sort of intuitively—somehow, the different rules for women and men and different attitudes toward women's and men's sexuality bothered me. And in this situation I was stopped one day by this bloke in a club, who said that I had a great T-shirt and that I was "theirs." The sign on the T-shirt was Lipsticks and bullets, which pretty much summarized what *Vicca* was about. Somehow, my love for feminism that connects social and gender issues emerged. Luna was a motivation for me to join the movement and actively create something. (activist Lenka)[4]

There was some overlap between the early and later groups, with some members of Luna later joining, even if temporarily, the FS8B collective. At the same time, later AFS activists distanced themselves from the early anarcho-feminist interest in spiritualism, as well as from ecofeminism with its, as they perceived it, essentialist understanding of gender roles.

THE FEMINIST GROUP OF THE 8TH OF MARCH (FS8B) WINS PUBLIC SPACE

FS8B, later renamed AFS, began taking shape in the year 2000, partly under the influence of the mass anti-globalization protests against the International Monetary Fund (IMF) and World Bank meeting in Prague. The zine *Bloody Mary*, rooted in the ideas of the American Riot Grrrls, provided another source of inspiration:

> I came across *Bloody Mary* by chance in the Gender Studies Library. The zine talked about a Global Women's Strike. The magazine provided what I had been missing, and the idea of a global strike in particular appealed to me. It combined the issue of women's position, which was central to me at the time, with social and economic issues. The Global Women's Strike idea made me think of organizing something like this here. (activist Lenka)

Thus, at the beginning of a specifically feminist anarchist tradition in the CR, we find FS8B/AFS along with the zine *Bloody Mary* both declaring an interest in organizing the Global Women's Strike in the CR. From the very beginning it was clear that this would not be just a temporary episode, although a more solid structure and a clearer conceptualization along the lines of anarchofeminism began emerging only after the strike in Prague in March 2001. In the CR, the Global Strike took the form of a large public event with a concert, a variety of accompanying events, and an informational campaign:

> We realized that something like an actual strike was beyond our organizational abilities. Plus we really had nothing we could offer the potential striking women in return. Thus we decided to organize a public event instead—at the Náměstí Míru in Prague, which is a busy intersection, guaranteeing that the event would be attended minimally by the passersby. That turned out to be correct. But a lot of people also turned up specifically to attend our event. The informational campaign was also a success, with information booths distributing our flyers. And we issued press statements, which were successful as well. We were featured by quite a few media stations. (activist Lenka)

The organizational meetings prior to the public event were well attended, often with about forty enthusiastic participants eager to be involved in the planning. Other groups active in the anarchist movement at the time were asked to participate as well. Although later there were generally more women than men in FS8B/AFS, a number of men participated in organizing the first Czech General Women's Strike. Along the way the established NGO the Gender Studies Centre provided institutional support; some of the meetings took place there. This is how activist Lenka remembers that time: "At first, there were not even enough chairs for all of us at the 'Gender'—there was almost not enough room to sit. We were surprised by the interest."

The first public event took place on March 8, 2001, in Prague. At the time, March 8 had strong negative connotations tied to the country's pre-1989 history. It was considered a relic of the past when the International Women's Day (IWD) used to be connected with a mandatory celebration of communism. Thus IWD was, and still to some extent is, perceived as a communist holiday forced on Czech society. A large portion of the public associated the day with a celebration of the socialist regime rather than with a memorialization of the struggle for women's rights. In the 1990s, there were efforts to replace IWD with Mother's Day (conspicuously associated with the West). To some extent against these efforts, it became one of FS8B's goals to disrupt the biased image of IWD and to return to it its original charge of highlighting the unequal position of women and men in society and celebrating women's struggle for equality. But in FS8B's conception, IWD was also about class issues and the unequal social and economic status of various groups.

The FS8B organizers of the 2001 Prague Global Women's Strike divided their agenda into four major areas: anarchofeminism versus liberal/institutionalized feminism, violence against women, the beauty ideal, and women in the capitalist market. Public discussions were held and flyers distributed around each of these topics. The FS8B group selected speakers from its midst and communicated intensively with the media and thus also with the broader public outside of Prague: "We were featured on a Czech Radio program focused on the Global Women's Strike and the IWD. During the discussion we raised the issue of capitalism and anarchism. That rather took the correspondent aback. He managed, but it was quite a shock for him" (activist Lenka). The media attended and covered the events, with one of the correspondents questioning the legitimacy of these events organized by participants of "violent" anti-IMF protests in September 2000. The Global Women's Strike events on March 8, 2001, repeated in 2002 and 2003, established the groundwork for a new understanding of IWD in the CR.

ANARCHOFEMINISM VERSUS LIBERAL FEMINISM

One of the key texts of AFS through which it entered public consciousness was the flyer "Institucionální feminismus vs. anarchofeminismus" (Institutionalized Feminism vs. Anarchofeminism).[5] The title referred to the institutionalization and ossification of liberal feminism, especially feminist NGOs, in the CR. The critique focused on the emerging phenomenon of professionalized global feminists perceived as traveling and navigating in the digital world and getting out of touch with the reality of actual women. As the flyer states:

> [In contrast to the established feminism] anarchofeminism does not aim at replacing the male elite with [a] female one but at eliminating elite as such. Its struggle against patriarchy is combined with a struggle to eliminate the state and capitalism. Dehumanization is another result of the third wave of liberal feminism. In contrast to the colorfulness and plurality of the 1960s, the current protagonists of liberal feminism have wrapped themselves in gray. They can be spotted in modern-looking offices, with a notebook and a cell, running from one conference to the next. Attending conferences has become not the means but the goal. As a result, their efforts have been distanced from women's everyday struggles.

AFS did not reject nonprofits entirely, however, and it particularly welcomed NGO programs focused on helping battered and poor women. Rather than completely dismissing them, AFS cooperated with and respected some

NGOS, and in fact to some extent the two spheres actually overlapped in membership. However, unlike Czech women's NGOS, funded by Western donors or (later) the European Union, FS8B/AFS unequivocally rejected capitalism and neoliberalism, repudiating any social system based on hierarchies, whether gender based or economic:

> When the media speak of feminism, it's connected with the cult of successful women. Usually, these are highly socially and economically successful women, with no children or with resources to hire childcare and household help. They are represented as the model of a socially acceptable feminism. We do not identify with this understanding of "feminism," and consider it a confusion of terminology. It confuses the elitism within the patriarchal order with feminism, which struggles for equal rights for all. For us, feminism does not mean gaining the highest possible position and prestige, but living our lives fully, making decisions about ourselves and being accountable for these decisions. While liberal feminism's goal is to place as many women as possible in leadership positions, our goal is to eliminate hierarchy as such. Privileges are unjust whether in the hands of men or women. ("Institutionalized Feminism vs. Anarchofeminism")

FS8B/AFS TOPICS

AFS emphasized not only topics of the social and economic revolution, trade unions, and post-revolutionary society but also everyday current issues reflecting women's problems in society, at work, at home, and within the anarchist movement. These issues included violence against women, rape, representations of women in the media, as well as the power of language to not just reflect but also coproduce reality. And as activist Darina articulated it, "Besides introducing new topics, we were also concerned with questions of relating to others and of how to facilitate discussions." According to many participants, these new foci contributed to the revitalization of the entire anarchist movement: "At the time, the anarchist movement was already ossified around historical dogmatism—questions of who is better—Malatest, Volin or Machno, globalization, NATO. AFS brought in new issues; its members were active, publishing a new magazine *Siréna*. There was a lot of good energy there" (activist Martin).

These topics were publicized not only through public happenings, informational booths, and events like the Global Women's Strike but also through magazines like *Přímá cesta* (Direct Way) or the bulletin *Siréna*. Published between 2001 and 2009, with ten issues, *Přímá cesta* focused on topics like family and education, pornography, gender roles in patriarchy, the role of language, women's roles in revolutions, women anti-fascist activists, sexual violence, anarchofeminism in everyday life, and many others. *Siréna* examined current topics and informed its readers about FS8B/AFS and other anarchist groups' events. Many of the topics the group discussed theoretically were put into practice as well. For instance, issues and ideas related to family, childrearing, and education found their practical application in anarchist summer camps for adults and children co-organized by FS8B/AFS.

One of the issues FS8B/AFS most emphasized was violence against women and the related topic of women's representations in the media. For the 2001 International Day for the Elimination of Violence against Women, FS8B/AFS organized a happening during which group members clad in burqas distributed flyers and protested both violence against women in Afghanistan and "the hypocritical politics of the United States and its allies . . . who after years of supporting or tolerating the Taliban and its practices are now calling for the protection of women's rights in Afghanistan."[6] The group was also pointing out that forced unveiling in the European context is similar to forced veiling of women in some Islamic countries and communities. This approach distinguished FS8B/AFS's position from the traditional, xenophobic perception of Muslim women.

Reflective of the central place of the anti-militarist and anti-capitalist struggle on the FS8B/AFS agenda, the group also joined protests against the 2002 NATO meeting in Prague. The call for anti-NATO demonstrations stated, "NATO defends the interests of the political and economic elites of rich countries. Thousands of innocent civilians die in wars waged for the purpose of economic gain."[7] While the anti-NATO events were not as well attended as the 2000 anti-IMF protests, they contributed to the further establishment of FS8B/AFS within the anarchist movement. However, the organization of these events was marked by growing internal problems and tensions in the movement.

Another key topic for FS8B/AFS, especially in the early 2000s, was women's reproductive rights. The FS8B/AFS activities in this arena were organized in opposition to the efforts of the civic society Hnutí pro život (Pro-Life Movement, HPŽ ČR), which, in cooperation with several conservative political parties, sought to change the traditionally liberal attitude of the Czech public toward abortion and to have abortions banned. In the CR, abortion has been legal since 1957, when it became permitted until the third month, both for medical and social reasons. While for several decades abortions required approval by a special committee, women saw these committees as a formality. The committees were abolished in 1986, making abortion entirely the woman's decision.

The first statement of FS8B/AFS against the HPŽ ČR's annual March for Life reads, "One of the main contradictions we see in their approach is that their emphasized respect for human life embraces only certain life. Homosexuality, children born out of wedlock, 'test tube' children are all, according to HPŽ ČR, socially harmful. We consider such an attitude to be part of a clero-fascist trend in our society."[8] FS8B/AFS not only sought to foreground the harmful effects of a potential abortion ban but also warned against the negative influence of the church. The public event that the group organized around this topic in 2002 used the image of the pope with bloodied hands. The image produced strong emotional responses among the March for Life participants and met with a strong negative public reaction, despite the CR's being one of the most atheistic countries in Europe.[9]

Anti-fascism was another important topic, one capable of mobilizing large numbers of anarchist and autonomous movements' sympathizers. The main focus of feminist critique in this area was the cult of power and violence, and the symbol of the male fighter, often invoked by the group Antifašistická akce (Anti-Fascist Action). According to FS8B/AFS, such stereotypes discouraged rather than attracted women's participation in anti-fascist, as well as anarchist movements: "There were only few girls participating really, and there was no such thing as a 'women's voice.' Girls either found their way into the existing organizations—where there were a couple of them—or they functioned as somebody's friends who would occasionally help out with things. But the atmosphere did not appeal to women. The cult of power and violence dominated these groups, and the atmosphere was quite macho" (activist Martina). The image of a male warrior, reliant on physical strength, discouraged women from participating, and women, not generally recognized for their physical strength, were not recruited by, or even accepted in, Czech anti-fascist groups.

WAS ANARCHOFEMINISM SEPARATISM?

The foundation of FS8B/AFS caused some negative response in the anarchist movement overall. In spite of the group's declaring from the very start that it was not separatist and welcomed both men and women, voices emerged arguing that the founding of the group was a needless step. It was necessary to explain repeatedly that feminism emphasizes men's participation as well and is not directed against individual men. Some FS8B/AFS members also stressed they would not welcome the formation of "women-only spaces" in Czech anarchism, as they existed for instance in Germany or Spain.

Jitka Kolářová, who studies Czech subcultures and feminism, observed in 2009 that some of the discussions between AFS and other anarchist groups were quite adversarial. But the end result was that feminist critique entered Czech anarchist consciousness, influencing its principles and functioning (see also Marta Kolářová 2009). As activist Darina has stated, "2002–2003, those were the golden years. . . . Other groups had much respect for us and wanted to work with us. People were joining and experiences were shared."

Still, the formation of an autonomous group devoted to anarchofeminism was a topic of much contention, and the AFS group was accused of dividing the movement. The topic of the unequal position of women was opposed and rejected by many conventional anarchists from the start. This phenomenon was not specific to anarchofeminism only but was reflective of a larger ongoing power struggle concerning which ideas and which groups would dominate the Czech anarchist movement. In this context, it was decided around 2003–4 to merge the individual groups into a single Federace anarchistických skupin (Federation of Anarchist Groups, FAS) with a single, united ideology.[10] Some AFS members disagreed with this decision and left AFS, joining other groups and contributing to *A-kontra*, which would become the most successful periodical of Czech anarchism in the 2000s. Others left the movement altogether. Overall, the struggle over whether the anarchist movement should or should not be dominated by a single umbrella organization was one of the main reasons behind the gradual decline of Czech anarchism, including the Anarchofeminist Group.

THE PERSONAL IS THE POLITICAL

One of the main principles of AFS was the feminist slogan "the Personal is the Political." According to AFS, topics of personal life, including domestic violence, sexual abuse, abortion, sexuality, and sexual violence overall, needed to be central in the anarchist movement. Untraditionally for anarchism, the group also embraced the theme of mental and emotional disorders, including depression, a highly personal issue but with a broad scope and impact in society as well as within the anarchist movement.

In its final years, AFS highlighted issues of sexual violence and consent. It was AFS who introduced the concept of explicit verbal sexual consent in the CR. This notion was criticized from many (including other feminist) points of view. AFS critiqued the stereotypical views of men's behavior in sexual relationships, which men are expected to initiate, while the group also focused attention on issues of public interference in intimate relationships. The AFS position on sexual violence was based on the principle that saying "no" should be sufficient to stop an unwanted sexual act. One of the critics of this position stated, "I am concerned about this assumption of violence automatically projected on all relationships. That doesn't seem right" (activist Radim). The issue of sexual consent became the main topic for AFS for a fairly long period of time. A special edition of *Přímá cesta* was devoted to this topic and many discussions were organized. The topic was also addressed in the lyrics of songs by groups sympathetic to AFS. All of this resulted in intensive discussions regarding sexual violence, not only among strangers but also among friends and partners, destroying another taboo including within the context of the anarchist movement. At the same time, the group was criticized by some for committing itself to a concept without adapting it to the Czech context. In the words of activist Martin: "It was a good impulse for new work, but somehow it went wrong. The slogan 'the personal is political' deteriorated into interference in people's lives. . . . The most intimate sphere was being politicized in the direction of social control. When people started criticizing my personal life I felt less free than in the mainstream bourgeois society."

THE SUCCESSES AND FAILURES OF CZECH ANARCHOFEMINISM

Some of the greatest successes of Czech anarchofeminism include an introduction of new topics, disruption of gender stereotypes, and leveling of the playing field inside anarchist and autonomous movements. Scholars vary in their assessment of the impact of Czech anarchofeminism. Marta Kolářová has argued that the rhetoric in the anarchist groups diverged from practice, where stereotypical thinking and unequal division of labor continued (2009). But participants generally agree that the topics of gender equality and struggle against sexism were successfully introduced into anti-authoritarian, squatters', and other anarchist movements. These topics were also embraced by the anarchist media, including magazines such as *A-kontra* and *Existence*. The AFS group's activities also principally influenced language use, leading to the rejection of the generic masculine in the anarchist press. Václav Tomek and Ondřej Slačálek have argued similarly that the anarchofeminist initiatives "contributed to a greater recognition of women's work in the anarchist movement and to the foregrounding of the issue of sex/gender discrimination in the agenda of anarchist groups" (Tomek and Slačálek 2006, 605). As activist Martina has stated it:

There have been many changes in representation; the image of the male fighter has practically disappeared, I think, the address is almost always correct. . . . It's probably also due to the fact that so many of active members today are women. This, I think, might be the biggest difference; it wasn't like this before. Also, we are discussing different topics today—more concrete and somehow softer, queer. In the past we discussed ideals and theory—like Bakunin, Kropotkin [laughter]. But what is clearly visible is that there are more girls involved today and that they are much more active. I would say that the path has been cleared for them and they might not even feel the need to explicitly call for feminism. Today, it's more about the superstructure.

An assessment of the impact of Czech anarchofeminism on mainstream society remains a more controversial matter. At its beginning, FS8B declared its interest in organizing various grassroots activities to specifically support women in crisis: "Problems need to be fixed today, we can't wait until 'after the revolution.' Grassroots projects, such as domestic violence shelters, or teaching victims of domestic violence how to actively protect themselves, could prevent many problems that affect women, while their realization would also contribute to involving people in active work and gaining sympathizers" ("Institutionalized Feminism vs. Anarchofeminism"). None of these ideas have been realized, however, nor were there significant efforts to realize them, although the group members did participate in Food Not Bombs activities.[11] And while the group organized a number of public lectures, it cannot be argued that these by themselves had a major impact on the broader Czech public. On the other hand, many former members of FS8B/AFS and the *Bloody Mary* collective were and continue to be involved in various ways with professional nonprofit groups, bringing their experiences and ideas from the anarchofeminist movement into these NGOs, and also into other spheres of life: "One cannot see a clearly visible impact. We organized workshops for the public, but how do you measure the effect of workshops? We don't live in an autonomous sphere; our lives permeate into other spheres. We lived it, and that has an impact on our surroundings" (activist Darina).

One of the notable changes FS8B/AFS managed to bring about is in the broader social view of March 8, no longer perceived negatively as a communist relic. This was partially achieved through a FS8B/AFS reconceptualization of the day in the public sphere. According to some activists, this affected established feminist organizations' approach to International Women's Day as well: "I think it also had an effect on academic and nonprofit feminists. They saw young feminists in the streets—celebrating the 8th of March of all the days. This was a completely different context, a completely different context" (activist Martin).

ANARCHOFEMINISM TODAY

A FS ended its activities in 2010, and *Bloody Mary* is no longer published. None of the above-discussed groups are active today, although its members do continue working in feminist or political spheres and some continue to further anarchofeminist principles and ideas by different means and in different contexts. None of the Czech anarchist groups in existence today continues in the tradition of A FS or *Bloody Mary*, even though some of them do highlight issues of gender inequality. But feminist topics are not taken up explicitly and intensely: "I am concerned that classical feminism/anarchofeminism might disappear completely. It seems as if in the fervor to deconstruct everything, the original idea gets lost and becomes difficult to pass on" (activist Martina).

A FS also introduced the topics of gays and lesbians into the Czech anarchist movement, and the *Bloody Mary* magazine further took up queer and transgender themes. A group of people around A FS and particularly *Bloody Mary* developed these themes further, organizing, for the first time in 2009 and later as part of Prague Pride, the cultural festival Gender Fuck Fest. In a way, we could view the hip-hop anarchist group Fakné, rooted in the gender fuck tradition, as an indirect successor of Czech anarchofeminism. Indeed, the queer movement operating within the larger Czech anti-authoritarian scene is sometimes considered to be indirectly continuing the anarchofeminist tradition. "Anarchofeminism still has much to say today," according to activist Darina. "It combines critiques of capitalism and of the heterosexual order. This interaction and combination is the attractive aspect that we do not find in the purely feminist tradition."

NOTES

1. See the website of FS8B: http://anarchofeminismus.ecn.cz/.
2. In October 2013, I conducted five interviews with three founders, one former member, and one sympathizer of FS8B/AFS. I myself am a cofounder and former member of AFS.
3. Dark Star Collective, ed., *Quiet Rumours: An Anarcha-Feminist Reader* (Edinburgh: AK Press/Dark Star), 2002, http://booksonline.website/book/624627.Quiet_Rumours.html.
4. This and all of the other interview quotations not sourced otherwise are from interviews I conducted with Czech activists in 2013. For more information see note 2.
5. http://fs8brezna.ecn.cz/files/anarchofeminismus.html.
6. http://anarchofeminismus.ecn.cz/files/25.listopad.html.
7. http://anarchofeminismus.ecn.cz/files/tiskantinato2.html.
8. http://anarchofeminismus.ecn.cz/files/prochoice02.html.

9. The pro-choice activists also faced some opposition from within the anarchist movement. See "Anarchofeministky, feministky nebo sufražetky?" [Anarchofeminists, Feminists or Suffragettes?], http://f58brezna.ecn.cz/files/rasputin.html.

10. This decision does not have a single interpretation and continues to be controversial. According to the FAS initiators, the goal was to unite and strengthen anarchist and autonomous movements, making their strategies more effective.

11. Food Not Bombs is an anti-authoritarian group that distributes food to the homeless and needy. The group cooks vegan and vegetarian food, usually using free products donated by supermarkets.

9 ASPECTS OF SEX AND GENDER IN ROMANY COMMUNITIES IN THE CZECH REPUBLIC

KAROLÍNA RYVOLOVÁ

WITH A CURRENTLY estimated population of (at least) 200,000, Roma constitute roughly 2 percent of the overall Czech population and are thus the largest ethnic minority living in the Czech Republic (CR).[1] Historically, both in the Czech lands and across Europe, Roma have long suffered economic discrimination and social exclusion, faced negative stereotypes and prejudices, and lived in poverty and frequently in inadequate and segregated housing. The CR in particular has been a target of international criticism for its harsh treatment of the Romany[2] population, and especially for its history of involuntary/forced sterilization of Romany women and the widespread practice of placing Romany children in "special schools" designed for children with learning disabilities.[3] Compared to *gadje* (non-Romany) women, Romany women living in the CR face many issues specific to their group, including their biased treatment by the majority population, severe unemployment, and traditional, in many respects quite limiting gender roles and practices within their community.[4]

Due to the relatively closed nature of Romany communities, there has been little feminist activity among Romany women in the CR, both prior to and post-1989. The few exceptions that I address in this chapter generally fall into two categories: political resistance, aimed at the misogynist and racially biased practices of the majority Czech population, and private resistance, turned inward and focusing on traditional gender relations behind the walls of Romany homes.

Despite its so-far marginal nature, a steady trickle of subtle but increasingly pronounced efforts at addressing issues of gender inequality have been under way, be it on the part of Romany women or Romany individuals from the LGBT spectrum. Recently, several prominent young Roma have come out, initiating a debate about one of the biggest taboos in the community and encouraging others to follow. Romany women have started taking action on issues such as forced sterilization and other examples of institutional abuse of power. And several Romany women writers have focused in their work on the specific experiences of Romany women within their community.

In this chapter, I discuss some aspects of gender roles and sexual relations in Czech Romany communities, using official data, results of my own participant observation research, as well as a consideration and interpretation of Romany oral and cultural tradition as textually embodied in Romany proverbs and fiction by Romany authors.[5] Increasing numbers of Romany women find writing to be a particularly suitable outlet for their gender-issues-related frustrations. Romany male writers, on the other hand, have tended, at least so far, to portray the conventional distribution of power among the Roma and the privileged male position in the community in mostly un-self-reflected and uncritical ways.

A NATION OR A SOCIAL GROUP?

Across Europe, the Roma, who represent Europe's largest ethnic minority group, estimated at roughly 8 to 10 million, share certain features of common identity, such as language and notions of ritual (im)purity, while also displaying a significant in-group differentiation, whether based on location, dialects of Romani (or the absence thereof), religion, or status. This heterogeneity has been cited by the European political establishment, and backed by some influential scholars (Okely 1983; Willems 1997; Jakoubek 2004), as the main reason behind the reluctance to recognize the Roma's claim to peoplehood. At best, Roma are viewed either as an ethnic group requiring the majority's assistance to integrate, or as a particularly challenging social group to grapple with. In either case, their future is viewed in terms of assimilation.

Gabriele Griffin and Rosi Braidotti, as well as Anikó Imre, have pointed out that whiteness is an important point of departure for post-communist countries in their struggles for clear-cut nationhood in a world that has moved past nation-states and toward greater European integration. "The myth of cultural homogeneity is crucial to the tale of European nationalism," they note (2002, 234). In the context of emphasized cultural (and ethnic) homogeneity, the Roma in Eastern Europe are perceived as an anachronism, and their only future is in merging with, and disappearing into, the majority populations. Their presence is perceived as a continuous disruption to the project of post-communist homogenous nation-states, which perhaps partly explains the resurgence of anti-Gypsyism after the fall of the Iron Curtain.

It is worth noting here that ever since the first Roma made their way from India via Persia, Armenia, the Byzantine Empire, and the Balkans into Europe in roughly the fifteenth century, they have been regarded as a threat and social nuisance, which it was advisable preferably to banish, and later in history to assimilate, but certainly not to tolerate or respect. Because of their traditionally itinerant lifestyle, distinct appearance and customs, unique language, and general reluctance to mingle with the societies they came into contact with, in Europe they have been regarded as the prime example of otherness.

The first systematic attempt to sedentarize Gypsies, as they became popularly known, in Central Europe, and to assimilate them forcefully into Austro-Hungarian society, occurred during the reign of Empress Maria Theresa in the latter half of the eighteenth century. Ever since then, new attempts to "do away with the Gypsy problem" have emerged periodically. Some of the milestones of Czechoslovak Roma's modern history include:

1927: A great Gypsy round-up was followed by the issuance of unique Gypsy identification cards.

1939–45: Based on the data collected during the round-up, the majority of the so-called Czech Roma were interned and subsequently disappeared in Nazi concentration camps, with only about six hundred returnees.

1958: Law No. 74 on compulsory sedentarization was passed by the Czechoslovak government, initiating a forty-year period of intense assimilation policy.

1965: A forced dispersal of communities with dense Romany population occurred.

1973: The first all-Czech Romany organization, the Gypsy-Roma Union, was dissolved by the communist authorities.

1993: A discriminatory Citizenship Act followed the dissolution of Czechoslovakia and the establishment of the Czech and Slovak Republics, which excluded a large percentage of Romany residents on Czech territory (but considered Slovak) from Czech citizenship.

The history of the Roma in the Czech lands has been one of persecution, bullying, and forced assimilation, accompanied by constant fear, which have all molded the Roma's generally cautious attitudes.

There are four dominant "sub-ethnic" groups of Roma in the CR, with the most numerous of them being the so-called Slovak Roma, whose predecessors in their majority came to the Czech part of Czechoslovakia in the wake of World War II. The idea behind the Slovak Roma's forced transfer was to populate the border regions of Czech Sudetenland, then semi-desolate following the deportation of the Sudeten Germans to Germany. The Roma were then employed as unskilled laborers in Czech industry.[6] The other three groups are Hungarian Roma, Vlax (Vlach) Roma, and the Sinti (or German Roma). The social structure of the Slovak Romany community partly overlaps with that of Hungarian Roma, and their respective dialects of Romani are mutually intelligible. Both the Vlax Romany and Sinti communities, on the other hand, have historically tended to be more socially conservative and intentionally isolated from their broader social context. To speak of the position of Vlax Romany women would require an insider, since, in general, the Vlax community tends to rigidly observe the traditional division of male and female realms, and a woman is still considered her husband's property with no voice of her own. "A Vlax woman's obligation is to run the household, raise children and obey her husband, and she always has to make ends meet, regardless of means," says Margita Lakatošová-Wagner, a rare example of a Vlax woman who speaks on Vlax women's issues outside her community (1994, 3).[7] Currently working for the Council of the Government of the CR for Romany Community Affairs, Lakatošová-Wagner's original decision to pursue higher education and a professional career was met with a lack of understanding on the part of her sisters and a feeling of loss by her mother, who said, "the *gadje* have stolen my daughter." Margita, on the other hand, maintains that an "educated Roma has a much stronger awareness of his or her identity," and that education reinforces an individual's desire to invest back in his or her community ("I Romové" 2007).

Slovak Roma (the focus of the rest of this article), as compared to Vlax Roma, are relatively more open to both external influences and outsider interest. The mass migration from the well-ordered social system of rural Slovakia to the individualized world of the industrialized CR following the end of World War II inaugurated a process of radical social change that has all but wiped out "the old ways," while at the same time also empowering some formerly disadvantaged segments of Romany society in unprecedented fashion.

THE TRADITIONAL WOMAN: *THE MAN WEARS THE HAT, THE WOMAN MERELY A SCARF / MURŠ HORDINEL STAD'I, DŽUVL'I ČA KHOSNO*

"Tradition" in common scholarly lexicons is defined as something "that is passed on, what has passed on naturally or what people are accustomed to" (Nünning 2008, 823)—a fairly loose definition to begin with. When used in

Czech academic papers as an attribute of the Roma, it frequently becomes an exceedingly versatile modifier that, depending on context, can stand for any one of a long list of adjectives, including "conservative," "rural," "true," "good old," "isolated," "primitive," or even "extinct." Writers often appear to presume that their readers share with them the same notion as to who "traditional Roma" are.

Without rejecting the term completely, I would like to see it used with better awareness of its limitations and with more specificity. Toward employing this term more concretely, when I use the term "traditional" in this chapter, I refer to what in Romani is called *romipen* (see below). The Slovak Roma in the CR often speak of *phure Roma* ("the old Roma"), whose practices and ways are viewed positively and worthy of following, as opposed to the current state of affairs in the Czech Romany urban community. What they refer to is an often-idealized image of their parents' and grandparents' homes in prewar rural Slovakia, where everybody knew their roles and place and everyone spoke Romani.[8] Removed both geographically and temporally, their predecessors are viewed as bearers of an unequivocally positive tradition, the sum of which is called *romipen* ("the-art-of-being-a-Rom"). With the Romany communities nowadays often plagued by a variety of negative, sometimes destructive social phenomena, such as gambling, drug abuse, prostitution, and usury, the practices of *phure Roma* represent a utopian world of the lost past. While some families preserved "the old ways" after their migration to the Czech lands and others did not, *romipen* continues to act as a complex set of unwritten rules regulating social contact among the Roma, and the majority relate to it, even if as to a distant ideal. Its importance and impact cannot be overemphasized.

Feminist and postcolonial thinkers such as Gayatri Chakravorty Spivak have noted that collective identities in general tend to display authoritarian and patriarchal tendencies, utilized to maintain and reproduce male power (1988). Roma are no exception, and *romipen* values and rules of behavior are strongly male-oriented, leaving women with a limited range of activities outside of child-bearing and the home. The world of the *phure Roma*, which many contemporary Roma tend to refer to as an ideal, is one in which emancipation and freedom of choice for women does not exist. The reliance on (patriarchal) tradition as one of the building blocks of their collective identity is reinforced by the centuries-long history of prejudice, discrimination, and exclusion the Roma have encountered in Europe, and the consequent cautious attitude of the Roma as a group (although not necessarily every individual) toward the majority society.

In the following section, I use Romany proverbs to illustrate some Romany traditions concerning gender roles and expectations. As folk wisdom repositories virtually frozen in time, proverbs can serve as a useful starting point to discuss traditional *romipen* ideals.

In traditional Romany families, children learn/ed by way of example. From early on they are expected to participate in decision-making, first as listeners but soon as contributors. Disciplining is rare and (unlike in many majority Czech families) so is smacking. As the old Roma used to say, *Smacks won't discipline your child; words will / Maribnaha na kereha čhavoreha ňič, ča laveha*, and *Why would I beat my child; I know I'm stronger than he is beforehand / Soske le čhavores te marav, th'avka džanav, hoj som zoraleder sar jov*. While children in general are loved and cherished, traditionally Romany girls are encouraged to quickly take on various gender-specific responsibilities. The eldest girl in the family, in particular, would substitute for the mother, who would often be either busy with the younger children or outside of the home procuring food for the family. Similar to many other patriarchal cultures, Romany girls have traditionally been considered less valuable than boys, as encapsulated in this proverb: *Ten boys are better than one girl / Feder deš murša sar jekh čhaj.* This is because boys represented power and security of the family in the face of adversity, and because sons traditionally learned their father's profession, thus multiplying the family's prestige and breadwinning capacity (Hübschmannová 1999, 46–48). In *phure Roma* families, the eldest brother also watched over his sisters' honor and innocence, because these were considered their greatest assets and their corruption would jeopardize the family's prestige.

Many of these traditions are reflected in contemporary Romany fiction. For instance, in Ilona Ferková's (born 1956) short story "Kal'i" (The Blackie), the father "really wanted a boy so that he could teach him how to play music, but God only granted them a girl." The father never loved the little girl, and he used to say, "You're a punishment on us, Kal'i! Why couldn't I have a boy?" (1996, 89).

Traditionally, Romany girls used to marry very young, so young in fact that they often still had not learned their expected roles as wife and mother. They had to finish their education by learning from their mothers-in-law. The young wife's status in the family of her new husband was initially very low, until she proved herself. According to Milena Hübschmannová, "The daughter-in-law could not talk back or complain; she had to put up with all the taunting, bullying, and ordering. . . . If she was a quick learner . . . she gradually gained a higher status in the family, her acceptance into its bosom became established and she was treated with increasing kindness, even respect" (1999, 55).[9] As the old Romany proverb illustrating this custom states, *On eating a tasteless meal, a good daughter-in-law will praise it for its tastinesss / Ajsi bori lačhi: chal bilondo, phenel londo.* Still, the so-called *amari bori* (our young bride) would often love her mother-in-law and would look up to her, according to Hübschmannová's research (1999, 55).

The importance of the new daughter-in-law's timidity and obedience, and the consequences for the family of this respectful behavior not being recognized and rewarded, is captured in Tera Fabiánová's 2006 short story "Eržika." Despite the heroine's genuine effort to please her mother-in-law, she continues to be mocked and mistreated. Furthermore, in consequence of her husband's frequent beatings and the hard work she does, she miscarries. As her acceptance into her husband's family does not follow the conventional path, and their marital life has not come to fruition, she is entitled to look for happiness outside of marriage. Leaving the community with her lover is a new beginning, but it is also a punishment. In this Romany settlement she has experienced social death: "The women who used to badmouth Bugo and sympathize with Eržika had all turned away from her. No one had stood up for her. People sided with Bugo. Him they felt sorry for, not her" (224).[10]

While the traditional marriage pattern model for Slovak Roma is patrilocal, that is, the young family moved in with, or near, the husband's parents, in rare situations, the new husband would move in with his wife's family. This may have happened if he was orphaned, if he was from an extremely impoverished background, or if he pursued a trade in which his father-in-law excelled. In these situations, the husband (*pristašis* or "tramp") enjoyed a similar position and treatment traditionally reserved for the young bride (Hübschmannová 1999, 32).

Romaňi daj—the Romany mother—is traditionally both an emblem as a giver of life and the axis of the family, as the following proverbs illustrate: *You can have a hundred wives, but only one mother / Šel piraňa—jekh dal,* and *When a father dies, the soul cries, when a mother does, it is the heart / Te merel dad, rovel o vod'i, te merel daj, rovel o jilo.* The mother's prominent role is, of course, in bearing children. Hübschmannová notes, "A woman without children was worthless. No one held it against her husband, if he left her" (1999, 45). And elsewhere she points out, "By nature, a woman between her first period and menopause is ritually unclean. This is why she has to compensate for her 'impurity' by all the other attributes of 'cleanliness,' which are at her disposal" (1999, 50). Such attributes are invariably linked to a clean/ritually pure household and perfectly performed chores. In *phure Roma* families, a woman during her period was not supposed to cook; before cooking, she had to wash her hands and cover her hair, lest her hair, considered an "unclean" item endowed with magic properties, fall into the food. On the other hand, a woman past menopause, sometimes referred to as *phuri daj* (old mother), was considered ritually clean and was revered as an experienced member of the community whose word weighed as much as a man's. In prewar Slovakia, a *phuri daj* was for example entitled to smoke publicly like a man and interrupt male conversations.

Today, with the continuing integration and assimilation of Roma into an urban environment, the traditional model of extended family is gradually being replaced with the nuclear kind. This, however, does not mean that the *phure Roma* categories (*bori, pristaš.s, phuri daj,* etc.) and values no longer apply. Rather, in many respects the traditional, gendered attitudes prevail, although they are becoming more subtle and covert.

NEW CIRCUMSTANCES, NEW CHALLENGES

In her article "Ženská romská próza jako zápas o sebevyjádření" (Romany Women's Writing as a Struggle for Self-Expression, 2010), Alena Scheinostová offers the following analysis of contemporary Romany writing: One group of authors draw directly on folklore, perpetuating the spoken word and its function as entertainment and instruction. They relate to the world of the old Roma in its idealized form, they declare their intention to capture and preserve its values, and their protagonists act on the repertoire of stock characters, rather than on individual will (see also Ryvolová 2005, 32). The other group, most of whom, significantly, are women, broach subjects formerly deemed improper (e.g., having to do with the female sphere of life and the woman's body) or look for answers and solutions to new situations, which *romipen* as a manual for everyday life does not cover.

A representative of *phure Roma* and a proponent of *romipen*, the short story writer Andrej G.ňa (born 1936) could be viewed as an example of the first trend. Frequently representing gender roles in the traditional prewar Romany community, Giňa's narratives often end up uncritically supporting traditional patriarchal structures. For instance, in his short story "Trin jandre" (Three Eggs), a wife comes to borrow eggs from her older friend. She mentions her husband has not returned from the Saturday dance and that he must be with his mistress. While clearly unhappy about his infidelity, she ultimately seems to accept the situation as she explains that she needs the eggs because her husband likes fried eggs when he returns from one of his flings. The two women discuss male womanizing, with the older one sharing that she even used to iron her husband's shirts when he went to see his lovers. Her husband is sitting within earshot, reading his paper. To his amazement, she declares, "If he tried any such nonsense today, I'd poison him" (2013, 192). The moral of Giňa's story seems to be that while the *phure Roma* might be a patriarchal community, with the husband's (but not the wife's) unfaithfulness not being considered a serious breach of marital life, a certain balance of power and authority emerges related to age. A young wife with children is powerless in the face of her husband's infidelity as she needs his support, but an aging man who has lost his virility and seeks happiness in the bosom of his family is dependent on his wife's care and can find himself at her mercy.

More interesting for the purposes of this essay is fiction by Erika Oláhová, a representative of Scheinostová's second trend in Romany writing. Oláhová's collections *Nechci se vrátit mezi mrtvé* (I Do Not Want to Go Back among the Dead, 2004) and *Matné zrcadlo* (The Opaque Mirror, 2007) give vent to the plight of the narrator/author as an abused woman. It is an open secret that Oláhová's own husband has often interfered with her public appearances at various Romany writing events to which she is invited, which become entirely impossible when he is away on business. Scheinostová, who discusses Oláhová's fiction in her essay, notes how the motif of domestic violence is at first acted out against a backdrop of traditional values in the world of *phure Roma* to be later replaced by much more contemporary circumstances, where the woman acquires her voice perhaps less dramatically but all the more realistically.

In Oláhová's "Beznaděj" (Despair; 2004, 5–10), the despairing wife murders her abusive husband but cannot live with the crime she has committed, not only against him but also against her designated role as a woman. The fear of her husband coming back to avenge himself in the form of a *mulo* (an evil ghost) eventually drives her insane. In a later story, "Matné zrcadlo" (The Opaque Mirror; 2007, 43–45), the scene has changed from an unspecified distant past to the modern city. The heroine—small, aging, ordinary, and therefore real—is keeping a painful soliloquy while fleeing from her drunken husband to various parts of the house. Eventually she makes a decision "to stop taking beatings, like a man, and to live!" (45). While Scheinostová, following Spivak's essay "Can the Subaltern Speak," reads Oláhová's abused Romany women characters as ultimately mute and in a position that makes it impossible for them to speak in a way that would be heard, she also remarks that Oláhová's character's seemingly trivial decision "to stop taking beatings . . . and to live" is a sign of great courage, "a leap into the great unknown" (2010, 260).

Traditionally in the Romany community, only extreme cases of domestic violence would be viewed as deserving notice and action, with women being encouraged not to take occasional beatings seriously, as illustrated by proverbs such as *Every woman has felt her husband's hand / Dojekh romňi prindžarel le romeskeri vast. Phure Roma* living in prewar Slovakia had specific mechanisms for condemning and dealing with extreme cases of domestic violence. Usually, a locally recognized authority—a storyteller or a singer—would speak or sing of the case publicly and in that way bring ritual shame on the husband. With these traditional ways passing in the increasingly atomized social environment of the CR, Romany women have begun to take action and speak up for themselves, similar to women in the majority population.

Another example of the increasing tendency of Romany women to challenge various abuses and thereby transgress the traditional role of Romany women is the well-known case of Elena Gorolová, who, while giving birth to her second son in 1990, aged twenty-one, was asked to sign documents allowing the medical staff to perform sterilization. As she was already in labor and in great pain, she did not read the documents or understand what her (supposedly) informed consent would result in. On finding out that she would never have the girl she and her husband longed for, she succumbed to depression. Her recovery process started many years later, in 2004, on meeting other Romany women in the same situation in a series of meetings organized jointly by the Ostrava organization Life Together, the League of Human Rights, and the European Roma Rights Center. Gorolová and other sterilization victims started to meet regularly to discuss their private issues but also to seek compensation and public acknowledgment of what had been done to them.[11] In 2007, Gorolová and Helena Baloghová made an appearance at the European Court of Human Rights in Strasbourg as representatives of sterilized Romany women from the CR. Following criticism of these practices from the Human Rights Court, in 2009 the Czech government officially expressed its regret.[12] As more and more cases continue to surface, Elena Gorolová continues to fight. Her story and the stories of others from her group have been portrayed in *Trial of a Child Denied*, a documentary film by Michelle Coomber (2008).[13]

The practice of forced sterilization, a continuation of the official Czechoslovak socialist state policy of forced assimilation, criticized in Charter 77's document no. 23 from December 1978, was amended in 1988 by the Czechoslovak Ministry of Health and Welfare's decree, which, in articles nos. 31 and

35, offered as an incentive considerable financial compensation to women who would undergo sterilization. The compensation was up to 10,000 Czechoslovak crowns in the Czech part of the country, and up to 25,000 in the Slovak part, with the latter sum roughly equaling an average year's salary at the time. Although the decree did not specify the ethnic or national status of the target persons, it was clearly aimed at Romany women. As Hübschmannová has commented, "the barbarian campaigns, which manipulated women to get sterilized by offering them financial 'incentives', broke up many a marriage" (1999, 45).

Ilona Ferková relates one such story in "Mosard'a peske o dživipen anglo love" (She Ruined Her Life over Money, 2006). A spendthrift wife who is afraid of her husband's anger for spending too much money travels to Slovakia to get sterilized in return for 25,000 crowns. Not only does the husband beat her up on finding out but the authorities eventually only send 8,000 crowns, which was indeed common practice (see Andrš and Pellar 1990).

Even after 1989, cases have continued to surface of medical staff both in Czech and Slovak maternity wards performing sterilizations on Romany women, now even without direct orders or financial incentives for either the women or themselves. Gorolová has exposed a case of an involuntary sterilization of a Romany woman from Frýdek-Místek from as recently as 2007. This continued practice of eugenics, which goes to show how deeply the ideas of Romany inferiority are internalized among the Czech public, including the Czech educated classes, is now finally being stopped thanks to the bravery of women like Gorolová. To go public with a story so deeply personal requires an enormous amount of courage, not only because among the more traditionally minded Roma the revelation of the woman's sterility shames the husband but because public speaking may also be considered a transgression against the strict *romipen* rules of woman's modesty.

THREEFOLD DISCRIMINATION

Until recently, the general assumption has been that there are no gay people of Romany origin. Hübschmannová offers no insight on the status of gay rights among the Roma, mirroring the groups' own prevailing attitude of silence on these issues. Victor Vishnevsky, a Brazil-based Romany writer of Russian origin, sums up the general sentiment: "We Gypsies get married very early . . . which is why I think we have very few homosexuals among our race. Our elders practically force us to go out and have sex after our fifteenth birthday . . .

to avoid having gay tendencies. I met a lot of Gypsies around the world of all tribes, and I heard of only few cases" (2006, 16).

In the strongly patriarchal and heteronormative Romany community, those of same-sex sexual orientation typically experience harsh treatment on coming out. Noted Romany gay-rights advocates Michal Miko and David Tišer have shared firsthand experiences about not being served food or drink in other people's homes, or finding that their refreshment would be served on an extra set of dishes, which would be set aside for only their use or thrown out straight after. As they are deemed ritually unclean, anything they touch must be discarded. As is common in many traditional heteronormative cultures, the popular belief among traditional Roma is that homosexuals are ill, and an ideal remedy is a swift marriage to a member of the opposite sex. Such practices force Roma from the LGBT spectrum into a double life, performing their prescribed gender and sexual roles for the community while seeking sexual satisfaction outside of wedlock.

Tišer maintains that Roma from the LGBT spectrum face triple discrimination: as Roma, as people with different sexual orientations, and as differently sexually oriented members of the Romany community. *Roma Boys—Příběh lásky* (Roma Boys—The Love Story), a student film directed by Rozálie Kohoutová in 2009 for which Tišer wrote the screenplay, was a groundbreaking project mainstreaming gay rights among the Roma in the CR for the first time.[14] The film tells Tišer's own story of falling in love with a young man from the highly conservative Vlax sub-group. On coming out, the young man was beaten by his brothers and forced into an arranged marriage. The consequence of his decision to flee the marriage and move to the capital with his boyfriend implies a (possibly lifelong) excommunication. To his Vlax family, he is as good as dead, and his mother only communicates with him via illicit phone calls outside of the male family members' hearing. An analogous story is told by the English Traveller Mikey Walsh in his coming-out narrative *Gypsy Boy* (2010), in which he relates the violence with which his sexual orientation was met by his father.

Romany lesbians face similar ostracism. Helena Krobotová, a female Romany truck-driver currently living in Canada, explained in an interview for the high-profile Czech weekly *Respekt*: "The Roma must not find out, otherwise it would bring shame on the whole extended family. The Roma hide their homosexuality and they are ashamed of it. A Romany woman only deserves respect when she is a mother of children" (2010, 41). Krobotová was placed in care as an infant and adopted by a non-Romany family. She thus represents what the Roma refer to as a "coconut"—dark on the outside, white on the inside. Her decision to move to North America with her Czech registered partner took care, according to her, of all three sources of discrimination she would be facing in the CR. In multicultural Canada she is a member of an invisible minority, her lesbian orientation is accepted, and she and her partner do not socialize with other Roma, making the fear of being shunned by Roma superfluous.

SUBJECT TO SOCIAL CHANGE

In this chapter, I have attempted to offer at least a partial window into some sex and gender issues in the communities of Slovak Roma in the CR. Fully aware that my access to the everyday life and understanding of Romany families is limited, I have relied on my own participant observation, on ethnographic research conducted by experts, and on representations of Romany life in fiction by Romany writers. I suggest that the division of roles and realms between the sexes among the Slovak Roma largely stems from prewar arrangements as coded and perpetuated by *romipen*, the "art-of-being-a-Roma." Nevertheless, the head-on collision with urban reality following the postwar migration from Slovakia has resulted in the atomization of the Roma as a group and in social change. Romany women speaking up concerning their traditional roles within their community and their well-being within the larger, racially biased Czech community, as well as Roma from the LGBT spectrum speaking out about their experiences, represent the beginning of a process that will clearly not stop there.

NOTES

1. Apart from the census, there exists no official tool to firmly establish what percentage of the Czech population identifies as Roma. The results of the censuses from 1991, 2001, and 2011, respectively, show a diminishing willingness among the Czech Roma to disclose their ethnic identity, related to their deteriorating social and economic status in Czech society. In the 1990s, the number of Czech Roma was officially estimated at 250,000–300,000, but in recent years more serious estimates based on demographic analysis point to a smaller number, roughly 200,000.

2. Throughout this article, I differentiate between "Romany" as an adjective meaning "pertaining to Roma," and "Romani" as a noun, meaning the language of the Roma.

3. The 2007 ruling of the European Court of Human Rights confirmed that Romany children in the CR had suffered damages due to this practice (cited in Koldinská 2009, 263). While the Czech government has responded to international criticism (and the ruling) by introducing pedagogical assistants for Romany children in primary schools, according to the latest (2012) governmental Report on the State of the Romany Minority, the situation has not significantly improved.

4. Koldinská points out that while the Czech majority women's unemployment rate in 2009 was only 4.5%, for Romany women living in the CR it was 45% (2009, 264).

5. I graduated from the Romany Studies department at the Faculty of Arts of Charles University in 2002, when Milena Hübschmannová, the founder of the department, was still the head of, and the main driving force behind, Romany Studies in the CR. While not a Roma myself, I have a good linguistic background in the Eastern-Slovak dialect of Romani and enjoy what I would call a "privileged access to the Roma" based on personal friendships and years of experience, which is naturally never completely devoid of outsider or colonial connotations. My main interest lies with Romany writing and the emerging Romany literature, and my recently completed dissertation (Ryvolová 2014) compares four life stories penned by Roma from different parts of the world in English, Czech, and Romani.

6. Sudetenland, or *Sudety* in Czech, was a largely German-speaking part of Czechoslovakia, mostly along the Czech-German border. In 1938, Sudetenland was annexed by the German Third Reich forces, following the Munich Agreement signed by Germany, Great Britain, Italy, and France in an attempt to appease Germany and prevent World War II. This act led to Germany's taking over the remaining part of the Czech Republic and turning it into its protectorate (while Slovakia became Germany's satellite state). After the war, the German population of Sudetenland, estimated at about 3 million people, was deported to Germany.

7. All translations from Czech and Romani are mine.

8. On the mutual complementarity of Slovak peasant society and "their" sedentarized Roma, see, e.g., Hübschmannová 1995, 28–29, and Hübschmannová 2005, 87–96.

9. Milena Hübschmannová (1933–2005) was a pivotal figure of Romany Studies in Czechoslovakia/Czech Republic, a pioneer who started her work among the Roma in the late 1950s as a student of Indology. Although she has been criticized for unproblematically promoting the Romany group's identity as that of an extraterritorial nation, the scope of her work and the degree of her influence over Romany Studies in the CR have been tremendous.

10. I am indebted to Alena Scheinostová's "Romany Women's Writing as a Struggle for Self-Expression" (2010) for pointing me in the direction of this text. Although our respective interpretations of the story partly overlap, I use it to a slightly different end.

11. For more information on forced sterilization of Romany women in Central and Eastern Europe, see, e.g., *Body and Soul* 2003; *Romani Women's Rights Movement* 2006, 19–37; and *Ambulance Not on the Way* 2006, 41–47.

12. The official apology has not been followed by financial compensation from the Czech government. The government has claimed that the cases are expired, although in a similar case of a Slovak Romany woman involuntarily sterilized at the age of twenty in the year 2000, the European Human Rights Court ordered Slovakia to pay her 43,000 euros in compensation.

13. Mortal Coil Media, 25 minutes.

14. *Roma Boys—Příběh lásky* [Roma Boys—The Love Story], directed by Rozálie Kohoutová, 2009, The Film and TV School of the Academy of Performing Arts, Prague, www.fdb.cz/film/roma-boys-pribeh-lasky/65579.

10 THE LIVES OF VIETNAMESE WOMEN IN THE CZECH REPUBLIC

MÁRIA STRAŠÁKOVÁ

THE HISTORICAL ROOTS of the Vietnamese community in the Czech Republic (CR) can be traced back to the 1950s, when then Czechoslovakia and the Democratic Republic of Vietnam forged strong ties within the Eastern bloc. Since that time thousands of Vietnamese have arrived in the country for study and work, laying the foundations of the current Vietnamese community, presently the third largest labor diaspora in the CR (after Slovakians and Ukrainians). Over time, three distinct social groups or classes have developed within that community, following three different migration waves of Vietnamese to Czechoslovakia/Czech Republic. Members of each wave have developed different lifestyles and are coping with divergent issues and varied modes of integration.

According to the 2013 Statistical Yearbook for the Czech Republic, there were roughly 57,000 Vietnamese citizens living in the CR in 2012, although other estimates claim that there could be over 100,000 Vietnamese present in the country.[1] While women constitute 43 percent of the community (Pechová 2007, 17), so far no study has focused specifically on their issues. The objective of this chapter is to provide an overview of the most pressing issues Vietnamese women face while endeavoring to integrate into Czech society. The primary focus here attends to four measures considered essential for successful immigrant integration by the Czech Ministry of Interior: knowledge of the Czech language, economic self-sufficiency, knowledge of the host society, and mutually beneficial relationships between immigrants and the majority. The Czech integration policy is calculated so as to avoid the creation of closed immigrant communities and their subsequent social isolation and exclusion. As far as the Vietnamese community in the CR is concerned, this goal has been only partially achieved, as the community is (still) perceived as closed and isolated (Kocourek 2007, 55).

Until the mid-1970s, migration studies as such ignored women, who were treated as more or less passive followers of men and presumed to be their dependents. The specificity of their lives and experiences was ignored and underresearched. This situation started to change with Mirjana Morokvasic's 1984 special issue of *International Migration Review* in which she demonstrated the male bias that still dominated both academic literature and the policymaking processes (discussed in Kofman 1999, 269–70). A gender perspective in the integration or incorporation process was similarly neglected for a long time (Itzigsohn and Giorguli-Saucedo 2005, 895; Tastsoglou and Preston 2005, 47). While there is not a perfect consensus on how to define integration on the intrastate or international level, recent leading perspectives emphasize that it is a two-way process of mutual adaptation between the host society and immigrants.[2] Furthermore, research has shown that men and women experience not only migration but also incorporation into the host society differently. Class and race impact the integration processes, generally pointing to more challenging circumstances for women of color (Tastsoglou and Preston 2005, 47).

Given the fact that so far there has been essentially no published research focusing solely on the integration of Vietnamese women in the CR, the present chapter is based on an analysis of selected surveys that have been conducted within the Vietnamese community as a whole. Particularly worth mentioning are studies conducted by the ethnologist Stanislav Brouček, the ethnologist Šárka Martínková, and Eva Pechová and Michal Krebs, who have carried out research on trafficked Vietnamese women in cooperation with the NGO La Strada. Furthermore, I find useful the results of research conducted by Krebs and his collective entitled *Stop Labour Exploitation—A Closer Look—Analysis of the Agency Employment of the Vietnamese in the Czech Republic* (2009), the objective of which is to shed light on labor recruitment and labor export from Vietnam, the role of intermediary agencies in hiring people, strategies of finding work, labor conditions, and wages, as well as exploitation faced by the Vietnamese during the 2008 economic recession in the CR. While focusing on the community as a whole, some of these surveys directly or indirectly touch on the experiences of Vietnamese women.

I assess the information and data from these surveys both against the existing relevant literature on the topic and my long-term experience of contact with the Vietnamese community.[3] This information is further augmented by my own small-scale field research, which I carried out with eight Vietnamese women living in the CR in the fall of 2013.[4] Since readers are not likely to have an emic understanding of the experience of Vietnamese women in integrating into Czech society, I have employed an interpretive, narrative approach with my research, hoping to provide the reader with a deeper understanding of Vietnamese women's lives within the host society.

From September to November 2013, I conducted a series of semi-structured narrative interviews at a venue and time of the respondents' choosing, with most of the interviews lasting between forty-five and ninety minutes. I found respondents for my research on the basis of a snowball technique. While the number of interview subjects selected in this manner precludes claims about them being widely representative of Vietnamese women in the CR, they do nonetheless provide useful insights into Vietnamese women's lives and interactions with the host society. It is my hope that my small-scale study will inspire further follow-up research on a larger scale.

SETTING THE CONTEXT: MIGRATION WAVES OF VIETNAMESE IMMIGRANTS AND THE STRUCTURE OF THE COMMUNITY

The first official contact between the two states can be traced back to 1950, when the Czechoslovak Socialist Republic (CSSR) officially acknowledged the Democratic Republic of Vietnam (DRV) and forged strong bilateral relations and mutually beneficial cooperation in many spheres (Kocourek 2007, 47). The collaboration between these two distant and culturally very different countries, which until then had little in common, was motivated by several factors. The CSSR and the DRV were both part of the socialist Eastern bloc, and the cooperation opened new markets for each. The DRV, which at the time was embroiled in a war against the French colonial occupation (the First Indochina War, 1946–54), was in a critical economic and social situation, and welcomed the assistance offered by Czechoslovakia. And Czechoslovakia on its part welcomed the cooperation and offer of Vietnamese guest workers, as it was in dire need of a larger workforce, especially in the Sudeten regions depopulated by the expulsion of its German residents after the end of World War II. Vietnamese workers were meant to help satisfy this demand. After 1950 a series of treaties were signed enabling Vietnamese people to travel to Czechoslovakia and work in engineering and light industry or study technical and economic fields, Czech language and literature, as well as marionette theater at Czech universities (Kocourek 2007, 47).

Socialist Czechoslovakia was not the only country in the Soviet bloc that forged these kinds of bilateral relationships with Vietnam. Other Soviet bloc countries, including Poland and the German Democratic Republic, developed similar student and worker exchange arrangements with the DRV. For instance, between 1970 and 1989, four thousand Vietnamese students and doctoral fellows (especially in technical sciences) came to Poland (Szulecka 2012, 169). In the case of Germany, both the Federal Republic of Germany (West Germany) and the German Democratic Republic (GDR, East Germany) set up special immigration/exchange programs for the Vietnamese, although these differed along Cold War lines. Similar to Czechoslovakia, East Germany's bilateral student and workers exchange programs with the DRV dated back to the 1950s. On the other hand, West Germany's programs for Vietnamese immigrants took place a bit later, going back to the late 1970s, when the Second Indochina War, fought between North Vietnam (supported by the Soviet Union) and South Vietnam (supported by the United States), ended with the fall of Saigon in 1975 and formerly Western-allied refugees were fleeing South Vietnam. West Germany accepted many of these refugees, eventually granting permanent residency to 38,000 people from South Vietnam, Cambodia, and Laos by 1984. Other refugees from South Vietnam migrated to the United States, France, Canada, and Australia (Huwelmeier 2008, 135).

Vietnamese students and exchange workers coming to Czechoslovakia prior to 1989 were usually eighteen to forty years old, of various levels of education, single or married, but without their families. Most of them were men (Brouček 2003, 15). They were located all over Czechoslovakia, but mostly in Prague, as the crucial industry fields tended to be concentrated around the capital (Martínková 2011, 173). These immigrants originated from the "elites" of their culture and were carefully selected by the Vietnamese authorities. Before their arrival they were all required to take Czech or Slovak language courses and lectures on Czechoslovak culture and society, and thus were relatively well informed about the living conditions and customs in the country. They continued in intensive language courses after their arrival and—with the help of the existing immigration support mechanisms—were quick to orient themselves in the Czechoslovak environment. In addition, the migrants were under strict surveillance from the Vietnamese embassy or assigned supervisors, who monitored their behavior and performance, and who could send them home for any transgression or for conduct perceived as "smearing" the good reputation of Vietnam, including poor study results or low working morale. All factors that might distract their attention from study or work were to be eliminated. For instance, until 1982, single Vietnamese working or studying in Czechoslovakia were forbidden (by Vietnamese officials) from pursuing sexual relationships with anyone during their stay. After 1982, sexual relations were tolerated on the condition that the woman did not get pregnant. In general, Vietnamese women's relationships with Czech men were not accepted well either by the Vietnamese community or Czech society. If the workers/students were married, they were allowed to visit their families in Vietnam every two years (Kocourek 2007, 48). Finally, prior to 1989, all of the Vietnamese were required to return home after their residency or study/work permits ended. This was the case in the GDR and Poland as well. In East Germany, Vietnamese workers were strongly discouraged from developing any kind of relationship with the local population, and their incorporation into the host society was not expected. Their stay in the GDR was viewed in terms of training, to last up to five years, and after that time they were expected to return to their home country (Huwelmeier 2008, 133–34).

The year 1989 represents a salient turning point in the bilateral ties between Vietnam and Czechoslovakia and a transformation of Vietnamese migration into the country. After the Velvet Revolution, in a rather clumsy attempt to break away from the communist past, Czechoslovak politicians voided all political and economic contracts with their communist counterparts around the world, including Vietnam. As a result, the Czechoslovak authorities started sending Vietnamese immigrants back to Vietnam. Nonetheless, many Vietnamese were able to capitalize on the legislative chaos that followed the rather unruly political, economic, and immigration reforms of the new system, and found a way to stay in the country. Most of them opted for getting business licenses, on the basis of which they could then obtain permanent residence permits (Martínková 2006, 90). A similar situation unfolded in post-1989 reunited Germany and in Poland. After the Berlin Wall came down, about two thirds of the Vietnamese contract workers were initially sent home from (now former) East Germany. However, many of them managed to return in the course of the 1990s, either legally or illegally, using their former networks and ties (Huwelmeier 2008, 134). In Poland after 1989, many of the former Vietnamese students managed to stay in the country and opened businesses, especially in services and catering (Szulecka 2012, 168).

The Vietnamese immigrants who came to Czechoslovakia prior to 1989 and who managed to stay in the country after the Velvet Revolution have laid the foundations of the current Vietnamese community in the CR. This community eventually split into three separate strata that all display different lifestyles and modes/levels of integration. A similar stratification has been observed among the Vietnamese in Poland as well (Szulecka 2012, 170). In Germany, the situation of social stratification among the Vietnamese is further complicated by the fact that the former contract workers who originally came to the GDR from socialist North Vietnam have little in common with the refugees who arrived in West Germany from South Vietnam (Huwelmeier 2008, 135). Furthermore, most of the Vietnamese in the western part of Germany have been granted citizenship and become economically well integrated, while the legal situation of many former East German Vietnamese contract workers, asylum seekers, and undocumented migrants is unclear and their situation precarious (135).

The highest social stratum of the Vietnamese community in the present-day CR is formed by the so-called first settlers—the immigrants who came to Czechoslovakia prior to 1989 (Brouček 2003, 22). These men and women find themselves at the top of the community both socially and economically, due to the fact that they studied or worked in Czechoslovakia prior to 1989 and thus speak Czech, are acquainted with Czech culture, and can navigate the Czech milieu with ease. After 1989 they were able to capitalize on their knowledge of the country and have become the leaders and elite of the Vietnamese community.

The Vietnamese who arrived in the country just after 1989 and in the decade following, whether from Vietnam or from other countries of the crumbling Eastern European bloc, form the middle rank or stratum of the community. This group's arrival was motivated primarily by economic reasons: "The Vietnamese do not intend to settle here, those who arrived here in their adult age plan to earn money or to support their children during their schooling and then want to fly back and die in Vietnam; as a person from our community once said: 'No Vietnamese has come to die in the Czech Republic'" (quoted in Krebs and Pechová 2009, 10).

Family reunification was the second most common reason for Vietnamese migration to the CR post-1989. The scenario where a male migrant would arrive first, set up a business, and create favorable conditions for his wife and children, who would then join him, was frequent. Furthermore, Vietnamese have continued to come to the CR for study, as the Czech government continues to offer scholarships to Vietnamese students. Yet another reason for migration post-1989 and still today is to "tuck away" problematic youth, who in Vietnam find "wrong" partners, experiment with drugs, or otherwise find themselves marginalized. Their parents might send them to relatives living in the CR in order to extract them from the problematic environment. Another common reason for choosing the CR is illustrated through the following quotation: "There are many Vietnamese here, because Czechs are nice and laws are stupid." In this sentence and context, "nice," unfortunately, appears to mean corrupt (Pechová 2007, 23). Shortage of accurate and reliable information is also perceived as a reason why the Vietnamese continue to migrate to the CR, as the country is still represented and viewed by many as a "dream land" where easy money can be made (Krebs et al. 2009). Finally, it should be noted that no Vietnamese women come to the CR as (mail-order) brides or in search of Czech marriage partners. Rather, Vietnamese men in the CR count on finding a bride in Vietnam.

The most recent migration wave of Vietnamese to the CR, also known as the "fresh wave," took place after 2000. Their arrival was stimulated by high demand on the part of Czech export-oriented factories for cheap yet skilled labor. Between 2006 and 2008, more than twenty thousand Vietnamese arrived to fill vacant places in Czech industry. Most of these men and women were recruited in the poorest provinces of northern and central Vietnam, often via unofficial intermediary agencies, and they had little knowledge of the reality awaiting them in Europe. They did not undergo language or any other training, and arrived in the country uninformed and unprepared. According to Michal Krebs, many of them did not even know the name of the intermediary agency that "secured" their transport to and work in the CR. The cost of these placement services ranged between $7,000–15,000, including visa, air ticket, registration at the Czech Financial Bureau, and a job for the client. In order to be able to pay for these services, most of these immigrants were left with no option other than to sell their land and their houses and indebt the whole family (Krebs et al. 2009, 50). However, when the economic crisis hit the Czech economy in the fall of 2008, most of the foreign guest workers from Asia were made redundant. The substantial number of unemployed Vietnamese immigrants subsequently destabilized the Vietnamese community and resulted in a series of negative consequences. This group of Vietnamese is the least integrated into Czech society, and they are particularly vulnerable to exploitation and abuse.

VIETNAMESE WOMEN AND THE KNOWLEDGE OF CZECH LANGUAGE

Mastering the host society's language is generally considered one of the most important elements in the integration of immigrants, as language proficiency plays a key role in communication with the local authorities, work, and increasingly with the immigrant's children (the 1.5 and 2nd generations) (Janská, Průšvicová, and Čermák 2011, 482).[5] As noted above, proficiency in Czech varies correlatively to the migration waves of Vietnamese, and women from the stratum of "first settlers" generally tend to speak better Czech than their compatriots who have migrated to the country more recently. Most post-1989 immigrants have much lower Czech language proficiency, with many only mastering the most useful phrases needed for communication with Czech customers. In my interviews, this was a common theme. For example, Hoa (age 24; 1.5 generation) noted, "[My parents] make themselves understood only concerning their basic needs in the shop, they just know common phrases to communicate with the customer." Nguyet (age 22; 1.5 generation) stated, "My parents know certain basics for their profession, like colors, sizes. . . . They can talk about the weather, how old they are, just the basics." Lan (age 26; 1.5 generation) commented on her mother's knowledge of Czech. "They can speak [Czech], my dad without any problems, but my mom has more problems, i.e., she understands everything, but she lacks the vocabulary. But when she is in the shop, she speaks with the elderly ladies about soap-operas, i.e., my mom knows all those phrases like 'I love you,' 'hug me,' 'I hate you.'"

Perhaps not surprisingly, the language proficiency of the last wave of Vietnamese workers who arrived in the country after 2008 is the lowest in the community (Krebs et al. 2009, 13). The rather low knowledge of Czech among the first generation of Vietnamese women also stems from the fact that it is possible to live and work in the country without knowing the local language, as the Vietnamese have developed an effective system of intermediary (*dich vu*) services, provided by men and women from the wave of first settlers. Should a Vietnamese need to go to the foreign police to prolong their stay, rent an apartment, see a doctor, or attend a parent-teacher meeting, they can simply call *dich vu* services and pay to have all arranged for them. While these services constitute substantial "social capital" and a safety net for newly arrived immigrants, they also hinder new immigrants' successful integration into Czech society, as the recent arrivals tend to rely completely on these services. As a result, the more recent immigrants have become dependent on the group of first settlers, who not only convince them of their indispensability but also often take advantage of their clients' ignorance of the Czech environment (Pechová 2007, 24; Rulíková 2012, 262). As Šárka Martínková points out, first-generation Vietnamese women in the CR spend most of their time running their businesses or taking care of their families. They have little time to learn Czech and are more vulnerable to both social isolation and exploitation (Martínková et al. 2010, 27).

Unlike the first-generation women, the one-and-a-half and second generation of Vietnamese (born in the CR) have mastered Czech, and many perceive it even as their main language. This phenomenon is also partially the result of the fact that Vietnamese women often hire Czech "grannies" and "aunties" (retired elderly ladies, young students, or Czech mothers on maternity leave) to look after their children so that they can fully concentrate on their business endeavors. Some children even live in the families of their babysitters; in extreme cases, they might spend weekdays in Czech families and only on weekends meet their parents. While this arrangement might have seemed advantageous at first, it often results in a culture gap between Vietnamese parents and their children, who are brought up in the Czech (Western) way, speak better Czech than Vietnamese, and are imbued with Western values (Martínková 2010, 36–37). The subsequent culture gap is further widened by the fact that Vietnamese family members rarely spend time together. Their contacts have become limited to seeing each other in the evening after work, or possibly on Sundays, providing the parents do not have to finish something at their shops (Martínková 2011, 180).

The second-generation children have also started functioning as interpreters when contact with the majority is necessary. They might run errands or communicate with the authorities and police, teachers, and so on (Janská, Průšvicová, and Čermák 2011, 482). However, having children and the need to communicate with them across linguistic contexts also encourages the integration of Vietnamese in the CR. Children are one of the reasons why Vietnamese parents tend to postpone their return to Vietnam, as they perceive education in Czech public schools as an important asset for their children. Their school-age children and the need to communicate with their teachers or friends often motivate especially Vietnamese women to take a greater interest in learning the Czech language.

WORK AND ECONOMIC INTEGRATION OF VIETNAMESE WOMEN IN THE CZECH REPUBLIC

Given the fact that the main reason for Vietnamese migration to the CR is economic, most Vietnamese women engage in a range of economic activities that vary according to the period of their arrival. Literature on gender and migration often highlights that the status of immigrant women vis-à-vis their male counterparts improves when they migrate to a new country due to their increased access to employment and resources in the country of destination as compared to the country of origin (Itzigsohn and Giorguli-Saucedo 2002, 897). This, however, does not necessarily apply to Vietnamese women, as even in Vietnamese traditional society, women were always economically active, whether in agriculture or trade. Given the Confucian ethic's stress on education and subsequent civil service, it was not desirable for Vietnamese men to engage in trade, perceived as a lowly profession. Conducting business has thus always been the realm of Vietnamese women. However, as one of my respondents, Mai (age 35; 1st generation), pointed out, what Vietnamese women do gain with immigration to the CR is greater freedom in conducting their private lives, as they find themselves under less scrutiny from their immediate family and neighborhood.

Currently, 70 percent of Vietnamese men are economically active in the long-term. On the other hand, the ratio of economically active women is 45–55 percent, which means that officially half of Vietnamese women in the CR are unemployed (Freidingerová 2014, 109). Tereza Freidingerová states three main reasons behind this phenomenon: (1) the persistence of traditional roles, wherein women are still expected to bear children and be on maternity leave and function rather as housewives, while men are the main breadwinners of the family; (2) rising numbers of young girls of preschool and school age inflate the percentage of economically non-active women; and (3) a stronger study ethic among girls, who more often continue their educations at universities and are thus outside of the job market longer than boys (109–10). However, most Vietnamese women who are officially unemployed are still economically active and help their husbands in running their businesses.

As noted above, Vietnamese women who arrived in the CR prior to 1989 are in general more economically successful than those who migrated later. Women from the class of first settlers are active in business, and most of them work as managers of commercial enterprises, either alone or in concert with their husbands (Leontiyeva and Tollarová 2010, 12). Many of them own large market halls, around which not only the economic but also the social and private lives of Vietnamese immigrants are centered. These Vietnamese businesswomen also commonly engage in importing consumer goods from Asia, which they then sell to the middle class of Vietnamese immigrants (Pechová 2007, 23). In addition, they often run the above-mentioned intermediary (*dich vu*) companies.

Women immigrants from the middle class of the Vietnamese community mostly earn their living as small vendors conducting business either alone or with their husbands. They spend much of their time at work, and their leisure time and social life are limited. Many of these women own and run shops selling clothes, shoes, or cheap electronic goods, or small local grocery shops. In the past few years, Vietnamese women have also frequently begun running nail studios, massage parlors, bistros, and restaurants (Pechová 2007, 24). The following comment, by a twenty-six-year-old woman, illustrates the everyday life of many Vietnamese women in the CR:

> Well, almost every day is the same. I get up at seven, have breakfast, and around eight I go and open the shop where I also live. It has a lot of rooms at the back, so my sister has made me a flat there, so that I could save money for rent and transport. I sell goods until half past eleven, then I close the shop, go inside to cook lunch and eat. Then I reopen the shop and sell until six p.m. I close again at six, then go shopping for groceries or tidy up the flat. I am alone at home in the evening. I don't do anything, I am at home, read newspapers or chat on the internet. I can't take any holiday at the moment, because I have a lot of debt and I must save money so that I can repay it. (quoted in Kocourek, Martínková, and Pechová 2012, 24–25)

Finally, Vietnamese immigrants from the last wave of "fresh newcomers" are the least economically integrated. Following the 2008 economic crisis, many of them have found themselves endangered by poverty and exploitation. Since returning to Vietnam without sufficient savings is not a conceivable option for them, due to a "loss of face," many of these immigrants end up in sweatshops, producing cigarettes, clothes, or alcohol, or as shop-vendors working in harsh conditions (Pechová 2007, 29; Nožina and Kraus 2012, 139). In addition, many poor Vietnamese women accept work in exchange only for housing and board as domestic servants for more affluent Vietnamese families, in order to repay their debts. Many of these servants are very young (Pechová 2007, 29).

My research also suggests that first- and second-generation Vietnamese often stay closely linked to their community or make use of their Vietnamese origins to make a living (a situation that has also been observed among the Vietnamese residing in Germany and Poland). As my interviews show, this is partly because it is still difficult, even for second-generation Vietnamese women, to enter the Czech labor market. As a result, the breadwinning activities of my respondents were all linked to the Vietnamese community. For instance, Mai (age 35; 1st generation) is a renowned fashion designer selling clothes that represent a blend of her Vietnamese heritage and Western influences. In the past, she and her mother also imported various goods (tea, ceramics, garments, and accessories) from Vietnam. Huong (age 30; 1st generation) first worked after her maternity leave as a hairdresser and makeup artist, and is currently running a popular Vietnamese bistro. Thuy (age 47; 1st generation) works as a freelance translator of and lecturer on the Vietnamese language. Phuong (age 49; 1st generation) runs a small shop in a town outside Prague. Nguyet (age 22; 1.5 generation) and Van (age 25; 1.5 generation) were studying at the moment. Lan (age 26; 1.5 generation) was not working at the time of the interview as she had just graduated and was on maternity leave, but she helps at her mother's shop when needed. Finally, Hoa (age 24; 1.5 generation), besides helping her parents run their business on weekends, is engaged in a civic society group whose objective is to train intercultural interpreters and mediators to help Vietnamese immigrants deal with everyday problems, teach them how to communicate with Czech authorities (thus reducing their dependence on *dich vu*), and encourage their interest in learning Czech and getting acquainted with the Czech environment (thus reducing their vulnerability to exploitation). Increasing numbers of second-generation Vietnamese women are becoming active in this field, helping to bridge the gap between the majority and Vietnamese populations and promoting their parents' integration into Czech society.

VIETNAMESE IMMIGRANTS' KNOWLEDGE OF CZECH SOCIETY

Undoubtedly, acquiring accurate basic knowledge of the host society's language, history, and customs, as well as the local legal and institutional system, job market, healthcare, and social security systems (preferably learning as much of this as possible prior to arrival), are indispensable to the integration of immigrants into the host society. Prior to 1989, the migration of Vietnamese to Czechoslovakia was government-orchestrated, and the migrants were quite well informed about the conditions in the country by the time of their arrival. Post-1989, however, most of those programs were abolished. As a result, recent immigrants largely depend on their relatives and acquaintances living in the CR for their information rather than on more reliable official sources ("Analýza přístupu" 2007, 17).

The most vulnerable group in the Vietnamese community are the women who arrived after 2000 to take up jobs in Czech factories. These women, as well as men, were recruited from the poorest provinces in Vietnam. As one female informant noted of this group:

> Vietnamese living in the countryside are very truthful, they have a simple way of thinking, are affable and confiding; what they say counts. Therefore, they can be easily abused. When people from the city come to the village, the village people believe everything they are told by them easily. They tell themselves: these are people who have experienced more than me, they have more money, they can earn money; therefore, they are more capable and know more things. When an intermediary comes to the countryside and people say he can do wonders, the whole village admires him. (quoted in Krebs et al. 2009, 16).

Unfortunately, the intermediaries often provide misleading information, thus making the immigrants more vulnerable to exploitation in the CR.

Many Vietnamese immigrants rely on a network of social relations based on family or community ties. This "social capital" substitutes for their lack of "cultural capital," that is, knowledge of language and everyday reality in the country ("Analýza přístupu" 2007, 17). Apart from relatives and acquaintances, *dich vu* companies are an important source of information for Vietnamese women as well. Research shows that Vietnamese immigrants trust even faulty information provided from within the community more than official sources, such as Czech institutions or nongovernmental organizations (NGOs). Compared to other foreigner groups, they display a lower level of trust in official information brochures and leaflets (31–32). As a result, these recently arrived first-generation Vietnamese tend to have a very low level of knowledge of Czech legislation, as well as of their own rights and obligations. In general, the Vietnamese do not trust authorities and tend to try to solve problems without their help (Martínková et al. 2010, 19). In the CR, they often avoid seeking the help of NGOs or government offices out of fear of possible persecution ("Analýza přístupu" 2007, 32).

Martínková and her colleagues point out that it is much more effective to publish information the Vietnamese might need in the Vietnamese press, which has been flourishing in the CR since 1997. Periodicals such as *Tuan Tin Moi* (Weekly News), *The Gioi Tre* (Young World), *Van Xuan* (Ten Thousand Springs), *Xa Xu* (Far from Home), *Suc Song* (Life Strength), *An Ninh The Gioi* (World Security), and *Thanh Nien* (Youth) are all edited in Vietnam but printed in the CR. These periodicals report about current events in the CR and within the community and provide practical information concerning all spheres of life in the CR, as well as printing serialized Czech language courses (2010, 19).

MUTUAL RELATIONS BETWEEN IMMIGRANTS AND THE MAJORITY POPULATION

Given that the vast majority of first-generation Vietnamese perceive their stay in the CR as temporary, they spend much of their time focusing on their business endeavors, which leaves them little time to participate in the life of the host society. In order to better explain the relations of Vietnamese women with Czech society, I make a distinction between formal and informal contacts, with the former encompassing necessary communications with Czech authorities and institutions, and the latter entailing interactions with Czech citizens on a personal level.

In general first-generation Vietnamese women speaking little Czech rarely come into contact with Czech authorities, and if they do, it is usually via *dich vu* services or their children, who often run errands for their parents. The following quotation by a thirty-two-year-old woman illustrates this situation well: "Last month I resorted to [*dich vu*] quite often. We were arranging a purchase of another shop. In winter I fell sick several times, so I saw the doctor with the interpreter several times. He used to accompany my daughter to see the doctor and get inoculation, but now our babysitter goes with her" (quoted in Kocourek, Martínková, and Pechová 2012, 24–25).

As suggested by my interviewees, when Vietnamese women do try to communicate with Czech officials, most of them find the experience frustrating. Mai (age 35; 1st generation) noted that Czech authorities (especially the Foreign Police) need to improve their efficiency and communication with immigrants, although she commented that, compared to the past, the services have improved somewhat. Czech institutions, and society in general, tend to treat foreigners with suspicion. Research suggests that Czech society, despite significant political, economic, and social changes in the last two decades, continues to be quite homogenous and closed when it comes to willingness to accept foreigners ("Analýza přístupu" 2007, 5). This was confirmed by one of my respondents, who has lived in the country for over twenty-five years but who still perceives Czech society as closed and unaccepting of foreigners. And a 2013 survey focused on the attitudes of Czechs toward ethnic minorities shows that only 20 percent of Czech respondents view the Vietnamese positively, while 36 percent view them negatively. Even more alarmingly, the most negative voices against the Vietnamese came from the youngest generation of Czechs, aged fourteen to nineteen (Červenka 2013, 1, 2).

As for informal (personal) contacts between first-generation Vietnamese immigrants and Czechs, they tend to be limited. First-generation Vietnamese rarely socialize outside of work or family. According to Stanislav Brouček, they rarely go to the cinema or theater or pursue other kinds of cultural activities typical of the host society (2003, 20). This was confirmed in my interviews. For instance, Lan (age 26; 1.5 generation) noted about her (first-generation) parents: "They don't have friends with whom they would socialize regularly. I think it results from the unsociability of the Vietnamese and their low self-esteem. My dad says he doesn't want to go anywhere, because he is small and ugly and feels that despite being small he stands out among the Czechs and everyone would notice him."

Surveys suggest that outside of work many Vietnamese women suffer from boredom and feelings of social isolation, and they miss their more lively social life in Vietnam. These feelings were confirmed by Mai (age 35; 1st generation), who despite being married to a Czech and being well integrated into the host society, has the majority of her family members in Vietnam and deeply misses them.

Most Vietnamese women of the first generation spend their evenings at home watching Vietnamese TV (channel VTV4), reading news on the internet, chatting with relatives on Skype, or, when there is time, meeting their Vietnamese relatives and friends who also live in the CR. This is especially true of the Vietnamese community in Prague (Martínková 2008, 199). Rather than developing contacts with the majority Czech population, Vietnamese women are active in a range of sociocultural transnational activities. They might maintain regular contacts with relatives and friends in Vietnam via post, email, chat, or phone, or occasionally return home for family occasions. Confirming this assessment, one of my respondents, Van (age 25; 1.5 generation), noted of her family's interactions: "Now that there is Skype we are in contact much more often than before. In the past we called relatives on the phone, but usually only when there was some occasion, like New Year Tet, a birthday, or when something happened."

The situation is, however, very different for the 1.5 and 2nd generation Vietnamese women. Unlike their mothers, they speak Czech fluently and, thanks to Czech babysitters and schooling, have a much wider array of personal contacts not only within the Vietnamese community but also among ethnic Czechs. Yet, even they note that the majority population sometimes makes them feel as "other" or "exotic." For example, Hoa (age 24; 1.5 generation) described her experience with the Czech majority:

> Sometimes I don't like the behavior of some people, who don't perceive one as an individual but tend to tar everyone with the same brush. . . . Often when you go shopping to Sapa [the Vietnamese wholesale center in Prague], the Czechs treat you terribly. . . . Sometimes they complain in the bus, why they can't have buses for Czechs only . . . and then everyone stares at you. There is no point in arguing with them. I also experience that every Sunday when I commute to Prague—many people just sit next to me and gossip about me as if I didn't understand . . . as if I was an extraterrestrial.

Her words confirm that Czech society is still not accustomed to, and resists, ethnically different cohabitants, and displays signs of racism and xenophobia. Other respondents also testified that they had experienced negative reactions from the Czechs, although they would always add that it "did not happen very often," perhaps once or twice in ten years.

CONCLUSION

The objective of this article is to provide an overview of the most relevant issues Vietnamese women face while integrating into Czech society. As the above cited surveys, studies, and testimonies suggest, the level of integration of Vietnamese women depends on the time of their arrival in the CR and on their socioeconomic status. While women from the first migration wave are the most integrated, women who arrived in the 1990s came primarily for economic reasons and tend to perceive their stay in the country as transitory, which does not motivate them to learn Czech, acquaint themselves with Czech culture, or socialize with the majority. Women who arrived as part of the last migration wave are the least integrated. Most of them were recruited by intermediary companies, and many of these women had to indebt themselves in order to pay for these services, which makes them particularly vulnerable to exploitation.

One-and-a-half- and second-generation Vietnamese women represent a special group. Unlike their parents, they speak Czech fluently, have studied in Czech schools, and have a good knowledge of the Czech environment, although even many of them feel that the Czech majority still does not fully accept them.

As my interviews suggest, Vietnamese women perceived the language barrier, cultural differences, different lifestyles, and isolated character of the Vietnamese community as some of the main factors inhibiting their integration into Czech society. Likewise, there are numerous factors inhibiting the integration of Vietnamese immigrants on the side of Czech society. Immigrants must overcome substantial bureaucratic and administrative barriers to acquire their long-term residence permits. This situation is aggravated by the overall lack of information on the part of Czech officials, who do not know how to, or do not want to, communicate with Vietnamese clients. Another salient inhibiting factor is racism and xenophobia in Czech society, which is still not accepting of foreigners, especially ethnically different foreigners. Furthermore, many Czech businesses state they are hesitant to employ foreigners out of fear of complicated administration linked to their employment. And on the state level, the strategies aimed at integrating immigrants remain insufficient as well.

As mentioned above, this article is limited by the fact that, to date, little gender-specific research has been carried out on the integration of Vietnamese women in the CR. The specificities of issues faced by Vietnamese women living in this country, and how they compare with issues faced by Vietnamese women in other European countries, deserve further study so that well-informed policy and other measures can be developed to help overcome these challenges.

NOTES

1. Almost 50% of the Vietnamese community is in the productive age of thirty-one to forty-five years old (Leontiyeva and Tollarová 2010, 8). Only 1% of the Vietnamese are of post-productive age (Pechová 2007, 25) as the Vietnamese prefer to spend the last years of their lives in Vietnam.

2. Most commonly, two levels of integration are discussed: structural and sociocultural. The former refers to the position of immigrants in the socioeconomic stratification, which entails such dimensions as the acquisition of rights and status within the core institutions of the receiving society, education, employment, housing, and political and citizenship rights (Heckmann 2005). Sociocultural integration refers to immigrants' conformity to the dominant norms of the receiving societies. This process entails proficiency in the majority language, social contacts, adoption of norms and values, and identification (Vancluysen, Van Craen, and Ackaert 2009, 6).

3. I spent my childhood in Vietnam (in the early 1980s) as my parents worked in that country. Fascinated by Vietnam and the people I met there, I later pursued a double degree (MA) in Vietnamese studies and sociology, followed by a PhD in Vietnamese Studies in Prague. My current position as a lecturer in Vietnamese and Asian Studies at the Metropolitan University in Prague has enabled me to cultivate relationships with second-generation Vietnamese students, who have stirred my current interest in the experiences of Vietnamese immigrants in the CR.

4. In order to safeguard their privacy I refer to my respondents by pseudonyms.

5. The 1.5 generation refers to people who migrated as children; the 2nd generation is children of immigrants born in the new country.

11 SEX WORK, MIGRATION, AND LAW

La Strada and Human Trafficking in the Czech Republic

SIMONA FOJTOVÁ

For NEARLY TWO decades now, the issue of human trafficking, especially in the context of Eastern and Central Europe, has been capturing a great deal of media, academic, and political attention.[1] This attention has been accompanied by a recent shift in the understanding of trafficking, which historically referred solely to the sex industry and often foregrounded concerns of morality, and only lately has expanded to include and prioritize labor issues. Along with the new reconceptualization of trafficking as (any type of) forced labor, the discourse has also been intertwined with immigration debates. Highlighting the role of women's nongovernmental organizations (NGOs) in the Czech Republic (CR), this paper focuses on La Strada Czech Republic, an NGO whose work centers on issues of human trafficking. Addressing the challenges faced by trafficked foreign nationals in the CR, I focus on La Strada's lobbying work in this area, especially with regards to national legislation pertaining to immigration. Furthermore, I examine La Strada's human rights approach to trafficking to demonstrate how their activities have helped shape public discourse and national legislation on trafficking with respect to human rights, immigration, and sex work.

In order to contextualize La Strada's activist efforts, I first briefly situate the issue of feminism in post-socialist Czech society in relation to the work of Czech women's NGOs. Throughout the 1990s and early 2000s, much of the scholarship examining the situation of women in post-socialist countries expressed concerns about the limited possibility of feminism coming to life in Eastern Europe. Many scholars noted the lack of vibrant feminist mobilization and advocacy for women's rights, and analyzed why women's movements in Eastern Europe did not become a stronger social force energized by the social transformation ushered in by political changes taking place in the CR. Among the former socialist countries, the CR came to be associated with the most pronounced opposition to Western-style feminism. Still, notwithstanding the lack of a mass-based women's movement, and despite dismissive attitudes toward feminism in Czech post-socialist discourse, it would be a mistake to interpret these factors as a complete absence of Czech social and cultural attention to women's issues. If there is one significant venue through which women's issues are addressed in contemporary Czech society, I would argue that women's NGOs constitute that venue. Not only have NGOs proliferated in post-1989 CR (there were about seventy registered women's NGOs in the first half of the 1990s), they have also been playing an increasingly stronger role in terms of advocating for women's issues. In the absence of a visible and massive women's or feminist mobilization in the CR, NGOs have focused on a variety of women's issues and on providing a wide range of needed assistance—from shelters for battered women to feminist libraries to information centers for equal employment opportunities. They have been the main source of training and education for women, publishing feminist materials, coordinating media campaigns, lobbying governmental bodies, and monitoring national legislation. In this context, NGOs have not only played a prominent role in terms of assisting women with legal, medical, psychological, and financial services; they have also brought a wider visibility to various issues such as human trafficking and violence against women.

Even though self-help, education, and social services represent the main focus of many Czech women's NGOs, there are several organizations whose activities and approaches extend beyond social repair work. La Strada's chapter in the Czech Republic (La Strada CR) can be counted among them.[2] Through their rights-based approach to the issue of human trafficking, La Strada CR has helped advance public discourse and policy regarding human rights in relation to migrant labor and migration issues. Established in Prague in 1995, La Strada CR is one of eight cooperating La Strada programs—in Belarus, Bulgaria, Macedonia, Moldova, the Netherlands, Poland, and Ukraine.[3] All are members of La Strada International (LSI), a European network originally established in the Netherlands that focuses on preventing trafficking in human beings in Central and Eastern Europe. La Strada CR shares with LSI their human rights approach and their goal of improving the position of women and promoting their universal rights, including the right to choose to emigrate and work abroad and be protected from violence and abuse.[4]

In addition to providing various forms of anonymous assistance (psychological, medical, financial, social, and legal) to women and children (and also increasingly men), La Strada CR places a great deal of emphasis on successful prevention, which they see as a significant defense mechanism against trafficking. Their prevention work consists of information dissemination tailored to specific target groups. While some of these groups (including sex workers and migrants living in or coming to the CR) are a relative constant, other, more peripheral groups vary over time. By way of example, La Strada CR has recently focused its prevention work on young Czechs living in institutional care facilities and on persons living in socially excluded areas. La Strada CR's forms of prevention have thus had to flexibly respond to changing trends, such as the recent development (2007–10) of perpetrators targeting vulnerable members of the Czech Vietnamese community. Still, even as La Strada CR believes that targeted prevention is essential, they also recognize that given the global nature of trafficking, the scope of the issue is much larger. Other factors need to be addressed as well, such as the shortage of sustainable livelihoods, increasingly unequal distribution of wealth in the world, gender discrimination, demand for sex work or cheap labor, war, armed conflict, and other forms of natural or socially constructed disasters that have played a significant role in the growth of trafficking in human beings

Over the years, La Strada CR has witnessed, tracked, and documented changes in the patterns, demographics, and gender of those trafficked into the CR. In the early 1990s, the CR functioned predominantly as a country of origin. Currently, while still functioning in that way, it has become more of a transit and destination place as well, in part because the Czech economy has become more stable during the last decade. Until the late 2000s, the majority of people exploited in the CR were not Czech citizens or documented foreigners; rather, they were persons with undocumented (or "unsure" in La Strada CR's definition) residence. In addition to people continuing to be trafficked to the CR from Ukraine, Moldova, the Philippines, and Vietnam, recently there has also been an increase in people trafficked into the CR from other European Union countries, especially Bulgaria and Romania. Due to the growing trend among perpetrators to take advantage of victims' vulnerable financial situations rather than relying on overt physical violence, the organization has been more frequently dealing with cases of unsettled wages and economic exploitation than with physical or emotional abuse. As I return to later in this discussion, these changes have created new challenges for prosecutors in their efforts to prove instances of trafficking.

In contrast to the mid- to late 1990s, when La Strada CR's monitoring of trafficking was limited to abuse in the sex industry, the organization has since expanded its scope to include trafficking in other economic sectors, such as domestic work, retail, construction, forestry, and agriculture. Changes in target industries have been accompanied by changes in the gender of trafficked people, and La Strada CR's assistance is now being sought by increasing numbers of men. According to La Strada CR's annual report, in 2011, 465 people contacted La Strada CR via their SOS and INFO lines, which represented a 50 percent increase compared to 2010. In terms of the gender composition of the people seeking help in 2011, there was almost an equal number by gender: 237 women and 228 men.[5] As the next sections illustrate, over the years, La Strada CR has played an important role in changing the legal definition of trafficking to encompass a broader set of practices than those associated only with the sex industry.

THE FEMINIST ACADEMIC DEBATE ON TRAFFICKING: CHALLENGING THE ASSOCIATION OF SEX WORK AND TRAFFICKING

The dominant discourse around trafficking has been shaped by competing conceptualizations of trafficking and differing agendas, which has affected how policies are implemented in various national contexts and who is recognized as a victim worthy of sympathy and assistance. As the sociologist Kamala Kempadoo has articulated it, "There are competing definitions of trafficking; little consensus or agreement among researchers, policy makers, and activists about the scope of the problem; and scant evidence or substantiation about actual trafficking practices. Moreover, much of what is pursued in the name of a war on trafficking has troubling consequences for the poor people around the world" (2005, vii–viii). An ideological divide remains between those who see trafficking as a labor and migration issue and those who see it primarily as a sexual exploitation issue, and this divide has played out in public and legislative spheres, generating considerable scholarly discussion. A brief examination of the main critiques of the dominant trafficking discourse is helpful for contextualizing La Strada's activities and their understanding of trafficking.

Numerous scholars have analyzed how the dominant discourse on trafficking as well as some anti-trafficking policies reflect general anxieties about sexuality, gender, and mobility, often becoming a means for promoting various morality and anti-immigration agendas (e.g., Agustín 2007; Andrijasevic 2010; Chapkis 2003; Chuang 2010; Ditmore 2005; Kempadoo 2005; Peters 2013). Much of this critique focuses on the problematic conflation of trafficking with sex work, a conflation that has resulted in ignoring or deemphasizing other forms of trafficking. The tendency to equate trafficking with commercial sex has a longstanding tradition, not only in general public discourse but also at the policy and legislative levels. As Melissa Ditmore points out, "Historically, trafficking in persons has been equated with prostitution. The forerunner to the latest anti-trafficking legislation is the United Nations 1949 Convention that exclusively addressed prostitution" (2005, 108). The current definition of trafficking, however, has expanded and, rather than focusing exclusively on sex work, now includes all sectors of the economy. This shift to a broader definition of trafficking is, to some extent, reflected in the most recent United Nations protocol on trafficking from 2000 (*UN Protocol to Prevent, Suppress and Punish Trafficking in Persons*). However, when it comes to academic discourse, and also to some national legislative and assistance contexts, conceptualizing trafficking as more than commercial sex and focusing on other economic sectors such as agriculture, domestic work, the garment industry, and construction, has *not* become more prominent. As Tanja Bastia has argued, "Research and action on trafficking of adults has largely focused on migrant women working in the sex sector" (2006, 21). Still, where some groups continue to view trafficking in women as always associated with sexual slavery and to conceptualize sex work as a form of violence, other groups, like La Strada, embrace the broader definition of trafficking and allow for the idea that some women might freely *choose* to engage in sex work.

The issue of sex worker agency—whether or not women even have the ability to freely choose sex work as an occupation—has been a divisive one among feminists, especially in the prostitution-as-violence versus prostitution-as-work debate. Often referred to as radical or abolitionist feminists, a group of highly vocal U.S.-based feminists (Janice Raymond, Kathleen Barry, and Donna Hughes), who see prostitution as a form of violence and refuse the idea of voluntary sex work, considers trafficking in women for purposes of sexual exploitation a separate category from trafficking for labor exploitation.[6] Believing force or coercion is implicit in the sex act itself, abolitionist feminists view prostitution always as a form of sexual exploitation and argue that sex work should be abolished. Due to abolitionist feminists' conflation of trafficking with prostitution and of prostitution with coercion and violence, the sociologist Alicia W. Peters has argued that "when they refer to 'sex trafficking,' abolitionist advocates on the one hand, and service providers and law enforcement on the other, are talking about two different things—the former referring to *prostitution* and the latter to *forced* prostitution" (2013, 237). Unlike the abolitionist advocates, non-abolitionist feminists and sex workers' rights activists, such as Kempadoo,

Jo Doezema, and Laura María Agustín stress women's agency in prostitution and insist on a distinction between trafficking and prostitution. They emphasize that the discursive slippage between prostitution and trafficking sweeps away any exercise of agency. These scholars and activists apply the "trafficking" label only to those cases that fit into the paradigm of forced or coerced labor.

Perhaps not surprisingly, the persistent conflation of trafficking with forced sex work (and often with prostitution as such, whether coerced or not) is not only confined to a particular corner of academic discourse but is also evident at the legislative level. As several scholars (Chapkis 2003; Chuang 2010; Peters 2013) have argued, "negotiations over new international and U.S. laws on trafficking" have become "the battleground for the prostitution debates" (Chuang 2010, 1672). For example, in her analysis of the Trafficking Victims' Protection Act of 2000 (TVPA), which is the cornerstone of U.S. federal human anti-trafficking legislation, the sociologist Wendy Chapkis points out that the law's "conflation of migrant abuse, trafficking, and sex slavery is a common rhetorical device in antitrafficking discourse" (2003, 926).[7] Commenting on the reductionist accounts that still associate all trafficking with sex work, Chapkis foregrounds the inconsistency of both the definition of trafficking as well as the statistics of trafficked persons: "In some accounts, all undocumented migrants assisted in their transit across national borders are counted as having been trafficked. In others, 'trafficking' refers exclusively to victims of sexual slavery. In some instances, all migrant sex workers are defined as trafficking victims regardless of consent and conditions of labor; in still others, abusive conditions of employment or deceptive recruitment practices in the sex trade are emphasized" (926). And in her 2013 analysis of the legislative history of TVPA, Peters examines how cultural understandings of gender and sexuality appear to influence conceptions of human trafficking and the implementation of U.S. anti-trafficking law and policy. Exposing the underlying anxieties over prostitution, victimization, and women's sexuality, Peters argues that "while the law instrumentally covers trafficking into all labor sectors, it symbolically privileges trafficking for forced commercial sex. In so doing, the law promotes a particular world view, one in which sex is different, unique, and special" (221–22). This view has resulted in the designation of severe and non-severe forms of trafficking in the law, with sex trafficking marked as a special category and distinct from other forms of forced labor.

The law's definition of trafficking, which in the U.S. case reflects the tendency to conflate trafficking with forced commercial sex, has affected how assistance and legal protection are provided to trafficked persons. As Peters argues, "in the case of the TVPA, a particular vision of trafficking (forced prostitution) and a specific type of victim (women forced into prostitution) are privileged in complicated ways that divert attention from trafficking into other labor sectors (e.g., agriculture, factory labor, or nude dancing) and from men altogether" (2013, 223). Many researchers and activists agree that the majority of trafficking cases involve non–sex sector trafficking and increasingly reflect the changing gender composition of victims. For example, as Peters points out, "in fiscal year 2009, 82 percent of identified victims were victims of 'labor trafficking' and 48 percent were men (USDOJ 2010). Yet, there was a sharp contrast between the reality of identified victims and the way the Bush administration represented the issue" (239). Discussing the gap between the "[U.S.] law on the books" and the "law in action," Peters argues that the privileging of sex trafficking affects how service providers and state agents define trafficking, identify victims, provide benefits and protection, and decide which cases they ultimately choose to prosecute.

As several scholars have also argued, the practical application of the concept of trafficking has been shaped by an anti-immigration agenda and the rejection of prostitution as work, as seen in the alliance of abolitionist feminists and conservative politicians. Even though U.S. abolitionist feminists represent a small group, they have wielded a significant influence on the trafficking discourse as well as anti-trafficking legislation in the United States, often taking advantage of their close alliance with conservative politicians and evangelical Christians. For this political coalition, anti-trafficking laws have become a legitimate vehicle for pursuing abolition of prostitution (Chuang 2010; Peters 2013). As Chuang notes, because these groups have been "unsuccessful in their efforts to criminalize prostitution as a matter of international law," they have politically aligned themselves in the effort to pass specific trafficking laws in the United States and have succeeded in incorporating a definition of trafficking that encompasses non-coerced prostitution in the U.S. anti-trafficking law (1677). Promoting a reductive understanding of trafficking wherein trafficking is primarily about prostitution, the abolitionist coalition has succeeded in controlling mainstream anti-trafficking discourse by prioritizing sex-sector trafficking and promoting an anti-prostitution agenda worldwide. As I discuss in the next section, U.S. abolitionist feminists have not only shaped anti-trafficking policies and discourse on trafficking and prostitution in the United States but have also worked to exert their influence in Eastern and Central Europe, such as through their attempts to sway public discourse on prostitution and trafficking in the CR

LA STRADA CR'S STANCE ON ISSUES
OF SEX WORK AND MOBILITY

There are several major international organizations that have played an influential role in the global discourse on trafficking and sex work. Among them, two prominent NGOs with opposing views on prostitution have become key players in the anti-trafficking lobby: the Coalition against Trafficking in Women (CATW) and the Global Alliance against Traffic in Women (GAATW). Prompted by the increased public awareness about trafficking that accompanied the late 1980s surge in "sex tourism," both organizations held their first conferences on trafficking in the early 1990s, shortly after being established. As an umbrella organization, CATW presently consists of regional networks and affiliated groups with national coalitions in fifteen countries in North America, Latin America, Asia, Africa, Australia, and Europe. GAATW is an alliance of more than one hundred NGOs in North America, Latin America, the Caribbean, Asia, Africa, and Europe.

Even though both organizations see themselves as feminist, they have very different views on sex work. GAATW rejects the abolitionist approach to prostitution. Conversely, CATW, which was spearheaded by U.S. radical academic feminists such as Kathleen Barry and Janice Raymond, views prostitution as a form of violence against women that should be abolished.[8] As Alison Murray explains, "The position of . . . [CATW] and Barry is that trafficking is part of [the] general exploitation of women according to the feminist principle that male sexuality under patriarchy is about power, not sex and thus all prostitution is coercive" (1998, 53). The organization conflates sex work with trafficking and uses a very narrow definition of trafficking that focuses only on sex trafficking. In this regard, it strongly opposes the perspectives of the GAATW and the sex workers' rights movement that has emphasized sex workers' agency.

Because La Strada CR is part of the LSI network, and because both La Strada CR and the LSI network are member organizations of GAATW, they share similar views on prostitution. La Strada CR's stance toward sex work has been feminist and non-abolitionist from the beginning, and its lobbying efforts have centered on separating sex work from trafficking in general and on shifting the focus from positions on morality to actual labor conditions.[9] La Strada CR questions the view that all prostitution is sexual slavery and differentiates between women's coercion into the sex trade and women's willing migration into sex work. Because La Strada activists believe curbing women's sexuality has been used as a way of curbing mobility, the organization has emphasized women's right to migrate and choose their work—including their right to work in the sex industry. Along with other activists and researchers around the world (Agustín 2007; Andrijasevic 2010; Chapkis 2003; Kempadoo 2005), La Strada CR believes that addressing the abuses of women working in the sex industry does not require closing the borders, and that women can consent to both economically motivated migration and to sex work. La Strada CR defines trafficking as a "movement of people by means of coercion for the purpose of exploitation" (interview with Irena Konečná, 2014). Arguing that prostitution and trafficking should not necessarily be linked, La Strada CR promotes women's agency, which is reflected in their prevention materials as well as in the way the organization provides assistance to victims of trafficking.[10]

While many NGOs—such as La Strada, the GAATW, and others—have been operating with this broader understanding of trafficking, other feminists, some of whom are very vocal and influential beyond the borders of their own countries, still focus exclusively on trafficking in women and girls for the sex industry and ignore other forms of trafficking. The U.S.-based academic Donna M. Hughes, who adopted her definition of trafficking from CATW, is one of the leading abolitionist feminists who has focused in her work on issues of trafficking and prostitution in Central and Eastern Europe. In her writing, she employs a definition of trafficking that centers only on prostitution. For example, in "The 'Natasha' Trade: Transnational Shadow Market of Trafficking in Women," Hughes defines trafficking as "any practice that involves moving people within and across local or national borders for the purpose of sexual exploitation" (2000, 626). Defining all prostitution as sexual exploitation and women's sex work migration as essentially violent, Hughes uses the terms "prostitution" and "trafficking" interchangeably in her writing. In her view, the traffic in women occurs whenever a migrating woman is involved in the sex industry, regardless of whether or not coercion is involved.

Differing views on prostitution between Hughes and Czech women's organizations, especially La Strada CR, became particularly prominent in the Czech media in the new millennium. For example, in 2004, when a bill proposing to legalize prostitution in the CR fueled public debate about sex work, Hughes actively lobbied against the legislative efforts of the Czech government to legalize prostitution. She published an article entitled "Legalizing Lies" in the *Prague Post*, an English-language newspaper, where she criticizes the Czech government's proposal to address the growing sex industry by regulating it and collecting taxes. Arguing that legalization of prostitution increases trafficking and does not bring desired government benefits and rights for women, Hughes reiterates her views that prostitution is not work but rather abuse and exploitation. While voicing her skepticism about the declared intended outcome of the proposed bill, Hughes also decries the lack of public protest against the bill, especially by Czech women's organizations:

> In the Czech Republic, women have not had an effective voice to protest the move to legalize prostitution. There are no civil-society organizations effectively speaking out against the harm of legalization to women, families and communities. In many countries, nongovernmental organizations (NGOs) protest attempts to subvert women's rights and the well-being of all of society by making such abuse and exploitation legal. In the Czech Republic, the best-known antitrafficking organization, La Strada-Czech Republic, is a member of a Dutch-founded network of antitrafficking NGOs. Consequently, this NGO speaks in a Dutch voice and supports its funder's view that prostitution can be work for women. It supports legalization of prostitution. Effectively, the women have been abandoned to the pimps and the sex tourists. (2004)

Even though Hughes frames the harms of prostitution and trafficking as questions of humanitarian concern about Czech women, she also focuses her critique on Czech women's organizations because they did not support her anti-prostitution campaign in the Czech media. While Hughes does not even mention La Strada CR in her 2000 article "The 'Natasha' Trade," where she discusses the alleged lack of response by Czech women's NGOs to issues of trafficking, she does acknowledge La Strada CR's existence in the 2004 newspaper article quoted above. However, she dismisses La Strada CR as presumably inauthentic because the organization allegedly does not have its own, locally grown philosophy regarding sex work. Without showing any real understanding of the organization's philosophy, Hughes assumes that Czech La Strada activists have uncritically adopted Dutch La Strada's perspective on prostitution as legitimate work, never considering the possibility that La Strada CR's views might have been actually developed by Czech activists as appropriate for the Czech location. In my interviews with Petra Kutálková, the vice director of La Strada CR, she stressed that the Czech activists' position on prostitution as legitimate work is not a foreign view but their own (2008). Perhaps ironically, Hughes criticizes Czech NGOs as trafficking in foreign ideas while not recognizing that she herself is campaigning to put Czech women in the service of a U.S. ideology.

Even though this debate mostly centered on the effects of state regulations of the sex sector, it turned out to be more than a public debate about prostitution. It exposed different feminist positions on sex work on the part of different interlocutors, and also revealed how women's agency and mobility are conceived of within these divergent positions on sex work. Not only did Hughes fail to acknowledge La Strada CR's past and ongoing work to help ensure the safety of sex workers; she also failed to mention another important local Czech women's NGO, Rozkoš bez Rizika (Bliss without Risk), which has been offering free health and social services to sex workers in the CR since 1992. Contrary to Hughes's assertions, prominent Czech women's organizations and researchers have been vocal about issues of sex work in Czech society and have worked to increase sex workers' rights. Rather than claiming that Czech women's organizations lacked an effective voice to protest the Czech government's bill to regulate sex work, Hughes should have examined more closely why Czech activists and feminist scholars refused to sign her petition opposing the bill. A more nuanced understanding of Czech activists' and scholars' views supportive of the legalization of prostitution would offer a more complex picture than the one Hughes has presented in which Czech women appear voiceless and without agency. Such an understanding would have to acknowledge the work and advocacy of Czech activists and scholars on behalf of sex workers, as well as the dynamic role of Czech women's NGOs since the fall of communism.

From a certain perspective, the encounters between Czech and U.S. feminists like Hughes and their opposing views on the proposed bill to regulate prostitution seem to continue U.S. debates from the 1970s and the 1980s about agency in relation to women's sexuality. These highly polarized discussions among U.S. feminists also generated opposing feminist politics and different proposals for change. One strand of second-wave U.S. feminists viewed sex as a site of oppression and danger, while the other advocated sexual freedom and pleasure as central to women's liberation. These opposing views appear to closely correspond to differing perspectives on prostitution. In these conflicting interpretations, some feminists see commercial sex as a form of violence and sex workers as victims of sexual slavery, while others stress the agency of sex workers and see commodified sex as potentially liberating or empowering for women. Czech feminists and activists, however, have not framed issues of sexuality in terms of women's right to pleasure nor have they stressed a liberating potential of sexuality for women. While Czech feminists and activists have not understood sexuality as a site of danger, and they do not see sex workers as victims of sexual slavery, they have been critical of the glamorization of prostitution and sexist portrayals of women in the Czech media, especially in advertising. As discussed above, the most prominent Czech activists have focused on improving the working conditions of sex workers rather than on debating questions about the morality of sexuality. Both La Strada CR and Rozkoš bez Rizika center their work on providing services and supporting sex workers' rights. While the debate on the issue of sex worker agency among Western feminists has intensified and become more polarized in relation to the issue of trafficking, these divisions are not prevalent in the Czech context. Even though Czech activists and academics whose attention centers on sex work are familiar with the two opposing positions, they agree in their view of sex workers as having agency. Taking into consideration the widely shared position among Czech activists on prostitution as legitimate employment and their work toward improving conditions in the sex industry, we can interpret Czech women's organizations' lack of protest against the bill differently than Hughes did, and understand that the reason behind their refusal to support Hughes's petition was far from indicative of their lack of an effective voice in the civic sphere.

In addition to their contributions to the public debate on sex work and their ongoing lobbying for sex workers' safety, La Strada CR has also exerted influence on Czech national legislation concerning trafficking. Along with direct assistance to victims and efforts to prevent trafficking, one of La Strada CR's important functions centers on developing strategies for improving national laws related to trafficking, and on enforcing the required compliance of Czech law with current international law. La Strada CR's lobbying efforts and monitoring of Czech anti-trafficking legislation reflect their understanding of trafficking as part of the broader issue of labor migration. While the 2000 UN protocol on trafficking defines trafficking in human beings as a breach of human rights, until 2004 the Czech criminal law only referred to cross-border sex trafficking and not to other forms of trafficking in humans. Even though forced labor is mentioned in the Czech Charter of Fundamental Rights and Freedoms, it was neither defined nor specifically addressed in Czech national legislation until the legislative change in 2004 when forced labor finally became specified as a crime in the Czech criminal code. Today, Czech anti-trafficking legislation does consider economic sectors beyond the sex industry, and it also includes intrastate, along with cross-border, trafficking. However, the CR has still neither signed nor ratified any of the most significant international conventions for the protection of migrant workers. La Strada CR continues to be critical of the current treatment of trafficked people in the CR, which remains unaligned with La Strada's approach to trafficking as a human rights issue. In their 2007 report, La Strada CR pointed out that there continues to be more focus on the punishment of the affected people for violations of immigration laws than there is on the protection of their rights.[11]

Another challenge that La Strada CR has faced concerns the on-the-ground interpretation of Czech anti-trafficking legislation by law enforcement. Even though the Czech criminal code now addresses forms of trafficking other than sex trafficking, La Strada CR and Czech law enforcement have tended to interpret the code's definition of trafficking differently. The main difference of opinion between the two groups concerns the question of what constitutes coercion and how to interpret the difference between trafficking and forced labor. La Strada CR works with a broader interpretation of the definition of trafficking than Czech law enforcement. In La Strada CR's view, because forced labor does not have to entail physical force, migrants might be in a position of vulnerability due to their lack of knowledge of Czech language, culture, and legislation; their lack of awareness of their own rights; or their lack of social networks in a foreign environment. La Strada CR understands that migrants' positions of vulnerability can be abused and they can consequently become exploited for labor purposes. However, what La Strada CR views as trafficking might not necessarily be understood as such by Czech police, and individual cases can thus be interpreted differently (interview with Irena Konečná, 2014).

The variations in the definition's interpretation between service providers and law enforcement bodies can affect the number of prosecutions for trafficking as well as the number of people assisted. In their efforts to improve the situation of trafficked workers, La Strada CR has critically reviewed the Czech governmental program providing assistance to trafficked persons, finding that the program still limits its offers of protection and support almost exclusively to persons trafficked for sexual exploitation. According to La Strada CR's 2007 report, only one person who was trafficked for a purpose other than sexual exploitation was accepted into the existing governmental program of assistance. Moreover, the number of crimes prosecuted for forms of trafficking other than sex work has remained low despite the 2004 change in the Czech criminal law. In fact, the first condemnatory judgment on labor trafficking was adjudicated only as recently as 2012, eight years after the amendment of the criminal code.[12]

According to La Strada CR's published documents and my interviews with La Strada CR's deputy director Petra Kutálková, the main challenge lies in the different interpretations by NGOs, governmental bodies, and the police when identifying instances of trafficking. Kutálková suggests that these different interpretations, and the challenging implementation that fails to distinguish between trafficking and labor exploitation, affect the forms of assistance available to trafficked victims, especially social services and the newly established protection program. In her 2010 report "Příliš úzká brána k lidským právům (A

Gate Too Narrow for Human Rights), Kutálková argues that the definition of trafficking remains conceptually vague, especially in areas other than sex work, which makes it challenging to identify those who qualify as trafficked persons who should have access to services and their rights defended. As Kutálková explains in the report, "The majority of trafficked people [in the CR] can't exercise their rights. They don't have access to legal representation, services, or sufficient information, or they are deported from the Czech Republic, or they are undocumented" (2010, 9). Critical of the narrow applicability of the existing definition of trafficking and its focus on crime rather than rights, Kutálková advocates for a better system of identifying trafficked persons in order to increase their access to services. Moreover, arguing that the concept of trafficking is artificially constructed, Kutálková wonders if a perspective that focuses on the phenomenon of exploitation itself could be more useful when approaching issues of trafficking.

Many scholars, researchers, and organizers have repeatedly stressed the importance of keeping anti-trafficking efforts centered on human rights. But as Kamala Kempadoo has cautioned, a recent new emphasis in the UN document on combating organized crime has negatively diverted attention away from the human rights focus, despite progressive international anti-trafficking conventions: "The changes in the UN definitions of trafficking . . . [have] been influenced by shifts in understandings among various feminists, researchers, activists, and community workers about prostitution, migrant work, and the global political economy. However, by prioritizing crime, punishment, and immigration control, the global government approach departs from the perspectives that have been generated from concerns with social justice and human rights" (2005, xiv). Two significant changes in the recent understanding of trafficking—first, the focus on actual labor conditions instead of conflating trafficking with sex work and, second, the emphasis on the agency and rights of women—have been emphasized by many anti-trafficking researchers and organizations, including La Strada CR.

In contrast to the mid-1990s, the issue of trafficking in human beings has become a widely acknowledged public policy concern in the CR, especially since 2004. La Strada CR's decade-long history of cooperation with the Czech government has produced some important changes with respect to addressing the problem of trafficking, especially in relation to foreign nationals. La Strada CR's successful lobbying, combined with pressure from international organizations, has not only resulted in drawing the attention of state-level decision-makers to issues of trafficking but has also compelled the state to generate new tools and efforts to help address the issue. Understanding that human rights violations have not abated under the existing anti-trafficking policies and legislation, La Strada CR continues to lobby for a human rights approach and argues that instead of deporting trafficked persons and returning them to the same conditions from which they had fled, state policies should create systems of safe migration. In this sense, La Strada CR members share the belief expressed by Kempadoo: "A common concern amongst many human rights and social justice advocates in such social movements is that the framework adopted by the UN supports the neoliberal economic interests of corporations, multilateral agencies, policy experts, and national governments, rather than those of the world's working and poor people" (2005, xiv).

Some scholars and policymakers believe that legal prostitution and open migration are significant factors stimulating trafficking. Therefore, they propose banning sex work and curbing migration to prevent it. This philosophy contrasts with those researchers and activists who use rights-based approaches to address the exploitative working conditions of migrant women and support legalization of prostitution and open migration. Espousing the latter position, La Strada CR functions as a strong advocate for social and legal protection for those affected by trafficking in the context of the Czech Republic.

NOTES

1. The author would like to thank Irena Ferenčíková Konečná, former director of La Strada Czech Republic, for reading and commenting on an earlier version of this chapter and for her helpful suggestions.

2. Other important NGOs include Nesehnuti, an environmental NGO with a strong gender focus, and several gay rights activist groups, such as Gay Initiative and Equal Family.

3. Bosnia and Herzegovina also had a member organization of La Strada until 2012.

4. http://www.lastradainternational.com/?main=informationlsi&section=aims philosophy.

5. http://www.strada.cz/en/who-we-are/annual-reports.

6. "Leading feminist thinkers in this camp include U.S.-based feminists identified with Catharine MacKinnon and sometimes referred to as 'radical feminists,' including Kathleen Barry and Sheila Jeffreys. These feminists recognize no distinction between 'forced' and 'voluntary' prostitution. In their view, choice and consent are not possible because prostitution is an institution of male dominance and results from the absence of meaningful choices" (Chuang 2010, 1664).

7. TVPA 2000 was reauthorized through the Trafficking Victims Protection Reauthorization Act (TVPRA) in 2003, 2005, 2008, and 2013.

8. Raymond, a prominent radical feminist scholar, was the co-executive director of CATW from 1994–2007 and now serves on the U.S. Board of Directors. During her

tenure, CATW expanded its international work, especially in the Baltic States and in Eastern and Southern European countries (but with no regional organization in the CR).

9. See http://www.strada.cz/en/our-activities/advocacy-and-lobbying.

10. In a more detailed definition, La Strada CR defines trafficking as "recruitment, transportation, transfer, harbouring, or receipt of persons by means of the threat or use of force or other forms of coercion, of abduction, of fraud, of deception, of the abuse of power or of a position of vulnerability for the purpose of exploitation" (Ferenčíková Konečná 2014).

11. See www.strada.cz/publikace-a-odkazy/vyrocni-zpravy?lang=cz&start=5.

12. La Strada CR's deputy director, Petra Kutálková, stated that in 2008, there were twenty-nine instances of trafficking identified as crimes but only ten of those were forms other than sex work. In 2009, there were only three cases of trafficking other than sex work out of the ten total cases identified as crimes (Kutálková 2010, 9).

12 IDLE ALLY

The LGBT Community in the Czech Republic

KATEŘINA NEDBÁLKOVÁ

THE PUBLIC SPACE of the gay and lesbian community in the Czech Republic (CR) is today generally situated in bars, cafés, restaurants, sex clubs, and saunas, especially in larger cities such as Prague, Brno, and Olomouc.[1] Although there is no geographically concentrated gay and lesbian community in particular neighborhoods or cities, Prague tends to be described in LGBT guidebooks as the gay metropolis of the former Eastern Europe. The private space of the subculture is constituted through informal groups of friends who meet in private households and do not opt for official gay and lesbian clubs. Another important part of the community consists of nonprofit LGBT organizations; there are several dozen of them in the CR. Media and especially the internet has become an essential part of the LGBT environment as well, and there are numerous servers devoted to LGBT issues.[2] The television program Q (formerly Legato) was broadcast by a state channel from 2004 to 2013. In 2007, the first lesbian publishing house, Le Press, was established. An annual queer film festival has been held since 2001, followed by regular Pride Marches since 2008.[3]

The transsexual community is concentrated predominantly in Prague around Transfórum, a civic association representing transpeople's interests. Given the fact that most transsexual people, after their sex reassignment, often desire assimilation into everyday society, transsexual communities are more likely to exist online. The first sex reassignment surgery was officially carried out in Czechoslovakia in the late 1960s. Nowadays, fifty to sixty people undergo the operation every year, and the surgery is covered by Czech national health insurance.[4] The most controversial part of the sex reassignment legislation is the requirement to terminate the reproductive function during the surgery. That means sterilization or castration. Persons who are not able or do not wish to undergo this intervention are excluded from the gender legal recognition, and they are barred from acquiring new personal documents and birth certificate number ("Zpráva o plnění" 2013, 19).

There are no official statistics available for hate crimes based on sexual orientation or gender identity, as the Czech Penal Code does not distinguish between the two, and neither qualifies as an aggravating circumstance. Regarding verbal aggression, bullying at schools is a major although often neglected problem. Minorities' rights are guaranteed by the Education Act, but the act does not mention sexual orientation explicitly. Based on data from nongovernmental organizations (NGOs) working with children and adolescents, it is clear that bullying represents a serious issue for gay and lesbian youth. Despite a growing number of prevention projects and peer-to-peer programs organized by NGOs, no unifying policy exists either for teachers or students.

In terms of public opinion, long-term research has shown that, compared to other Central and Eastern European countries, the CR is relatively tolerant regarding same-sex marriage and child adoption.[5] Public perceptions of homosexuality have been associated with medicine and sexology, a discipline that actually facilitated the decriminalization of homosexuality in Czechoslovakia in the socialist period (1961). The CR was also second among post-communist countries to legalize registered partnership for same-sex couples in 2006.

THE AIM OF THIS STUDY AND ITS METHODS

Several fundamental questions concerning the Czech LGBT situation are taken up throughout this text. What forms has the LGBT movement been taking in this legal and social context? How has the Czech gay and lesbian community changed in recent decades, and what is its relationship to the feminist movement? In an attempt to address these issues as fully as possible within the scope of a relatively brief chapter, I draw on two data sources: gay men and lesbian women's recollections of, and reflections on, the community in the 1980s and interviews concerning the topic of lesbian parenting. The chapter thus focuses on two different generations and two disparate contexts, including both pre-1989 Czechoslovakia and the post-1989 Czech Republic. Time-wise, it covers the period between the 1980s and 2010. I draw on twelve interviews with gay men and two interviews with lesbian women that I carried out regarding the gay and lesbian community in the communist era, as well as interviews with seventeen lesbian families (thirty-four women) that I conducted as part of my 2004–9 postdoctoral research. Comparing and combining information about the experiences of (mostly) gay men in pre-1989 socialist Czechoslovakia with those of contemporary lesbian mothers in the CR provides an opportunity to explore different aspects, strategies, and phases of the community, as well as questions concerning identity politics, legality/illegality, formal and informal organizing, and private and public expressions of these communities.

Respondents for the "gay/lesbian community under state socialism" interviews were selected based on their age: I looked for people over the age of forty-five for the interviews to be relevant. Thanks to my fifteen years of experience within the Brno gay and lesbian community, I was able to find potential respondents either directly or through a contact person.[6] The lesbian families involved in my second set of interviews were contacted based on the snowball effect. The first lesbian couple I interviewed was active in the public debate on parenting. I was able to meet two other families through them, eventually reaching the seventeen couples. My limited results in identifying lesbians for inclusion and participation in the "gay/lesbian community under state socialism" interview set confirms the findings of other researchers about the lesser visibility of lesbians in Czech public life (Taylor 2008; Valentine 2000).

INFORMAL AND PRIVATE COMMUNITIES

Social sciences conceptualize the gay and lesbian community using a variety of different perspectives and paradigms, which is also reflected in the terminology used. In this text, I primarily use the terms "community" and "movement": "community" refers to spaces where gay men and lesbian women spend time or meet; "movement" refers to organized activities with political goals.[7] Logically, in the section focused on the socialist Czechoslovakia, the term "community" appears more frequently as the 1989 regime change first enabled the birth of a social movement in the Czech context.

Even though homosexuality was not criminalized under socialism, homosexuals were expected not to "cause public nuisance." Also, the age limit for consensual homosexual intercourse was eighteen while it was fifteen for heterosexuals.[8] This regulation served as a potential tool for coercion of homosexuals by the secret police, who gathered, according to some, names of homosexuals in order to blackmail them (see Schindler 2013, 291; and Seidl 2013, 82).

During the communist regime, civil society was severely constrained. Homosexuality was treated merely in medical terms under the guidance of sexology. There were no officially existing gay and lesbian bars, clubs, or organizations, and no publications dealing with LGBT issues.[9] Compensating for this absence of LGBT organizations to some extent were the so-called socio-therapeutic clubs—a network of therapy groups led by sexologists or similarly trained "experts," where people would discuss homosexuality-related issues and concerns. Participation in a therapy group of this sort was also well known to be one of the few officially condoned ways of avoiding the mandatory two-year military service.[10] Similarly to informal gay scenes, this formally established and scientifically sanctified institution of therapeutic groups was dominated by men.

Besides this formally established activity, in the pre-1989 period, elements of gay and lesbian community could be found in various locations:

> Gay life happened on two basic levels. The first was one that I particularly love reminiscing about and will never forget—these home gatherings. There were groups of people who would agree to get together on Saturdays to party: dancing, drinking, chatting. Obviously, or evidently, the bonds among people were a whole lot tighter than they are today. There are so many gathering places these days. And the second level of community formation, that was the underground level (and I have experienced that type of community also abroad, in England and Australia), those cruising areas where people would have fleeting encounters. Public toilets, I suppose, were among them, but one did not simply act on sexual urges or the promise of anonymous sex there, of tea-rooming, cottaging, as they say. That was of course made possible there and happened a lot, too, but one also used it as an opportunity to meet someone like oneself. Every boy growing aware of his homosexuality would suddenly see these pornographic and vulgar inscriptions there at the public toilets. Somebody like that had been there, one of them had peed here. Gradually, it would dawn on the boy. (respondent Václav)

This quotation suggests the interconnectedness of two seemingly disparate community platforms: private parties organized in people's apartments on the one hand, and public spaces enabling anonymous sex on the other. Public toilets represented an important part of the Czech gay subculture before 1989, a time when identification at the hands of a vigilant secret service included considerable risks. Public toilets—and other places such as saunas, swimming pool showers, parks, and railway stations—functioned partly as cruising areas and represented one of the few opportunities (for men) to meet persons of the same sexual orientation.[11]

This second type of gay community space lent itself particularly well to the enactment of homosexuality: it was possible to gain visibility as a gay man in the eyes of the other, to make oneself discernible, decodable, intelligible, and accessible as a gay male:

At the urinal, you show each other what you've got (laughter) and then you either nod to the other to show you will go someplace together or you do not. You could enter a stall then or we would go to the university library or other public toilets. Things could happen right at the urinal, too. That was attractive to some people because you could be seen, or there was the potential that another person would arrive. (respondent Marek)

This space provided the possibility of noncommittal sex but also was one of the few opportunities to meet and get initiated into smaller private groups and networks:

There was a huge meeting place for homosexuals in front of the main railway station in Brno; they would stroll the area day and night. One person introduces you to another. That is how I got hooked up with a group of boys. It had an almost anti-establishment character: I learned to listen to the 80s hippies, they were banned; it was illegal to play such music out loud. Initiation is always crucial; these men taught us about the 60s culture and music, the stuff that is again so popular nowadays. They taught us how to live in the socialist structures as gay people, how to keep one's own homosexuality a secret, how to put ads in the papers (to search for a boy to go vacationing with). (respondent Michal)

Through newly established connections, the individual was acquiring what we could call, with Pierre Bourdieu, cultural capital (1986, 171), a sort of cultural taste, be it in music, film, or literature. Moreover, one would pick up highly practical skills, such as how to avoid mandatory military service or how to advertise in the papers at a time when open same-sex advertisements were forbidden.

These interview excerpts are telling in their mono-gendered quality. In Michal's narrative, "homosexual" clearly means a gay man. While it could be argued that both gays and lesbians were invisible in socialist Czechoslovakia, lesbian women faced a double disadvantage: they did not have access even to the handful of unofficial spaces that were available but dominated by gay men.

Several of the men habituating the so-called gay spaces in pre-1989 Czechoslovakia with whom I spoke were reluctant to view gays and lesbians in terms of a community:[12]

K: I don't really feel there is a community.

R: There are people who are ill and it is as if one referred to them as a community, too. What do we have in common? The range of these folks is so wide, each one has their own interests, and the only common denominator is that we are "bent" [teplí]. . . . That's as if we were saying that people in wheelchairs were a community, because they give each other tips on fine-working wheelchairs to be had. I think it is a community only if and when people act together in some common interest.

K: I don't think so, it could be people with common interests but there may
be no end result. The people have to feel they belong together, be ready to
stick up for one another. But if you go to the public toilets and some gypsies
[sic] assault you, will the others at the urinals stick up for you? They won't.
Homosexuality itself is not a community as much as it may get represented
as such these days.

While the idea of a general (gay and lesbian) homosexual community is
rejected in these comments, other interviewees (such as Michal above) were
clearly invoking a sense of community. Gays (and lesbians) shared tips, ideas,
and experiences on how to live a day-to-day, fairly ordinary life as a homosexual person; where to look for potential life or sex partners; or how to avoid military service and police raids. The often articulated sense that "people used to be
there for each other more" during the communist period was closely related to
the stronger need at the time to hide one's homosexuality if one did not wish to
run the risk of being stigmatized and discredited. The female respondents also
reminisced about the pre-1989 times with a certain sense of nostalgia, emphasizing the underground character of the anti-establishment rebellion for which
they came to find no more need after the regime change. They compared the
commercial and consumerist character of the club scene now and the domestic,
supportive, and often private or secretive aspects of the community prior to
1989.

Sexological discourse remains the dominant way of knowledge production
in the field of human sexuality in the CR (Sokolová 2005; Lišková 2009, 2011).
This characteristic, of course, affects the conceptualization of (homo)sexuality
within the Czech community, where homosexuality has often been seen as a
clear-cut, fixed, and unchanging characteristic.[13] It also reflects Michel Foucault's theory that connects sexuality and truth (1990), where sexuality, viewed
as a presumed source of an "authentic truth" about the self, comes to char-
acterize and determine the individual in modern times. It becomes modern
individuals' duty to seek the truth about themselves in their own sexuality,
and this presumed truth is then perceived as having an unchanging, definite
nature. Such a normative image of a presumably true, proper gay person is an
illustrative example of the problematic phenomenon of homonormativity as
discussed elsewhere (Valentine 2000; Bell 2001b; Taylor 2008). Yet in the context of the CR, sexology, while playing a limiting role to some extent, has also
played an enabling role. While differentiating itself from other discourses dealing with gay and lesbian issues,[14] and claiming, quite problematically, a position
of "objective, scientific truth" about sexuality, sexology also played a key role

in homosexuality's early decriminalization and acceptance (in a medicalized form) in Czech society.

To summarize, homosexuality in Czechoslovakia under the communist regime was removed almost exclusively into the private space. It was stigmatized, which reinforced the fear of coming out in the family or workplace (Schindler 2013, 295). The actors themselves used the term "community" cautiously, often preferring the term "minority," a label that is symptomatic in its implicit reference to a majority. For many Czech men and women, their homosexual identity was determined by their same-sex preference, while in other respects, they emphasized their conformity with the majority population. Some of the interviewed homosexual men and women also tended to define themselves against other subgroups within the community, such as bisexuals, cross-dressers, transsexuals, or transgender people. This normalizing tendency reappears in the second part of this chapter addressing lesbian families, where the family as an institution can be seen as a prime normalizing instrument.

Overall, the stronger bonds within the gay (and also lesbian) community prior to 1989, repeatedly invoked in the interviews, can be assumed to have resulted from general societal circumstances. Compared to the CR nowadays, the society in socialist Czechoslovakia was much more homogeneous and also organized around fairly unambiguous social norms. The post-1989 political regime change led to a shift in the entire social structure and social fabric.

REGIME CHANGE: THE BEGINNINGS OF FEMINIST AND LGBT POLITICS AND ORGANIZING

In the post-1989 period, Czech society, previously marked by state regulation and limited disparities in terms of wages and property, turned into one beginning to deliberately cultivate, create, and reproduce a range of social inequalities as a result of market liberalization and privatization (Večerník 2010, 484). Yet this was also a period when civil society institutions started to gradually form, and conditions for re/organizing of gay and lesbian space and community were created. Since the regime change in 1989, several public LGBT organizations have been established. A number of LGBT internet servers have been created, and dating websites have appeared where personal ads can be posted. Studies, nonfiction, and fiction books (of varying quality) are now being published, and courses on sexuality are offered at several Czech universities. The community has moved from private flats to formal and public institutions.

The European Union (EU) accession negotiations, which started in the second half of the 1990s, were also significant with respect to the changing public landscape and emerging variety of LGBT organizations. With the completion of the EU accession process, the CR joined the European Human Rights protection system. These changes brought about *inter alia* the adoption of the Anti-Discrimination Act in 2009, which introduced the prohibition of discrimination on the grounds of sexual orientation and gender identification in a number of areas, such as access to employment, education, healthcare services, and housing ("Zpráva o plnění" 2013). The Registered Partnership Act was enacted in 2006, although it took several years of negotiations in the Czech Parliament. While the act was a milestone achievement, the extent of partners' rights (and obligations) remains disadvantageous in comparison with marriage, which remains reserved for two people of different sexes. Registered partners cannot jointly own property or jointly rent their home, and there are no tax advantages for them in the manner that exists for a husband and wife. Likewise, there is no right to a widow/widower pension, and for the purposes of inheritance and gift taxes, the partners are included in a less advantageous class than husbands and wives. All of these factors can contribute to the destabilization of same-sex partnerships and seriously disadvantage children in the family ("Zpráva o plnění" 2013, 15).

After 1989, other social movements, including feminism, started (re)emerging in the CR as well. Unlike the LGBT movement, women's movements have a long Czech tradition dating back to the nineteenth century and interwar periods. As discussed elsewhere in this volume, following World War II, the communist regime enacted its own version of women's emancipation via full employment, and it formally established women's committees and Communist Party–controlled women's organizations (with no real decision-making powers). But since 1989, various Western social movement concepts, ideas, and arguments have been adopted in the CR.

Comparing gender politics in the United States and Germany, Myra Marx Ferree (2012) has introduced a useful analytical tool, distinguishing between two different types of gender politics: gender as class (Germany) and gender as race (United States). The gender as race model views individuals (in this case women) as presumably carrying or embodying the characteristics that disadvantage them in the male-dominated society. The emphasis here is on women's rights, individual choice, institutional gender desegregation, and the value of women's anti-stereotypical behavior. According to Ferree, this framework is institutionalized in canonical American texts. Gender as class politics, on the other hand, treats women as a group situated in a complex web of structural exclusions and oppressions and also perceives them as an appropriate object of state intervention. Government is here viewed as having a responsibility to mitigate the consequences of inequalities. This model is based on the idea of a "typical woman" and suggests supportive measures in her favor. Gender mainstreaming is one of the government-managed strategies that is supposed to eliminate existing gender inequalities. Since, however, gender is here foregrounded above other structuring categories, such as race, age, ethnicity, or sexual orientation, this model's disadvantage is that it does not account for diversities among women. The EU (and the CR as well) has taken the route of gender mainstreaming in gender politics. The problem with this politics is that it tends to generalize men as well as women as unified and homogeneous groups. In contrast, as I argue below, Czech LGBT movement's politics is closer to the race model in Ferree's framework.

Whereas in the post-1989 period and throughout the early 2000s, large umbrella LGBT organizations and activities were established, by today more specialized organizations have emerged, focusing specifically on students, gay teens, queer film fans, or promoting specific political goals. The differentiation of the meeting spaces, along with the achievement (in 2006) of the unifying (for a while) political goal of registered partnership, has also meant the disintegration of the idea of a unified community. Individuals as well as organizations have had to cope with the community's ever more apparent internal diversity. In the next section, I focus on one facet of this diversity: the emergence of lesbian families.

LESBIAN FAMILIES: DEALING WITH DIFFERENCE AND DIVERSITY

In the U.S. context, lesbian and gay families have been researched extensively over the past five decades (Green 1978; Golombok and Tasker 1996; Stacey and Biblarz 2001; Almack 2008; Sullivan 2004; Taylor 2009). The topic of lesbian families raises conceptually rich and challenging questions for the social sciences, as it changes our perception about the nature of kinship, family, and intimacy (Butler 2002; Weston 1591). I chose to study this subgroup because I see it as an illustrative example of the processes of differentiation within the Czech LGBT community in recent decades. I focus on how such families relate to the larger lesbian community and whether the manner of their relating is similar to or different from gay men's attitudes as described in the first part of the chapter.

I also discuss strategies invented and embraced by Czech lesbians as they have struggled to overcome various obstacles to becoming parents.

Many of my lesbian mother-respondents described the "bar scene," which figured so prominently in my earlier respondents' image of community, as the exact opposite of home or pride. Instead of a place where masks could be discarded, where one could be who one really is, the bar scene for them is a place of pretense and exhibitionism. For instance, one of the respondents, Mirka, found the environment of a lesbian bar "strange and dirty." Rather than representing a space where a shared sense of identity could emerge, the community serves as a negative frame of reference. One respondent, Kamila, stated, "We've got nothin' in common with 'em. We are depressed by the community, it makes us sad. We are somewhere else." Czech lesbian families tend to consciously distance themselves from other lesbians, and from the stereotypical image of a lesbian (discussed below), which they, surprisingly, share with the majority population.

Agata and Eva provide another example of this phenomenon. They run a coffeehouse where they occasionally host meetings of lesbian or feminist groups. The two women commented on their own position in the community: "They are shocked by us and we are shocked by them because we are quite different from all those girls that come to our coffeehouse; they are so terribly promiscuous, or just y'know so terribly . . . really!" (Eva). The excerpt draws a picture of the "typical lesbian" as promiscuous, feasting on an hedonist life, so distant from a family life with children. The quotation also suggests an otherwise fairly atypical connection between Czech feminist and lesbian communities, as the coffeehouse owners offer their space also for feminist literary group meetings. Literature (especially nonfiction) could be seen as a potential meeting point for the two movements, as exemplified by the Slovakian project Aspekt, one of the first sources of translated and local feminist writing in the region.[15] Aspekt combines feminism and lesbianism to a much higher degree than Czech feminism does.[16]

As is generally acknowledged in broader LGBT scholarship, gays and lesbians do not constitute a monolithic community; the "homosexual identity" is a social construct rather than an expression of inner characteristics informing particular kinds of behavior or lifestyles (Binnie and Valentine 1999). However, from the activism perspective, it is sometimes useful to refer to unity and uniformity, as that can facilitate the pursuit and achievement of what might be viewed as common goals. This is what happened during the debates and negotiations about the Czech registered partnership law, when leading activists (mostly gay men) decided pragmatically not to include parental rights for gays and lesbians in their demands. Their fears that any mention of gay and lesbian parenting would spoil the chances of getting the law passed were likely grounded in reality, but many Czech lesbians expressed their disappointment at the time. In 2002, several lesbian activists initiated an appeal that drew attention to the issue of parental rights in the proposed legislation. Their voices and efforts, however, were not heeded. In the rest of this chapter, I discuss the paths Czech lesbian women have taken to fulfill their wish to have children, hindered by the non-inclusion of parental rights in the 2006 Registered Partnership Act, and I note how their plans often have been adjusted as they encounter various obstacles to parenting on their way.

Until several decades ago, Czech lesbians were still born into a society where it was difficult to meet other women and live openly as a lesbian couple. If women did find the courage to live in a lesbian relationship, it usually meant giving up on the desire to have children. Marriage and starting a heterosexual family was the most imaginable and feasible way of fulfilling the desire to have children. Today, however, this former intrinsic link between heterosexuality and procreation on the one hand and homosexuality and childlessness on the other no longer holds. Personal ads are one of the areas where the changes in Czech lesbians' options, and also of their attitudes to parenting, can be traced. Whereas prior to 1989 homosexual orientation could not be openly expressed in personal ads, today there are many printed and online meeting platforms for gays and lesbians. Furthermore, the wish to have children is a frequent and openly articulated component of an envisioned lesbian partnership life. While this is particularly true for women, the theme of parenting is relevant for gay men as well, as evidenced in Věra Sokolová's research (2009).

Overall, in my research, the idea of a baby born in the context of a same-sex couple was much more frequent and real for Czech lesbians in their twenties and thirties than for those in their forties or fifties. There was a clear generational difference. This does not mean, of course, that all younger women are attracted to the idea of starting a family or that parenthood is unimaginable for lesbian women of the older generation.

Lesbian motherhood allows us to understand the two main ways of conceptualizing motherhood—as a natural and inevitable part of womanhood or as an active plan or life choice. Due to the necessary assistance of a third party, parenthood is always a planned act in a lesbian relationship. Thinking parenthood through in a lesbian relationship is far from focused just on the yes/no question. The way to lesbian pregnancy is a strenuous, step-by-step effort, always more accessible for those with the necessary financial resources. And the women need to consider specific forms of conception. Certain authors liken the situation of same-sex couples in this respect to heterosexual partnerships encountering difficulties with getting pregnant and using the services of assisted reproduction clinics (Sullivan 2004, 11).

Leaving families with children from previous marriages or previous heterosexual partnerships aside, assisted reproduction at a specialized clinic might seem the most frequent path to parenthood and is indeed the strategy most often discussed in international studies dealing with lesbian parenthood (Stacey and Biblarz 2001). This option, however, is officially unavailable to lesbian women in the CR, as the Healthcare Services Act (Act No. 373/2011) states,

> Assisted reproduction may be performed based on a written application of a woman and a man who intend to undergo this treatment together (hereinafter "infertile couple") if, due to health reasons, it is not likely or is completely ruled out for the woman to get pregnant in a natural way or if there is a demonstrable risk of the transmission of genetically conditioned diseases or defects. The application requires the man's consent. . . . The consent must be repeatedly expressed before each artificial insemination. The application must not be older than 24 months, it forms part of the woman's health documentation.[17]

The Czech law thus classifies infertility as a health condition requiring treatment, that is, an illness. The situation is somewhat different in cases where the partner is classified as infertile (the biological capacity of conception is missing) or the partner is altogether absent (the case of single women or lesbian couples). Whereas in the first case (if the man is infertile) another man's (anonymous donor's) sperm is provided to the couple and the term "treatment" loses its original meaning, in the second case (if the man is absent in the family) the woman is not entitled to another man's sperm. The Czech legislation here, not surprisingly, reproduces and guards the traditional concept of family as a unit exclusively formed by one man, one woman, and children.

In practice, both heterosexual and homosexual couples apply for assisted reproduction at Czech clinics, with one fundamental difference between them. Whereas heterosexual couples come in accordance with the law, lesbian couples often find themselves in situations where they have to hide their orientation. Some lesbian couples attempt to simulate the state-sanctioned family ideal by substituting a friend or acquaintance into the missing position in the conventional family constellation for the purposes of clinic visits. He takes up the future father role, including the rights and obligations to the child, but does not implement this commitment after the birth and is usually not stated as a father on the birth certificate. The women who chose this option often mentioned the emotional effort and work related to coping with this situation. For other couples, the idea of having a baby this way was unacceptable.

In some instances, it has also proved possible for the conventionally restrictive family reproductive legislation to be circumvented without a fictitious partner. For instance, Simona and Petra looked up several Czech private assisted reproduction clinics on the internet and contacted them via e-mail, describing their situation openly. Then they visited three of them. According to Simona, "this is happening at all clinics, and it is probably generally known. But they use different legal covers. In one they wanted a notarially certified signature of a male friend[18], in another they did not care if we faked it, and the third one did not want anything at all." The Czech internet portal dedicated to lesbian and gay parenting—drbna.cz—features dozens of requests for suggestions for open-minded local clinics or doctors willing to perform insemination for lesbian couples. Considering that disclosures about this illegal insemination might be detrimental for the clinic, it is not surprising that the server does not provide specific addresses.

Only one of my study's respondent families chose the transparent and legal way through a foreign clinic openly performing inseminations for lesbian and single women. Ivana stated, "It's also business for them; they reassured us high and low, they gave us the feeling that it's normal. It was also interesting for me, it was the first and last time when some official institution saw us as a couple, so when I received a letter Dear Ivana and Michaela, I was over the moon." Whereas for Czech clinics lesbian families are invisible in the eyes of the law, in this case, in a Belgian clinic, the women represented a legitimate couple as well as a family eligible to reproduce.

Apart from insemination performed at a clinic using anonymous donor sperm, three of the women I interviewed used a sperm donor they found themselves through an ad. The donor then either visited the clinic with them or provided the sperm at home. At the lesbian parenthood server mentioned above, the "Parenting ads" section contains dozens of offers like the following: "Sperm donation: I would like to help lesbian couples or women. I am 33/176 [i.e., 33 years old, 176 cm high], secondary school education, without health issues. I will impregnate women who are interested or donate my sperm for home insemination. Discreetly, no entitlement to the child." Most of the ads facilitate sperm exchange between men and lesbian women; rarely do we see an ad accounting for the possibility of shared parenting between lesbians and gays.

Apart from the options of insemination at a clinic or seeking a donor via ads, there are other paths emerging in the Czech context for lesbian parenthood planning. One of the ways is insemination with the sperm of a known man. Several women I interviewed mentioned help offered by a doctor-gynecologist, provided that the women find the sperm on their own. In one case, a recommended sexologist actually offered to inseminate the woman using his own sperm during coitus. These anecdotal accounts of the situations lesbian women sometimes step into when seeking to get pregnant suggest a significant longing for a child, as well as a considerable inventiveness in the search for ways to get pregnant.[19] Informal paths to pregnancy often substitute for the institutional support and solutions that are researched and described in places like the United States, where (at least in urban areas) there are not only specialized clinics focused on lesbian women or single mothers but also a range of self-help groups for gay and lesbian parents.[20]

Most Czech lesbians in families do not view themselves as courageous pioneers of new and experimental relationships, which is how some researchers abroad conceptualize homoparental relationships (Weeks, Heaphy, and Donovan 2001). For some of these women, starting a family means leaving activism, while for others the family presents a new platform for so-called private activism in the form of providing opinions and interviews to the media. Czech lesbian women in families often long for an essentially conventional image of their relationship and family, where the unusualness consists only in both parental positions being taken by women. They have usually perceived and represented themselves as similar to other women and other families, and tend to insist on their own "normality" and similarity with the so-called majority society.

CONCLUSION

LGBT life and community in the CR has changed significantly in recent decades, which have witnessed a transition from a seemingly united identity of "the homosexual" to a range of different identities within (and outside of) the community. Whereas prior to 1989, identity for many gays and lesbians unfolded within a narrow personal circle of shared coming out, the organizations emerging after 1989 have become a platform for the development of various alternative identities. While previously the minority/majority polarity represented the dominant axis of comparison for Czech gays and lesbians, today the presence of further differentiating categories is much more visible. This multiplicity represents a new opportunity to define oneself against difference with which one does not identify (lesbians against gays and vice versa, lesbians in families against non-parents, activists versus non-activists), but it can also be mobilized as a political strategy—as has been the case of a newer LGBT association called PROUD.

Two significantly different stages of identity politics can thus be distinguished in the Czech LGBT community's history. At the movement's onset, it was constructed around a united and uniting category of "homosexual," sanctioned officially by the Czech sexological discourse and differing from the majority population only in sexual orientation. Today the term "queer" is embraced by some, especially the younger generation, and is sometimes even used as an umbrella category for various groups and identities within the Czech LGBT community.

The idea behind the term "queer" in terms of queer theory is to disturb the conventionally presumed continuity between the categories of sex, gender, sexuality, and normality. If sexual orientation does not form an essential identity component, it might then be easier to form alliances among different social movements and to fight on different fronts connected to varied experiences of inequality (LGBT parenting, elderly LGBT, etc.). In the case of newer LGBT organizations like PROUD, identity politics gives way to human rights rhetoric. In the LGBT movement, this strategy (the implementation of the race-like model in Ferree's rhetoric) replaces the earlier, united homosexual identity politics. Whereas the established Czech feminist movement still struggles with the idea of universal womanhood and generally focuses on efforts to have gender issues included in government-sponsored official gender politics through (tamed) gender mainstreaming, the LGBT movement perhaps appears more ready to experiment with alliance building along different inequality and disadvantage axes, including sexual orientation, class, ethnicity, and age.

NOTES

1. Short portions of this essay have appeared in Kateřina Nedbálková, "Community at the Backstage: Gays and Lesbians in the Czech Republic," *Queer Presences and Absences*, ed. Yvette Taylor and Michelle Addison (London: Palgrave Macmillan, 2012), 31–48.

2. For a list of relevant organizations and short descriptions of their activities in Czech, see http://www.stud.cz/komunita/glbt-adresar/. For a historical account of the emancipation of homosexuality in the Czech context, see Seidl 2012.

3. See the festival website at http://www.mezipatra.cz/.

4. Among postoperative transsexuals in the CR, female-to-male transsexuals prevail at a ratio of up to 5:1. This trend is also characteristic of other post-communist countries,

while data from Western Europe suggest an opposite trend. Possible explanations for this variation include different social conditions under socialism, more difficult self-enforcement of male-to-female gender roles, or differences in diagnostic criteria (Fifková 2008, 18).

5. See *Češi jsou vůči sňatkům* (2005) and *Special Eurobarometer 393* (2012), especially pages 34–43.

6. Brno is the second largest city in the CR with approximately 400,000 inhabitants.

7. For a more detailed theoretical and empirical framing of the LGBT community, see Stein 1997; Binnie and Valentine 1999; Binnie and Skeggs 2004; Švab and Kuhar 2005; Taylor 2007; Béres-Deák 2007; and Jörgens 2007.

8. Paragraph 244 of the Czech Penal Code.

9. Several informants mentioned the book *Well of Loneliness* by Radclife Hall, translated to Czech in 1969, as the only available source for potential identification prior to 1989.

10. Military service was mandatory for all men (not women) until 2004.

11. For interpretatively rich accounts of public toilets in relation to broader social structures, see Skeggs 2001 and Bell 2001a.

12. This might be a good place to comment on terminology. Prior to 1989 the term *minorita* (minority) was often used rather than "community." Under socialism, *homosexuál* (homosexual) was common, and the use of this medical term was reflective of the role of sexology at that time. Other, more informal terms include *náš* (ours), *našinec* (ours, one of us), *je na chlapy* (he is after guys), and *je na ženský* (she is after women). The term "queer" is also becoming popular nowadays, especially among the younger generation.

13. The Czech-Canadian sexologist Kurt Freund's research and publications in the field of male homosexuality strongly argued for homosexuality as an inborn characteristic that cannot be changed by therapy or medical treatment (Seidl 2013).

14. Namely, feminist theory, anthropology, or social sciences in general.

15. Founded in the early 1990s in Slovakia, Aspekt is a feminist educational and publication project, or a set of projects, under the patronage of a handful of women (see *Kto je kto alebo Aspekt'áčky 2007*, http://archiv.aspekt.sk/about.php).

16. As defined by the Czech Women's Lobby, Czech feminisms' main topics include gender equality, gender stereotypes, violence against women, work/life balance, and rights of migrants. There is no mention of the rights of sexual minorities in the three-page document. See http://www.czlobby.cz/content/files/CZL_postoje_aktual.pdf.

17. For the full text of the law, see Právní informační system (Law Information System), Czech Ministry of the Interior, www.mvcr.cz/clanek/pravni-informacni-system.aspx.

18. In the clinic's documentation on the case, he would then act as the child's father.

19. If readers miss adoption in this list of potential paths to parenthood, it is because none of the families I interviewed considered this option, partly because heterosexual couples are given clear preference in the adoption process and because registered partnership law rules out adoption.

20. In the Czech context, this alternative is represented by two servers: lesba.cz and drbna.cz. Drbna.cz has been in operation since 2007 and, in the administrator's words, "the content is for anyone interested in homosexuality, and specifically in lesbian (and gay) parenting." In the seven years of its existence, over two hundred texts (all with dis-

cussion options) have been published and seven hundred advertisements placed there, in which women search for a partner, sperm donor, active father, or another lesbian family to meet and share experiences. Similarly, men use the personal ads to search for a partner, a lesbian woman or couple with whom to share parenthood, or to offer sperm to lesbian women for insemination. The stejnarodina.cz server was established in 2008 in the same shop (administered by the same person as the server above) and is a site presenting the activities of the Stejná rodina (The Same Family) association. The association aims to "achieve legal equality of homosexual families with heterosexual families." The server is more formal in content and form and primarily provides information on the legal environment for gay and lesbian families.

13 CONDEMNED TO RULE

Masculine Domination and Hegemonic Masculinities of Doctors in Czech Maternity Wards

IVA ŠMÍDOVÁ

WITH THIS CHAPTER focused on a generally neglected dimension of sociological research, I set out to provide an empirically based study of masculinity within a particular contemporary site of Czech professional work. While the so-called crisis of masculinity or the supposed unsustainability of the conventional male role are topics increasingly visible in Czech public discourse, the prevailing context characteristically marked by the dominance of men and the mechanisms of reproduction of male dominance have received marginal attention. The question of whether it is Czech men who are in crisis, whether the crisis pertains to the current concept and representation of masculinity, or rather whether there is no crisis and men remain powerful deserves a thorough reflection and analysis. My response to these questions attends to, and seeks to comprehend, a key paradox that I have encountered in my research: men as a group continue to hold a dominant position in Czech society, but this position does not necessarily assure a satisfying life experience.

The concept of hegemonic masculinity as developed within the field of Critical Studies on Men and Masculinities (CSMM) provides a useful analytical handle for understanding this phenomenon. The framework of hegemonic masculinity takes into consideration and explores the complicated relationship between actor and structure, and it highlights understandings of social structures as gendered and patriarchal. It helps us explore the mechanisms that bring men to dominance and helps us understand why structural masculine domination can be perceived by individual men as involuntary and imposed. In this chapter, I use this concept to analyze the statements of respondents working in a professional setting that has long been prestigious and publicly respected: physicians in the obstetric wards of Czech hospitals.

Czech physicians are well-known for their active engagement in political affairs in the Czech Republic (CR) and for high voter support, suggestive of a significant level of public trust. With the CR ranking highly in the field of modern (bio)medicine, including throughout its communist past, this field, and specifically obstetrics, offers an opportunity to study a context that is influential and prestigious, as well as conspicuously filled and shaped by gender stereotypical patterns of behavior.

HEGEMONY: THE PRIVILEGE AND BURDEN OF MEN—OR AN INDICATOR OF CRISIS?

A couple of years ago, an older man knocked at my door looking for someone "who does the gender thing," as he put it. He showed me what he considered an alarming set of statistics about the ratio of men and women studying at the Veterinary and Pharmaceutical University in Brno. Himself a medical doctor and retired professor, he was concerned that some fields of study were becoming so predominantly filled by young women that the few young men left would be, in his words, "condemned to become upper administrators and professors" without necessarily aspiring to do so. They would have little choice but to serve in these positions, which in his eyes was a major injustice. My visitor was also concerned that women pursuing a career in veterinary and human medicine would be unable to fulfill their maternal roles and raise children—according to him, women's primary responsibility.

This conversation prompted me to reflect (once again) on the ambivalent relationship between the dominant place of men in today's Czech society on one hand and the reported experiences of masculinity on the other. Why would this (male) professor and physician conclude that the situation that lifts men into highly placed decision-making positions is in some ways a structural disadvantage?

In one of my earlier research projects I followed the careers of men working in professions associated with protecting the environment. These careers too brought many men into highly placed positions, and here too I encountered evidence of the governing organizational structure and personal advancement in which Czech men apparently unwittingly found themselves involved. They spoke of "service to their country" and of responsibilities that men must not shirk but that they themselves did not choose (Šmídová 1999; 2002; 2004).

A 2005 British study by Caroline Gatrell found that women professionals who are mothers regarded their professions also as (among other things) "service to their country." Besides wanting to hold onto their jobs because they liked them or because they had worked hard to achieve their professional position, these mothers of small children also reported feeling a moral duty to their society. They felt a sense of responsibility, sometimes even an imperative, to continue in their paid work despite becoming parents (152–53). Yet, compared to the responses I received from Czech men, there seems to be no hint in Gatrell's text that her women respondents regarded their "service" as inevitable doom. Gatrell's women respondents described their well-deserved high positions as something they had to work hard for, whereas the Czech men I interviewed were simply "glad to accept" and took for granted the positions offered to them. I see in this distinction the outline of a symbolic gender order by which men's and women's lives are oriented in distinctly different ways.

Pierre Bourdieu's concept of somatized (masculine) dominance and symbolic violence might be useful in this context. While structural dominance in the vast majority of cases disadvantages the subordinated, that is, women, the impact on men can be negative as well. The system of structures prescribes and inscribes bodily passions to men, resulting in their feelings of "social mission" reported above, and producing in them their "dispositions to rule," with which, however, individual men do not necessarily align (1998). Other researchers have framed the gendered difference in access to prestigious positions through the analogies of a glass ceiling for women and a glass elevator for men. This approach, however useful otherwise, does not help to explain the apparent passive or non-volitional role in the whole process men reported in my research. It does not account for these men's reported sense of being compelled into leading ranks as if they were powerless cogs in the social machinery, condemned to dominance.

I believe the concept of hegemonic masculinity offers a way to account for the ambiguous relationship between men's structural privilege on one hand and their often reported perceived personal lack of individual freedom and control over their own fates on the other. While clearly visible in my interviews with Czech medical professionals, this phenomenon is in fact observable across cultural and political spheres. This situation, where structural advantages granted to men are accompanied by individual feelings of powerlessness, cries out for analysis, particularly in the under-researched context of social and political transformation of the former Soviet bloc countries.

HELPLESS HEAD DOCTORS AND POWERFUL MASCULINITY

In yet another study I conducted and that included interviews with male and female Czech obstetricians, (male) department heads complained about men leaving the field of obstetrics. Explanations for this trend included fear of litigation, whose numbers are rising, but also the fact that obstetrics as a field mainly requires a conservative, patient, wait-and-see approach. It thus fails to offer opportunities, presumably sought by men entering the medical profession, for the kind of technological innovation and intervention expected from those who wish professional visibility and fast career advancement. Moreover, in the Czech context of mostly state hospitals, and where medical professionals are prohibited from delivering children outside of certified medical facilities, obstetrics does not pay as well as other, more lucrative private employments.[1] Aging department heads (especially in regional hospitals) are thus lacking successors who would meet their stereotypical gendered expectations.

Women obstetricians in hospital teams were portrayed by their bosses as conscientious and competent (except in the area of operations, for which ward heads almost always choose men), but also as facing the supposedly insurmountable handicap of motherhood, automatically associated with a Czech woman's life trajectory.[2] Citing examples from their own practices, head doctors argued that when women returned from parental leave they preferred to take assistant positions to that of a senior doctor. Women's (presumably inescapable) biological role as mothers (presumably unavoidably) placed them at an a priori professional disadvantage in relation to men, and gender inequality was reinforced.

The hospital—as a strongly hierarchical organization with strict rules in which the ward heads play a strong authoritative role (chief of clinic, head doctor)—socializes medical graduates into the routine of hospital practice, whose regime is often compared to life in the military. It is a setting in which (gendered) power hierarchy is constantly reinforced, whether between the senior and younger doctors or between them and the other hospital personnel (midwives, nurses, etc.). Young women doctors often speak about having to work much harder to achieve recognition in the eyes of middle-level staff (often skilled women) than their male counterparts, who tend to be the center of attention and enjoy various advantages. In contrast, women doctors later in their careers are systematically relied on by the middle medical staff—because of their perceived conscientiousness and willingness—to carry out bureaucratic tasks or communication with patients, even on behalf of their male colleagues. Combined with the above-mentioned preference by head doctors for male assistants in surgery and as successors in head positions, the professional world of obstetric and gynecological wards seems to be strongly gender biased.

The privileges of (male) ward heads, however, are being weakened today by various phenomena that relate to general trends in current medicine. Physicians in general find themselves in newly difficult positions as their previously unquestioned medical authority is no longer automatically recognized. This understandably has a greater impact on those in positions of formal responsibility for the workplace. Armed with knowledge from the internet, women patients increasingly seek to become partners in their own care instead of remaining its passive recipients. Doctors find themselves having to explain and defend their actions to the "object" of their work, a role many of them refuse to accept. This is a situation in many ways symptomatic of post-Soviet national healthcare systems, characterized by a tradition of paternalistic and authoritative approaches to patients. The practice of exercising power and authority increasingly clashes with a more democratic, customer-service-focused approach demanded by patients today under the new political and economic regime.

The situation for doctors and head doctors is further complicated by their choices and decisions being to a great extent circumscribed by recommendations coming from professional associations. This formal guidance is usually put together by teams from large research clinics or adopted from abroad, and failure to observe the recommendations can place doctors in legal jeopardy or result in the loss of collegial backing. These set rules and standards are sometimes at odds with the capabilities of smaller wards in regional hospitals or in conflict with a conservative approach to birth (minimizing intervention in the birth process), which many experienced doctors of the "old school" still practice and know how to do.[3] The autonomy of individual ward heads is thus bound by strong guild hierarchies.

Furthermore, the doctor's aura of glory, enhanced in the case of obstetricians through their role as "bearers of joyful news," can in fact be experienced in everyday practice by doctors as exhausting. Meanwhile, many women doctors feel that this professional glory is achieved by men much more easily.

The situation reflects the still highly accepted expectation among the general Czech public, so clearly expressed by the retired professor whom I recounted knocking on my door, of different life trajectories for men and women, trajectories organized along sharply polarized gender lines. The persistence of these conventional and stereotypical expectations (man/career versus woman/motherhood) might be surprising in the context of the CR. After all, similar to other countries of the former Soviet bloc, the CR is characterized by high rates of employment and education among women, as well as by a (still relatively high) state subsidy for maternity, parenthood, and institutional care for children.

Few researchers have analyzed the conditions of men and masculinities under socialism in the Czech context. Hana Havelková (1997), Jiřina Šiklová (1996) and Ivan Vodochodský (2008) have suggested that the structural situation of men under socialism was weaker in comparison to capitalist contexts. As I have argued elsewhere (Šmídová 2004, 2006a, 2009), the still-dominant position of men in the social hierarchy under socialism was attained through consent to the communist ideology, by membership in the Communist Party and apparatus. With the social transformation of the country post-1989, major changes have been expected toward more conservative (capitalist) gender relations, and indeed some of the trends in the political and social transformation of Czech society come hand in hand with trends to "re-feminize" Czech women and place masculinity unambiguously in a dominant position. Of course, as my male respondents have suggested, the lived experience can be at odds with such presumptions. But even if actual men feel insecure and as individuals do not fit the expectations connected with hegemonic masculinity, as long as they believe that their aspirations to hegemonic masculinity will bring them privileges, they will work to maintain and support it.

HEGEMONIC MASCULINITY IN THE
LIGHT OF DELIVERY ROOMS

The concept of hegemonic masculinity was developed within CSMM to account for and explore the complex and often contradictory nature and experience of masculine domination, sometimes interpreted as privilege while other times perceived as inevitability. CSMM understands masculinity as a relational, unsettled, and non-uniform construct. Guided by feminist historical explorations of femininity, CSMM attends to historical changes in masculinity while also exploring its different forms among different social classes, as well as in relation to age, sexual orientation, religion, ethnicity, and other factors. Taking seriously feminist theoretical insights concerning gender aspects of power relations, CSMM studies masculinity within the framework of patriarchal social order, characterized by unequal power positions and masculine domination. It seeks to contribute to our understanding of the notable tendency across societies, and especially in societies of Western capitalism, for men to dominate both structurally and interpersonally in most aspects of life (Hearn 2004, 51).

Jeff Hearn points out that power forms a determining, prevalent aspect of men's social relations, actions, and experiences, and that these issues continue to be overlooked by mainstream social science. According to Hearn, the key topic of analysis should be the persistent presence of accumulations of power and powerful resources by certain men, the enacting of power and dominance in many men's practices, and the pervasive association of the social category of men with power. Men's power and dominance can be structural or inter-personal, public or private, accepted and taken for granted or recognized and resisted, obvious or subtle. It also includes violations and violences of all kinds (Hearn 2004, 51).

The vast majority of men take masculine domination in society for granted and, with the consent of some women, help to maintain patriarchal power rela-tions (Hearn 2004, 52). The hegemony of such power refers to the fact that it acts on the level of everyday, unquestioned ideas and actions, and that it oper-ates with the active consent of the dominated. The concept of hegemony, origi-nally developed by Antonio Gramsci, relates to the ruling group's ability to im-pose their definitions, understandings, and interpretations, and to determine the rules by which others interpret events, discuss issues, formulate ideals, and define morality.

The concept of hegemonic masculinity has evolved. Australian sociologist Raewyn W. Connell originally described hegemonic masculinity as a form of masculinity, or a particular set of gender practices, that stands in contrast to other, subordinate forms of masculinity (1995, 77–81). Hegemonic masculinity characteristically entails a status tied to the possession and mastery of certain gender practices essentially unavailable to other subordinate men (Hearn 2004, 57; Carrigan, Connell, and Lee 1985, 586). Some groups of men thus occupy a disadvantageous structural position to various degrees similar to the main group subordinated by the patriarchal gender order—women.

Among types of non-hegemonic masculinity Connell lists complicit mas-culinity, subordinated masculinity, and marginalized masculinity (1995, 77–81). Complicit masculinity is particularly useful in the context of this present article. It is founded in the advantage that men acquire through a "patriarchal dividend," a share of power received by helping to maintain the hegemonic model, even though they may not exercise the practices or embody the model of hegemonic masculinity themselves (79–80). It is crucial to realize that the strongest defenders of the cultural ideal of hegemonic masculinity may not be the most powerful individual actors. In reality, some holders of power may in fact depart significantly from hegemonic masculinity as a cultural ideal that they actively profess or perform. Between hegemonic and complicit masculin-ity there exists tension and differentiation. In contrast, subordinate and mar-ginalized masculinities are in direct opposition to hegemonic masculinity, although they still work in complex harmony with other key social characteris-tics, such as class or ethnicity, to "authorize" the hegemonic masculinity of the ruling group (76–81, 242).

CSMM authors describe masculinity as a dynamic concept that works through constant monitoring and reinforcement. In order to succeed in the world of masculine domination, men must constantly demonstrate their masculinity, before the eyes of other men, in the form of public self-control and in their relationships to women. They also must distance themselves from everything viewed as feminine (Bourdieu 1998). At the same time, hegemonic masculinity need not adhere to the most common patterns of everyday life of boys and men. Rather, it operates by positing authoritative symbols to which men are meant to aspire.

Although hegemonic masculinity is a widely used framework, different authors use it in various ways. Furthermore, it is difficult to identify hegemonic masculinity in everyday practice, because it is not always clear what constitutes anti-/non-hegemony. Being perceived by some as too broad and ambiguous, the concept of hegemonic masculinity has been repeatedly questioned (Hearn 2004; Beasley 2008; Howson 2006; Connell and Messerschmidt 2005). Authors wishing for a clearer and narrower definition of the term have asked whether it refers to cultural representation, everyday practice, or institutional structure. Hearn has even proposed abandoning the framework, opting instead for the more empirically pragmatic and less conceptually abstract "men's practices." Advocating for an informed return from masculinity to men, Hearn suggests that scholars should focus on deconstructing the social category of "men" (2004, 58). Doing so, he argues, we could "begin to face the possibility of the abolition of 'men' as a significant social category of power" (66).

Other scholars have defended the continued usefulness of the concept of hegemonic masculinity. Raewyn Connell and James W. Messerschmidt, for instance, value its focus on the contextual and structural dependence of gender relations (rather than on sets of stereotyped psychological traits), and on the plurality of masculinities and their hierarchies. According to these authors, the framework of hegemonic masculinity is broadly applicable in that it encompasses cultural representation and everyday activities, as well as institutional structures. Other conversations within CSMM focus on the ways in which the social structures of masculinity are embodied and rooted in men's bodies (Connell and Messerschmidt 2005, 846–53; Bourdieu 1998). The male body surely plays a role in the symbols of approved masculinity, in acknowledged prestige, and in the establishment of men's reputations within their peer groups (Connell and Messerschmidt 2005, 851). The body, and its attributed and proven capacities, plays a role in the performance of professionally demanding activities and in adrenaline situations, such as medical operations for doctors.

Connell and Messerschmidt in this context explicitly point out gender patterns in the areas of health, illness, and treatment. Expensive modern technologies are being invented specifically with an eye to serving and contributing to the enhancement of the physical strength of the bodies of elite men (851–52). Here, the gendered patters appear to work in similar ways in the cultural context of the CR or the United States.

MASCULINITY IN THE DELIVERY ROOM

In the CR, the medical field of childbirth, currently the focus of heated public debates, constitutes one of the areas in which demonstrations of masculinity are formalized, contested, unraveled, and, for the most part, reinforced. In the Czech environment today, the high-tech interventionist methodology of modern biomedicine stands in sharp contrast to the conservative approach of some old-school doctors in smaller hospitals, as well as to the assisting approach to childbirth represented by midwifery ideology and by a segment of Czech women. The former, interventionist style aligns with hegemonic masculinity, while the latter, wait-and-see, meticulous approach rooted in patience is perceived and represented as feminine (and thus inferior), whether actually carried out by men or women. Action, qualified intervention, and physical robustness, linked with skill in using modern technological equipment, are regarded as progressive and associated with a more masculine approach to medicine. The concept of hegemonic masculinity can help us understand the processes through which alternative (non-interventionist) approaches to childbirth continue to be delegitimized in the Czech context. Such a delegitimization is in line with Connell's and Messerschmidt's argument that hegemonic masculinity tends to insist on a central discursive position and operates through the marginalization of alternatives (2005, 846).

What constitutes hegemonic masculinity does change over time, reflecting broader social processes. The phenomenon of feminization in healthcare can, in concrete contexts, alter the rigid professional rivalry and gender establishment of the hospital's medical hierarchy, as well as the consideration of alternative approaches to obstetrics. This, in turn, can potentially enhance the position of the bearers of alternative masculinity. However, considering that despite the fact that the majority of Czech doctors today are women, little if any change in the existing rules and gender relations in the hospital environment has occurred, we need to proceed carefully and avoid oversimplification. Obviously, achieving lasting changes, changes that would make a mark on the social structure, is a complex matter. In today's environment, women doctors tend commonly to appropriate the characteristics of hegemonic men in their professional career, thus becoming "complicit women." The persistent inertia of the professional hierarchy and organization of hospital wards should lead to a renewed scholarly focus on femininity and on the role played by women in the shaping of particular forms of masculinity. Connell and Messerschmidt bring up the concept of "emphasized femininity" in this context, as a model of femininity that accentuates asymmetrical and polarized positions of masculinity and femininity.

I need not go far for illustrations of this sort of emphasized or complicit femininity as playing a hand in assisting in the reproduction of hegemonic masculinity in Czech maternity wards. In the following quotation, a woman doctor with two certificates and more than ten years of hospital practice describes and legitimizes the asymmetrical gender symbiosis in the operation room of her district hospital:

> In my opinion they [men] are able to decide better and faster. . . . I think that both the woman, and the man simply have a certain role. For instance, I was most satisfied in the role of assistant at the operating room of my head doctor. He was an excellent surgeon. . . . He knew exactly what to do; in a crisis situation he knew how to deal with it. And then I was capable, with my female element, to make it comfortable for him there. How to set it up well for him, sometimes say something so he would feel better. I think this made a kind of a good team and that in the end we were all happy. I did not have the ambition to be as good as he was. But then I knew that I can do things he can't. Right, he made a terrible assistant, yeah? So if you know what I mean, everyone has a bit of a different role.

Under different circumstances, particularly in larger hospitals, this kind of complementarity is not considered desirable. The hospital rules grant considerable power and authority to the head doctor, while junior men and women colleagues are expected to behave in accordance with stereotypical gender expectations presumed to predetermine their professional competencies. In the words of one woman doctor:

> When I came on as a graduate . . . two thirds were men doctors and a third of us were women doctors, and the men really made it into the operating room while we stood in the corner during the indications for surgery, where it is decided which treatment the patient is to undergo, what procedure is to be carried out. There is always like the chief of the clinic and several men doctors who decide what to do. We [women doctors] just stood there and we really wanted to make at least assistant or stand there and hold something.

And it was . . . hard, and I think that men really, really had a privilege, that they really started to put us women more in the outpatient office and we do these other things, or we are in the small [outpatient] operating room. . . . But we, not that we wanted to operate all of the time, but all the same for the certification we needed some procedures. . . . We do enjoy doing something manually, sew something up; we needn't do some kind of heroic surgeries, but since we've gone into the profession, to do something, and it was a little harder to get anywhere. . . . Well, it's a little bit, that "these girls"—most of the women doctors, are whooshed to the ambulance, because they are like more meticulous, hardworking, they can withstand the routine of seeing one patient after another and type it up. . . . These guys don't have much patience, and they just try more to get into surgery. Well . . . I think they have an easier time of it.

This respondent illustrates the practice by which routine bureaucratic tasks and "red tape," presumably unsuitable for "impatient, active men," end up being done by women. The more attractive, adrenaline-filled jobs in the delivery room are offered to women only when there are "no men available," a phenomenon repeatedly observed by Gender Studies scholars and described in other contexts as a temporary solution at best.

In my research I have also encountered examples of explicit discrimination against capable women doctors, as illustrated through the following comment. Here again the conventional perspective is maintained (despite clear evidence to the contrary) that the best doctors/surgeons are men:

She is extremely talented and . . . really an excellent surgeon—if she got her space, which she did not, because she got it at the beginning and then went on maternity leave. Now she's come back but it's already like the end. She would have shown all those men that she's simply much better. She is really very good, precise, super-talented, and now she's returned after maternity leave. . . . Well, she, she's just a much better surgeon than he [the head doctor] is, and he sees that, you know. So, he found that out a couple of times. Then he completely stopped writing her down for the operating room, and she basically told me that he doesn't let her at anything since then. What's more she's good looking; it's just like, it's, it's simply a disaster, see?

The reproduction of masculine domination through a (likely conscious) use of power by the supervisor appears here to be backed up by the overall social structure with its accepted gender stereotypes (expressed through the comment about the woman doctor's looks). Unfortunately, in the Czech context, similar situations are rarely perceived by powerful men actors as abuse, and they are rarely even perceived by them in terms of an exercise of power. Men like the supervisor are supported in their practices by their perception that the stereotypes they hold concerning gender are not "just" their attitudes, because they see these values and practices articulated and reproduced everywhere in the larger Czech society.

The author of the following quotation, the head of the obstetrics department of a smaller hospital, acknowledges the gendered division of labor at the hospital, and presents it as resulting from the way in which the broader society is structured. Despite this apparent awareness, even this physician appears resigned to having no power to modify it:

> In outpatient service I think these women have a number of advantages and privileges; on the other hand in the whole field, hospitals and surgery, there I think it's more complicated for them to get ahead. . . . There is also a certain limitation by the family, that's clear, because a guy can just say: I'm on duty, I'm going. And the woman takes care of the kids and it's just that I think in the Czech Republic it won't work that a guy would be as involved in family life as the woman. The woman is always saddled with that. I know what I'm talking about—my mother was a doctor, my wife is a doctor, my sister is a doctor, my daughter is a doctor—so I know how it is for every generation, and we have gone through a lot, and it's always the guy who says first: I'm going. When there are two doctors, it's the woman who has to be more with the family. If you ask me, maybe it will change now, but I don't believe many guys would say: Hey, sorry, I can't take the shift, because my wife already has something. . . . Yep, it's harder for them to get ahead. In regard to knowledge, skill, attention to detail, the women may have a lot of advantages. But society is set up so that a guy is a guy. It's the way it still is. |

This statement concerning the maternal role of women is by no means isolated, and the expected need for women to be available both for work and their family is often emphasized by Czech women doctors (and generally accepted by them). Many women who face the dual role as professionals and as mothers responsible for childrearing accept (likely for pragmatic reasons) the above views and the status quo. These women doctors generally welcome that they do not have to serve on weekends, and, as they seek to harmonize work with personal and family life, commonly volunteer to fill the role of assistant doctor. There was no available role in the profession (at the time of my research) that would allow doctor-mothers to work part-time. This is a problem faced by Czech women in many other professions as well.

Returning to the framework of hegemonic masculinity, the attributes of dominant masculinity in the profession of obstetrics are at work not only in the hierarchical environment of the individual hospital workplace but also at professional forums. The annual conference of the Czech Association of Gynecologists and Obstetricians serves as a prime example. Power relations are here negotiated through the ways in which discussions are conducted, the arguments the actors use to support their assertions, whom they cite, and with which school of child-delivery they align themselves. Decisions are reached not necessarily on the basis of the strength of an argument or with sensitivity to local conditions but on the basis of alliances. Through their service on professional councils and commissions, physicians from larger clinics are often in a position to mandate procedures to be used in maternity wards in smaller hospitals, or even make decisions about these smaller wards' continued existence or closure. Thus, while the obstetrics department heads at small hospitals can be representatives and beneficiaries of hegemonic masculinity in certain contexts, such as in their own wards, at other times, such as in the larger context of the profession, they find themselves pawns in somebody else's game.

Therefore, while structurally lifting men as a group into dominant positions, hegemonic masculinity here once again does not necessarily translate into satisfying life experiences. The practiced and tolerated hegemonic masculinity remains hegemonic to the extent to which it is able to resolve these tensions while stabilizing patriarchal dominance or re-establishing it under new conditions (Connell and Messerschmidt 2005, 853).

WARD HEAD DOCTORS, PROFESSORS, AND MOTHERS

How are we to summarize the conceptualization of hegemonic masculinity in relation to the question of why Czech men are still "condemned to rule" while women are still expected to either produce children or "assist men" in their careers? And what to make of the fact that status privilege begins to be represented by many Czech men as a disadvantage, an unwanted bonus? The state policy under socialism mandated women's emancipation and encouraged the blurring of gender differences in the workplace. However, the fact that we today continue to assign men to leading work positions while women are to care for children and the household suggests that the patriarchal gender ideology was never completely disassembled and is today having a significant resurgence.

As opposed to former state policy under socialism, within the current conditions created by the country's transformation to neoliberalism, the polarized dual role of women and men is represented as "natural" and strongly enforced. An emphasis is placed on the biological nature of motherhood and presumably instinctive female care. With this conceptualization, women's sexuality and (in the language of medical authorities) pregnant women's "hormonal imbalance" presumably turn women giving birth into irrational beings who are in no condition to be making decisions, not even about their own bodies, especially when the life of a child is at stake. Calls by Czech women to transform the way their children are born are represented as nothing but hysterical expressions of irresponsible and uninformed risk-taking actors. While conducted as a seemingly professional dispute over alternative approaches to childbirth, the current Czech public debate over childbirth frequently degenerates into a strongly gendered screed about irresponsible mothers and risk-taking independent women midwives on the one hand, and the rational, reasoned, benevolent "masculine" experts who promise maximum safety for child delivery in fully equipped maternity wards. There, needless interventions into the process of giving birth are routine; there the men remain the "bearers of good news" (while much of the work is done by others). With the post-1989 re-imposition of the conventional, essentializing concept of gender relations, the men in expert medical positions are encouraged in their feelings of carrying out their "masculine mission."

The status quo is not reproduced without problems, however. The second wave of Western feminism pointed out women's general dissatisfaction with being assigned to the private sphere, while in recent years some men have spoken out against their rule as painful and limiting. So far, the dominant, symbolically powerful edifice of "bosses and mothers" in the Czech context demonstrates a high level of durability, despite its many cracks. To some extent, the inertia (or stubbornness) of the current hegemonic masculinity in obstetrics can be understood as a form of public control maintained by various players partly out of loyalty to the established (male) members of their profession.

The above analysis of interviews concerning practices and gender dynamics in Czech maternity wards reveals mechanisms that both rely on and perpetuate the glorification of polarized feminine or masculine conduct that falls into the patriarchal pattern. Those who challenge the gender status quo in the profession or who represent alternative perspectives within the (gendered) debate around the prevalent interventionist approach to childbirth are being marginalized.

Still, as the debate continues, some influential male obstetricians appear to be becoming more open to arguments for non-interventionist delivery and are beginning to question the future sustainability of the given system, including its gender order. Returning to the statistics presented to me with some alarm by the retired male medical professor, it is likely that the continued feminization of the profession will force its structural changes and might even lead in directions where "the few men left" will no longer be "condemned to rule."

NOTES

1. Prior to 1989, the state socialist era amplified divisions of tasks between medical doctors and midwifes; the latter profession was almost eliminated and downgraded to nurses (with secondary school education and thus limited qualifications and responsibilities). The lack of qualified midwifes, together with a centralized approach to health processes, has influenced the arrangement of childbirth in the CR. The status quo has been resistant to changes despite significant advancements in the educational professionalization of midwives since 1989. Childbirth is not only required to take place in a hospital setting, but medical personnel can even have legal action brought against them for assisting at a home-birth.

2. As noted in other chapters in this volume, the CR offers an unusually long paid parental leave. With the birth of one child, a mother can stay at home two, (most often) three, or up to four years. The more children she has, the longer the interruption in her career. The Czech system of childcare assumes that the child will be cared for within the family, and since the dissolution of socialism, there has been a lack of (state-run, subsidized) care facilities for children under three. Furthermore, the Czech labor market is organized in such a way that part-time employment is almost nonexistent.

3. In many respects these physicians, sometimes with professional experience from abroad, are unacknowledged allies of the "birth-assisting" model of birth advocated by midwives, that is, woman-centered with minimum interventions, responsibility shared by mother and midwife, and with physicians called only in emergencies.

14 SOME ISSUES AND CHALLENGES FACED BY ELDERLY AND RETIRED WOMEN IN THE CZECH REPUBLIC

JIŘINA ŠIKLOVÁ

WRITING ABOUT SUCH a general category of people as "old or elderly women in the Czech Republic" is a challenging task. The immediate question that comes to mind is, who belongs in this category? Is our criteria here given by or specific to a particular society? Might the labels of "old" or "elderly" be self-defined, something seen more in the eye of the beholder? And however it comes about, is there some concrete demographic of women who consider themselves elderly, either in respect to the fact of biological age or prevailing perceptions? Czech opinions on the matter form some consensus around biological criteria, generally dubbing post-fertile women over sixty as "old." This cohort of women tends to be retired, almost always (in the Czech context) with adult children who might well have their own families. Demographically speaking, with average lifespans on the increase and birthrates long remaining low in the Czech Republic (CR), "old people" are among the most populous age groups. And among this group, women predominate. This reality underscores the importance of taking seriously this group that is often overlooked in feminist and other academic research circles.

While age and sex are among the most frequently invoked demographic categories, differentiating women based on their biological age only, without considering other age-related social criteria, would certainly not be sufficient for arriving at any meaningful understanding of what elderly Czech women contribute to the distinctiveness of Czech culture today. And to put our finger on these differentiating characteristics, it might be useful to review some of the main historical and social events that this generation of women lived through and in which they participated. In this way we can delineate the specificity of this group as a *generational group formed by concrete sociohistorical events.*

Without this sociohistorical approach, a person's age remains just a simple, culturally abstract chronological dimension of one's existence, a mechanical tool employed in the categorization of an individual. Our goal here is rather to arrive at the distinctness of this age- and sex-specific group as a whole, to explicate what characterizes this group of women we today label as old and who live in the CR in the second decade of the twenty-first century. Many of them have lived here since the middle of the twentieth century, some even longer. Curiously, they are a generation who have (in some instances more than once) outlived the political society they were born into. The political and economic events of the second half of the twentieth century, now part of our history books, all directly touched on the lives of these women.

In this chapter, I use the term "old women" to refer to women born on or before 1940. Recent scholarship refers to this period in human life as the "fourth dimension of the third age," an advanced stage of old age (Bútorová et al. 2013). According to another commonly used definition, this group is divided into the "young old," a term used up to the age of seventy-five, and the "old-old," a term referring to those over seventy-five. This latter group of the "old-old" is one with a particularly rapid growth in numbers when compared to other age groups, especially at present times of continuing low birthrates.

While birthrates in the CR have (recently) been increasing slowly, according to the 2005 World Bank projections for Eastern Europe and the former Soviet Union (as cited by Chawla, Betcherman, and Banerji 2007, 7), the CR can expect a population decrease (-5%) by 2025. This challenge is one shared by other countries in the region, with Poland's projected population decrease by 2025 being -4 percent, Hungary -8 percent, Slovakia -8 percent, and Ukraine -24 percent. The same 2005 World Bank report projects that the proportion of population aged 65+ will be much higher in the region by 2025, with the CR's increase of that demographic group expected to be around 14 percent, as compared to about 12 percent in Slovakia, 13 percent in Poland, and 15 percent in Hungary (7). Indeed, according to the same report, the CR can expect the highest projected increase of life expectancy for males, and the second (after Slovenia) highest projected increase in life expectancy for females in the region (59).

Regarding the "young-old" and "old-old" groups of people, in both of these groups, women are clearly predominant in the CR (and around the world). Demographic studies suggest that Czech women live on average seven years longer than men, and in the age group of sixty-five years and older, there are one third more women than men. In the higher age category, women even make up three quarters of the group. To be more specific, in the 60–69 age bracket, there are 122 women for every 100 men; in the 70–79 age bracket, it is 163 women for 100 men; and in the over 80 age bracket, there are 237 women for each 100 men (*Zaostřeno na ženy a muže* 2013). These statistical trends are shared by many other Central and Eastern European national communities, as well as by economically developed countries, and as suggested by the World Bank projections, the trend is not expected to change anytime soon. These figures thus call for an increased emphasis on scholarship dedicated to women (including Czech women) as they age; not doing so would be to neglect to understand a significant portion of the population.

What distinguishes "old women" in the CR from other age groups? While this group of women are often represented and popularly thought of as conservative or inflexible, I do not necessarily agree with this characterization. After all, this generation lived through and adapted to several major socioeconomic transformations, accompanied by fundamental realignments in values in both public and private spheres. They survived, or even actively participated in bringing about, these transformations, either accepting or rejecting them but not being broken down by them. In their childhood, the generation of currently old women survived the occupation of Czechoslovakia by the Nazis in 1939, World War II, and the re-establishment of Czechoslovakia in 1945. They lived through the postwar time of poverty; they witnessed the postwar German population transfer from Czechoslovakia's border regions, and the repopulation of these regions by tens of thousands of people, including women, arriving from the eastern part of the country. They lived through a short period of democracy, which ended with the communist overthrow in February 1948, followed by the incorporation of the country into the Soviet bloc. They witnessed and likely participated in the socialist nationalization of private capital, including small farms and businesses, only to see—after several decades—a re-privatization of property and a return to private farming and enterprise. Remarkably, they managed to adapt to all of these shifts and changes.

Thus, rather than characterizing them as conservative, inflexible, or old-fashioned, I would look for the specificity of this remarkably resilient group somewhere else. First of all, this is a highly educated cohort of women; they are the first generation of Czech women with a fairly high level of education, including university education. Most of them worked full time for a large portion of their lives; they had their own careers, usually besides being wives and mothers. Only a very small number of them relied financially on their partners or husbands. Consequently, today they tend to have their own pensions, although, as I point out below, their pensions are on average lower than men's.

Furthermore, as Alena Wagnerová discusses in her chapter in this volume, this is a generation of women who were emancipated "from above" (however inaccurate the term), in some cases against their will, through centrally prescribed and induced sociopolitical mandates with deep implications for the private lives of families and especially women. It is a generation for whom contraception and the right to make their own decisions about having children was a fairly taken-for-granted matter. In the public sphere, these women were encouraged to and many did participate in politics, joined political parties, and sometimes were persecuted, just as men, for their political activities. Some in this group of today's old women were active in political dissent against the communist regime and even spent time in jail as political prisoners.[1]

The political transformations this generation of women has lived through fundamentally changed the very texture of the social structure, including assumptions about family life and the position of women. These formative experiences explain why those who lived through them might have a very different attitude than today's young or middle-aged women toward such issues as extramarital relationships, divorce, contraception, lesbian love, and also emancipation and feminism. Today's generation of "old women" tends not to be overtly interested in activism for women's emancipation. In a way, this is paradoxical: this cohort of Czech women largely rejects terms like "emancipation" or "feminism," in spite of the fact that throughout their lives they more often than not actually realized and lived feminist principles, and many could indeed be viewed as feminist role models! When during my public lectures I point out to "old women" in the audience this fact—that they realized many feminist principles in their own lives—they are often surprised and dismissive of the idea. After all, as other chapters in this volume discuss, until 1989 feminism was represented in this country as a bourgeois ideology threatening to divide the proletariat and derail the working masses from their task of building a new, socialist society. And the concept of women's emancipation became unattractive to many in this older generation because the term was often invoked to call on women to work harder, to organize, and to be "politically engaged" (*angažované*), all in the service of the socialist state and economy. As these activities were required and actively enforced by authorities, today's old Czech women often explicitly reject political "engagement." At the same time, we see them attending public lectures and discussing political issues, perhaps even to a greater extent than younger women. Czech women, especially old women, tend to be the foundation of local cultural and civic life, particularly in smaller towns, although they do not tend to be majorly engaged in political parties.

They do not organize political interest groups that would advocate for their rights and interests. Their political engagement tends to be minimal—almost as if they had been exhausted by their earlier, mandated participation.

Still, we should not forget that this generation of women was the first to start building the so-called third or civic sector, which had been missing in the Czechoslovak socialist context prior to 1989. After 1989, Czech men were much more than women attracted (and encouraged) to try their hand in business, gradually developing and getting involved in the so-called second, private sector (the first sector refers to state organizations). Czech women, on the other hand, were much more populous in the arena of nonprofit organizations. While prior to 1989 all civic organizations had to be approved by the Communist Party, after 1989 establishing civic groups became much easier. This third sector—what today we call nonprofit organizations—has in the CR been dominated by women from the start. And it is today's old women who first delved into the task of building up this sector in the 1990s. Throughout that decade they were involved with such issues as help for released political prisoners and assistance for immigrants and asylum seekers—especially from the Balkans—as well as with various other human rights initiatives. They were also involved with numerous local civic projects, such as setting up kindergartens and extracurricular groups for children or organizing various educational initiatives. Some of these women either still remembered similar civic activities from the pre-1948 period or they had heard about them from their own parents' stories. By renewing this civic sector, they were involved in reviving Czech democratic society from below. The publication *Alty a soprány II* (2005) lists sixty-two new civic groups and initiatives that were established in the first period post-1989. Many of them were established by this generation of women, and many of the organizations that still exist are run by women. As these women are getting older and leaving the initiatives, too often they are not being replaced by the younger generation, who are generally, it would seem, less interested in this sort of public organizing.

As mentioned above, the vast majority of today's old Czech women worked full time for most of their lives. As a result, they live on their own pensions, although in the CR, women's pensions are about 10 percent lower than men's. According to the Czech Statistical Office, the average monthly salary in the CR in 2012 (the latest available data) was 25,112 Czech koruna (kc), and the average monthly pension was 10,422 kc. Yet, differentiated by gender, the average pension for men was 11,924 kc while for women it was only 9,511 kc. Furthermore, women represent only 16.7 percent in the highest pension category (*Zaostřeno na ženy a muže* 2013).

As in many other national contexts, this discrepancy is not due to some explicit and express gender discrimination in the law itself but is a result of accepted practices in how pension benefits are calculated, reproducing inequalities of working life into the terms of retirement. Basically, the gender pension gap results from the gender pay gap, the financial discrepancy between men's and women's salaries, which, historically, has been prevalent both under socialism and capitalism. It is interesting to observe that in the Czech context, the gender pay gap is most pronounced in the 30–39 age group, and it is lowest in the 60–64 age bracket, during the time when women do not care for children anymore, and when the gap is "only" 6.6 percent (*Zaostřeno na ženy a muže* 2013). During most of their productive lives, Czech women—of the old generation and to a lesser degree still of the younger generation as well—tend to take for granted that although they work full time, child- and household care is still their main responsibility at home, and many of them might "voluntarily" give up on their careers during this period of their lives. As women age and their children grow up, their family responsibilities gradually decrease, which might perhaps be one of the reasons why the gender pay gap decreases as well. Yet, since pension benefits depend on the wages throughout one's career (not just the last several years), women end up with lower pensions than men.

The relative greater poverty among old women as compared to old men in the CR is further related to the high divorce rate in the country, which is almost 62 percent. While men usually remarry for the second and often even third time, and thus in their old age tend to live in a shared household with two salaries or two pensions, old divorced women are much more likely to live on their own without a partner. Furthermore, if old women become widowed, they on average live in the widow status twice as long as widowed men, which is related to women's longer lifespan and the fact that Czech women tend to be younger than the men they marry (which seems to be the tradition in most European countries). This again translates to higher poverty levels, especially among old-old women. Statistically speaking, only 40 percent of Czech men over the age of 80 are widowers; a typical old Czech man over the age of 65 is married. On the other hand, only 8 percent of women over 80 are married (Pechholdová and Šamanová 2006, 264).

Elderly women living in the CR today began entering the productive life stage in the mid-1950s—the period of the so-called building of socialism. During this era, women were strongly encouraged to join the workforce. It was presumed that the state and society would take over childrearing, thus releasing women to realize themselves fully at work, including in professions previously closed to women. What this meant in practice, to use myself as an example (born in 1935), was that when I first went to school, only three of my classmates' mothers worked outside of the home. When I graduated from high school at the age of eighteen, only three of my classmates had mothers who were not employed—and they were all at home because they were taking care of small children. Unless women had small children to take care of or were handicapped, they were obliged to work; if they did not, they were considered social "parasites" living off the work of others I still remember vividly the day my mother went to work at the age of fifty because my father, a successful physician, could no longer support his family of two children on his salary alone. My mother's salary was pitiful, but it was necessary to feed the family. This was the first time I saw my father cry—out of shame for not being able to support his wife and family.

Myself and my generation already took women's employment entirely for granted. The ideology behind this development was that everybody (including women) was supposed to contribute to building a better and more just society, and in the 1950s and early 1960s, these were not yet empty phrases. So that citizens, including women, understood and accepted the ideology, films were produced in Czechoslovakia, and especially in the Soviet Union, about women who could fulfill not only their role as mothers and caregivers but who also worked full time and, furthermore, excelled in their work. The titles of these films are telling. For instance, I remember the film *Žena na kolejích* (Woman on the Rail), which featured a female character who was a mother as well as a tram driver. Even strange men admired her accomplishments. Another film was about a woman who was a wife and mother while also serving in the army. Yet another novel and film told the story of a woman who, besides being a mother and full-time worker in a job in which she excelled, studied long distance in the evenings and organized special extra shifts! It probably did not occur to anybody in the audience to think of this woman's double/triple shift as an example of women's exploitation.

Life was not easy when today's old women were young in the 1950s and 1960s. There was a shortage of apartments, and young couples with children often lived in a single household with their aging parents. Socialist nurseries and kindergartens were only beginning to be built at that time. Most people ate their lunches at work and at school cafeterias. When some of today's old Czech women criticize young people who wish to live together unmarried, or for any other reason, often they might be projecting desires on these young people that they themselves could not fulfill in their own lives—such as a traditional church wedding followed by a life in their own apartment.

During the period of so-called Normalization (1969–89), the situation of women in Czechoslovakia changed. First of all, birthrates plummeted in the 1980s, which was seen as a social and political problem. Simultaneously, many factory tasks were mechanized, which relieved women's work duties somewhat. As a result, paid maternity leave was extended from the original four months to a year and later even three years. More public kindergartens were built for children over the age of three, and free afterschool services were set up for school children. The ideology behind this system of public childcare was to help raise a "new socialist person." All of this is important to remember if we want to understand the views of the old generation of women on such issues as employment, education, their own old age, as well as feminism or Gender Studies. Simply speaking, this oldest generation of Czech women takes for granted some of the goals (especially around women's employment) that Western feminism has been fighting for, which in some cases leads to a sort of anti-feminism on their part. It could be said that these women were emancipated without feminism. They thus often reject feminism as unnecessary and useless, even if in the next sentence they might state that what matters is that women get equal pay for equal work, that they can equally utilize their education and qualifications, that women are not discriminated against just because they are mothers doing extra work by bringing the next generation to life. But feminism? That sounds too ideological, too much like the propaganda of "pseudo-problems." Only after a clarification of basic terms and aims are they willing to listen to feminist theory.

I know what I am talking about from firsthand experience. I myself belong in this generation born before World War II, and I observe these opinions and attitudes among my peers and colleagues, as well as readers of my books, who often write to me. For them, terms like "emancipation" or "political engagement" are contaminated by the communist past of compulsory political and civic engagement and emancipation enforced from above. After 1989, there were so many changes to keep up with that little time was left for these busy women to be catching up on feminist terminology and theory. Furthermore, in the 1990s, many tended to consider any criticism of capitalism, including criticism of women's positions in the job market under capitalism, as propaganda. After all, this was a period of relative economic prosperity in the United States and Western Europe, and after decades of compulsory, full-time employment, many Czech women were fascinated by the fact that women in the West (at least as they figured in Czech cultural imagination) did not have to work and that their husbands could support them on a single salary. Today, this might sound absurd—but we need to place these opinions in their appropriate historical context if we want to understand why today's old Czech women were, and often continue to be, dismissive of feminism when it started arriving in our country after 1989. Similar negative and dismissive attitudes were registered among women in East Germany, as well as in Slovakia and many other countries of the former Soviet bloc.

What are Czech old women busy doing after they retire? Foreign visitors, especially those coming from the United States, are often surprised to see how closely different generations tend to live in the CR today. This tradition was even more pronounced under socialism. Czech retired women are often highly involved in helping their daughters and sons raise their children. Under socialism, and still to a great extent today, it was considered "normal," indeed it was almost expected, for grandmothers to help out by picking up grandkids from kindergarten, by walking school-age grandchildren to and from school (school buses are not the norm, and Czech children usually walk to school), or by taking care of grandkids during summer school holidays and on weekends. The reason for this close involvement of grandparents, and especially grandmothers, in the lives of young families has been a high level of full employment among Czech mothers (not to mention fathers) of small children, a lack of part-time jobs in both socialist Czechoslovakia and today's Czech Republic, and (especially in the past) frequent young families' cohabitation with grandparents caused by a shortage of affordable housing. This tradition of active involvement with the young generation increases the sense of "worth" of elderly women in Czech society, although many would say it can lead to intergenerational conflicts as well, as the grandparents' opinions on childrearing often differ from those of the young parents. Yet, the system was, and to a great extent continues to be, set up in such a way that grandparents' help is almost necessary. The assistance coming from grandparents, especially grandmothers, was, and still often is, financial as well. This is not necessarily a matter of inheritance but rather of "helping out" with a young family's rent, their vacation expenses, automobile and gas expenses, and so on. This again has tended to increase the perception of elderly women's "worth" in Czech society, although it also limits what old women can afford to do, as most of them live on small pensions.

Finally, while living through much social and political change in Eastern Europe provides me with a grounded understanding about specificities of Czech women's experiences in the historical realities we have inhabited, it also occurs to me that some of the greatest challenges facing women today increasingly cut across individual cultures. This realization has come to me out of my

expanded chance to travel and interact with others beyond old political bound-
aries in the time since the dissolution of the Eastern bloc. During the late 1990s,
while attending a feminist conference organized in the United States for deliberations concerning war and sex crimes against women, specifically prompted
by atrocities taking place in the Balkans at the time, we were reminded that the
world has watched silently too often as similar brutalities against women have
been routinely perpetrated in Africa, Latin America, and other conflict-ridden
places outside of Europe. This reminder made me realize how the pre-1989 socialist borders had kept me and other Eastern European women of my generation from exploring the rest of the world and from learning about the plight of
women of color around the globe.

In this regard, it seems we have a dual challenge: to be activist-citizens
in the country to which we are born and to be involved in the world of others
alongside whom we necessarily exist. There are some things best understood
from the view up close. But there are also hazards of seeing the world from
only one cultural locality. Coming to today's challenges informed by various
cultural perspectives offers women speaking to each other across borders and
political blocs an opportunity to approach our future together more creatively
than if navigated each alone.

NOTES

1. Political dissent in Czechoslovakia developed in the period of the so-called Normalization, 1969–89, and included the signatories of the Charta 77 declaration, of whom
more than one third were women. These women not only copied and distributed banned
texts, a dangerous task for which some ended up in prison, but formulated and wrote
these texts as well.

15 THE EAST SIDE STORY OF (GENDERED) ART

Framing Gender in Czech and Slovak Contemporary Art

ZUZANA ŠTEFKOVÁ

To NARRATE A history is always tricky and so is my attempt to present the story of the past twenty-five years of gendering Czech and Slovak art. With any of the possible versions of the story, too much must be left out: training attention on certain events and their protagonists leads to the omission of others. Also, in speaking of events that one has lived through and sometimes even helped to shape, the (hi)story-teller risks becoming partisan: in order to avoid the Scylla of the "view from nowhere," one faces the Charybdis of an excessively subjective perspective. Furthermore, there are other traps of history-telling typical of the genre: the lure of a narrative arc, the temptation of concluding with a climax, the tendency to neglect and discard fissures and ruptures, and replace them with smooth cascades of causalities.

With these questions and issues in mind, my aim is to present this story as a contested field rather than a grand narrative. From among the many possible versions of the story, I have chosen one that demonstrates four different modes of framing the gender discourse in Czech and Slovak visual art since 1989.[1] The following text chronicles the development of gendered terminology, the changing approach to art-making as a socially conditioned and gender specific activity, and the representation of the gendered self of the artist in Czech and Slovak contexts. Another aim of this chapter is to offer an overview of different curatorial strategies that have helped to introduce gender-centered approaches into Czech and Slovak exhibition practice, and to instigate a gendered critique within the domain of visual art. Related to this is a focus on the institutional framing of gender as manifest in gallery policies on one hand and art pedagogy on the other.

Of course, this theme is not a *tabula rasa*. There is abundant information regarding the topic, including exhibition catalogues, as well as theoretical volumes and conference proceedings addressing gender in Czech contemporary art (Pachmanová 2001; Štefková 2003, 2012; Bartlová and Pachmanová 2008; Hanáková 2010; Putna 2011). However, the majority of these texts have been published in Czech or Slovak, making them essentially inaccessible to non-speakers. As the Czech art historian Martina Pachmanová notes in her seminal essay "In? Out? In Between?" save for a few token artists, the Western art world largely ignores post-socialist Eastern bloc art dealing with gender. According to Pachmanová, the reason for this omission is that, from the Western perspective, Eastern Europe is "neither in nor out": "It is similar, yet different, but not different enough to be in the position of the postcolonial 'Other' that is today an integral part of contemporary feminist and gender debates about art and visual culture" (2009, 37).

Another reason for the underexposure of gender discourse in Eastern European art is the anthropological/sociological focus of local gender discourse. As Bojana Pejić observed in her preface to the *Gender Check: A Reader*, research targeting gender in post-socialist countries has been primarily conducted from sociological and anthropological, rather than art theory, perspectives. At the same time, "the production of knowledge in the fields of art history and visual culture [continues to be] informed, for the most part, by a gender-neutral approach" (2010, 15).

Finally, in the rare cases when information on gendered aspects of Eastern European art gets published, it often presents all of Eastern Europe and its art as a uniform, monolithic entity. While it is true that artists from the countries of the former Soviet bloc share common historical experiences, there are important differences among the individual countries and hence the art produced in various locations. A good example of such difference would be the varying role that religion plays in art dealing with gender and sexuality across Eastern European countries. For example, in Poland, with the dominant place of the Catholic Church, artists frequently deploy religious symbols when addressing issues of sexuality, and their critique often focuses on the traditional, patriarchal gender role models championed by church authorities. By contrast, these kinds of topics tend to be marginal in, for instance, Czech art. This should not surprise us given the fact that the Czech Republic is renowned for its self-proclaimed atheism. Seen from the outside, these distinctions might get overlooked, yet these specific social realities generate artistic responses that vary from state to state.

This chapter seeks to redress the absence of information in English on the subject of gender in the visual art of Eastern Europe, and specifically in the Czech and Slovak contexts, while suggesting the possibility to rethink feminist knowledge assumptions from within this marginal perspective. As numerous feminist scholars have suggested, the perspective of an outsider can sometimes offer the extra piece of knowledge that the dominant discourse lacks. From this point of view (which feminist epistemology claims as its very own domain), the marginal story of the production of gendered discourse regarding visual art embedded in the specific conditions of the Czech and Slovak context can enrich the range of perspectives on gender informing global feminist thought.

FRAMING THE DISCOURSE: ASKING QUESTIONS

The beginnings of gendered discourse in Czech art date back to a time long before the fall of the Iron Curtain. However, after an initial lively phase that coincided with activities of the feminist movement around the turn of the twentieth century and again during the interwar period (see Pachmanová 2004 and also Huebner in this volume), the use of gendered, if not feminist, perspectives in art came to an abrupt halt, remaining dormant until its reintroduction in the 1990s. There were many reasons for this silence: lack of information and dialogue with the West; lack of solidarity among women and of a collective effort to change; surviving domination of the modernist tradition and the notion of art as a category presumably transcending social and psychic processes; skepticism toward all "-isms" (regarded with suspicion and often denounced as the danger of a new "totality"); absolute mistrust of political art, discredited by the official propaganda of the communist regime; and, last but not least, sexism and misogyny, permeating all layers of society (Pachmanová 2013, 35–37).

This does not mean that there were no attempts to use a gender-specific approach to art prior to 1989, yet these rare examples engaging gender criteria did so in a way that avoided politicization of gender and bypassed contemporary Western feminist discourse. Gender aspects of art were treated as presumably "natural" outcomes of the artist's sex, and its attributes discernible in art were seen as individual responses to one's sensitivity or as a purely aesthetic problem.[2] Furthermore, gendered perspective was reserved for women only. Without exception, art criticism presented art made by women as marked by their gender—unlike the art of men.

With the opening of Western borders after 1989, the Czech art scene saw the arrival of new discursive practices and the establishing of gender-sensitive theoretical frameworks. The term "gender" was not used in Czech writing about art until the end of the 1990s, yet already in 1993, *Visual Arts* magazine published a special issue dealing with art made by women. Among the various texts that it presented, this issue featured a survey focused on gender-related topics whose respondents were Czech women artists of several generations. The survey—polemically entitled *Women's Art Does Not Exist*—delineated many of the topics driving the Czech gender discourse of the early 1990s. The survey questions addressed gender roles, examined the working conditions of women artists, identified characteristic traits of art made by women, and, for the first time in the Czech art world context, attempted to use gender-specific terminology.

Without further specification or explanation, the author of the survey, art historian Věra Jirousová, used the expression "women's art" in order to underline similarities in art produced by women. Yet the reception of the term was marked by doubt and suspicion. As the responses suggest, there was no consensus as to what the term actually meant. Some appeared to view the notion of "women's art" as meaningless (for instance Zorka Ságlová, the author of the quote used in the survey's title), or even as misleading and inappropriate. Irena Jůzová considered it "a convention that misuses a biological given matter . . . to gain attention or to stir interest in an inappropriate way," while Martina Riedelbauchová declared that she pictures women's art as "something really disgusting; some sort of lavender mustiness of crochets" (quoted in Jirousová 1993, 45, 46).[3] Věra Janoušková connected the term with feminism, albeit in a way that was ultimately negative: "I have to admit I don't like the term 'women art.' I am not a fan of feminism and the whole emancipation movement has led to the enslavement of women" (50). Finally, Jana Žáčková championed the relevance of the notion for women artists: "Women's art is something that relates directly to her and says: I am here, I am a woman, I have a body and a soul" (47).

Besides coining gender-specific terminology, the survey diverged from the then-dominant perception that viewed art as essentially divorced from the social realities of the artist. By posing the question, "Do you think a woman is as free in her work as a man, or do you perceive any concrete physical or social determination?" (42), Jirousová suggested that men and women artists might be influenced by their respective social conditions, which are invariably different. Still, the majority of respondents rejected any ties between social conditions and art. In the words of Jůzová: "There should be no external determinations in art" (45). This statement reflected a belief in the autonomy of art that was not as much an outcome of some a priori formalist theoretical framework as it was a response to the experiences of the situation prior to 1989, in which nonconformist artists sought to keep their freedom and avoid control by the state regime.

Another opinion that the respondents shared was that freedom or lack thereof is a matter of personal responsibility. For instance, Janoušková suggested it is up to every individual to defend *her* freedom: "It depends on the woman, how much freedom she can preserve" (quoted in Jirousová 1993, 50). Only a minority of artists perceived any influence of established gender roles on their work, but even then this impact was not perceived as an automatic disadvantage. Adriena Šimotová maintained, "I feel a certain social determination, but the perception of freedom or the lack of it can have many forms" (52). And Olga Karlíková even saw traditional women's duties or the proverbial second shift as potentially enriching: "If she has a family, children she wants to take care of, she has to divide her time. To some extent she is limited by this while at the same time this opens up another realm of understanding" (51).

As for the concept of gender itself, the phrasing of the questions and answers alike demonstrated an absence of distinction between the concepts of sex and gender in the Czech context. The theoretical divide between sex and gender, typical of Western discourse, did not enter Czech theoretical discourse until the 2000s. The survey questions were formulated from an essentialist perspective and presented the categories of "man" and "woman" as homogeneous, stable, and natural.[4]

CURATORIAL STRATEGIES

In 1992, the all-women exhibition entitled *Kolumbovo vejce* (Columbus's Egg), curated by Vlasta Čiháková-Noshiro for the Behémot Gallery, became the first post-1989 exhibition in the Czech context whose concept and selection criteria were based on gender. It became the first out of several women-only projects characteristic of the 1990s.[5] The egg metaphor suggested an unspecified problem and its innovative solution while simultaneously evoking the traditional symbol of the female principle. In a published curatorial text, Čiháková-Noshiro declared her pro-feminist stance: "We have not experienced feminism at its best so far. We want to experience it and bring joy by means of this experience" (1992a). This surprisingly positive perception of feminism was, however, compromised in the text of the catalogue. Speaking of the feminist movement, the curator maintained that "emancipation did not bring about any new imaginative approach. It engendered women, who were fat, worn out, and prematurely senescent" (1992b). In the catalogue the curator quoted the 1991 text of the Czech sociologist Jiřina Šmejkalová entitled "What Is Feminism? What to Do with Her/Him?" and concluded that "the WOMAN becomes a problem that has to be researched" (1992b). According to Čiháková-Noshiro's understanding of feminist theory, "WOMAN" is defined "firstly as a subject of inquiry, the plane on which meanings reveal themselves (for instance in the history of art), and secondly as a subject of female perception, the plane where meanings are created (for example the specific female way of art expression)" (1992b). To Čiháková-Noshiro, desirable feminism was one without a struggle for emancipation. She perceived feminism in general as an ideology in line with the officially sanctioned employment of women during the forty years of socialist rule, which had realized full employment for women, introduced them into traditionally masculine professions, and granted them partial financial independence while also imposing the burden of the double shift. What the curator on the other hand envisioned was a joyful feminism or feminism without the "tragedy of the second sex."

This fairly favorable approach toward feminism was the exception rather than the rule. Far more typical was a refusal of feminism and gender perspectives in art, with both perceived as Western imports. As the art critic Lenka Lindaurová commented, "No debates have evolved regarding female or feminist art here. This term is treated with unease, as it is perceived as a capitalist relic. Even if we indulge ourselves in some relics with pleasure, feminism simply does not belong among the good manners of an intelligent Central European woman" (quoted in Vodrážka 1998, 65; my translation). As if in an attempt to stay away from the unpopular misalliance with feminism, the other all-women exhibitions of the 1990s were characterized by a lack of theoretical framing or proclaimed a stance uninformed by feminism (*Women Homes I* and *II*). The Czech-German exhibition *Muzzle*, initiated by German curator Juliette Güthlein, was labeled as a foreign import out of sync with local sensibilities. As Pachmanová has argued, "In order to hear the Czech women artists' voices, and to show them in a gendered—as opposed to a gender-neutral—context, the initiative had to be taken not from within but from outside, and the discourse had to be signified as a foreign one" (2001).

A good example of this determination to appear untouched by (presumably) imported feminist theories—a determination that more often than not resulted in an essentialist approach—was the 1998 show *Tělo jako důkaz* (Body of Evidence), curated by Štěpánka Müllerová.[6] Müllerová here brought together and exhibited art dealing with the topic of embodiment. In her curatorial text, she presented the women artists' preoccupation with the body as presumably biologically given while maintaining that women's bodies and minds are more tightly interconnected than men's because of women's hormonal cycles: "A woman has a more varied register of bodily experience tied to her psyche through her hormonal system" (1998, 9). By so elevating the role of the female hormonal and physiological "nature," the curator reproduced the gender stereotype that sees women as being closer to the somatic, material, and vegetative existence as opposed to men and their links to the spiritual realm. Müllerová emphasized gender-based qualities of art produced by women, yet she also characterized them deterministically as symptoms of hormonal and (alleged) neurobiological differences supposedly without any social and cultural determination.

Müllerová's take on feminism was similarly essentialist. According to her, "The fundamental goal [of feminism] is to liberate woman into "womanhood," into finding her place within the current system" (10). This notion of "womanhood" seems problematic and could be easily challenged from feminist social-constructivist perspectives, maintaining that every fixed definition of "womanhood" precludes liberation that could be only reached by means of transgressing essential categories.

The first project in the Czech and Slovak context to critically reflect on gender-centered curatorial strategy was the 2003 exhibition *5 žen, 5 otázek* (5 Women, 5 Questions), curated by Pavlína Morganová for the Jelení Gallery. The exhibition comprised interviews conducted by the curator and four young women artists, Lenka Klodová, Petra Cíklová, Silvie Vondřejcová, and Patricie Fexová, with five male artists and one art historian. The starting point for this audio-exhibition about women's art was the question posed by the curator: "Does it make sense to produce an all-women exhibition and what should it look like? Should it emphasize its femininity or downplay it? When five men make an exhibition nobody would declare it to be a male exhibition. When women are concerned, one of the first remarks will surely be that it is a female exhibition. How can women in this situation produce a normal exhibition?"

Already the first question in the interview demonstrated the self-reflexive and critical approach toward selection based on (female) gender. The women asked their male colleagues whether they would take part in a women-only exhibition had they been women. Perhaps not surprisingly, some men found it problematic. Michal Pěchouček, for example, thought of it as "slightly offensive. And . . . somehow passé." Jiří Surůvka was more open to the idea. He was also the one to comment on the gender bias in favor of all-men exhibitions: "As a man, I take part in men's exhibitions and I don't think about it. If I were

Figure 15.1. Ivan Mečl, design for *5 žen, 5 otázek* [5 Women, 5 Questions], exhibition catalogue, 2003.

a woman I would participate in a women's exhibition, but maybe I would ask why there are only women." Even the exhibiting women themselves were not certain whether it was a good idea to participate in an all-women show. In the exhibition catalogue, Klodová stated, "The answer depends on many circumstances—who would invite me to participate, who would exhibit there, where would the exhibition be, and what would be the aim of the exhibition, whether to claim something or to question." Vondřejcová was even more hesitant: "I am a woman and to be honest I would hesitate. Until Pavlína [Morganová] suggested it, I would not consider myself as a woman artist."

Another exhibition to question gender as a curatorial and artistic strategy was *A Room of Their Own* by Slovak artists Anetta Mona Chişa and Lucia Tkáčová.[7] The exhibition took place in Medium Gallery in Bratislava, Slovakia, also in the year 2003. Starting with the title, the project worked with citations and appropriations whose primary goal was a critical reception of "clichés appearing in art produced by women in the recent time." Authors were critical of the "emptiness of the language of women's art, its means of communication and the tired expression of women artists and their persistently repeating interpretations" (Čarná 2003, 89). The exhibition itself comprised works appropriating topics and approaches stereotypically linked with women's or feminist art. On display were installations made of women's magazines, toys, used tampons, cosmetics, and cut hair. Another part was conceived as a "feminist bunker" with textural works resembling the "Truisms" by Jenny Holzer and a series featuring a Barbie doll raped by Superman, Batman, Ironman, and Spiderman action figures. Included were works that critiqued pornography using porn magazines, figurines combining attributes of both genders, and a set of stereotypically masculine objects encased by crocheting. A room dedicated to the theme of domesticity and fashion contained, among other items, a display of women's underwear, tea towels with embroidered French phrases on the theme of love, paintings of kitchen still-lifes, casts of the interiors of handbags, videos showing details of depilation of various bodily parts, and so on.

The artists intended their exhibition to be deliberately sarcastic and filled with clichés, an ironic criticism of the stereotypical art and theoretical framework that conventionally interprets certain approaches and themes as presumably quintessentially feminine. However, as illustrated by a (positive) review published in *Profile* magazine, in spite of the artists' statement, the majority of visitors did not get the intended point. When recalling the exhibition later, Tkáčová commented on this misinterpretation: "Looking back now, I have the feeling we did it too early. Both of us had seen a lot of art of this type and to us they were all tired empty forms. But people in the Slovak scene didn't see them that way yet" (quoted in Štefková 2012, 336). With this project the authors realized a post-feminist critique of a supposedly worn-out language of women's visual art in a context where the majority of local artists and gallery goers did not even start to perceive gender as a relevant category.

In spite of their different concepts and aims, all of these exhibitions shared a preoccupation with female gender. Throughout the 1990s, the gender discourse tended to refer to women's art alone. Yet already in 1993, there was a gender-themed exhibition of male artists entitled *Jako ženy* (*Just Like Women*), curated by Petr Písařík for the Nová síň Gallery in Prague. The exhibition presented works of thirteen male artists working from the position of their "inner women." The catalogue contained texts by psychologists (male and female) interpreting the artists' relationships to their feminine inner personalities, or "anima" in Carl Jung's terminology. The featured artists were trying to picture their versions of female art, feminine topics, and sensitivity, yet the outcome was mostly a portrayal of gender stereotypes and fragments of female physiognomy. At the same time, the concept of playing with one's imaginary gender allowed for a notion of a more flexible, constructed, and/or androgynous gender identity. The plan to interpret artwork by men as if it had been created by women also enabled the audience (at least in theory) to untie the causal links between the gendered aspects of the representation and the gender of the artist, and instead to perceive gender as a construction in the eyes of the beholder.

A similar experiment, this time with an openly feminist twist, was the exhibition *On je rád Feministka* (He Likes To Be a Feminist; translated into English as *Happy Macho Feminist*), which took place in Buryzone Gallery in Bratislava, Slovakia, in 2002. The curators, Petra Hanáková and Alexandra Kusá, presented their all-male selection as an exhibition by women feminist artists.[8] They chose works that could be viewed as "sympathetic to gender or feminist issues, or that reflected new themes until today usually not spotted in the oeuvre of Slovak artists . . . including works tackling clichés tied with gender and sexuality."[9] The curators re-contextualized some older works in order to reveal their latent gender-related content. They also focused on themes traditionally described as feminine or issues that had been explored by the feminist movement but presented them as freely available to men, thus stressing their strategic use rather than their "natural" relatedness to any particular gender. Whereas the curators of the *Just Like Women* exhibition urged their male artists to work as if they were women in order to explore "men's notion of femininity," in their 2002 exhibition Hanáková and Kusá used the featured works to the end of deconstructing that very notion.

The last step taken in the process of considering gender discourse in Czech (and Slovak) curatorial practice was the inclusion of other than heterosexual artists and of themes of transgender identity. Only in the most recent curatorial strategies are we witnessing a more complex schema that entertains and invites a fluid notion of gender. This shift, for instance, was reflected in an exhibition concerned with "lesbian art" entitled *Coming Soon*, organized in 2011 under the umbrella of the Queer Eye festival in Prague. In *Coming Soon*, the Slovak curator/artist Tamara Moyzes decided to present a non-essentialist, consciously political, open-ended exhibition whose main aim was not to constitute a category of lesbian art or to define a fixed lesbian identity but to pose questions regarding the roles of sexuality and gender in art production. In her unpublished text for the exhibition, she asked whether "lesbian art can be produced by a heterosexual woman, a man, a homosexual or transgender person etc." Rhetorically Moyzes left these questions unanswered; however, by including women who identify themselves as alternately lesbian, bisexual, and/or queer, she opted for an identity-based definition of "lesbian art." The exhibition consisted of seven women and one transgender artist—Michal/Michelle Šiml—who at the time went under his masculine identity.[10] The inclusion of a transgender artist suggested that while acknowledging self-identification with lesbian desire is a condition *sine qua non* for lesbian art, the curator simultaneously thwarted the traditional dualist opposition of homo- vs. heterosexuality where lesbians are identified as women.[11]

INSTITUTIONS

In 2005, the philosopher and feminist activist Mirek Vodrážka organized a happening critiquing gender bias within the exhibition practice of the leading Prague exhibition hall Rudolfinum. In the following year he produced a "slightly chaotic underground document" entitled *Mlha a moc aneb nechod'te za Knížákem* (Fog and Power; or, Don't Go to Knížák).[12] Between Rudolfinum's reopening in 1994 and 2005, this major gallery hosted twenty solo shows of Czech male artists but not a single one by a Czech woman artist. In an interview, the longtime director of the gallery and its chief curator, Petr Nedoma, stated that he contacted one Czech woman artist (Adriena Šimotová) regarding a solo exhibition, but she declined his offer. According to Nedoma, no other Czech woman artist was fit to have a one-woman show in the prestigious gallery. Apparently, they did not reach the standards of production of the foreign women artists whose works the gallery had presented (for example, Louise Bourgeois, Cindy Sherman, Nan Goldin, and Rineke Dijkstra). The director maintained that the unbalanced selection was not an outcome of his gender bias but of an impartial aesthetic judgment, with his gender having nothing to do with it (Vodrážka 2006).

Unfortunately, Rudolfinum Gallery is not an exception. This case of a supposed gender-blind approach that masks bias toward women artists is widespread among Czech gallery institutions. A quick look at the exhibition policy of another major public institution, City Gallery Prague, shows a similar if not

Figure 15.2. Mirek Vodrážka, photograph from a happening in front of the Rudolfinum Exhibition Hall, 2005, later captured in Vodrážka's video document *Mlha a moc aneb nechoďte za Knížákem* [Fog and Power; or, Don't Go to Knížák], 2006. Translation of the Czech text in the image: "The proportional representation of Czech male vs. Czech female artists in solo artist shows at the gallery Rudolfinum between 1994–2005." (The list to the left consists of male artists' names; the list to the right consists of zero female artists' names.)

as blatant imbalance. Between 2000 and 2009, there were fifty solo shows by men and eleven one-woman exhibitions. Curiously, this ratio seems to reflect the long-term, unsatisfactory standard characteristic of the art world in general.[13] Another phenomenon typical of the institutional exhibiting policy is the above-mentioned double standard that highlights gender whenever women are involved while deeming it invisible when presenting works by men. A good example would be the exhibition entitled *Space for Intuition* in the City Gallery Prague in 2007, where the curator, Jiří Machalický, brought together fourteen men and no woman yet no review branded the project as "masculine" or a "men-only" exhibition.

The link between a pretense of gender blindness and male curators on one hand and gender sensitivity and women curators on the other is not an inescapable rule. Still, it is no accident that the majority of exhibitions conceptually foregrounding gender have been put together by women. This tendency of women curators to deal (critically) with gender in visual art is a well-documented trend that can be explained by their higher level of interest in the issues at stake. As Martina Pachmanová has put it:

> As members of the sex that was marginalized in the history (and art history) [women curators] seek to uncover the reasons behind this marginalization, while reflecting on the uneven position of women and men in the contemporary culture, society, and politics. On the contrary, male curators pay far less attention to these issues; unlike their women colleagues, they have fewer reasons to deconstruct and undermine art and art historical canons (including the curatorial practice) that cater to the dominance of the masculine element and stem from the patriarchal tradition. (quoted in Štefková 2008)

The time of the 2005 happening organized by Vodrážka corresponds with the emergence of art interested in questioning the figure of a curator and relations within the art world and art institutions. An example of this institutional critique was a video by Lucia Tkáčová and Anetta Mona Chişa entitled *Dialectics of Subjection 2* (2005), made for Praguebiennale 2. In this video the artists compared—tongue in cheek—the sex appeal of Giancarlo Politi and Milan Knížák, the chief curators of two rival biennials concurrently taking place in Prague at the time. Using irony, they turned around the objectifying gaze typically coded as male, although they simultaneously flared the traditional, even if often suppressed, power relations whereby young women offer their sexualized bodies to older men in positions of power in exchange for various prospective benefits.

Another piece dealing critically with gender of a curator/art historian/art theoretician, albeit in an oblique way, was the final-exam work of Lukáš

- And would you sleep with Križak for a show in National Gallery?

- I would maybe give him a blowjob...

Figure 15.3. Anetta Mona Chişa and Lucia Tkáčová,
Dialectics of Subjection 2 2005, stills from video.

Haruštiak, at the time a student at the Academy of Visual Arts in Bratislava, Slovakia. The installation, entitled *Party after Dinner* (2005), reacted to the perceived dominance of women among Slovak art historians at the time.[14] The title referred to the famous *Dinner Party* by Judy Chicago (1974–79) realized as a tribute to key women figures. Similar to Chicago, Haruštiak used the manual labor of a group of women, yet unlike Chicago, he commissioned students of a school of applied arts to embroider pieces of cloth (cut from the artist's bedsheets) with names of rapists and mass murderers of women (interview with Haruštiak in Geržová 2011, 41). Not knowing whose names were being commemorated, the students were asked to attach their personal mark (such as a flower) to each name. Haruštiak then copied these marks onto another set of pieces of cloth and stained them with his semen (41). The artist explained his work as a response to clichés in feminist and gender-specific art made by women promoted by a strong group of women art curators at the time. In the theoretical part of his diploma work, Haruštiak concluded: "In Slovakia, which is at the present moment flooded with women curators, it is tempting to make women's art or at least art that deals with gender" (Haruštiak 2005, 15–16; my translation). This statement suggests that—likely for the first time in Slovak art history—a young male artist felt the art scene was being dominated by women emphasizing gender-specific art, and responded with a piece reacting to this condition. Thus it is possible to understand *Party after Dinner* as a symptom of male self-consciousness and as a backlash to the appearance of women in positions of power.

The analysis of this last example brings us to the art academy as another type of institution that shapes the gender canon of art practice. In spite of the self-proclaimed gender-egalitarianism of the teachers and the growing number of female students enrolled in their courses,[15] art academies in Czech and Slovak contexts have a strong masculine tradition, and they still tend to champion men over women among their ranks.[16] While awareness of gender-related issues among students (male and female alike) increases, this transformation is not always followed by a corresponding change on the teachers' part.

There are still many faculty whose comments and evaluations bespeak their presumption of female artistic inferiority. Pachmanová recalls examples from the Academy of Art, Architecture, and Design in Prague. While one instructor there suggested giving a better grade to a female student because she is "just a woman," another wanted to downgrade a different student for presumably behaving like a "prima donna" (2002). It seems that particularly works that are either perceived as excessively feminine or are informed by feminist concepts tend to provoke condescending, confrontational, or downright hostile responses from (especially) male professors.

Other times, the reaction is not necessarily directly or overtly hostile but inept or oddly off the mark. This was the case of faculty response to the work of Lenka Vráblíková at the Faculty of Arts in Ostrava. In her staged self-portrait entitled *Interpreting VALIE EXPORT* (2006), the student appropriated the photographic gesture of the Austrian artist Valie Export wearing split-crotch trousers while posing with a gun. In her version of the feminist classic *Genital Panic*, Vráblíková reversed the nude and dressed parts, flaring her unshaven legs in an homage to the exposed genitalia in the original image, and replaced the ominous looking weapon with a toy water gun, thus rephrasing the threatening original gesture with a playful one. The male faculty, according to the student's recollection, "lacked the foundation for understanding the work as a feminist critique" and hence dismissed it, resorting to irrelevant comments about the unshaven calves of their student.[17]

Figure 15.4. Lenka Vráblíková, interpretation of Valie Export photograph, 2006.

Another example where an explicit interest in feminist discourse on the part of a (female) student clashed with the approach of her (male) professors occurred with respect to the research of Zdenka Řezbová, a student at the Faculty of Visual Arts, Technical University Brno. As part of her thesis she conducted a survey on "visual arts and gender" among her pedagogues. During the interviews Řezbová was confronted with some animosity from her male teachers. One of them refused to respond to her questions, dismissing the theme of her study as a "sly marketing strategy" (2007, 15). Another professor agreed to the interview but appeared to deliberately spice up his answers with a dose of overtly sexist comments (50).

These examples demonstrate some of the challenges faced by young artists who openly declare their feminist stance while trying to instigate polemics with the supposedly gender-blind attitudes of their teachers and fellow students on one hand and older feminist art on the other. Unlike in the 1970s U.S. context, where women-only activities like the Feminist Art Program at Cal Arts helped to stimulate exchange and cooperation among women, in today's Czech Republic there are no art programs intended specially for women. However, there are studios with a majority of female students or even all-female collectives, even if they do not tend to be a result of a conscious strategy but rather the outcome of a convergence toward certain charismatic women artists.

A case in point is the Studio of Body Design at the Faculty of Arts in Brno, established during the 1998–99 academic year. The title of the studio suggests design, but its proclivities are more conceptual, with a focus on performance and mixed-media art. Since its founding, this studio has continued attracting female students predominantly.[18] Under Jana Preková and later Lenka Klodová, the studio has evolved into an interdisciplinary conceptual art program dealing with themes of gender and the body. Unlike the otherwise (locally) predominant notion of performance and body art as an existential (and essentially gender-less) expression of the authorial Artist-Subject, this studio conceives of the body as closely tied to the social-political climate, and its media make the issue of gender the core of its pedagogical approach.

CONCLUSION

Due to the isolation of the countries of the Eastern bloc during the Cold War, gender in art in the Czech and Slovak context was not critically discussed until after 1989. With the opening of borders, Western gender theory and comparable visual material became available, yet what followed should not be seen as a passive acceptance of Western (feminist) terminology and strategies by the local art scene. Contrary to the still-popular belief that feminist and gender perspectives were incongruently implanted into Czech art (their proponents often being accused of following a "fad" or "Western import"), the evolution of a local gendered discourse correlated with changes in Czech society as a whole.

The transition from state socialism to capitalism brought along a return to more traditional practices of gender expectations, a growing gap between men's and women's salaries, as well as financial insecurity on the part of (among others) socially vulnerable women (single mothers, unemployed senior women, pensioners). Another problematic phenomenon connected with the opening of borders was the proliferation of sex tourism and prostitution in Prague and in the border regions along the former Iron Curtain. These issues then precipitated a response, if not downright critique. In the field of visual art, the main object of contention and criticism was the exploitation of (especially women's) bodies in advertising, pornography, fashion, and the beauty industry. On a different note, an important development in the local grounding of the theoretical gender framework of art production involved the establishing of Gender Studies as an academic curriculum taught at the university level in 1998. Six years later, Gender Studies became officially accredited at Charles University. Last but not least, the implementation of gender (art) discourse was aided by the coming of age of the generation that grew up after the dissolution of the socialist regime.

At the same time, the story of framing Eastern European gendered art cannot be portrayed as a simple echo of the development of gender discourse in the West. In spite of many similarities and overlaps with feminist issues in art of the 1970s (namely the attempts of art critics and curators to identify form and content characteristic of art made by women and to establish terms to describe it—only to critique the essentialism, one-sidedness, and heterosexism of this approach a decade or so later), there was a key difference to the process. Unlike in the United States and Western Europe, Eastern European art dealing with gender was not created in the context of a popular feminist movement, and most of the leading Czech women artists would reject not only an association with feminism but even their art being interpreted as gender specific.

The limits of applying Western feminist terminology and theory can be demonstrated through a series of digital photographs entitled *Views* (1996) by Veronika Bromová. These large-scale, digitally manipulated images show portions of the artist's body (crotch, stomach, brain, etc.) that are seemingly dissected and cut open. According to the curator Olga Malá, the photos were a response to "the wider social basis with its various aspects (for example feminism)" (1998). And in his response to Bromová's photo series, the curator and art theorist Karel Srp evoked the (feminist) theory of the gaze when speaking of the camera "as a phallus or even more precise a phallus terminating with a collective eye" (1998). Yet these interpretations were out of sync with the interpretation of her work by Bromová herself, who saw her pieces as a celebration of the "wonderful" interior of the body: "I wanted to suggest that inside we are all the same, soft, and vulnerable . . . to draw attention away from the surface to the interior that functions quite independently from what we see from the outside. What is under the skin is also very interesting and so complicated that it is a real miracle that we are here, that we function" (quoted in Müllerová 1998, 21; my translation). On a different occasion, Bromová came up with a sexier interpretation. Regarding the split crotch image she noted, "Everyone has seen a wide open cunt in a porn magazine a thousand times. I wanted to show it from the other side, so that one could see that—in its own way—the body is pretty on the inside too" (Bromová 1998, 36; my translation). Given these different stated motivations, one should be careful when ascribing to *Views* primarily critical or feminist intentions. Yet even the author's own interpretation can change over time. Some fourteen years after producing *Views* Bromová concluded, "I was definitely reacting to . . . the boom in pornography and the mindless way in which the female form was used in advertising" (quoted in Štefková 2012, 275).

What makes *Views* a particularly good example of the ways in which gendered art tends to be discussed in the Czech context is the open-endedness and shifting nature of interpretations here. This openness to a variety of interpretations should not be mistaken for a lack of clarity or a missing (or somehow confused) opinion on the part of the artist. As the American artist Mira Schor noted in her interview with Pachmanová: "Art is not 'dumb'; it produces by itself an amazing amount of ideas and discourses, and even though in most cases they are not explicitly verbally or textually pronounced, they are there" (2001, 73). In this sense, the varied and sometimes discordant interpretations stem from the plurality of meanings that are implicitly coded in the work itself.

The institutional framing of *Views* followed a similar pattern. It premiered at the *Urban Legends* exhibition at Kunsthalle in Baden-Baden, Germany, where it readily assumed a position within the identity discourse typical of the

1990s, and in 1998 it was presented at *Close Echoes* in Prague alongside feminist artists like Elke Krystufek and Mona Hatoum. Yet even in this context, and in spite of the curatorial effort to bring up possible feminist readings of the series, its socially critical potential was lost on the majority of viewers and not embraced by the author herself either.

Since the 1990s, Bromová's work dealing with issues of embodiment, intimacy, identity, and female archetypes became a prime example of Czech "gender art." Her institutionalization as a "woman artist" played an important role in this process. This in turn illustrates the way in which art produced by women artists is perceived as gender specific, unlike the art of men. Bromová has been interviewed in various surveys targeting women artists (for instance, in the catalogues of *Body of Evidence*, 1998, and *Inter View,* 2010), and her work has been included in issues of art journals dealing with women in art (*Labyrint, Umělec*) and women-only exhibitions. Simultaneously, Bromová rose in prominence. In 1999, she represented the Czech Republic at the Venice Biennial; between 2001 and 2010, she was in charge of the Studio of Photographic and Digital Image at the Academy of Fine Arts Prague, bringing up dozens of students—many of them women. In 2009, the City Gallery Prague organized a major exhibition of her work. Bromová's take on (her own) femininity became a canonical example within the Czech discourse on gender in art.

As this present study demonstrates, the story of Czech and Slovak art dealing with gender cannot be complete without an analysis of the discursive tools and institutions that help to produce "gendered art." Through the analysis of several relevant surveys and curatorial texts this chapter examines the conception and development of gender-specific terminology and gendered iconography in post-1989 Czech and Slovak art and art criticism. The study delineates how the changing social conditions gradually transformed the notion of gender both in the larger society and in art. It outlines how after the initial stage of conflating gender with biological sex and/or mistaking it for femininity, art exhibitions started embracing the notion of male gender and transgender as well. Finally, the chapter seeks to manifest how Czech and Slovak art institutions (galleries and schools) produce gender difference, and gender bias, while at the same time denying their own role in this process. To sum up, the story this chapter tells might be missing a narrative arc, but it seeks not to miss the greater picture. By tying art to the institutions that frame and contextualize it, the story highlights key challenges pertinent not only to gendered discourse in the Czech and Slovak art contexts but to Czech and Slovak societies in general.

NOTES

1. While this volume focuses primarily on gender in the Czech context, this chapter includes some examples of Slovak art. My aim here is to underscore the interconnectedness of Czech and Slovak art scenes that survives to this day, in spite of the division of Czechoslovakia in 1993. Even today, Czech and Slovak artists keep close ties—as demonstrated by the number of Slovak artists who study or teach at Czech art academies.

2. This was particularly the case of Jindřich Chalupecký, an influential Czech art critic and theorist, who saw gender as a relevant category in connection to Czech women artists but in a deliberately depoliticized way.

3. All translations from Jirousová, as well as from other sources written originally in Czech or Slovak and cited in this chapter in English, are mine.

4. Jirousová's own notions of femininity and masculinity—as apparent in her other texts that deal with the issue of gender—could best be described as a relationship of two complementary principles within each individual, or as the anima and animus in the Jungian sense.

5. Other women-only exhibitions organized in the early 1990s included *Ženské domovy I* (1992) and *Ženské domovy II* (1993; Women Homes I and II); *Ženské umění* (Women Art; 1993); and the Czech-German exhibition *Náhubek* (Muzzle; 1994).

6. The exhibition was organized by the Museum of Art Olomouc in 1998. All translations from Müllerová are mine.

7. The original title of the exhibition was *A Room on Their Own*.

8. In Slovak, the word "feminist" is grammatically gendered, so the original title suggested that the artists in the show are happy to be not only feminists but also women.

9. Unpublished curatorial text.

10. The poster suggested that only women artists took part in the exhibition, yet Michal Šiml is a masculine name and surname.

11. When I asked Michelle/Michal Šiml about her/his self-identification, s/he concluded, "I am a spiritual lesbian." Personal communication, October 13, 2010.

12. Milan Knížák was at that time the director of the National Gallery.

13. According to 1984 statistics for the United States, women represented on average 20–25% of exhibiting artists in U.S. galleries and museums (Collins and Sandell 1984, 23). This statistic from 1984 would need to be adjusted today to reflect the growing numbers of working women artists. In 2003, 46% of professional artists in the United States were women (Lovelace 2013).

14. This strong position of women art historians in the Slovak context at the time is discussed in Hanáková 2010.

15. Based on online sources and catalogues of graduate exhibitions, the percentages of female graduates from the Academy of Fine Arts Prague are as follows: 2002, 33%; 2003, 37%; 2004, 38%; 2005, 39%; 2006, 42%; 2007, 41%; 2008, 51%; 2009, 34%; 2010, 32%; 2011, 57%; 2012, 50%; 2013, 47%; 2014, 52%; 2015, 56% (https://www.avu.cz/document/absolventi-avu-1990-2014-3509).

16. As of 2014, in the Academy of Fine Arts, out of eighteen studios, only one was led by a woman professor. Based on information published by the respective art institutions

online, the ratio of women among the heads of the studios in Czech art academies in 2014 was between 6 and 33%.

17. Vráblíková, personal communication, July 27, 2015.

18. In the catalogue published on the tenth anniversary of the Faculty of Fine Arts, there was one man among fifteen students of the Studio of Body Design.

16 TYPOLOGICAL DIFFERENCES BETWEEN LANGUAGES AS AN ARGUMENT AGAINST GENDER-FAIR LANGUAGE USE?

JANA VALDROVÁ

The issue of nonbiased treatment of women and men in language, that is, gender-fair language, has been studied extensively in the context of both English and German, and has now begun to gain attention within the Czech-language community as well. Prior to 1989, Czech press, radio, and television broadcasting were censored, and scientific research was controlled by the Communist Party.[1] Issues of gender inequality were not to be problematized or studied since, in socialist societies, all were supposed to be already equal.

The first (mostly dismissive) reports on international gender linguistic research appeared in Czech scholarly discourse around 1995. Most Czech linguists at the time did not accept arguments about language, and specifically Czech language, as a tool of sexism. As Jana Hoffmanová wrote in 1995 in her review of Deborah Tannen's texts, feminist linguistics is nothing more than a "new fashion trend." Some Czech scholars specifically maintained that the problem of sexism as discussed in English- or German-language contexts was irrelevant in relation to the Czech language because of typological specifics of Czech. For instance, according to František Daneš and colleagues, "the structure of Czech will not allow for such reforms to come about" (1997, 259).

In 1996, the Pedagogical Faculty in Ústí nad Labem organized the conference Žena—jazyk—literatura (Woman—Language—Literature), the first event of its kind on the topic of gender in Czech language and literature. According to Marek Nekula, who reviewed the conference proceedings, the issues of feminist linguistics present "a great intellectual potential" for Czech scholars (1998, 215). As Nekula stated, one of the tasks is to "demonstrate that language, even in its constructedness, is a social phenomenon and to offer remedies for the potential discrimination implied in linguistic acts, depending on needs and possibilities." In this context the question is "whether the problem might be located in the language system, in the linguistic categories and their relations," as they reflect and (partially) determine "our way of thinking and evaluations of reality, i.e., our value classifications" (217).

By today, some Czech nongovernmental organizations (NGOs), administrative institutions, and, to some extent, also the media do show efforts to use language in a gender-fair way, and they sometimes turn to Czech linguistics experts for help and advice. Unfortunately, Czech linguistic research regarding gender is still markedly behind the United States and Western Europe. For example, there is not a single thesis paper on gender in Czech linguistics. Many scholars working in the field come from the structuralist tradition of linguistics established by Vilém Mathesius, Bohumil Trnka, Bohuslav Havránek, Jan Mukařovský, Roman Jacobson, and others, and developed by the legendary Pražský lingvistický kroužek (Linguistic Circle of Prague) of the 1930s. The emphasis is on studying language at the level of typology (*langue*) rather than focusing on how language is used in everyday speech acts within the language community, how that use might disadvantage various groups of people, and how language use can be reformed in ways that would treat all fairly.

The present chapter distinguishes between the phenomena of language typology (*langue*) on the one hand and those of language use (*parole*) on the other. While attending to gender-relevant typological characteristics of Czech in comparison to other Western languages, especially English as the reference point for our readers, the main focus is on Czech language *use*. I argue that in spite of Czech-language speakers facing specific, gender-related language issues as compared to speakers of analytic languages like English, gender-fair language use is feasible in Czech. Analyzing examples from newspaper headlines, advertisements, legal formulations, administrative texts, and so on, I suggest simple and practical ways in which the so far frequently gender-biased usage of Czech language can be modified in more gender-fair directions.

CZECH AS A SYNTHETIC AND HIGHLY INFLECTIONAL LANGUAGE

In this section I first seek to explain for readers who might not be familiar with the Czech language some of the relevant typological differences between Czech and English that play a role in defining specific issues needing to be addressed when seeking to use the Czech language in nonsexist ways. Unlike English, an analytic language that conveys grammatical relationships to a great extent (although not only) through sentence structure, Czech (similar to German) belongs among synthetic languages, and many of the grammatical values conveyed in English syntactically are in Czech expressed through inflectional morphology—specifically through word endings and suffixes. For instance, in the example below, the Czech verb *cestovat* takes on different endings depending on the subject of the sentence, while in English, the verb *travel* does not take on different endings (with the exception of the third-person singular). The subject must be explicitly stated in English, while in Czech it can be conveyed through the verb's morphology:

> I travel—Cestuji. You travel—Cestuješ. He/She travels—Cestuje.
> We travel—Cestujeme. You travel—Cestujete. They travel—Cestují.

In this highly inflectional language, not only verbs but also nouns and other parts of speech convey many values through word endings, and one of these values is grammatical gender. Compared to English, Czech is a highly morphologically gendered language. As I discuss in more detail below, nouns, pronouns, adjectives, and some numerals, as well as verbs take on different endings for masculine, feminine, and neuter grammatical genders.

Czech also has linguistic tools for specifying the gender of almost all surnames: *Navrátil* names a man, *Navrátilová* names a woman; *Nový* names a man, *Nová* names a woman. Even foreign female names get inflected (Bill Clinton keeps his name, but Hillary Rodham Clinton becomes Hillary Rodhamová Clintonová in Czech), although there is an ongoing discussion around this issue, and some Czech speakers are beginning to avoid inflecting foreign women's last names. Speaking of names, stringent rules apply to Czech first names, and Czech parents (with some exceptions) are obliged to choose names for their children from a list of registered names. Most first names, furthermore, are gender specific, and there are very few gender-neutral first names that can be given to babies born in the Czech Republic—for example, *Alex, Nikola* (or *Nicola*), *René,* and *Saša.*

All Czech nouns are classified as grammatically either masculine, feminine, or neuter. Nouns denoting male humans mostly belong in the masculine category (taking on masculine suffixes or endings) and nouns denoting female human beings belong in the feminine category (taking on feminine endings or suffixes). Nouns denoting children, young animals, or immature beings belong, as a rule, in the neuter grammatical category.

As a result of typological features of words classifying as grammatically either masculine, feminine, or neuter, almost all titles of occupations or professions can have both masculine and feminine versions in Czech:

učitel (*masc.*)—učitelka (*fem.*) [teacher]
doktor (*masc.*)—doktorka (*fem.*) [doctor]
advokát (*masc.*)—advokátka (*fem.*) [lawyer]
zemědělec (*masc.*)—zemědělkyně (*fem.*) [peasant], and so on

While not unknown to English, the tendency to create feminine counter-parts for existing words naming occupations is not as widespread, with some rare examples including *actor-actress*. Nouns like *teacher, professor, lawyer*, and so on are gender indistinct in English (but: *waiter-waitress*), and thus when used for instance in job advertisements, their use itself does not lead to sexist language. In Czech, the situation is different. Since feminines and masculines exist for these nouns (*učitel-učitelka, student-studentka, politik-politička*, etc.), using *učitel, student, politik*, or the like when referring to both men and women could be perceived as gender biased and as making women invisible.

Some representatives of Czech structural Bohemistics (the study of the Czech language) maintain that the use of grammatically masculine words in such cases is not perceived as gender biased because the words here function as "generic masculines" (Daneš 2007b). These arguments are reminiscent of earlier, now rejected, arguments in the English-speaking context about the generic masculine pronoun *he* and the generic *man*. Czech linguists support their position by using the concept of markedness and unmarkedness. Feminines like *studentka* are perceived always as marked, as female-specific. On the other hand, masculines like *student* can, depending on the context, be perceived as either unmarked (generic masculine) and as referring to both men and women, or as marked and male-specific. Constructions with generic masculines are very common in Czech, and sometimes women use grammatically masculine versions of professional titles when referring to themselves: for example, *Zástupce starosty* (*Deputy Mayor masc.*), *Ing. Bláhová* (*female name*) instead of *Zástupkyně* (*fem.*) *starosty Ing. Bláhová*. In such cases, the issue is not language typology but rather the extent to which speakers are or are not sensitive to gender bias in language. Furthermore, examples like the above are also reflective of the state of Czech language reform. There are no official materials available for the Czech public that would systematically list masculine and feminine versions of job titles. And the same absence of guidance is found with regard to official and internationally recognized lists of professional titles issued by the Czech Ministry of Labor.[2]

Most examples of the use of generic masculines in Czech are cases where a gender-fair alternative would be recommended and easily feasible. Examples like the following are abundant in Czech language use:

Má student (masc.) právo vyjádřit své názory ve škole?
Does a student (masc.) have a right to express his/her views at school?

The solution here would be quite simple:

Má student/studentka (masc./fem.) právo vyjádřit své názory ve škole?

or

Má student/ka (masc./fem.) právo vyjádřit své názory ve škole?

or even (using the German alternative with plural participle):

Mají studující (masc./fem.) právo vyjádřit své názory ve škole?

Presumably, Czech readers would read statements like the original sentence with *student* as pertaining to both men and women because the word here functions in its generic mode. However, as I have stated elsewhere, from today's perspective, the argument about unmarkedness looks rather vague and empirically difficult to support. My own study with primary and secondary Czech students (2008) suggests that generic masculines tend to invoke images of men, thus rendering women invisible, to a much greater extent than the discourse of established Czech linguistics presumes. These results echo similar experiments and surveys in other language contexts, including English and German (Klein 2004; Irmen and Linner 2005), refuting the supposition that generic masculines would be cognitively associated equally with males and females. Furthermore, Iva Baslarová and Pavlína Binková (2007), Tereza Kynčlová (2006), and others provide evidence that generic masculines in Czech language use are distributed in a selective manner, implying status elevation for men and thus a reinforcing of the existing gender hierarchy.

GENDER-FAIR LANGUAGE USE VERSUS GRAMMATICAL CONGRUENCE?

In Czech, not only nouns but also adjectives, pronouns, and some numerals take on different endings depending on the grammatical gender of the controlling noun (the grammatical congruence rule), with these endings (similar to nouns) classifying as masculine, feminine, or neuter. Furthermore, verbs also have to enter into grammatical agreement with the subject, and in the past tense this means that the verb takes on an ending that expresses grammatical gender (including in the first person). The following example illustrates how the agreement principle works in a sentence and how the Czech sentence is in the end much more explicitly gendered than its English equivalent. Note how in Czech, the form of the numeral, adjective, and verb change depending on whether the leading noun is masculine or feminine:

> The English sentence *Two of our excellent students went to the USA* has two possible Czech translations, depending on whether one speaks of female or male students:
>
> *Dvě (fem.) naše (fem.) výborné (fem.) studentky (fem.) odjely (fem.) do USA.*
>
> *Dva (masc.) naši (masc.) výborní (masc.) studenti (masc.) odjeli (masc.) do USA*

Furthermore, if a group referred to in a sentence is mixed, the verb takes a masculine form, even if there is only one male in the group!

> *Padesát našich studentek (fem.) a jeden student (masc.) odjeli (masc.) do USA.*
>
> *Fifty of our female students and one male student went (masc.) to the USA.*

As a result of grammatical congruence rules, it is virtually impossible to speak about somebody in Czech without knowing if the person is a man or a woman. The popular way—in English-speaking transgender communities—of gender-neutralizing statements by substituting *they* for gender specific nouns *he* or *she* is not applicable to the Czech context, since *they* exists in two, feminine and masculine, forms—*oni (masc.)* and *ony (fem.)*—accompanied by gender-specific congruence of verb endings in the past tense. Adding yet another special challenge to transgender and transsexual Czech speakers, in the past tense (although not in the present or future tenses), it is grammatically impossible for the speaker not to express the person's own gender. The English phrase *I went* can be translated only in a gender-specific way: *Šla jsem [I-female-went]* or *Šel jsem [I-male-went]*. The gender neuter form *Šlo jsem [I-it-went]* is not used, and it would (at least at the moment) be perceived as very strange and highly marked, and would invoke childishness or an inanimate creature. Czech transgender speakers agree that the grammatical gender problem makes their identity processes even more difficult.

Returning to the issue of the congruence rule, the morphology of the entire sentence (adjectives, pronouns, some numerals, verbs) must be congruent with the leading noun's grammatical gender. Thus when seeking to make women grammatically visible in Czech, not just the noun but the whole sentence must be modified. The so-called gender splitting, frequently used in English in cases such as *he/she*, is often explicitly discouraged by Czech linguists as presumably too cumbersome for the inflectional Czech language. For instance, Světla Čmejrková constructs the following Czech sentence—as a supposedly deterring example—in a highly artificial way:

> *The reader is invited to reveal for himself/herself the consequences of revising language paradigms.*
> *Čtenář/i/ky (masc./fem.) jsou vyzýváni/y (masc./fem.), aby sam/i/y (mas./fem.) odhalil/i/y (masc./fem.) důsledky revidování jazykového paradigmatu pro text.*
> (1995, 51)

While this example might demonstrate that Czech speakers face extra challenges compared to English speakers when trying to use their language in a gender-fair way, I do not see this frequently cited example as a valid argument against the feasibility of an equal linguistic treatment of women and men in Czech.[3] There are various other, uncomplicated, and elegant gender-fair ways to modify sentences such as the above. An acceptable modification might be, for instance:

> *Vyzýváme čtenářskou obec, aby sama odhalila důsledky revidování jazykového paradigmatu pro text.*
> *We ask the reader community itself to discover the consequences of revising language paradigms.*

In many other cases, we can follow the German language as our model, as German, also a synthetic language with gender-specific endings for nouns and some other parts of speech, is typologically closer to Czech than is English. I suggest that where splitting appears too cumbersome in Czech sentences, using nominalized participles (*the studying [ones], the teaching [ones]*)—admittedly sounding strange in English but not in Czech or German—can often solve the problem. Participles have proven to be one of the most suitable language tools for building nonsexist constructions in German, a language in which (similar to Czech) achieving gender-fair use sometimes requires more effort than in English.

NOMINALIZED PARTICIPLES, CREATIVE PHRASING, AND OTHER WAYS OF MAKING CZECH LANGUAGE USE NONSEXIST

In Czech, linguistic forms such as *pracující* (*working [one]*), *cestující* (*traveling [one]*), *kupující* (*buying [one]*), and many others have been used for decades. The nominative singular is identical for both genders, which allows for an unproblematic use in all cases where the nominalized participle does not trigger agreement in other parts of the sentence. Thus masculine generic nouns such as *student, učitel*, can be replaced by *studující, vyučující* (*studying [one], teaching [one], masc./fem.*), for example, in forms, on websites, and so on.

For instance, reading the study regulations of the Pedagogical Faculty in České Budějovice for 1995–96, I noted 205 masculine generics and one feminine form (referring to mothers-to-be). Using gender splitting and nominalized participles, the prevalence of generic masculine forms in official policy text could be considerably reduced. For instance, §8 states:

> *Student, který nezískal zápočet nebo klasifikovaný zápočet v uvedených termínech, nesplnil podmínky pro zápis do vyššího ročníku.*
> *A student (masc.) who did not obtain (masc.) an attestation or classified attestation at the appointed time does not meet (masc.) the requirements for being enrolled in the higher term.*

In 1996, I suggested the following rewording, which replaced the generic masculine form with nominalized participles and gender splitting:

> *Studující, který/á nezískal/a zápočet nebo klasifikovaný zápočet v uvedených termínech, nesplnil/a podmínky pro zápis do vyššího ročníku.*

And my subsequent 2008 version shifted the sentence to plural, thus reducing the number of slashes:

> *Studující, kteří nezískají zápočet nebo klasifikovaný zápočet v uvedených termínech, nesplní podmínky pro zápis do vyššího ročníku.*

As František Daneš pointed out, using nominalized participles certainly would not work in all cases, since when used as a noun in a generic function, the participle requires masculine agreement in all dependent parts of the sentence.[4] Four years later, Daneš even rejected the "presumably unmarked circumlocution" *osoba kupující* (*buying person*), because the noun *osoba* (*person*, a grammatically feminine noun in Czech) is "evidently feminine," which may, in turn, "insult men" (2001, 45). However, whereas Daneš and colleagues cited this as another reason to reject calls for gender-fair language reform (1997, 258), I maintain that the participle can function as a nonsexist alternative in constructions where no additional sentence elements are controlled by the gender of the participle, such as in headings. Thus *Rozvrhy učitelů* (*Timetables of teachers, masc.*), which relies on a generic masculine noun, can be easily replaced with gender-neutral *Rozvrhy vyučujících* (*Timetables of the teaching [ones]*).[5] Or *Kupé pro matky s dětmi* (*Compartment for mothers with children*), which used to be very frequent, can and is being replaced with the gender-unmarked alternative *Kupé pro cestující s dětmi* (*Compartment for passengers traveling with children*).

Another feature that can support Daneš's position that Czech is typologically unsuitable for nonsexist language reform relates to pronouns such as *kdo* (who). Unlike in English and German, in Czech, pronouns like *kdo, někdo, kdokoli* (*who, someone, whoever*), and so on, and *každý, žádný* (*everyone, no one*) require masculine verb agreement in the past tense, such as in Daneš's example: *Kdo to udělal?* (*Who[masc.] did this?*) (2001, 43). This sentence does not exist in a grammatically feminine version, and it would indeed be perceived by Czech speakers as gender indistinct. However, sometimes, applying the above grammatical rule can lead to rather absurd statements, such as the following:

> *Kdyby se mě někdo jiný zeptal, kde rodit, řekla bych mu, aby šel do porodnice.*
> *Protože už jen to, že se ptá, ukazuje, že není na porod doma zralý.*
>
> *If somebody (masc.) asked (masc.) me where to give birth, I would tell him he should go to the hospital. The mere fact that he is asking shows that he is not prepared to give birth at home.*[6]

And:

> *Mateřství není pro každého. Pro mne ale ano.*
> *Motherhood is not for everyone (masc.), but it is for me.*[7]

Although the pronoun *někdo* (*someone, everyone, masc.*) can be easily substituted by *některá* (*everyone, fem.*), it is not (yet) the standard or norm in Czech statements of this type. For the average speaker, the feminine form would be semantically loaded for gender and might sound unusual, no matter how logical it would be in connection with motherhood and birth. In contexts like this, I would recommend looking for a creative reformulation. Indeed, one of the principles of gender-fair language is "creative phrasing," explicitly referred to in the title of a brochure issued by the Austrian Ministry of Women (Karlg et al. 1997). Through creative reformulation, the second example above could be easily modified to the more gender-specific *Mateřství není pro každou ženu* (*Motherhood is not for every woman*). And in the larger context, the feminine form of the pronoun, *každá* or *každá z nás* (*every or each of us, fem.*), could be used instead of the masculine generic *každý*.

Finally, this might be the right place to at least mention other ways in which Czech language use continues to be sexist. Czech speakers, including serious newspapers and media personalities, continue to perpetuate gender stereotypes through frequent references to stereotypical gender role patterns, for example, in statements such as *"Muži mají nevěru v genech"* (Being unfaithful is in men's genes), as well as through continued gender-stereotypical designations of persons, for example, of women as *"něžná stvoření"* (tender beings), used even in a "serious" newspaper article on female employees in a Swiss company.[8] These forms of sexist language use are perpetuated in the media thanks to their "marketability." They have nothing to do with language typology and everything to do with the continued blindness of Czech users to sexism. Eliminating this type of gender stereotyping and bias is a matter of educating the Czech public.

GENDER AND CZECH LANGUAGE USE
ON THE WORLD WIDE WEB

While the traditional and regular channels of public life still include some significant challenges in addressing expressions of gender bias, the expansive role of the internet in everyday life also deserves attention. The Czech world wide web is replete with examples of generic masculines and gender-biased language use, such as the following:

a. *Chceš pokračovat nepřihlášený?*[9] *Do you want to continue without logging in (masc.)?*

b. Interactive computer games for preschool children: *To jsi hezky zvládl. Jsi šikovný. You did (masc.) well. You are smart (masc.)!*[10]

c. Google advertisement, September 26, 2011: "*MUDr. Výborná Daniela je doporučený jako Velmi dobrý gynekolog České Budějovice. www .znamylekar.cz/ . . . /mudr-vyborna . . . /gynekolog/ceske-budejovice.*"[11] *Dr. Výborná Daniela (female name) is recommended (masc.) as a Very good (masc.) gynecologist (masc.).*

An equal linguistic treatment in online texts (a task for specialists in linguistics and information technology) could help improve the mode of address and create a user-friendly communicative climate for both male and female users. There are linguistic alternatives for all of the above three gender-biased cases. For the first example, it is not linguistically necessary to address all internet users in the masculine form only. Use of endings for both genders as in *Chcete pokračovat nepřihlášen/a?* or of alternatives such as *Chcete pokračovat bez přihlášení?* (*Do you want to continue without registration?*) would address women and men in a gender-fair way. The second example illustrates how girls are encouraged from early on to start accepting masculine forms of language as referring to themselves. The little girl's reaction, mentioned in endnote 10, suggests that masculine forms of address are resented and resisted by at least some girls and can possibly disrupt the developing female linguistic identity in a girl. Gender-neutral expressions such as the following would be an easy solution: *Jsi šikulka!* (the noun *šikulka* [*smart girl/boy*] can be masculine as well as feminine), *Výborně!, Musím tě pochválit!* [*Excellent! You deserve praise!*]. The final example contains numerous mistakes (orthography, punctuation), but the mismatch of biological and grammatical gender appears particularly awkward. There are easy solutions for this case as well. Depending on the context, the heading *gynekolog (masc.)* could be replaced with gender neutral *gynekologie (gynecology)*. And the list of names could be introduced with this gender-fair phrase: *Doporučujeme Vám tyto známé lékaře a lékařky (We recommend the following well-known male and female doctors).*

GERMAN AS A STARTING POINT FOR GENDER-FAIR LANGUAGE IN CZECH AND CONCLUSION

Based on an examination of linguistic means for equal treatment of women and men in present-day Russian, German, English, Polish, and Slovak (Bruns 2007; Doleschal 2004; Běličová 1998; Roelcke 1997; Hellinger 1990; Jiráček 1986; Dvonč 1966; and others), in 2010, non-mandatory alternatives to traditional language use were published for Czech as the first Slavic language to formally address these issues (Valdrová, Knotková-Čapková, and Paclíková 2010).[12] As I have demonstrated throughout this text and elsewhere (Valdrová 2001), in Czech various alternatives to masculine generics exist, with one of the most important means of making women linguistically visible being derivation, that is, the use of feminine suffixes.[13] In German—as a synthetic language that to some extent faces similar morphology-related issues to Czech—ways of making women visible in official language use are by now well-established. As I show in table 1 below, with a few exceptions, similar measures can be applied in Czech as well.

The Czech language, similar to German, thus offers many ways of expressing equality of women and men. Of course, when formulating recommendations for gender-fair language use in Czech, as in any other language, typological specifics that structurally might exclude certain forms of expression have to be considered. As a highly inflectional language with a grammatical congruence principle, Czech does not lend itself easily to using feminine-masculine word pairs in longer stretches of text. However, examples cited above from the 1996 version of the Pedagogical Faculty's study regulations do suggest that the use of word pairs is feasible in written policy language. In other cases, there are numerous stylistic alternatives to gender-biased language use.

Research shows that the problem of gender-fair language lies in language use. The main source of resistance rests in the lack of consideration for the people concerned and in speakers' lack of willingness to use language in a respectful

TABLE 16.1. Linguistic methods of making language gender-fair: Comparison between German and Czech

LINGUISTIC METHODS OF MAKING LANGUAGE GENDER-FAIR	GERMAN EXAMPLES	CZECH EXAMPLES	TRANSLATION
Specification of gender, above all use of feminine suffixes and feminine-masculine word pairs	L. Irmen ist Psycholinguistin	L. Irmen je psycholingvistka	L. Irmen is a psycholinguist (fem.)
	Sehr geehrte Wählerinnen und Wähler.	Vážené voličky, vážení voliči	Dear voters (fem.) and voters (masc.)
	Sie ist eine erfolgreiche Wissen-schaftlerin (instead of Sie ist ein erfolgreicher Wissenschaftler...)	Ona je úspěšná vědkyně (instead of Ona je úspěšný vědec)	She is a successful scientist (fem.) (instead of She is a successful scientist [masc.])
	Kfz-Mechaniker/-in	automechanik/-čka	car mechanic (masc./fem.)
Neutralization	die/der Studierende	studující	the (fem.)/the(masc.) student
Abstraction	Person, Personal, Team, Kraft, Dekanat, Professur,	osoba, personál, tým, síla, děkanát, profesura,	person, staff, team, employee (unspecified), deanship, professorship,
	Schule in XY organisiert... (instead of Schüler in XY organisieren...)	škola v XY organizuje... (instead of školáci v XY organizují...)	school in XY organizes... (instead of pupils [masc.] in XY organize...)
Paraphrase	Ihre Unterschrift (instead of Unterschrift des Bewerbers)	Váš podpis (instead of podpis uchazeče)	Your signature (instead of Applicant's [masc.] signature)
Avoidance of the masculine	Eine Maßnahme für Behinderte (instead of behinderte Mitbürger)	Opatření pro postižené (instead of postižené spoluobčany)	A measure in favor of disabled [ones] (instead of disabled citizens [masc.])

way. In this context, it is encouraging to observe that the initial Czech public resistance against linguistic visibility of women is giving way to a more gender-fair
use of language. Nowadays job advertisements are formulated in more gender-
sensitive ways than was the case decades earlier. In 2010, the Czech Ministry
of Education replaced the categories on its homepage, originally worded in the
masculine, with gender-fair expressions (see MSMT): e.g., *Média (Media)* instead
of *Novinář (Journalist, masc.)*. And in the summer of 2011, a member of the Sen-
ate was publicly cautioned not to address the audience in a "macho" fashion with
Vážení páni senátoři (Dear [Mr.] Senators, masc.), and to take female representatives into account. All of this is encouraging considering that sociological and
linguistic research on gender construction and gender hierarchies in the history
and present of the Czech language continue to yield new insights into the inter-
play of gender roles and power mechanisms in society.

In conclusion, typological differences, such as those between Czech and
German, or Czech and English, do not prevent the use of gender-fair language
in Czech. The alternatives are already in the language; it is "simply" a matter of
will on the part of Czech speakers to use them.

NOTES

1. An earlier version of the second half of this chapter has been published by the author in German as "Typologische Unterschiede zwischen Sprachen als Argument gegen
geschlechtergerechte Sprachkritik und Sprachpflege?" in *Bilingualer Sprachgebrauch
und Typologie: Deutsch-Tschechisch*, ed. Marek Nekula, Kateřina Šichová, and Jana Valdrová (Tübingen: Julius Groos Verlag, 2012), 141–58. The author has obtained permission
to republish the section in English in this present volume.

2. See the website of Národní soustava povolání (Czech National System of Occupations), www.nsp.cz.

3. This example can be also found, in an adjusted way, in Čmejrková 2003 (50), as
well as in Daneš et al. 1997, 2001, 2007a and 2007b.

4. But there are certain cases where the masculine and feminine endings are hom-
onymous, cf. *Rozvrhy vyučujících* further below in the text.

5. Following my suggestion, this was changed on the website of the Pedagogical
Faculty in České Budějovice (ROZVRHY online), www.pf.jcu.cz/stru/katedry/vkz_old
/KS_informace-posluchaci.pdf.

6. This example is cited from Klára Mandausová, "Je porod doma hazard?" (Is giving birth at home dangerous?), *MF Dnes*, August 6, 2009, 9.

7. Salma Hayek, quoted in translation in the Czech daily *Metro*, November 30,
2007, 7.

8. Plesnik, quoted in the daily newspaper *Právo*, November 10, 2011, 2.

9. Inquiry after shutting down the e-mail program in the portal Centrum (CEN-
TRUM; online), www.centrum.cz/.

10. Evidence in Valdrová, Smetáčková-Moravcová, and Knotková-Čapková (2005). The five-year-old daughter of a colleague protested against the masculine form of address as she was not a boy.

11. Verbatim entry, including all mistakes.

12. Published on behalf of the Ministry of Education and available on the ministry's website (www.msmt.cz), retrievable under the title of the publication.

13. In this context, present-day Russian and Polish (also Slavic languages, like Czech) could not serve as models from which to derive recommendations, as human nouns with feminine suffixes are mostly perceived as pejorative in these two languages. A comparative study of Czech and Slovak from the perspective of gender-fairness has, to my knowledge, not yet been published.

BIBLIOGRAPHY

Acker, Joan. 1992. "Gendered Institutions. From Sex Roles to Gendered Institutions."
    Contemporary Sociology 21:565–69.
Agustín, Laura María. 2007. *Sex at the Margins: Migration, Labour Markets and the
    Rescue Industry*. London: Zed Books.
Almack, Kathryn. 2008. "Display Work: Lesbian Parent Couples and Their Families of
    Origin Negotiating New Kin Relationships." *Sociology* 42:1183–99.
Alty a Soprány II: Kapesní atlas iniciativ na podporu rovných příležitostí pro ženy a muže
    [Altos and Sopranos II: A Pocket Handbook of Women's Organizations]. 2005.
    Prague: Gender Studies Centre
Ambulance Not on the Way: The Disgrace of Health Care for Roma in Europe. 2006.
    Budapest: European Roma Rights Centre. www.errc.org/cms/upload/media/01
    /E6/m000001E6.pdf.
"Analýza přístupu žen imigrantek a mužů imigrantů ke vzdělávání a na trh práce v ČR"
    [Analysis of Female and Male Immigrants' Attitude toward Education and Labor
    Markets]. 2007. Prague: Ministerstvo práce a sociálních věcí.
Andrijasevic, Rutvica. 2010. *Migration, Agency and Citizenship in Sex Trafficking*. New
    York: Palgrave Macmillan.
Andrš, Zbyněk, and Ruben Pellar. 1990. *Statistical Evaluation of the Cases of Sexual
    Sterilisation of Romany Women in East Slovakia—Appendix to the Report on the
    Examination in the Problematic Sexual Sterilisation of Romanies in Czechoslovakia*.
    Košice, Slovakia: Center for Civil Human Rights.
Argent, Angela. 2003. "Post-Communism and 'Women's Experience'?" In *Feminist
    Approaches to Social Movements: Community and Poser*, vol. 2, *Partial Truths and
    the Politics of Community*, edited by Robin L. Teske and Mary Ann Tetreault, 35–66.
    Columbia: University of South Carolina Press.
———. 2008. "Hatching Feminisms: Czech Feminist Aspirations in the 1990s." *Gender
    and History* 20.1:86–104.
Bakić-Hayden, Milica. 1995. "Nesting Orientalisms: The Case of Former Yugoslavia."
    Slavic Review 54.4:917–31.
Balibar, Étienne. 1992. "Is There a 'Neo-Racism'?" In *Race, Nation, Class*, edited by Eti-
    enne Balibar and Immanuel Wallerstein, 17–28. London: Verso.
———. 2005. "Europe as Borderland." The Alexander von Humboldt Lecture in Human
    Geography, University of Nijmigen, the Netherlands, November 10. http://gpm
    .ruhosting.nl/avh/Europe%20as%20Borderland.pdf.
Balkenende, Teresa J. 2004. "Protecting the National Inheritance: Nation-State Forma-
    tion and the Transformation of Birth Culture in the Czech Lands, 1880–1938." PhD
    diss., University of Washington.

Bánhegyi, F. 1967. *Sociólogia súčasné rodiny* [Sociology of the Present-Day Family]. Bratislava: N.p.

Baršová, Andrea. 2002. "Partnerství gayů a lesbiček: Kdy dozraje čas pro změnu?" [Partnerships of Gays and Lesbians: When Will the Time Be Ripe for a Change?]. *Sociální studia* 7:173–85.

Bartlová, Milena, and Martina Pachmanová, eds. 2008. *Artemis a Faust: Ženy ve službách* [Artemis and Faust: Women at Service of Art History]. Prague: Academia.

Baslarová, Iva, and Pavlína Binková. 2007. *Mediální obraz českých političek v období voleb do Poslanecké sněmovny v roce 2006: Rovné příležitosti vs. promeškaná příležitost? Analýza diskurzů* [The Image of Female Czech Politicians in the Media at the Time of the 2006 Parliamentary Elections: Equal Opportunities or a Missed Opportunity? Discourse Analysis]. Brno: Fórum.

Bastia, Tanja. 2006. "Stolen Lives or Lack of Rights? Gender, Migration and Trafficking." *LABOUR: Capital and Society* 39.2:20–47.

Beasley, Chris. 2008. "Rethinking Hegemonic Masculinity in a Globalizing World." *Men and Masculinities* 11.1:86–103.

Běličová, Helena. 1998. *Nástin porovnávací morfologie spisovných jazyků slovanských* [A Comparative Sketch of the Morphology of Slavic Literary Languages]. Prague: Karolinum.

Bell, David. 2001a. "Fragments for a Queer City." In *Pleasure Zones: Bodies, Cities, Spaces*, edited by David Bell, 84–102. Syracuse, NY: Syracuse University Press.

———, ed. 2001b. *Pleasure Zones: Bodies, Cities, Spaces*. Syracuse, NY: Syracuse University Press.

Béres-Deák, Rita. 2007. "Values Reflected in Style in a Lesbian Community in Budapest." In *Beyond the Pink Curtain: Everyday Life of LGBT People in Eastern Europe*, edited by Roman Kuhar and Judit Takács, 81–93. Ljubljana: Peace Institute.

Bezouška, Jiří, and Josef Vytlačil. 1963. "Šetření o využití času obyvatelstva v Československu" [Survey of the Use of Time by the Citizens of Czechoslovakia]. *Demografie* 4.4:321–29.

Binnie, Jon, and Beverley Skeggs. 2004. "Cosmopolitan Sexualities: Disrupting the Logic of Late Capitalism." *Sociological Review* 52:39–62.

Binnie, Jon, and Gill Valentine. 1999. "Geographies of Sexuality—A Review of Progress." *Progress in Human Geography* 23:175–87.

Blagojević, Marina. 2010. "Feminist Knowledge and the Women's Movement in Serbia." *Aspasia* 4:184–97.

Body and Soul: Forced Sterilisation and Other Assaults on Roma Reproductive Freedom in Slovakia. 2003. Center for Reproductive Rights and Poradňa pre občianske a ľudské práva. www.reproductiverights.org/sites/crr.civicactions.net/files/documents /bo_slov_part1.pdf.

Borovoy, Amy, and Kristen Ghodsee. 2012. "Decentering Agency in Feminist Theory: Recuperating the Family as a Social Project." *Women's Studies International Forum* 35:153–65.

Bourdieu, Pierre. 1986. *Distinction: A Social Critique of the Judgement of Taste.* London: Routledge.

———. 1998. *La domination masculine.* Paris: Seuil.

Boxer, Marilyn. 2007. "'Communist Feminism' as Oxymoron? Reflections of a 'Second-Wave' Feminist Historian of European Socialism and Feminism." *Aspasia* 1:241–46.

Boxer, Marilyn, and Jean H. Quataert. 1978. *Socialist Women: European Socialist Feminism in the Nineteenth and Early Twentieth Centuries.* New York: Elsevier.

Brabencová, Jana. 1996. "Pražské ženy v procesu vývoje českého dívčího vzdělávání ve 2. polovině 19. století" [Prague Women in the History of Czech Girls' Education in the Second Half of the Nineteenth Century]. In *Žena v dějinách Prahy* [Woman in the History of Prague], edited by Jiří Pešek and Václav Ledvinka, 203–11. Prague: Scriptorium.

Braidotti, Rosi. 2011. *Nomadic Subjects: Embodiment and Sexual Difference in Contemporary Feminist Theory.* 2nd edition. New York: Columbia University Press.

Brockmann, Stephen. 1994. "Weimar Sexual Cynicism." In *Dancing on the Volcano: Essays on the Culture of the Weimar Republic,* edited by Thomas W. Kniesche and Stephen Brockmann, 165–80. Columbia, SC: Camden House.

Bromová, Veronika. 1998. "Sexkontakt s Veronikou Bromovou" [Sexcontact with Veronika Bromová]. *Živel* 10. http://www.zivel.cz/archiv?magazin=12&kapitola=204.

Brouček, Stanislav. 2003. "Aktuální problémy adaptace vietnamského etnika v ČR" [Current Problems of Adaptation of the Vietnamese in the Czech Republic]. In *Integrace cizinců na území České republiky* [The Integration of Foreigners on the Territory of the Czech Republic], edited by Zdeněk Uherek, 7–184. Prague: Etnologický ústav Akademie Věd Česká Republika.

Bruns, Thomas. 2007. *Einführung in die russische Sprachwissenschaft* [Introduction to Russian Linguistics]. Tübingen: Narr Verlag.

Bucur, Maria. 2008. "An Archipelago of Stories: Gender History in Eastern Europe." *American Historical Review* 113.5:1375–89.

Buden, Boris. 2010. "The Children of Postcommunism." *Radical Philosophy* 159. http://www.radicalphilosophy.com/article/children-of-postcommunism.

Bullough Bonnie, and Vern L. Bullough. 1993. *Cross Dressing, Sex, and Gender.* Philadelphia: University of Pennsylvania Press.

Bullough, Bonnie, Vern L. Bullough, and James Elias, eds. 1997. *Gender Blending.* Amherst: Prometheus Books.

Burgess, Adam. 1997. *Divided Europe: The New Domination of the East.* London: Pluto Press.

Busheikin, Laura. 1993. "Is Sisterhood Really Global? Western Feminism in Eastern Europe." In *Bodies of Bread and Butter: Reconfiguring Women's Lives in the Post-Communist Czech Republic,* edited by Susanna Trnka and Laura Busheikin, 69–76. Prague: Gender Studies Centre.

Butler, Judith. 2002. "Is Kinship Always Already Heterosexual?" *Journal of Feminist Cultural Studies* 13:14–44.

Bútorová, Zora, et al. 2013. *Štvrtý rozmer tretieho veku: Desat kapitol o aktívnom starnutí* [Fourth Dimension of The Third Age: Ten Chapters on Active Aging]. Bratislava: Inštitút pre verejné otázky.

Čarná, Lucia. 2003. "Feminizmus nie je to, za čo ho považujete" [Feminism Is Not What You Think]. *Profile,* January.

Carrigan, Tim, Bob Connell, and John Lee. 1985. "Toward a New Sociology of Masculinity." *Theory and Society* 14.5:551–604.

Cavanagh, Clare. 2004. "Postcolonial Poland." *Common Knowledge* 10.1:82–92.

Čermáková, Marie, et al. 2000. *Relations and Changes of Gender Differences in the Czech Society in the 90s.* Prague: Institute of Society of the Academy of Sciences of the Czech Republic.

Čermáková, Marie, and Hana Havelková. 1995. "Úvodem k monotematickému číslu *Gender v sociálních vědách a otázky feminismu*" [Introduction to the Special Issue, *Gender in Social Sciences and Feminist Issues*]. *Sociologický časopis* 31.1:3–5.

Černá, Marie, et al. 2002. *Romové mezi Čechy, Češi mezi Romy* [Roma among the Czechs, Czechs among the Roma]. Final report, Grantová Agentura UK, 301/99. Prague: Karlova Univerzita.

Červenka, Jan. 2013. "Vztah Čechů k národnostním skupinám žijícím v ČR–březen 2013" [Attitude of the Czechs toward Ethnic Minorities Living in the CR–March 2013]. Prague: Centrum pro výzkum veřejného mínění, Akademie Věd Česká Republika. http://migraceonline.cz/doc/brezen_13.pdf.

Červinková, Hana. 2012. "Postcolonialism, Postsocialism and the Anthropology of East-Central Europe." *Journal of Postcolonial Writing* 48.2:155–63.

Cerwonka, Allaine. 2008. "Traveling Feminist Thought: Difference and Transculturation in Central and Eastern European Feminism." *Signs: Journal of Women in Culture and Society* 33.4:809–32.

Češi jsou vůči sňatkům a registrovanému partnerství homosexuálů vstřícnější než Poláci, Maďaři a Slováci [Czechs are More Tolerant toward Registered Partnerships of Homosexuals than the Poles, Hungarians and Slovaks]. 2005. Public Opinion Research Centre of the Institute of Sociology of the Academy of Sciences of the Czech Republic. http://www.cvvm.cas.cz/upl/zpravy/100533s_ov51128.pdf.

Chapkis, Wendy. 2003. "Trafficking, Migration, and the Law: Protecting Innocents, Punishing Immigrants." *Gender and Society* 17.6:923–37.

Chatterjee, Partha. 1993. *The Nation and Its Fragments: Colonial and Postcolonial Histories*. Princeton, NJ: Princeton University Press.

Chawla, Mukesh, Gordon Betcherman, and Arup Banerji. 2007. *From Red to Grey: The "Third Transition" of Aging Populations in Eastern Europe and the Former Soviet Union*. Washington, DC: World Bank.

Chřibková, Marie, ed. 1999. *Feminismus devadesátých let českýma očima* [Feminism of the Nineties through the Czech Eyes]. Prague: One Woman Press.

Chuang, Janie A. 2010. "Rescuing Trafficking from Ideological Capture: Prostitution Reform and Anti-Trafficking Law and Policy." *University of Pennsylvania Law Review* 158.6:1655–728.

Čiháková-Noshiro, Vlasta. 1992a. "Ke koncepci výstavy Kolumbovo vejce" [Toward the Concept of Columbus's Egg Exhibition]. *Ateliér* 10:7.

———. 1992b. *Kolumbovo vejce* [Columbus's Egg]. Exhibition catalogue.

Císař, Ondřej, and Kateřina Vráblíková. 2010. "The Europeanisation of Social Movements in the Czech Republic: The EU and Local Women's Groups." *Communist and Post-Communist Studies* 43:209–19.

Čmejrková, Světla. 1995. "Žena v jazyce" [Woman in Language]. *Slovo a slovesnost* 56. 1:43–55.

———. 2003. "Communicating Gender in Czech." In *Gender across Languages*, edited by Hadumond Bussmann and Marlis Hellinger, 27–57. Amsterdam: John Benjamins.

Cohen, Gary B. 1981. *The Politics of Ethnic Survival: Germans in Prague, 1861–1914*. Princeton, NJ: Princeton University Press.

Collins, Giorgia, and Rene Sandell. 1984. *Women, Art and Education*. Reston, VA: National Art Education Association.

Connell, Raewyn W. 1995. *Masculinities*. Berkeley: University of California Press.

Connell, Raewyn W., and James W. Messerschmidt. 2005. "Hegemonic Masculinity: Rethinking the Concept." *Gender and Society* 19.6:829–59.

Cornwall, Mark. 2002. "Heinrich Rutha and the Unraveling of a Homosexual Scandal in 1930s Czechoslovakia." *Gay and Lesbian Quarterly* 8.3:319–47.

———. 2012. *The Devil's Wall: The Nationalist Youth Mission of Heinz Rutha.* Cambridge, MA: Harvard University Press

Crenshaw, Kimberle. 1989. "Demarginalizing the Intersection of Race and Sex: A Black Feminist Critique of Antidiscrimination Doctrine, Feminist Theory, and Antiracist Politics." *University of Chicago Legal Forum* 14:538–54.

———. 1991. "Mapping the Margins: Intersectionality, Identity Politics, and Violence against Women of Color." *Stanford Law Review* 43.6:1241–99.

Czech Women's Club in Prague. 1906. *Ženský klub český: Naše snahy I: Svůj k svému* [Czech Women's Club in Prague: Our Efforts I: Support Your Own]. Prague: Nákladem Ženského klubu českého.

———. 1901. *Ženský klub český v Praze: Přednáška pí Terézy Novákové* [Czech Women's Club in Prague: Presentation by Teréza Nováková]. Prague: Komitét pro zřízení ženského klubu.

Dahlström, Edmund. 1967. *The Changing Roles of Men and Women.* London: Druckworth.

Daneš, František. 2001. "Univerzália a specifika češtiny v období globalizačních proměn" [Universals and Specifics of the Czech Language at the Time of Globalization]. In *Čeština—univerzália a specifika* 3 [The Czech Language—Universals and Specifics 3], edited by Zdenka Hladká and Petr Karlík, 37–47. Brno: Ústav českého jazyka, Filozofická Fakulta Masarykovy univerzity.

———. 2007a. "Genderová lingvistika se do práva nehodí" [Gender Linguistics Has No Place in Law]. *Lidové noviny*, October 16, 7.

———. 2007b. "Ještě jednou 'feministická lingvistika'" ["Feminist Linguistics" One More Time]. http://nase-rec.ujc.cas.cz/archiv.php?art=7412.

Daneš, František, et al. 1997. *Český jazyk na přelomu tisíciletí* [The Czech Language at the Turn of the Millennium]. Prague: Academia.

David, Katherine. 1991. "Czech Feminists and Nationalism in the Late Habsburg Monarchy: 'The First in Austria.'" *Journal of Women's History* 3.2:26–45.

Davis, Angela. 1981. *Women, Race, and Class.* New York: Random House.

Dean, Carolyn J. 2001. "History, Pornography and the Social Body." In *Surrealism: Desire Unbound*, edited by Jennifer Mundy, Vincent Gille, and Dawn Ades, 227–43. Princeton, NJ: Princeton University Press.

de Haan, Franciska, Krassimira Daskalova, and Anna Loutfi, eds. 2006. *A Biographical Dictionary of Women's Movements and Feminisms: Central, Eastern, and South Eastern Europe, 19th and 20th Centuries.* Budapest: Central European University.

———. 2006. "Introduction." In *A Biographical Dictionary of Women's Movements and Feminisms: Central, Eastern, and South Eastern Europe, 19th and 20th Centuries*, edited by Franciska de Haan, Krassimira Daskalova, and Anna Loutfi, 1–15. Budapest: Central European University Press.

Descarriers, Francine. 2014. "Language Is Not Neutral: The Construction of Knowledge in the Social Sciences and Humanities." *Signs: Journal of Women in Culture and Society* 39.3:564–69.

Ditmore, Melissa. 2005. "Trafficking in Lives: How Ideology Shapes Policy." In *Trafficking and Prostitution Reconsidered: New Perspectives on Migration, Sex Work, and*

Human Rights, edited by Kamala Kempadoo with Jyoti Sanghera and Bandana Pattanaik, 107–26. Boulder, CO: Paradigm.

Doleschal, Ursula. 2004. *Genus als grammatische und textlinguistische Kategorie: eine kognitiv-funktionalistische Untersuchung des Russischen* [Gender as a Category of Grammar and of Textlinguistics: A Cognitive-Functionalist Investigation on Russian]. München: Lincom Europa.

Donaldson, Mike. 1993. "What Is Hegemonic Masculinity?" *Theory and Society* 22.5: 643–57.

Drakulić, Slavenka. 1991. "A Letter from the United Stated." In *How We Survived Communism and Even Laughed*, 123–33. New York: Norton.

Dunovský, Jiří. 1971. "Mateřství zaměstnaných žen" [Motherhood of Employed Women]. *Sociologický časopis*, 155–57.

Dvonč, Ladislav. 1966. *Morfológia slovenského jazyka* [Morphology of the Slovak Language]. Bratislava: Slovenská akadémia vied.

Einhorn, Barbara. 1991. "Where Have All the Women Gone? Women and the Women's Movement in East Central Europe." *Feminist Review* 39:16–36.

———. 1993. *Cinderella Goes to Market: Citizenship, Gender and Women's Movements in East Central Europe*. London: Verso.

———. 2005. "Citizenship in an Enlarging Europe: Contested Strategies." *Czech Sociological Review* 41.6:1023–39.

Encyklopedie mladé ženy [Young Woman's Encyclopedia]. 1972. Prague: Avicenum.

Fabiánová, Tera. 2006. "Eržika." In *Čalo vod'i. Sytá duše. Antologie prozaických textů romských autorů z ČR* [Anthology of Fiction by Czech Romany Authors], edited by Jana Kramářová and Helena Sadílková, 208–24. Brno: Muzeum romské kultury.

Feinberg, Melissa. 2006. *Elusive Equality: Gender, Citizenship and the Limits of Democracy in Czechoslovakia, 1918–1950*. Pittsburgh: University of Pittsburgh Press.

Ferber, Marianne A., and Phyllis Hutton Raabe. 2003. "Women in the Czech Republic: Feminism, Czech Style." *International Journal of Politics, Culture, and Society* 16.3:407–30.

Ferenčíková Konečná, Irena. 2014. Personal correspondence, June 16.

Ferková, Ilona. 1996. "Kal'i." In *Čorde čhave: Ukradené děti* [Čorde čhave: Stolen Children], 89–90. Brno: Společenství Romů na Moravě.

———. 2006. "Mosard'a peske o dživipen anglo love/Zničila si život kvůli penězům" [She Destroyed Her Own Life for Money]. In *Čalo vod'i. Sytá duše. Antologie prozaických textů romských autorů z ČR* [Anthology of Fiction by Czech Romany Authors], edited by Jana Kramářová and Helena Sadílková, 304–6. Brno: Muzeum romské kultury.

Ferree, Myra Marx. 2012. *Varieties of Feminism: German Gender Politics in Global Perspective*. Stanford, CA: Stanford University Press.

Ferro, Marc. 1997. *Colonization: A Global History*. London: Routledge.

Fifková, Hana. 2008. *Transsexualita a jiné poruchy pohlavní identity* [Transsexuality and Other Sexual Identity Disorders]. Prague: Grada.

Forrester, Sibelan, Magdalena J. Zaborowska, and Elena Gapova, eds. 2004. *Over the Wall/After the Fall: Post-Communist Cultures through an East-West Gaze*. Bloomington: Indiana University Press.

Foucault, Michel. 1990. *The History of Sexuality, Volume I : An Introduction*. New York: Random House.

Frankl, Michal. 2007. *"Emancipace od Židů": Český antisemitismus na konci 19. století* ["The Emancipation from the Jews": Czech Anti-Semitism in the Late 19th Century]. Prague-Litomyšl: Paseka.

Fraser, Nancy. 1997. *Justice Interruptus: Critical Reflections on the "Postsocialist" Condition*. New York: Routledge.

Fraser, Nancy, and Axel Honneth. 2003. *Redistribution or Recognition? A Political-Philosophical Exchange*. Transl Joel Golb, James Imgram, and Christiane Wilke. London and New York: Verso.

Freidingerová, Tereza. 2014. *Vietnamci v Česku a ve světě: Migrační a adaptační tendence* [The Vietnamese in the Czech Republic and in the World: Migration and Integration Tendencies]. Prague: Sociologické nakladatelství.

Fukalová, Dagmar. 1967. "Ekonomická aktivita žen v ČSSR" [Economic Activity of Women in the Czechoslovak Socialist Republic]. PhD diss., Ústav Marxismu-Leninismu, Universita Karlova.

Funk, Nanette. 1993. "Feminism East and West." In *Gender Politics and Post-Communism*, edited by Nanette Funk and Magda Mueller, 318–30. New York: Routledge.

———. 2004. "Feminist Critiques of Liberalism: Can They Travel East? Their Relevance in Eastern and Central Europe and the Former Soviet Union." *Signs: Journal of Women in Culture and Society* 29.3:695–726.

Funk, Nanette, and Magda Mueller, eds. 1993. *Gender Politics and Post-Communism: Reflections from Eastern Europe and the Former Soviet Union*. New York: Routledge.

Gabb, Jacqui. 2004. "Critical Differentials: Querying the Incongruities within Research on Lesbian Parent Families." *Sexualities* 7:167–82.

Gal, Susan, and Gail Kligman. 2000. *The Politics of Gender after Socialism: A Comparative-Historical Essay*. Princeton, NJ: Princeton University Press.

Gapova, Elena. 2007. "On the Political Significance of the Sexual Division of Labour." *Aspasia* 1:231–35.

Garton Ash, Timothy. 1939 (1986). "Does Central Europe Exist?" In *The Uses of Adversity: Essays on the Fate of Central Europe*, 179–213. New York: Random House.

Garver, Bruce M. 1985. "Women in the First Czechoslovak Republic." In *Women, State and Party in Eastern Europe*, edited by Sharon L. Wolchik and Alfred G. Meyer, 64–81. Durham, NC: Duke University Press.

Gatrell, Caroline. 2005. *Hard Labour: The Sociology of Parenthood*. Maidenhead, UK: Open University Press.

Geržová, Barbora. 2011–2012. *Inter-View 2*. Nitrianska galéria, Nitra, Slovakia. http:// nitrianskagaleria.sk/event/inter-view-ii/?lang=en.

Ghodsee, Kristen. 2004. "Feminism by Design: Emerging Capitalisms, Cultural Feminism, and Women's Nongovernmental Organizations in Post-Socialist Eastern Europe." *Signs: Journal of Women in Culture and Society* 29.3:727–53.

———. 2012. "Rethinking State Socialist Mass Women's Organizations: The Committee of the Bulgarian Women's Movement and the United Nations Decade for Women, 1975–1985." *Journal of Women's History* 24.4:49–73.

Giňa, Andrej. 2013. "Trin jandre/Tři vejce." In *Pat'iv: Ještě víme, co je úcta* [Pat'iv: We Still Know What Honor Means], 192–95. Prague: Triáda.

Goffman, Erving. 1997. "Frame Analysis of Gender." In *The Goffman Reader*, edited by Charles Lemert and Ann Branaman, 201–28. Malden: Blackwell.

———. 1999. *Všichni hrajeme divadlo: sebeprezentace v každodenním životě.* Czech translation of *The Presentation of Self in Everyday Life.* Transl. Milada McGrathová. Prague: Nakladatelství Studia Ypsilon.

Goldberg, David Theo. 2006. "Racial Europeanization." *Ethnic and Racial Studies* 29.2:331–64.

Goldstücker, Eduard. 1999. "K dějinám českého antisemitismu." [Issues in the History of Czech Anti-Semitism]. In *Hilsnerova aféra a česká společnost 1899–1999* [The Hilsner Scandal and the Czech Society, 1899–1999], edited by Miloš Pojar, 146–51. Prague: Židovské Museum.

Golombok, Susan, and Fiona Tasker. 1996. "Do Parents Influence the Sexual Orientation of Their Children? Findings from a Longitudinal Study of Lesbian Families." *Developmental Psychology* 32.1:3–11.

Green, Richard. 1978. "Sexual Identity of 37 Children Raised by Homosexual or Transsexual Parents." *American Journal of Psychiatry* 135:692–97.

Griffin, Gabriele, and Rosi Braidotti. 2002. "Whiteness and European Situatedness." In *Thinking Differently: A Reader in European Women's Studies*, edited by Gabriele Griffin and Rosi Braidotti, 221–36. London: Zed Books.

Grossmann, Atina. 1995. *Reforming Sex: The German Movement for Birth Control and Abortion Reform, 1920–1950.* Oxford: Oxford University Press.

Guild, Elspeth, and Sergio Carrera. 2013. "Introduction: International Relations, Citizenship and Minority Discrimination. Setting the Scene." In *Foreigners, Refugees or Minorities? Rethinking People in the Context of Border Controls and Visas*, edited by Didier Bigo, Elspeth Guild, and Sergio Carrera, 1–20. Burlington, VT: Ashgate.

Háková, Libuše. 1966. "Ženy v sociální struktuře naší společnosti" [Women in the Social Structure of Our Society]. In *Sociální struktura socialistické společnosti* [Social Structure of the Socialist Society], edited by Pavel Machonin et al., 547–64. Prague: Svoboda.

———. 1970. "Uvahy a podněty k chápání společenských funkcí ženy" [Toward the Understanding of Women's Social Roles]. *Sociologický časopis* 5:443–49.

Hall, Timothy M. 2007. "Rent-Boys, Barflies, and Kept Men: Men Involved in Sex with Men for Compensation in Prague." *Sexualities* 10.4:457–72.

Hanáková, Petra. 2010. *Ženy-inštitúcie? K dejinám umeleckej prevadzky devät'desiatych rokov* [Women-Institutions? On the History of Art Practice of the Nineties]. Bratislava: Slovart.

Haruštiak, Lukáš. 2005. "Nežné pohlavie" [Fair Sex]. Thesis, Academy of Visual Arts, Bratislava.

Hašková, Hana. 2005. "Czech Women's Civic Organizing under the State Socialist Regime, Socio-economic Transformation and the EU Accession Period." *Czech Sociological Review* 41.6:1077–110.

———. 2011. "Establishing Gender Studies in Czech Society." *Aspasia* 5.1:146–57.

Hašková, Hana, and Christina Klenner. 2010. "Why Did Distinct Types of Dual Earner Models in Czech, Slovak and East German Societies Develop and Persist?" *Zeitschrift für Familienforschung/Journal of Family Research* 22.3:266–88.

Hašková, Hana, and Zuzana Uhde, eds. 2009. *Women and Social Citizenship in Czech Society: Continuity and Change.* Prague: Institute of Sociology of the Academy of Sciences of the Czech Republic.

Hašková, Hana, Zuzana Uhde, and Kateřina Pulkrábková. 2011. "The Framing of Care Claims by Czech Women's Groups in a Post-Socialist Context." In *Politics of Care*, edited by Majda Hrženjak, 61–84. Ljubljana: Peace Institute.

Hauser, Eva. 1994. "How and Why Do Czech Women Organize?" *Canadian Woman Studies/Les Cahiers de la Femme* 16.1:85–89.

Havelková, Barbara. 2014. "The Three Stages of Gender in Law." In *The Politics of Gender Culture under State Socialism: An Expropriated Voice*, edited by Hana Havelková and Libora Oates-Indruchová. 31–56. London: Routledge.

Havelková, Hana. 1993. "A Few Prefeminist Thoughts." In *Gender Politics and Post-Communism*, edited by Nanette Funk and Magda Mueller, 62–73. New York: Routledge.

———. 1995. "Liberální historie ženské otázky v Českých zemích" [Liberal History of the Woman Question in the Czech Lands]. In *Existuje středoevropský model manželství a rodiny?* [Does a Central European Model of Marriage and Family Exist?], edited by Hana Havelková, 19–30. Prague: Divadelní ústav.

———. 1997. "Transitory and Persistent Differences: Feminism East and West." In *Transitions, Environments, Translations: Feminism in International Politics*, edited by Joan W. Scott, Cora Kaplan, and Debra Keates, 56–62. New York: Routledge.

Havelková, Hana, and Libora Oates-Indruchová. 2014. "Expropriated Voice: Transformations of Gender Culture under State Socialism." In *The Politics of Gender Culture under State Socialism: An Expropriated Voice*, edited by Hana Havelková and Libora Oates-Indruchová, 3–27. London: Routledge.

Hearn, Jeff. 2004. "From Hegemonic Masculinity to the Hegemony of Men." *Feminist Theory* 5.1:49–72.

Heckmann, Friedrich. 2005. *Integration and Integration Policies*. Bamberg: European Forum for Migration Studies. http://www.efms.uni-bamberg.de/pdf/INTPOL%20Final%20Paper.pdf.

Heczková, Libuše, and Kateřina Svatoňová, eds. 2012. *Jus Suffragii: Politické projevy Boženy Vikové-Kunětické z let 1890–1926* [Jus Suffragii: Political Speeches by Božena Viková-Kunětická, 1890–1926]. Prague: Ústav T.G. Masaryka.

Heitlinger, Alena. 1979. *Women and State Socialism: Sex Inequality in the Soviet Union and Czechoslovakia*. Montreal: McGill-Queen's University Press.

———. 1993. "The Impact of the Transition from Communism on the Status of Women in the Czech and Slovak Republics." In *Gender Politics and Post-Communism: Reflections from Eastern Europe and the Former Soviet Union*, edited by Nanette Funk and Magda Mueller, 95–107. New York: Routledge.

———. 1996. "Framing Feminism in Post-Communist Czech Republic." *Communist and Post-Communist Studies* 29.1:77–93.

Hellinger, Marlis. 1990. *Kontrastive feministische Linguistik: Mechanismen sprachlicher Diskriminierung im Englischen und Deutschen* [Contrastive Feminist Linguistics: Mechanisms of Linguistic Discrimination in English and German]. Ismaning: Max Hueber.

Hendrychová, Soňa. 1992. "Z historie ženského hnutí v Československu" [From the History of the Women's Movement in Czechoslovakia]. In *Lidská práva, ženy a společnost* [Human Rights, Women and Society], edited by Hana Havelková, 9–15. Prague: Evropské středisko UNESCO pro výchovu k lidským právům.

Herder, Johann Gottfried. 1966 (1784). *Outlines of a Philosophy of the History of Man*. Transl. T. Churchill. New York: Bergman.

Hoffmanová, Jana. 1995. "Feministická lingvistika?" [Feminist Linguistics?] *Naše řeč* 78.2, http://nase-rec.ujc.cas.cz/archiv.php?art=7234.

Hölderlin, Friedrich. 1979. *Hyperion*. Frankfurt am Main: Souhrkamp.

Honzáková, Albína. 1935. *Studie práce a osobnosti F.F. Plamínkové* [Study of the Work and Personality of F. F. Plamínková]. Prague: Ženská národní rada v Praze.

Honzík, Karel. 1963. *Ze života avantgardy* [From the Life of the Avant-Garde]. Prague: Československý spisovatel.

hooks, bell. 1984. *Feminist Theory: From Margin to Center*. Boston: South End Press.

Horská, Pavla. 1983. "K ekonomické aktivitě žen na přelomu 19. a 20. století (Příklad Českých zemí)" [The Economic Activity of Women at the Turn of the 19th and 20th Century (The Example of the Czech Lands)]. *Československý časopis historický* 21.5:711–42.

Howson, Richard. 2006. *Challenging Hegemonic Masculinity*. New York: Routledge.

———. 2009. "Deconstructing Hegemonic Masculinity: Contradiction, Hegemony and Dislocation." *NORMA: Nordic Journal for Masculinity Studies* 4.1:6–24.

Hübschmannová, Milena. 1995. *Šaj pes dovakeras. Můžeme se domluvit* [Šaj pes dovakeras: We can Understand Each Other]. Olomouc: Vydavatelství Univerzity Palackého.

———. 1999. "Několik poznámek k hodnotám Romů" [Several Notes on the Values of the Roma]. In *Romové v České Republice (1945–1998)* [The Roma in the Czech Republic (1945–1998)], 16–66. Prague: Socioklub.

———. 2005. *"Po židoch cigáni": Svědectví Romů ze Slovenska 1939–1945* ["After the Jews, Gypsies": Testimonies of the Roma from Slovakia 1939–1945]. Prague: Triáda.

Huebner, Karla. 2008. "Eroticism, Identity, and Cultural Context: Toyen and the Prague Avant-Garde." PhD diss., University of Pittsburgh.

———. 2010a. "Fire Smolders in the Veins: Toyen's Queer Desire and Its Roots in Prague Surrealism." *Papers of Surrealism* 8, www.surrealismcentre.ac.uk/papersofsurrealism /journal8/acrobat%20files/Articles/Huebner%20final%2019.05.10.pdf.

———. 2010b. "The Whole World Revolves around It: Sex Education and Sex Reform in First Republic Czech Print Media." *Aspasia* 4:25–48.

———. 2011. "Girl, Trampka, or Žába? The Czechoslovak New Woman." In *The New Woman International: Representations in Photography and Film from the 1870s through the 1960s*, edited by Elizabeth Otto and Vanessa Rocco, 231–51. Ann Arbor: University of Michigan Press.

———. 2013. "In Pursuit of Toyen: Feminist Biography in an Art-Historical Context." *Journal of Women's History* 25.1:14–36.

Hughes, Donna M. 2000. "The 'Natasha' Trade: Transnational Shadow Market of Trafficking in Women." *Journal of International Affairs* 53.2:625–51.

———. 2004. "Legalizing Lies." *Prague Post*, May 20, http://www.uri.edu/artsci/wms /hughes/legalizing_lies.pdf.

Hull, Gloria T., Patricia Bell Scott, and Barbara Smith, eds. 1982. *All the Women Are White, All the Blacks Are Men, But Some of Us Are Brave: Black Women's Studies*. Old Westbury, NY: Feminist Press.

Huwelmeier, Gertrud. 2008. "Spirits in the Marketplace: Transnational Networks of Vietnamese Migrants in Berlin." In *Transnational Ties: Cities, Migrations and Identities*, edited by Michael Smith and John Eade, 131–44. London: Transaction.

Imre, Anikó. 2005. "Whiteness in Post-Socialist Eastern Europe: The Time of the Gypsies, The End of Race." In *Postcolonial Whiteness: A Reader on Race and Empire*, edited by Alfred J. López, 79–102. Albany: SUNY Press.

International Organization for Migration (IOM). 2012. "Zpráva o situaci v České republice: Migrantské organizace a orgány státní správy v ČR" [Report on the Situation in the Czech Republic: Migration NGOs and State Administration Bodies]. Prague: European Local Cooperation for Integration. http://www.iom.cz/.

Irmen, Lisa, and Ute Linner. 2005. *Die Repräsentation generisch maskuliner Personenbezeichnungen: Eine theoretische Integration bisheriger Befunde* [The Representation of Masculine Person Reference: A Theoretical Integration of Existing Findings]. *Zeitschrift für Psychologie* 213:167–75.

"I Romové mají svoji elitu: Jaká je?" [Even the Roma Have Their Elite: What Is It Like?]. 2007. *Magazín Práva*, October 22. http://www.romea.cz/cz/zpravy/i-romove-maji-svoji-elitu-jaka-je.

"Institucionální feminismus vs. anarchofeminismus." [Institutionalized Feminism vs Anarchofeminism]. 2001. FS8B/AFS leaflet. January. http://anarchalibrary.blogspot.com/2010/10/institucionalni-feminismus-vs.html.

Itzigsohn, José, and Silvia Giorguli-Saucedo. 2002. "Immigrant Incorporation and Sociocultural Transnationalism." *International Migration Review* 36.3:766–98.

———. 2005. "Incorporation, Transnationalism, and Gender: Immigrant Incorporation and Transnational Participation as Gendered Processes." *International Migration Review* 39.4:895–920.

Jakoubek, Marek. 2004. *Romové—konec (ne)jednoho mýtu* [The Roma—The End of A(nother) Myth]. Prague: Socioklub.

Jánská, Eva, Alena Průšvicová, and Zdeněk Čermák. 2011. "Možnosti výzkumu integrace dětí Vietnamců v Česku: Příklad základní školy Praha-Kunratice" [The Potential for Research on the Integration of Vietnamese Children in the Czech Republic: The Case of Primary School Prague-Kunratice]. *Geografie* 116.4:480–96.

Jelínek, František. 1924. *Homosexualita ve světle vědy* [Homosexuality in the Light of Science]. Prague: Obelisk.

Jiráček, Jiří. 1986. *Morfologie ruského jazyka* [Morphology of the Russian Language]. Prague: Státní pedagogické nakladatelství.

Jirousová, Věra. 1993. "Žádné ženské umění neexistuje" [Women's Art Does Not Exist]. *Výtvarné Umění* 1:42–52.

Johnson, Lonnie R. 1996. *Central Europe: Enemies, Neighbors, Friends.* Oxford: Oxford University Press.

Jonáš, Karel. 1872. *Žena ve společnosti lidské, zvláště v Anglii a v Americe* [Woman in Society, Especially in England and America]. Prague: J. Otto.

Jörgens, Frédéric. 2007. "East Berlin: Lesbian and Gay Narratives of Everyday Life, Social Acceptance, and Past and Present." In *Beyond the Pink Curtain: Everyday Life of LGBT People in Eastern Europe,* edited by Roman Kuhar and Judit Takács, 117–39. Ljubljana: Peace Institute.

Jusová, Iveta. 2000a. "*Fin-de-Siècle* Feminisms: The Development of Feminist Narratives within the Discourses of British Imperialism and Czech Nationalism." PhD diss., Miami University of Ohio.

———. 2000b. "Imperialist Feminism: Colonial Issues in Sarah Grand's *The Heavenly Twins* and *The Beth Book*." *English Literature in Transition* 43.3:298–315.

———. 2005. "Gabriela Preissová's Women-Centered Texts: Subverting the Myth of the Homogeneous Nation." *SEEJ* 49.1:63–78.

———. 2010. "Figuring the Other in Nineteenth-Century Czech Literature: Gabriela Preissová and Bozena Viková Kunětická." In *History of the Literary Cultures of East-Central Europe*, vol. 4, edited by Marcel Cornis-Pope and John Neubauer, 367–78. Amsterdam: John Benjamins.

Kalibová, Květa. 1999. "Romové z pohledu statistiky a demografie" [Roma from the Point of View of Statistics and Demography]. In *Romové v České Republice (1945–1998)* [The Roma in the Czech Republic (1945–1998)], 91–114. Prague: Socioklub.

Kapusta-Pofahl, Karen, Hana Hašková, and Marta Kolářová. 2005. "Only a Dead Fish Flows with the Stream: Subversive Voices, NGOization and Czech Women's Organizing." *Anthropology of East Europe Review* 23.1:38–52.

Karlg, Maria, et al. 1997. *Kreatives Formulieren: Anleitungen zu geschlechtergerechtem Sprachgebrauch*. Bd. 13 der Schriftenreihe der Frauenministerin [Formulating Creatively: Instructions for Gender-Balanced Language Use. Volume 13, Series of the Ministry for Women]. Vienna: Ministry for Women.

Kelly, T. Mills. 2006. *Without Remorse: Czech National Socialism in Late-Habsburg Austria*. New York: Columbia University Press.

Kempadoo, Kamala. 2005. "Introduction: From Moral Panic to Global Justice: Changing Perspectives on Trafficking." In *Trafficking and Prostitution Reconsidered: New Perspectives on Migration, Sex Work, and Human Rights*, edited by Kamala Kempadoo with Jyoti Sanghera and Bandana Pattanaik, vii–xxxiv. Boulder, CO: Paradigm.

Kiczková, Zuzana, et al. 2006. *Pamat' žien: O skúsenosti sebautvárania v biografických rozhovoroch* [Women's Memory: The Experience of Self-Formation in Biographical Interviews]. Bratislava: IRIS.

Kieval, Hillel J. 1988. *The Making of Czech Jewry: National Conflict and Jewish Society in Bohemia, 1870–1918*. Oxford: Oxford University Press.

———. 2000. *Languages of Community: The Jewish Experience in the Czech Lands*. Berkeley: University of California Press.

Klein, Josef. 2004. "Der Mann als Prototyp des Menschen—Immer noch? Empirische Studien zum generischen Maskulinum und zur feminin-maskulinen Paarform" [Men as the Human Prototype—Still? Empirical Studies on Masculine Generics and on Feminine-Masculine Word Pairs]. In *Duden. Thema Deutsch 5. Adam, Eva und die Sprache. Beiträge zur Geschlechterforschung* [Duden. Theme German 5. Adam, Eve and Language. Contributions to Gender Research], edited by Karin M. Eichhoff-Cyrus, 292–307. Mannheim: Dudenverlag.

Kocourek, Jiří. 2006. "Vietnamci v současné ČR" [The Vietnamese in the Contemporary Czech Republic]. In *S vietnamskými dětmi na českých školách* [With Vietnamese Children at Czech Schools], edited by Jiří Kocourek and Eva Pechová, 102–18. Jinočany: Nakladatelství H+H.

———. 2007. "Vietnamci v ČR" [Vietnamese in the Czech Republic]. *Sociologické studie* 6.10:46–62.

Kocourek, Jiří, Šárka Martínková, and Eva Pechová. 2012. *Aktuální sociálně-ekonomická situace a problémy Vietnamců v Chomutově* [Current Socio-Economic Situation and Problems of the Vietnamese in Chomutov]. Prague: OS Klub Hanoi.

Kocourková, Jiřina. 2007. "Potratovost" [Abortions]. In *Populační vývoj české republiky, 2001–2006* [Population Trends in the Czech Republic, 2001–2006], edited by Milan Kučera, 39–44. Prague: Přírodovědecká fakulta Univerzita Karlova.

Kofman, Eleonore. 1999. "Female Birds of Passage a Decade Later: Gender and Immigration in the European Union." *International Migration Review* 33.2:269–99.

Köhler-Wagnerová, Alena. 1974. *Die Frau im Sozialismus-Beispiel ČSSR* [Woman in Socialism—A Case Study: The Czechoslovak Socialist Republic]. Hamburg: Hoffmann und Campe.

Kolářová, Jitka. 2009. "Za genderovou rovnost subkultur!" [Toward Gender Equality in Subcultures!]. *A2* 18. http://www.advojka.cz/archiv/2009/18/za-genderovou-rovnost-subkultur.

Kolářová, Marta. 2009. *Protest proti globalizaci: Gender a feministická kritika* [Protest against Globalization: Gender and Feminist Criticism]. Prague: Sociologické nakladatelství.

Koldinská, Kristina. 2009. "Multidimensional Equality in the Czech and Slovak Republics: The Case of Roma Women." In *European Union Non-Discrimination Law: Comparative Perspective on Multidimensional Equality Law*, edited by Dagmar Schiek and Victoria Chege, 249–77. London: Routledge.

Kovačević, Nataša. 2008. *Narrating Post/Communism: Colonial Discourse and Europe's Borderline Civilization*. New York: Routledge.

Krásnohorská, Eliška. 1881. *Ženská otázka česká* [Czech Woman Question]. Prague: Grégr.

Krchová, Andrea, Hana Víznerová, and Alena Kutálková. 2008. *Ženy migrantky v České republice: Uvedení do problematiky* [Women Migrants in the Czech Republic: Introduction to the Issue]. Prague: Friedrich-Ebert-Stiftung.

Krebs, Michal, et al. 2009. *Stop Labour Exploitation—A Closer Look—Analysis of the Agency Employment of the Vietnamese in the Czech Republic*. Prague: La Strada CR.

Krebs, Michal, and Eva Pechová. 2009. *Vietnamese Workers in Czech Factories—Research Report—Excerpt*. Prague: La Strada CR.

Krobotová, Helena. 2010. "Jsem kokos" [I Am a Coconut]. *Respekt* 6:38–41.

Kutálková, Petra. 2008. Personal correspondence, July 7.

———. 2010. "Příliš úzká brána k lidským právům" [A Gate Too Narrow for Human Rights]. http://www.strada.cz/cz/ke-stazeni-a-odkazy/publikace-a-vystupy-la-strada-cr.

Kynčlová, Tereza. 2006. "Rozbor webových stránek informační a osvětové kampaně, Žiješ, protože tě rodiče chtěli' z hlediska kritické diskurzívní analýzy" [Analysis of the Websites of the Sex Education Campaign "You Live Because Your Parents Wanted You"]. *Gender, rovné příležitosti, výzkum* 7.2:51–57.

Lakatošová-Wagner, Margita. 1994. "Některé zvyklosti olašských Romů" [Some Traditions of the Vlach Roma]. In *Romano džaniben: Journal of Romany Studies* 1.3:2–13.

Lang, Sabine. 1997. "The NGOization of Feminism." In *Transitions, Environments, Translations: Feminisms in International Politics*, edited by Joan Wallach Scott, Cora Caplan, and Debra Keates, 101–20. New York: Routledge.

Langmeier, Josef, and Zdeněk Matějček. 1974. *Psychická deprivace v dětství* [Psychological Deprivation in Childhood]. Prague: Avicenum.

Le Brun, Annie. 2001. "Toyen ou l'insurrection lyrique" [Toyen or Lyrical Insurgency]. *Nouvelle revue française* 559:131–50.

Lenin, Vladimir Ilyich. 1961. *Werke Bd. 30 (An die Arbeiterinnen)* [Works. Vol. 30 (To the Workers)]. Berlin: Dietz Verlag.

Leontiyeva, Yana, et al. 2006. *Menšinová problematika v ČR: Komunitní život a reprezentace kolektivních zájmů* [The Minority Issue in the CR: Community Life and Community Interests]. Prague: Sociologický ústav, Akademie Věd Česká Republika.

Leontiyeva, Yana, and Blanka Tollarová. 2010. *Results from a Survey of Foreigners' Incomes, Expenditures, and Remittances*. Prague: Institute of Sociology, Akademie Věd Česká Republika.

"Let's Be Pro-Choice! Why Feminist Group 8. March Comes Out against Hnutí Pro Život ČR." 2002. Unpublished leaflet of FS8B, March.

Lima, Alvaro. 2010. *Transnationalism: A New Mode of Immigration Integration*. Boston: Mauricio Gastón Institute for Latino Community Development and Public Policy, University of Massachusetts.

Linch, Amy. 2013. "Introduction. Postcommunism in a New Key: Bottom Up and Inside Out." In *Postcommunism from Within: Social Justice, Mobilization, and Hegemony*, edited by Jan Kubik and Amy Linch, 1–21. New York: New York University Press.

Lippold, Gregor. 1967. "Mezinárodní srovnání časového rozvrhu domácích prací" [An International Comparison of the Timetable of Domestic Work]. *Populační zprávy* 4:23–26.

Lišková, Kateřina. 2009. "Defining Pornography, Defining Gender: Sexual Citizenship in the Discourse of Czech Sexology and Criminology." In *Intimate Citizenships: Gender, Sexualities, Politics*, edited by Elżbieta H. Oleksy, 147–56. New York: Routledge.

———. 2011. "Released from Gender? Reflexivity, Performativity, and Therapeutic Discourses." In *Sociological Routes and Political Roots*, edited by Michaela Benson and Rolland Munro, 189–204. Oxford: Blackwell.

Lorber, Judith. 2010. *Gender Inequality: Feminist Theories and Politics*. Oxford: Oxford University Press.

Lovelace, Carey. 2013. "Women in Art, A Status Report." Paper presented at the College Art Association Conference 2013, section "Gender Politics in the Workplace."

Lukič, Jasmina, Joanna Regulska, and Darja Zaviršek, eds. 2006. *Women and Citizenship in Central and Eastern Europe*. Burlington, VT: Ashgate.

Lutz, Helma, Maria Teresa Herrera Vivar, and Linda Supik, eds. 2011. *Framing Intersectionality: Debates on a Multi-Faceted Concept in Gender Studies*. Burlington, VT: Ashgate.

Machonin, Pavel, et al. 1969. *Československá společnost* [Czechoslovak Society]. Bratislava: Epocha.

———. 1994. "Social and Political Transformation in the Czech Republic." *Czech Sociological Review* 2:71–87.

MacMaster, Neil. 2001. *Racism in Europe, 1870–2000*. New York: Palgrave.

Macura, Vladimír. 1995. *Znamení zrodu: České národní obrození jako kulturní typ* [Sign of Revival: The Czech National Revival as a Cultural Type]. Prague: Melantrich.

———. 2010. "Dream of Europe." In *The Mystifications of a Nation: The "Potato Bug" and Other Essays on Czech Culture*, edited and translated by Craig Cravens and Caryl Emerson, 13–26. Madison: University of Wisconsin Press.

Mahmood, Saba. 2001. "Feminist Theory, Embodiment and the Docile Agent." *Cultural Anthropology* 16.2:202–36.

———. 2005. *Politics of Piety: The Islamic Revival and the Feminist Subject*. Princeton, NJ: Princeton University Press.

Malá, Olga. 1998. "Metamorfózy těla" [Metamorphoses of the Body]. In *Close Echoes*. Prague: City Gallery Prague.

Malečková, Jitka. 1996. "Gender, Nation and Scholarship: Reflections on Gender/Women's Studies in the Czech Republic." In *New Frontiers in Women's Studies: Knowledge, Identity and Nationalism*, edited by Mary Maynard and June Purvis, 96–112. London: Taylor and Francis.

———. 2000. "Nationalizing Women and Engendering the Nation: The Czech National Movement." In *Gendered Nations: Nationalisms and Gender Order in the Long Nineteenth Century*, edited by Ida Blom, Karen Hagemann, and Catherine Hall, 293–310. Oxford: Berg.

———. 2004. "The Emancipation of Women for the Benefit of the Nation: The Czech Women's Movement." In *Women's Emancipation Movements in the 19th Century: A European Perspective*, edited by Sylvia Paletschek and Bianka Pietrow-Ennker, 167–88. Stanford, CA: Stanford University Press.

———. 2009. "Looking at First-Wave Feminism from Eastern Europe." In *Wie Frauenbewegung geschriebenwird: Historiographie, Dokumentation, Stellungnahmen, Bibliographien* [Writing the Women's Movement: Historiography, Documentation, Commentaries, Bibliografies], edited by Johanna Gehmacher and Natascha Vittorelli, 263–65. Vienna: Erhard Löcker.

Marling, Raili Poldsaar. 2010. "Out of the Room of One's Own? Gender Studies in Estonia." *Aspasia* 4:157–65.

Martínková, Šárka. 2006. "Česko-vietnamské vztahy" [Czech-Vietnamese Relations]. In *S vietnamskými dětmi na českých školách* [With Vietnamese Children at Czech Schools], edited by Jiří Kocourek and Eva Pechová, 85–92. Jinočany: Nakladatelství H+H.

———. 2008. "Sociabilita vietnamského etnika v Praze" [The Sociability of the Vietnamese Ethnic Group in Prague]. In *Cizinecké komunity z antropologické perspektivy: Vybrané případy významných imigračních skupin v České Republice* [Foreign Communities from the Anthropological Perspective: Selected Cases of Significant Immigrant Groups in the Czech Republic], edited by Zdeněk Uherek, Zuzana Korecká, and Tereza Pojarová, 167–210. Prague: Etnologický ústav Akademie Věd Česká Republika.

———. 2010. *Vietnamská komunita v Praze* [Vietnamese Community in Prague]. Prague: Muzeum hlavního města.

———. 2011. "The Vietnamese Ethnic Group, Its Sociability and Social Networks in the Prague Milieu." In *Migration, Diversity and Their Management*, edited by Zdeněk Uherek et al., 133–200. Prague: Institute of Ethnology, Akademie Věd Česká Republika.

Martínková, Šárka, et al. 2010. *Vietnamci, Mongolové a Ukrajinci v ČR* [The Vietnamese, Mongolians and Ukrainians in the Czech Republic]. Prague: Ministerstvo vnitra ČR.

Masarykův slovník naučný IV [Masaryk's Encyclopedia IV]. 1929. Prague: Československý kompas.

Mayer, Tamar, ed. 2000. *Gender Ironies of Nationalism: Sexing the Nation*. New York: Routledge.

McClintock, Anne. 1995. *Imperial Leather: Race, Gender and Sexuality in the Colonial Contest*. New York: Routledge.

McEwen, Brita. 2003. "Viennese Sexual Knowledge as Science and Social Reform Movement, 1900–1934." PhD diss., University of California at Los Angeles.

McLaren, Angus. 1999. *Twentieth-Century Sexuality: A History.* Oxford: Blackwell.

Mikulášek, Alexej. 2000. *Antisemitismus v české literatuře 19. a 20. století. Teoretická a historická studie* [Anti-Semitism in Czech Literature of the 19th and 20th Centuries: Theoretical and Historical Study]. Prague: Votobia.

Mínění žen o zaměstnání, domácnosti a rodině [Women's Views on Employment, Housework, and Family]. 1972. Prague: Ústav pro výzkum veřejného mínění ČSAV.

Ministry of Interior, Czech Republic. 2012. "Integration of Foreigners within the Territory of the Czech Republic." http://www.mvcr.cz/docDetail.aspx?docid=44811&docType=ART.

Miroiu, Mihaela. 2007. "Communism Was a State Patriarchy Not State Feminism." *Aspasia* 1:197–201.

Mlinarević, Gorana, and Lamija Kosović. 2010. "Women's Movements and Gender Studies in Bosnia and Herzegovina." *Aspasia* 4:128–38.

Mohanty, Chandra Talpade. 1984. "Under Western Eyes: Feminist Scholarship and Colonial Discourses." *Boundary 2* 12.3–13.1:333–58.

———. 2002. "'Under Western Eyes' Revisited: Feminist Solidarity through Anticapitalist Struggles." *Signs: Journal of Women in Culture and Society* 28.2:499–535.

Moraga, Cherrí, and Gloria Anzaldúa, eds. 1983. *This Bridge Called My Back: Writing by Radical Women of Color.* New York: Kitchen Table Press.

Morganová, Pavlína. 2003. *5 žen, 5 otázek* [5 Women, 5 Questions]. Prague: Jelení Gallery 2003.

Müllerová, Štěpánka. 1998. *Tělo jako důkaz* [Body of Evidence]. Olomouc: Museum of Art Olomouc.

Musil, Jiří. 1961. "Časový rozvrh žen" [Women's Timetable]. *Demografie* 2:68–71.

Murray, Alison. 1998. "Debt-Bondage and Trafficking: Don't Believe the Hype." In *Global Sex Workers: Rights, Resistance, and Redefinition*, edited by Kamala Kempadoo and Jo Doezema, 51–64. New York: Routledge.

Narayan, Uma. 1997. *Dislocating Cultures: Identities, Traditions, and Third World Feminism.* New York: Routledge.

Nash, Rebecca. 2002. "Exhaustion from Explanation: Reading Czech Gender Studies in the 1990s." *European Journal of Women's Studies* 9.3:291–309.

Nebeský, Václav. 1937. *L'Art Moderne Tchécoslovaque, 1905–1933* [Czechoslovak Modern Art, 1905–1933]. Paris: Felix Alcan.

Nečasová, Denisa. 2011. *Buduj vlast—posílíš mír! Ženské hnutí v českých zemích, 1945–1955* [Build Your Country—Strengthen Peace! Women's Movement in the Czech Lands, 1945–1955]. Brno: Matice moravská.

Nekula, Marek. 1998. "Review of D. Moldanová: *Žena-jazyk-literatura.*" *Sborník prací Filozofické fakulty brněnské university A* 46:215–19.

Němcová, Jana. 1971. "Postoje k ekonomické činnosti žen" [Attitudes toward Women's Economic Activity]. *Demografie* 12:11–19.

Neudorfl, Marie. 1990. "Masaryk and the Women's Question." In *Thinker and Politician, vol. 1 of T. G. Masaryk (1850–1937)*, edited by Stanley B. Winters, 258–82. New York: St. Martin's Press.

Nezval, Vítězslav. 1965. *Z mého života* [From My Life]. Prague: Československý spisovatel.

Nožina, Miroslav. 2010. "Crime Networks in Vietnamese Diasporas: The Czech Republic Case." *Crime Law Social Change* 53:229–58.

Nožina, Miroslav, and Filip Kraus. 2012. *Bosové, vojáci a zrnka rýže: Vietnamské kriminální sítě v ČR a jejich mezinárodní dimenze.* [Bosses, Soldiers and Grains of Rice: Vietnamese Criminal Networks in the CR and Their International Dimensions]. Prague: Koniasch Latin Press.

Nünning, Ansgar, ed. 2008. *Lexikon teorie literatury a kultury* [Lexicon of Literary and Cultural Theory]. Brno: Host.

Nyklová, Blanka. 2013. "Krajinou současného feminismu" [The Landscape of Contemporary Feminism]. *Gender, rovné příležitosti, výzkum* 14.1:25–62.

Oates-Indruchová, Libora. 2002. *Discourses of Gender in Pre and Post 1989 Culture.* Pardubice: Pardubice University Press.

Occhipinti, Laurie. 1996. "Two Steps Back? Anti-Feminism in Eastern Europe." *Anthropology Today* 12.6:13–9.

Okely, Judith. 1983. *The Traveller-Gypsies.* Cambridge: Cambridge University Press.

Oláhová, Erika. 2004. *Nechci se vrátit mezi mrtvé* [I Do Not Want to Go Back among the Dead]. Prague: Společná budoucnost.

———. 2007. *Matné zrcadlo* [The Opaque Mirror]. Prague: Triáda.

Ottův slovník naučný [Otto's Encyclopedia]. 1893, 1901. Vols. 6, 17. Prague: J. Otto.

Pachmanová, Martina. 2001. "The Muzzle: Gender and Sexual Politics in Contemporary Czech Art." *ArtMargins.* http://www.artmargins.com/index.php/2-articles/362-the -muzzle-gender-and-sexual-politics-in-contemporary-czech-art.

———. 2002. "Primadona, múza, popelka" [Prima Donna, Muse, Cinderella]. *Lidové noviny,* February 16, 15.

———. 2004. *Neznámá území českého moderního umění: Pod lupou genderu* [Unknown Territories of Czech Modern Art: Through the Looking Glass of Gender]. Prague: Argo.

———. 2006. "Les Femmes Artistes d'Aujourd'hui: Czech Women Artists in the Context of International Modernism." In *Local Strategies, International Ambitions: Modern Art in Central Europe, 1918–1968,* edited by Vojtěch Lahoda, 65–70. Prague: Ústav Dějin Umění Akademie Věd Česká Republika.

———. 2009. "In? Out? In Between? Some Notes on the Invisibility of a Nascent Eastern European Feminist and Gender Discourse in Contemporary Art Theory." In *Gender Check: Femininity and Masculinity in the Art of Eastern Europe,* edited by Bojana Pejić, 241–48. Cologne: Walter König.

———. 2013. "Mlčení o feminismu a ženskost jako výtvarná hodnota: České umělkyně očima Jindřicha Chalupeckého" [Silence about Feminism and Femininity as an Aesthetic Value: Czech Women Artists through the Eyes of Jindřich Chalupecky]. *Sešit pro umění, teorii a příbuzné zóny* 14:34–43.

Paletschek, Sylvia, and Bianka Pietrow-Ennker. 2004. "Women's Emancipation Movements in Europe in the Long Nineteenth Century: Conclusion." In *Women's Emancipation Movements in the Nineteenth Century: A European Perspective,* edited by Sylvia Paletschek and Bianka Pietrow-Ennker, 301–33. Stanford, CA: Stanford University Press.

Pavlík, Petr. 2006. "Originální experiment české vlády aneb jak prosazovat politiku rovných příležitostí bez odpovídajícího institucionálního zabezpečení" [An Original

Experiment of the Czech Government; or, How to Enact the Politics of Equal Opportunities without Appropriate Institutional Backing]. In *Mnohohlasem: Vyjednávání ženských prostorů po roce 1989* [In Multiple Voices: Negotiating Women's Spaces Post-1989], edited by Hana Hašková, Alena Křížková, and Marcela Linková, 132–41. Prague: Institute of Sociology of the Academy of Sciences of the Czech Republic.

Pech, Stanley Z. 1969. *The Czech Revolution of 1848*. Chapel Hill: University of North Carolina Press.

Pechholdová, Markéta, and Gabriela Šamanová. 2006. "Úmrtnost seniorů v České republice: Trendy a perspektivy" [The Death Rate among Seniors in the Czech Republic: Trends and Perspectives]. In *Životní cyklus. Sociologické a demografické perspektivy* [The Life Cycle: Sociological and Demographic Perspectives], edited by Dana Hamplová, Petra Šalamounová, and Gabriela Šamanová, 247–66. Prague: Sociologický ústav Akademie Věd Česká Republika.

Pechová, Eva. 2007. *Migrace z Vietnamu do České republiky v kontextu problematiky obchodu s lidmi a vykořisťování* [Migration from Vietnam to the Czech Republic in the Context of Human Trafficking and Exploitation]. Prague: La Strada the CR.

Pečírka, Jaromír. 1931. "Bilder-Ausstellung von Jindřich Štyrský und Toyen in der 'Umělecká Beseda'" [Exhibition of the Art by Jindřich Štyrský and Toyen in "Umělecká Beseda"]. *Prager Presse,* December 4, 8.

Pejić, Bojana, ed. 2010. *Gender Check: Reader.* Cologne: Walter König.

Peters, Alicia W. 2013. "'Things That Involve Sex Are Just Different': US Anti-Trafficking Law and Policy on the Books, in Their Minds, and in Action." *Anthropological Quarterly* 86.1:221–56.

"Poznámky a informace: Nová literatura" [Notes and Information: Newly Published Literature]. 1933. *Nový hlas* 2.5:78–80.

Preissová, Gabriela. 1896 (1889). "Gazdina roba" [Farmer's Woman]. In *Obrázky bez rámu,* 72–117. Prague: J. Otto.

Procházková, Jaroslava. 1897a. *Český lid a český Žid: Časové úvahy* [The Czech People and the Czech Jew: Timely Reflections]. Prague: Josef Jirman.

———. 1897b. *Českým mužům: Ani my nejsme spokojeny s Vámi!* [To Czech Men: Neither Are We Satisfied with You!] Prague: N.p.

Putna, Martin C., ed. 2011. *Homosexualita v dějinách českého umění* [Homosexuality in the History of Czech Art]. Prague: Academia.

Pynsent, Robert B. 2004. "Neplodní 'Staří mládenci' jako výplod feministické ideologie Boženy Vikové Kuněticské" ["Infertile Old Bachelors" as the Fruit of Božena Viková Kunětická's Feminist Ideology]. *Slovo a smysl* 1:66–87.

———. 2008. *Ďáblové, ženy a národ* [Devils, Women, and the Nation]. Prague: Karolinum.

———. 2010. "Czech Feminist Anti-Semitism: The Case of Božena Benešová." In *History of the Literary Cultures of East-Central Europe: Junctures and Disjunctures in the 19th and 20th Centuries,* vol. 4, *Types and Stereotypes,* edited by Marcel Cornis-Pope and John Neubauer, 344–66. Amsterdam: John Benjamins.

Ramet, Sabrina P. 2007. *The Liberal Project and the Transformation of Democracy: The Case of Eastern Europe.* College Station: Texas A&M University Press.

Regulska, Joanna, and Magdalena Grabowska. 2012. "Post-1989 Women's Activism in Poland." In *Women and Gender in Postwar Europe: From Cold War to European Union,* edited by Joanna Regulska and Bonnie G. Smith, 212–30. New York: Routledge.

———. 2013. "Social Justice, Hegemony and Women's Mobilizations." In *Postcommunism from Within: Social Justice, Mobilization, and Hegemony*, edited by Jan Kubik and Amy Linch, 139-90. New York: New York University Press.

Regulska, Joanna, and Bonnie G. Smith, eds. 2012. *Women and Gender in Postwar Europe: From Cold War to European Union*. New York: Routledge.

Reiger, Kerreen. 2008. "Domination or Mutual Recognition? Professional Subjectivity in Midwifery and Obstetrics." *Social Theory and Health* 6.2:132-47.

Renne, Tanya, ed. 1997. *Ana's Land: Sisterhood in Eastern Europe*. Boulder, CO: Westview.

Řezbová, Zdenka. 2007. "Vizuální umění a feminismus" [Visual Art and Feminism]. Thesis, Faculty of Visual Arts, Technical University Brno.

Roelcke, Thorsten. 1997. *Sprachtypologie des Deutschen* [Typology of the German Language]. Berlin: de Gruyter.

Romani Women's Rights Movement. 2006. A special issue of *Roma Rights: Quarterly Journal of the European Roma Rights Centre* 4. http://iiav.nl/ezines/DivTs/RomaRights /2006/No4Part1.pdf

Roth, Silke, ed. 2008. *Gender Politics in the Expanding European Union: Mobilization, Inclusion, Exclusion*. New York: Berghahn Books.

Rulíková, Markéta. 2012. "Responses to the Economic Crisis among Immigrants in the Czech Republic: Impeding and Inhibiting Factors for Staying." *Comparative Populations Studies—Zeitschrift für Bevölkerungswissenschaft* 31.1–2:247-70.

Ryvolová, Karolína. 2005. "Jinakost, perzekuce, diaspora" [Otherness, Persecution, Diaspora]. *Svět literatury* 31:31–49.

———. 2014. "Romany Letters in the Making: Testing the Frontiers of Legitimate Literature. A Comparative Analysis of Four Romany Life Stories." PhD diss., Charles University.

Sanghera, Jyoti. 2005. "Unpacking the Trafficking Discourse." In *Trafficking and Prostitution Reconsidered: New Perspectives on Migration, Sex Work, and Human Rights*, edited by Kamala Kempadoo with Jyoti Sanghera and Bandana Pattanaik, 3–24. Boulder, CO: Paradigm.

Saxonberg, Steven. 2003. *The Czech Republic before the New Millenium: Politics, Parties and Gender*. New York: Columbia University Press.

Saxonberg, Steven, Hana Hašková, and Jiří Mudrák. 2012. *The Development of Czech Childcare Policies*. Prague: Sociologické nakladatelství.

Scheinostová, Alena. 2010. "Ženská romská próza jako zápas o sebevyjádření" [Romany Women's Fiction as a Struggle for Self-Expression]. In *Česká literatura v perspektivách genderu* [Czech Literature through Gender Perspectives], edited by Jan Matonoha, 253–63. Prague: Academia-Akropolis.

Schindler, Franz. 2013. "Život homosexuálních mužů za socialismu" [Life of Homosexual Men under Socialism]. In *Miluji tvory svého pohlaví: Homosexualita v dějinách a společnosti českých zemí* [I Love the Same Sex: Homosexuality in the History and Society of the Czech Lands], edited by Pavel Himl, Jan Seidl, and Franz Schindler, 271–386. Prague: Argo.

Seidl, Jan. 2007. "Úsilí o odtrestnění homosexuality za první republiky" [Struggle to Decriminalize Homosexuality in the First Republic]. MA thesis, Masarykova Univerzita.

———. 2012. *Od žaláře k oltáři: Emancipace homosexuality v Českých zemích od roku 1867 do současnosti* [From Jail to the Altar: The Emancipation of Homosexuality in the Czech Lands from 1867 to the Present]. Brno: Host.

——. 2013. "Teplí" [Bent]. In *Kmeny 0* [Stocks 0], edited by Vladimir 518 et al., 78–109. Prague: BiggBoss and Yinachi.

Seifert, Jaroslav. 1999. *Všecky krásy světa* [All the Beauty of the World]. Prague: Eminent/Knižní klub.

Šiklová, Jiřina. 1993. "Are Women in Central and Eastern Europe Conservative?" In *Gender Politics and Post-Communism*, edited by Nanette Funk and Magda Mueller, 74–83. New York: Routledge.

——. 1996. "Jiný kraj, jiné ženy. Proč se v Čechách nedaří feminismu" [Different Countries, Different Customs: Why Feminism Isn't Doing Well in the Czech Republic]. *Respekt* 13:17.

——. 1997a. "Feminism and the Roots of Apathy in the Czech Republic." *Social Research* 64.2:258–80.

——. 1997b. "McDonalds, Terminators, Coca-Cola Ads—and Feminism? Imports from the West." In *Ana's Land: Sisterhood in Eastern Europe*, edited by Tanya Renne, 76–81. Boulder, CO: Westview.

——. 1998. "Why We Resist Western-Style Feminism." *Transitions* 5.1:30–35.

Skeggs, Beverley. 1997. *Formations of Class and Gender: Becoming Respectable*. London: Sage.

——. 2001. "The Toilet Paper: Femininity, Class and Mis-recognition." *Women's Studies International Forum* 24.3–4:295–307.

Slavova, Kornelia. 2006. "Looking at Western Feminisms through the Double Lens of Eastern Europe and the Third World." In *Women and Citizenship in Central and Eastern Europe*, edited by Jasmina Lukič, Joanna Regulska, and Darja Zaviršek, 245–64. Burlington, VT: Ashgate.

Slavova, Kornelia, and Ann Phoenix. 2014. "Living in Translation: Voicing and Inscribing Women's Lives and Practices." *European Journal of Women's Studies* 18.4:331–37.

Slepičková, Lenka, Eva Šlesingerová, and Iva Šmídová. 2012. "Biomoc a reprodukční biomedicína v České republice" [Biopower and Reproductive Medicine in the Czech Republic]. *Sociologický časopis/Czech Sociological Review* 48.1:85–106.

Sloat, Amanda. 2005. "The Rebirth of Civil Society: The Growth of Women's NGOs in Central and Eastern Europe." *European Journal of Women's Studies* 12.4:437–52.

Šmejkalová, Jiřina. 1991. "Co je feminismus? (Kam s ní/m?)" [What Is Feminism? (Where to Place Her/Him?)]. *Tvář*, 37–41.

——. 1998. "Strašidlo feminismu v českém 'porevolučním' tisku: U'vaha doufejme historická" [The Specter of Feminism in Czech "Post-Revolution" Media: A Reflection Hopefully Historical]. In *Žena a muž v médiích* [Woman and Man in the Media], edited by Hana Havelková and Mirek Vodrážka, 16–19. Prague: Nadace Gender Studies.

Šmejkalová-Strickland, Jiřina. 1993. "Do Czech Women Need Feminism? Perspectives on Feminist Theories and Practices in the Czech Republic." In *Bodies of Bread and Butter: Reconfiguring Women's Lives in the Post-Communist Czech Republic*, edited by Susanna Trnka and Laura Busheikin, 13–18. Prague: Gender Studies Centre.

——. 1995. "Revival? Gender Studies in the 'Other' Europa." *Signs: Journal of Women in Culture and Society* 20.4:1000–1006.

——. 1998. "Strašidlo feminismu v českém 'porevolučním' tisku: Úvaha, doufejme, historická" [Specter of Feminism in the "Post-Revolution" Czech Press: A (Hopefully)

Historical Reflection]. In *Žena a muž v médiích* [Woman and Man in the Media], edited by Hana Havelková and Mirek Vodrážka, 16–18. Prague: Gender Studies.

Šmídová, Iva. 1999. "Men in the Czech Republic." *Sociologický časopis/Czech Sociological Review* 7.2:215–22.

———. 2002. "Muži v České republice podle jiných mužů" [Men in the Czech Republic According to Other Men]. *Sociální studia* 7:89–117.

———. 2004. "Jiní muži: Alternativní životní dráhy mužů v České republice" [Different Men: Alternative Life Strategies of Men in the Czech Republic]. PhD diss., Masarykova Univerzita.

———. 2006a. "The Czech Republic: Domination and Silences." In *Men and Masculinities in Europe*, edited by Keith Pringle et al., 49–58. London: Whiting and Birch.

———. 2006b. "Kritická mužská studia" [Critical Masculinity Studies]. In *Gender a společnost: Vysokoškolská učebnice pro nesociologické směry magisterských a bakalářských studií* [Gender and Society: College Textbook for Non-Sociology BA and MA Students], edited by Jana Valdrová, 59–70. Ústí nad Labem: Universita J. E. Purkyně.

———. 2009. "Changing Czech Masculinities? Beyond 'Environment and Children Friendly' Men." In *Intimate Citizenships: Gender, Subjectivity, Politics*, edited by Elzbieta H. Oleksy, 312–34. New York: Routledge.

———. 2011. "Childbirth, Authoritative Knowledge in Reproductive Medicine and Masculine Hegemony." GEXcel Work in Progress: Gendered Sexualed Transnatialisations, Deconstructing the Dominant: Transforming Men, "Centres," and Knowledge/Policy/Practice 15 (Spring). Linköping University, 167–74.

Smith, Barbara, ed. 1983. *Home Girls: A Black Feminist Anthology*. New York: Kitchen Table/Women of Color Press.

Snitow, Ann. 1997a. "Appendix: A Postscript to Laura Busheikin." In *Ana's Land: Sisterhood in Eastern Europe*, edited by Tanya Renne, 238–39. Boulder, CO: Westview.

———. 1997b. "Response." In *Transitions, Environments, Translations: Feminisms in International Politics*, edited by Joan W. Scott, Cora Kaplan, and Debra Keates, 176–84. New York: Routledge.

———. 2006. "Cautionary Tales." In *Women and Citizenship in Central and Eastern Europe*, edited by Jasmina Lukič, Joanna Regulska, and Darja Zaviršek, 287–97. Burlington, VT: Ashgate.

Sodano, Valeria. 2011. "The New Division of Labor in the Globalized Economy: Women's Challenges and Opportunities." *Forum for Social Economics* 40.3:281–98.

Sokolová, Věra. 2005. "Identity Politics and the (B)Orders of Heterosexism: Lesbians, Gays and Feminists in the Czech Media after 1989." In *Mediale Welten in Tschechien nach 1989: Genderprojektionen und Codes des Plebejismus* [The World of the Media in the Post-1989 Czech Republic: Gender Projections and Codes of Plebeianism], edited by Jiřina van Leuween and Nicole Richter, 29–44. München: Kubon und Sagner.

———. 2009. "Otec, otec a dítě: Gay muži a rodičovství" [Father, Father and Child: Gay Men and Parenting]. *Sociologický časopis* 45.1:115–45.

Soukupová, Blanka. 2007. "Národněpolitické protižidovské stereotypy v české společnosti na konci 19. století." [Nationalistic Anti-Jewish Stereotypes in the Late 19th Century Czech Society]. In *Protižidovské stereotypy a křesťanská společnost na přelomu 19. a 20. století* [Anti-Semitic Stereotypes and Christian Society at the Turn of the 20th Century], edited by Zbyněk Vydra, 13–49. Pardubice: Univerzita Pardubice.

Special Eurobarometer 393: Discrimination in the EU in 2012. 2012. European Commission. http://ec.europa.eu/public_opinion/archives/ebs/ebs_393_en.pdf.

Spivak, Gayatri Chakravorty. 1988. "Can the Subaltern Speak?" In *Marxism and the Interpretation of Culture*, edited by Cary Nelson and Lawrence Grossberg, 271–313. London: Macmillan.

Srp, Karel. 1998. "Převrácené ráje" [Perverted Paradises]. In *Close Echoes*. Prague: City Gallery Prague.

Stacey, Judith, and Timothy Biblarz. 2001. "(How) Does the Sexual Orientation of Parents Matter?" *American Sociological Review* 66.2:159–83.

Statistická ročenka ČSSR, 1958–1972 [The Year in Statistics for the CR, 1958–1972]. 1958–72. Slovenský štatistický úrad v Bratislave; Federální statistický úřad; Český statistický úřad. Prague: Státní nakladatelství technické literatury.

Štefková, Zuzana. 2003. "Obraz ženy přelomu tisíciletí ženskýma očima" [Image of the Woman of the Turn of the Millennium through Women's Eyes]. *Umění* 51:219–28.

———. 2008. "O ženách a otázkách aneb jak postavit vejce na špičku" [On Women and Questions; or, How to Stand an Egg on Its Tip]. In *Artemis a Faust*, edited by Milena Bartlová and Martina Pachmanová, 62–63. Prague: Academia.

———. 2012. *Svědectví: Ženským hlasem. Rozhovory s českými a slovenskými umělkyněmi a teoretičkami umění.* [Testimonies: In a Female Voice. Interviews with Czech and Slovak Women Artists and Art Theoreticians]. Prague: Vysoká škola uměleckoprůmyslová.

Stein, Arlene. 1997. *Sex and Sensibility: Stories of a Lesbian Generation.* Berkeley: University of California Press.

Stenning, Alison. 2012. "Where Is the Post-Socialist Working Class? Working-Class Lives in the Spaces of (Post-)Socialism." *Sociology* 39.5:983–99.

Sternstein, Malynne. 2006. "Ecstatic Subjects: Citizenship and Sex in Czech Surrealism." In *The Invention of Politics in the European Avant-Garde (1906–1940)*, edited by Sascha Bru and Gunther Martens, 113–31. Amsterdam: Rodopi.

Stryker, Susan. 2008. *Transgender History.* Berkeley: Seal Press.

Suchland, Jennifer. 2011. "Is Postsocialism Transnational?" *Signs: Journal of Women in Culture and Society* 36.4:837–62.

Sullivan, Maureen. 2004. *The Family of Women: Lesbian Mothers, Their Children and the Undoing of Gender.* Berkeley: University of California Press.

Švab, Alena, and Roman Kuhar. 2005. *The Unbearable Comfort of Privacy: The Everyday Life of Gays and Lesbians.* Ljubljana: Peace Institute.

Svoreňová-Királyová, Vlasta. 1968. *Žena dvacátého století ve světě práce* [Woman of the Twentieth Century in the World of Labor]. Prague: Práce.

Szulecka, Monika. 2012. "The Right to Be Exploited: Vietnamese Workers in Poland." In *Human Rights and Migration: Trafficking for Forced Labor*, edited by Christien van den Anker and Ilse van Liempt, 161–89. New York: Palgrave.

Tastsoglou, Evangelia, and Valerie Preston. 2005. "Gender, Immigration and Labour Market: Where We Are and What We Still Need to Know." *Atlantis: A Women's Studies Journal/Revue d'études sur les femmes* 30.1:46–59.

Taylor, Yvette. 2007. *Working Class Lesbian Life: Classed Outsiders.* Basingstoke, UK: Palgrave Macmillan.

———. 2008. "'That's Not Really My Scene': Working-Class Lesbians In (and Out of) Place." *Sexualities* 11.5:523–46.

———. 2009. *Lesbian and Gay Parenting: Securing Social and Educational Capital*. Basingstoke, UK: Palgrave Macmillan.

———, ed. 2010. *Classed Intersections*. New York: Ashgate.

Tereskinas, Arturas. 2012. "Post-Soviet Masculinities, Shame, and the Archives of Social Suffering in Contemporary Lithuania." In *Women and Gender in Postwar Europe: From Cold War to European Union*, edited by Joanna Regulska and Bonnie G. Smith, 194–211. New York: Routledge.

Tilly, Charles, and Sidney Tarrow. 2007. *Contentious Politics*. London: Paradigm.

Titěra, František. 1913. *České dítě patří do české školy!* [A Czech Child Belongs in the Czech School!]. Prague: Národní jednota pošumavská.

Tlostanova, Madina. 2012. "Postsocialist≠Postcolonial? On Post-Soviet Imaginary and Global Coloniality." *Journal of Postcolonial Writing* 48.2:130–42.

Tomek, Václav, and Ondřej Slačálek. 2006. *Anarchismus: Svoboda proti moci* [Anarchism: Freedom versus Power]. Prague: Vyšehrad.

Třeštík, Dušan. 1999. *Češi: Jejich národ, stát, dějiny a pravdy v transformaci: Texty z let 1991–1998* [Czechs: Their Nation, State, and History of Transformations: Texts from 1991–1998]. Brno: Doplněk.

Trinh, Minh-ha T. 1989. *Woman, Native, Other: Writing Postcoloniality and Feminism*. Bloomington: Indiana University Press.

Tripp, Aili Mari. 2006. "The Evolution of Transnational Feminisms: Consensus, Conflict, and New Dynamics." In *Global Feminism: Transnational Women's Activism, Organizing, and Human Rights*, edited by Myra Ferree and Aili Mari Tripp, 51–78. New York: New York University Press.

True, Jacqui. 2003. *Gender, Globalization, and Postsocialism: The Czech Republic after Communism*. New York: Columbia University Press.

Uchalová, Eva, et al. 1996. *Czech Fashion, 1918–1939: Elegance of the Czechoslovak First Republic*. Edited by Andreas Beckmann. Translated by Štěpán Suchochleb. Prague: Olympia Publishing House in cooperation with the Museum of Decorative Arts.

Uhde, Zuzana, et al., eds. 2009. "Report on the Activities and Political Claims of Majority Women's NGOs and Minoritised Women's and Gender-Based NGOs or Groups on Care, and Specifically on Childcare in the Czech Republic since the End of the Second World War." FEMCIT working paper. Prague: Akademie Věd Česká Republika. www.femcit.org/files/WP2_WorkingpaperNo2.pdf.

UN Protocol to Prevent, Suppress and Punish Trafficking in Persons, Especially Women and Children. 2000. https://treaties.un.org/Pages/ViewDetails.aspx?src=IND&mtdsg_no=XVIII-12-a&chapter=18&lang=en.

Václavíková-Helšusová, Lenka. 2006. "Genderová vědecká komunita vlastníma očima" [Gender Studies Community through Its Own Eyes]. In *Mnohohlasem: Vyjednávání ženských prostorů po roce 1989* [In Multiple Voices: Negotiating Women's Spaces Post-1989], edited by Hana Hašková, Alena Křížková, and Marcela Linková, 165–80. Prague: Institute of Sociology of the Academy of Sciences of the Czech Republic.

Valdrová, Jana. 2001. "Novinové titulky z hlediska genderu" [Article Headings from a Gender Perspective]. *Naše řeč* 84.2:90–96.

———. 2008. "Žena a vědec? To mi nejde dohromady" [A Woman and a Scientist? That Doesn't Seem to Match]. *Naše řeč* 91.1:26–38.

———. 2010. "Reprezentace generidky maskulinních názvů osob: Teoretická integrace dosavadních poznatků (Komentář ke stati Lisy Irmen a Ute Linner)" [The Represen-

tation of Masculine Generic Person References: A Theoretical Integration of Existing Findings. (A Commentary on the Publication by Lisa Irmen and Ute Linner)].
Gender, rovné příležitosti, výzkum 11.2:3–15.

———. 2012. "Typologische Unterschiede zwischen Sprachen als Argument gegen ge-
schlechtergerechte Sprachkritik und Sprachpflege?" [Typological Differences between
Languages as an Argument against Gender-Sensitive Language Critique and Lan-
guage Planning?]. In *Bilingualer Sprachgebrauch und Typologie: Deutsch-Tschechisch*
[Bilingual Language Use and Typology: German-Czech], edited by Marek Nekula,
Kateřina Šichová, and Jana Valdrová, 141–58. Tübingen: Julius Groos Verlag.

Valdrová, Jana, Blanka Knopková-Čapková, and Pavla Paclíková. 2010. *Kultura
genderově vyváženého vyjadřování* [The Culture of Gender-Balanced Expression].
Prague: Ministerstvo školství, mládeže a tělovýchovy.

Valdrová, Jana, Irena Smetáčková-Moravcová, and Blanka Knotková-Čapková. 2005.
Příručka posuzování genderové korektnosti učebnic [Handbook for Evaluating
Gender-Correctness of Schoolbooks]. Prague: *Ročenka genderových studií FHS UK*
[Yearbook of the Gender Studies Department, School of Humanities, Charles Uni-
versity], 03–04:173–96.

Valentine, Gill. 2000. *From Nowhere to Everywhere: Lesbian Geographies*. New York:
Routledge.

Vancluysen, Kris, Maarten Van Craen, and Johan Ackaert. 2009. "Transnational Activities and Social-Cultural Integration of Moroccan and Turkish Descendants in Flem-
ish Belgium." Paper presented by Kris Vancluysen at the 26th International Union
for the Scientific Study of Population Conference, Marrackech, Morocco, October 1.
http://iussp2009.princeton.edu/papers/90999.

Večerník, Jiří. 2010. "Střední vrstvy v české společnosti a výzkumu: Mizející, nebo zapo-
menuté?" [The Middle Classes in the Czech Society and in Research: Disappearing
or Forgotten?]. *Lidé města* 12.3:475–97.

Veliković, Vedrana. 2012. "Belated Alliances? Tracing the Intersections between Postcolonialism and Postcommunism." *Journal of Postcolonial Writing* 48.2:164–75.

Vermeersch, Peter, and Melanie H. Ram. 2009. "The Roma." In *Minority Rights in Central and Eastern Europe*, edited by Bernd Rechel, 61–73. London: Routledge.

Viková Kunětická, Božena. 1897. *Medřická*. Prague: F. Šimáček.

———. 1910. *Vzpoura* [Revolt]. Prague: F. Šimáček.

———. 1919. *Vyznání: Řeči a studie (1906–1918)*. [Confessions: Speeches and Studies
(1906–1918)]. Prague: Unie.

Vishnevsky, Victor. 2006. *Memories of a Gypsy*. Cheverly, MD: Salo Press.

Vodochodský, Ivan. 2008. "Muži-rodina-socialismus: Mužství a generace v biblio-
grafických vyprávěních o manželství a otcovství v 70. letech 20. století" [Men-
Family-Socialism: Oral Stories of Fatherhood and Husband-hood in the 1970s].
PhD diss., School of Social Sciences, Charles University.

Vodrážka, Mirek. 1998. "Ženské umění ve výtvarné řeči nových médií" [Women's Art in
the Visual Language of New Media]. *Aspekt* 2:65–70.

———. 2006. *Mlha a moc aneb nechod'te za Knížákem* [Fog and Power; or, Don't Go to
Knížák]. Video. http://blisty.cz/art/28746.html.

Volet-Jeanneret, Helena. 1988. *La femme bourgeoise à Prague, 1860–1895: De la philan-
thropie à l'émancipation* [The Bourgeois Woman in Prague, 1860–1895: From Philanthropy to Emancipation]. Geneva: Slatkine.

Vráblíková, Kateřina. 2006. "Český anarchofeminismus" [Czech Anarchofeminism]. *Rexter* 2, www.rexter.cz/cesky-anarchofeminismus/2006/11/01/.

Vrba, Rudolf. 1898. *Národní sebeobrana: Úvahy o hmotném a mravním úpadku národa českého.* [National Self-Defense: Reflections on the Material and Moral Decay of the Czech Nation]. Prague: N.p.

Wagnerová, Alena. 1995 "Emancipace a vlastnictví" [Emancipation and Property]. *Sociologický časopis* 31.1:77–84.

Walsh, Mikey. 2010. *Gypsy Boy.* London: Hodder and Stoughton.

Walters, Garrison. 1988. *The Other Europe: Eastern Europe to 1945.* New York: Dorset.

Weeks, Jeffrey, Brian Heaphy, and Catherine Donovan. 2001. *Same Sex Intimacies: Families of Choice and Other Life Experiments.* New York: Routledge.

Weiner, Elaine. 2007. *Market Dreams: Gender, Class, and Capitalism in the Czech Republic.* Ann Arbor: University of Michigan Press.

Weiss, Petr. 2002. *Sexuální Deviace: Klasifikace, Diagnostika, Léčba* [Sexual Deviation: Classification, Diagnosis, Treatment]. Prague: Portál.

West, Candace, and Don Zimmerman. 1987. "Doing Gender." *Gender and Society* 1.2:125–51.

Weston, Kath. 1991. *Families We Choose: Lesbians, Gays, Kinship.* New York: Columbia University Press.

Willems, Wim. 1997. *In Search of the True Gypsy: From Enlightenment to Final Solution.* London: Frank Cass.

Wincapaw, Celeste. 2000. "The Virtual Spaces of Lesbian and Bisexual Women's Electronic Mailing Lists." *Journal of Lesbian Studies* 4.1:45–59.

Wolchik, Sharon L. 1991. *Czechoslovakia in Transition: Politics, Economics, and Society.* New York: Pinter.

———. 1995. "Women and the Politics of Transition in the Czech and Slovak Republics." In *Women in the Politics of Post-Communist Eastern Europe*, edited by Marilyn Rueschemeyer, 3–27. New York: M. E. Sharpe.

Wolff, Larry. 1994. *Inventing Eastern Europe: The Map of Civilization on the Mind of the Enlightenment.* Stanford, CA: Stanford University Press.

Young, Amy Dawn. 2004. "'Das Gesprengte Korsett': Gender in Lesbian Periodicals in Berlin, 1924–1933." PhD diss., University of Nebraska.

Zahra, Tara. 2008. *Kidnapped Souls: National Indifference and the Battle for Children in the Bohemian Lands, 1900–1948.* Ithaca, NY: Cornell University Press.

Zaostřeno na ženy a muže 2013 [Focus on Women and Men 2013]. 2013. Prague: Český statistický úřad. http://www.czso.cz/csu/2013edicniplan.nsf/p/1413-13.

Zheng, Wang. 2005. "'State Feminism'? Gender and Socialist State Formation in Maoist China." *Feminist Studies* 31.3:519–51.

Zinn, Maxine Baca, and Bonnie Thorton Dill, eds. 1994. *Women of Color in U.S. Society.* Philadelphia: Temple University Press.

Zhuzhenko, Tatiana. 2010. "Gender Studies between Post-Communist Transition and Nation Building." *Aspasia* 4:176–84.

"Zpráva o plnění Doporučení CM/Rec(2010)5 Výboru ministrů členským státům ohledně boje proti diskriminaci na základě sexuální orientace a genderové identity Českou republikou" [Report on the Implementation by the Czech Republic of the Recommendation CM/Rec(2010)5 of the Committee of Ministers of the Council of Europe on Measures to Combat Discrimination on Grounds of Sexual Orientation

or Gender Identity]. 2013. PROUD. http://www.proudem.cz/o-proudu/dokumenty
.html.

"Zpráva o stavu romské menšiny v ČR za rok 2012" [Report on the State of the Roma
Minority in the CR for 2012]. 2013. Prague: Office of Human Rights, Government of
the Czech Republic. https://www.google.com/#q=zprava+o+stavu+romske+mensiny
+2012.

CONTRIBUTORS

IVETA JUSOVÁ is Professor of Women's and Gender Studies, and Director of the Women's and Gender Studies in Europe program at Carleton College (previously with Antioch University). Jusová's research areas include Czech and British literatures, European feminisms, and postcolonial studies. Her book *The New Woman and the Empire* explores the intersections of gender and colonial issues in the work of British New Women writers. Her articles have appeared in *Feminist Theory, Camera Obscura, Women's Studies International Forum, Social Text, Tulsa Studies in Women's Literature, Theatre History Studies,* and *Slavic and East European Journal.*

JIŘINA ŠIKLOVÁ, is an acclaimed Czech sociologist, writer, former dissident, and one of the most influential Czech feminists. She was dismissed from her teaching post in sociology at Charles University for participation in the Prague Spring in 1968, and imprisoned in 1981–82. Post-1989, she returned to Charles University, where she cofounded and headed the Department of Social Work. She also founded the feminist library and nongovernmental organization (NGO) the Gender Studies Centre in Prague. Šiklová is the recipient of several prestigious awards, including the Woman of Europe Award (1995). She serves on the boards of trustees for Vize 1997, Nadace Charty 77, and Konto Bariéry. Her books include *Žena v dnešní rodině* (under a pseudonym; Woman in Today's Family), *Deník staré paní* (The Diary of an Old Lady), *Dopisy vnučce* (Letters to a Granddaughter), *Matky po e-mailu* (E-mail Mothers), *Stoupenci proměn* (Followers of Changes), and *Vyhoštěná smrt* (Banished Death).

SIMONA FOJTOVÁ is Associate Professor and Director of Women's, Gender and Sexuality Studies at Transylvania University, Lexington, Kentucky. Fojtová's research areas include Western feminist theory, Czech feminism, Czech women's nongovernmental organizations, lesbian activism in post-socialist Czech society, and gender and sexuality in contemporary Czech women's writing. Her work has appeared in *Aspasia, Contemporary Literature, NWSA Journal,* and *Journal of Lesbian Studies,* as well as in the collection *Queer Visibility in Post-Socialist Cultures.*

PAVLA FRÝDLOVÁ is a feminist activist, film director, screenwriter, and publicist. She is also a founding member of the NGO Gender Studies Centre in Prague, where she has led the international oral-history project "Women's Memory: Searching for Identity under Socialism." On the basis of interviews with women from different generations and backgrounds she has put together a series of books: *Všechny naše včerejšky* (All of Our Yesterdays), *Ženská vydrží víc než člověk* (Woman Endures More than a Human), and *Ženám patří půlka nebe* (Women's Half of the Sky), and a documentary film *War in Women's Memory*.

HANA HAŠKOVÁ is Senior Research Fellow at the Institute of Sociology of the Czech Academy of Sciences and teaches at Charles University. Her research focuses on the sociology of gender, family, reproduction, and intimate lives, and policies, discourses, and practices of care. Hašková has held visiting fellowships at the University of Groningen, Rutgers University, McGill University, and Central European University. She has headed several research projects; cofounded the academic journal *Gender and Research*; and published articles on gender roles, work-life balance, and family policies in East Central Europe. Her authored and coauthored books include *Women and Social Citizenship in Czech Society, Fenomén bezdětnosti* (The Phenomenon of Childlessness) *The Development of Czech Childcare Policies*, and *Vlastní cestou? Životní dráhy v pozdně moderní společnosti* (One's Own Way? Life Courses in a Late Modern Society).

KARLA HUEBNER is Associate Professor of Art History and affiliate faculty in Women, Gender and Sexuality Studies at Wright State University. Her research areas include the history of gender and sexuality, surrealism, women artists, and Czech modernism from 1890 to 1950. Her articles on Toyen, surrealism, and sex reform in the Czechoslovak First Republic have appeared in collections including *The Flâneur Abroad: Historical and International Perspectives, Competing Eyes: Visual Encounters with Alterity in Central and Eastern Europe*, and *The New Woman International*, as well as in the *Journal of Women's History, Papers of Surrealism*, and *Aspasia*.

JITKA MALEČKOVÁ is Associate Professor and Head of the Turkish Studies Program at the Institute of Near Eastern and African Studies of the Faculty of Arts, Charles University, and Senior Researcher at the Center for Economic Research and Graduate Education–Economics Institute. Her research interests include gender and nationalism in nineteenth- and twentieth-century Central and Eastern Europe, Middle Eastern history, and terrorism. Her book *Úrodná půda: Žena ve službách národa* (The Fertile Land: Woman in the Service of the Nation) compares Turkish national discourses on women in the late Ottoman

Empire with five other societies of post-Enlightenment Europe. Malečková's recent articles have appeared in *Rethinking the Space for Religion: New Actors in Central and Southeast Europe, The Contested Nation: Ethnicity, Religion, Class and Gender in National Histories*, and *European History Quarterly*.

KATEŘINA NEDBÁLKOVÁ is Associate Professor of Sociology at the Masaryk University, Brno. Her research focuses on working-class, gay and lesbian families and on men's and women's prisons. She has authored two books: *Matky kuráže: Lesbické rodiny v pozdně moderní společnosti* (Mothers' Courage: Lesbian Families in Late Modern Society) and *Spoutaná Rozkoš: (Re)produkce genderu a sexuality v ženské věznici* (Handcuffed Bliss: The Reproduction of Gender and Sexuality in a Women's Prison). In 2013, she was a Fulbright Scholar at the University of California at Berkeley.

KAROLÍNA RYVOLOVÁ received her doctorate from Charles University in 2015 with a dissertation on "Romany Letters: Testing the Frontiers of Legitimate Literature." She regularly contributes to Czech magazines and journals, including *Respekt*. Her essays thematizing Romany communities have also appeared in *Roš chodeš, A2, Host, Plav, Svět literatury, Nový prostor, Transcript Review, Romano džaniben*, and *Romano vodi*. She is a translator from English and Romany, and has translated texts by Ronald Lee, Joanna Kavenna, and Ian Hancock. She has also coedited/cotranslated a selection of Andrej Giňa's best short stories, *Pat'iv: Ještě víme, co je úcta* (Pat'iv: We Still Know What Honor Means), and a selection of contemporary Romany women's prose, *Slunce zapadá už ráno* (The Sun Sets Already in the Morning).

IVA ŠMÍDOVÁ is Associate Professor in the Gender Studies Division of the Sociology Department, Faculty of Social Studies, Masaryk University, Brno. Šmídová has held visiting fellowships at the New School for Social Research and the Institute for Advanced Studies in the Humanities at the University of Edinburgh, and she holds an Open Scholar position at the GEXcel, University of Linköping. Šmídová's research concentration is in Critical Studies on Men and Masculinities, focusing on alternative life courses of men, men on parental leave, men at childbirth, and men "condemned to rule." Her articles have appeared in *Men and Masculinities in Europe; Intimate Citizenships: Gender, Subjectivity, Politics; Diversity Is Reality;* and *European Perspectives on Men and Masculinities*.

LINDA SOKAČOVÁ is a sociologist and director of Alternativa 50+, where she is responsible for projects requiring expert knowledge of age management. Her other research areas include family policies, equal opportunities, and discrimination issues. Until 2011 she worked at the Gender Studies Centre in Prague, where she served as director from 2007 to 2011. Sokačová has conducted commissioned research focused on access to healthcare in the Czech Republic by Romany people and migrants from post-Soviet countries (for the European Agency for Fundamental Rights), as well as an analysis of migration trends in Northern Bohemia (for the Agency for Social Integration in Romany Communities).

ZUZANA ŠTEFKOVÁ teaches at the Academy of Arts, Architecture, and Design and at the Institute for Art History, Charles University. She also cofounded c2c Circle of Curators and Critics, and works as a freelance curator (currently affiliated with Artwall Gallery) and art critic. Her essay on homosexuality in contemporary Czech art appeared in *Homosexualita v dějinách českého umění* (Homosexuality in the History of Czech Art), and her chapter "Naked Babes, Macho Feminists, and Queer Eyes: Curating Gender in Contemporary Czech and Slovak Exhibition Practice" was published in *Curating "Eastern Europe" and Beyond: Art Histories through the Exhibition*.

MÁRIA STRAŠÁKOVÁ is Senior Lecturer in the Department of Asian Studies at Metropolitan University Prague, and also teaches at the Institute of Far East, Faculty of Arts and Letters, Charles University. Strašáková's research areas include Vietnamese history and literature, with special emphasis on colonial modernity, as well as Czech-Vietnam relations and the Vietnamese community in the Czech Republic. She has coauthored *Vietnamese History* and the *Dictionary of Vietnamese Writers*, and has also published articles in *Nový Orient*.

ZUZANA UHDE specializes in social and feminist theory, globalization and migration, and recognition struggles, as well as the concept of care and its relationship to global justice. She is a researcher at the Institute of Sociology of the Czech Academy of Sciences and editor in chief of the academic journal *Gender and Research* (www.genderonline.cz). Uhde has held a Fulbright fellowship at the University of California at Berkeley and a number of short-term fellowships. She has published numerous chapters and articles, and coauthored and edited several scholarly books in Czech.

JANA VALDROVÁ is Lecturer and Senior Researcher in the Department of German Studies, the University of South Bohemia, České Budějovice, the Czech Republic. Her research areas include gender linguistics, gender-sensitive pedagogy, and German lexicology. Valdrová has been involved in several Czech gender projects and training courses. Since 2009, her team has been conducting, as part of the international project *Language-Cognition-Gender*, research into

Czech and Italian language use from a gendered point of view. Valdrová also authored the first guidelines for non-sexist Czech language. Her articles have appeared in *Kosmas; Naše řeč; Sociologický časopis; Gender, rovné příležitosti, výzkum; Wiener slawistischer Almanach; Specimina Philologiae Slavicae;* and *Open Society* handbooks.

ALENA WAGNEROVÁ is an independent writer, publisher, oral historian, and translator. Born and educated in Czechoslovakia, she immigrated to West Germany in 1969. Since 1989 she has lived and worked both in Saarbrucken, Germany, and in Prague. She is a member of Sektion Frauen- und Geschlechterforschung in der DSG—Deutschen Gesellschaft für Soziologie. Wagnerová has published monographs, oral histories, and essays on women and gender under socialism and on specific Czech women writers. Her publications (in German) include *Die Frau im Sozialismus* (Woman in Socialism), *Mutter, Kind, Beruf* (Mother, Child, Occupation), *Scheiden aus der Ehe* (Divorcing from Marriage), *Milena Jesenská: Biographie, Prager Frauen: Neun Lebensbilder* (Women of Prague: Nine Portraits), *Die Familie Kafka aus Prag* (The Kafka Family from Prague), *Das Leben der Sidonie Nádherný* (Life of Sidonie Nádherná), and *Helden der Hoffnung- die anderen Deutschen aus den Sudeten, 1935–1989* (Heroes of Hope: Other Germans from the Sudeten, 1935–1989). Several of her books have been published in Czech translations.

INDEX

abortion, 12, 19, 26n11, 68, 132, 152, 153; committees, 16, 87, 151; under social-ism, 13, 15, 16, 21, 69, 84, 86–87, 92, 97, 122, 127, 151. *See also* reproductive rights

Africa/African, 36, 38, 196, 246

Amerling, Karel Slavoj, 58n4

anarchism, 6, 144–157; anarchofeminism, 21, 144–157

Anarchofeminist Group, the, 144, 145–156

Anglo-American, 6, 24, 25, 118, 123, 126. *See also* feminism: Anglo-American

Anti-Discrimination Act, 212

anti-Semitism, 40, 47, 54–58, 58n2, 59n12, 59n15, 59n17

artificial insemination, 216–218, 221n20

Austria/Austrian, 8, 9, 11, 13, 32, 35, 47, 48, 50, 58, 63, 68, 75, 122, 262, 278. *See also* Austro-Hungarian Empire

Austro-Hungarian Empire, the, 11, 52, 61, 75, 83, 160. *See also* Austria/Austrian; the Habsburg Empire

Balibar, Étienne, 40, 45n5, 45n7

Balkans, the, 59n18, 160, 241, 246; "Bal-kanization," 37

Barry, Kathleen, 193, 196, 203n6

Bebel, August, 81, 85

birth control. *See* contraception

birthrate, 87, 136, 237, 238; socialism and, 16, 17, 87, 90, 104, 244

bisexuality, 6, 69, 70, 211, 257

Black Rose and Siren, the, 146

Bloody Mary zine/collective, 144, 146, 147, 155, 156

Bohemia, 11, 47, 50, 52, 53, 54, 55, 58n5, 59n13, 61

Bourdieu, Pierre, 209, 224, 229

bourgeois, 13, 61, 62, 154, 240; feminism, 15, 26n9, 92, 112

Boxer, Marilyn, 10, 17, 26n9

Braidotti, Rosi, 44, 159

Bromová, Veronika, 265–267

Buden, Boris, 35

Bulgaria/n, 16, 21, 22, 26n13, 42, 190, 191

Busheikin, Laura, 111, 120

Canada/ian, 19, 30, 42, 112, 124n3, 128, 129, 169, 170, 175, 220n13

capitalism: anarchofeminism and, 144, 145, 146, 149, 150, 151, 156; anti-, 144, 145, 151; Eurocentrism and, 41; global, 35, 40; the Great Depression and, 13; Marxist theories of, 80, 82, 91; men and, 35, 91, 93, 227; modernity and, 39; transition to, 6, 91, 93n3, 142, 144, 265; women and, 78, 79, 81, 91, 92, 93n8, 149, 156, 227, 242, 244. *See also* market economy; neoliberalism

Cavanagh, Claire, 38

Čelakovský, František Ladislav, 48, 56, 58n6

Central Europe, 37, 41, 67, 71, 74, 107n4, 117, 160, 189, 195. *See also* East Central Europe; Eastern Europe

Čermáková, Marie, 127

Červinková, Hana, 39–40

Cerwonka, Allaine, 3, 30, 41

Chapkis, Wendy, 194

Charta 1, 25n1, 77, 89, 90, 94n25, 94n27, 167, 246n1

childbirth/child-delivery: approaches to, 230, 234, 235; conservative, 226, 236n3; home, 236n1; interventionist, 235, 235n1. *See also* midwives; obstetrics childcare, 21, 126, 127, 133, 134–139, 142, 143n6, 143n8, 150, 236n2; socialism and, 15, 16–17, 85–86, 88, 89, 101, 104, 105, 244. *See also* grandmothers; kindergartens; nurseries

Chişa, Mona Anetta, 255, 259, *260, 261*

Churchill, Winston, 32

Čiháková-Noshiro, Vlasta, 251–252

Císař, Ondřej, 131, 132

Civic engagement, 89, 90, 127, 128, 151, 183, 200, 205, 240, 241, 244

class (social), 50, 53, 61, 68, 69, 79, 82, 146, 148, 173, 219, 227, 228; antagonism, 15; as a category of analysis, 2, 20, 116, 120–121, 124n5, 145, 212; classless, 25n5; lower, 54; middle, 10, 12, 48, 50, 111, 116, 122, 137, 181; struggle, 75; upper, 50, 59n11; Vietnamese minority and, 172, 181; working, 10, 12, 49, 50, 62, 69, 146. *See also* bourgeois; Marxism; working-class women

Čmejrková, Světla, 275, 282n3

Coalition Against Trafficking in Women, the, 196, 197, 203n8, 204n8

Cold War, the, 29, 30, 32, 99, 175, 264

colonial/colonialism, 4–5, 18, 21, 34, 36, 38, 39, 42, 46, 58, 171n5, 174. *See also* imperialism

communism: and abortion, 122; and class antagonism, 15; the fall of, 21, 112, 114, 199; and feminism, 26n9, 117, 118, 119, 120, 121, 123; and individual autonomy, 17; and International Women's Day, 148; and marriage, 13; and othering of Eastern Europeans, 40; post-communism, 25n5, 35; the term, 25. *See also* socialism

concentration camps, 14, 15, 160

Connell, Raewyn W, 41, 228–231, 234

contraception, 13, 63, 68, 69, 86, 87, 240

creative phrasing, 276, 278. *See also* language (Czech)

Crenshaw, Kimberle, 124

cross-dressing, 67, 211

Czechoslovak Communist Party, the, 12, 14, 77, 79, 82, 83, 89, 93n14, 241

Czechoslovak Women's Union, the, 128, 132, 134, 143n3

Czech Women's Club, the, 50, 53, 56, 57

Czech Women's Lobby, 128, 132–134, 137, 220n16

Daneš, František, 270, 273, 277, 278, 282n3

Daskalova, Krassimira, 17, 124n3

de Haan, Franciska, 17, 124n3

dich vu (intermediary), 179, 181, 183, 184, 185. *See also* Vietnamese minority

divorce, 13, 62, 68, 101, 105, 240, 242, 250

Dutch: colonialism, 4, 41; funding, 198; La Strada, 190, 198

democracy: communism and, 83, 91, 117; Czech debates about, 11–12, 25n7, 47, 58; Czech feminists and, 11, 12, 47, 58, 118, 122, 123; in interwar Czechoslovakia, 10, 11, 18, 61, 63, 75, 79, 117, 118, 122, 123, 239; Masaryk and, 11; meaning of, 11, 25n7, 76; post-1989, 18, 93n3, 226, 241

dissidents, 1, 18, 25n1, 36, 37, 89, 90, 94n25, 113, 240, 246n1

Ditmore, Melissa, 193

domestic work. *See* housework

donors: financial, 20, 37, 129, 130, 133, 150 (*see also* funding); sperm, 215, 217–218, 221n20

double burden, 16, 17, 88, 90, 103, 124n4, 134

Dunovský, Jiří, 94n21

East Central Europe: feminism in, 24–25, 43, 44, 121; postcolonial theory and, 36, 38, 40–41, 43; representations of, 34; Roma in, 42–43; socialism in, 5, 99; study of, 3–4, 19, 31, 39; the term, 25n4, 36–37, 41. *See also* Eastern Europe; Central Europe; feminism: Eastern/East Central European

Eastern bloc, 2, 3, 4, 16, 18, 19, 20, 22, 25, 172, 174, 246, 248, 264

Eastern Europe: art in, 248–249, 265; birthrates in, 238; communism/socialism in, 5, 6, 14, 15, 16, 25n5, 40, 95, 246; gays and lesbians in, 205, 206; in the interwar period, 11; life span in, 239; neo-liberalism in, 18, 19; postcolonial theory and, 38, 39, 40, 41, 248; representations of, 2–3, 19, 20, 21, 29–30, 31–36, 37–40;